LEWIN OF GREENWICH

LEWIN OF GREENWICH

THE AUTHORISED BIOGRAPHY OF
ADMIRAL OF THE FLEET LORD LEWIN

RICHARD HILL

FOREWORD BY
H.R.H. THE PRINCE PHILIP,
DUKE OF EDINBURGH,
KG, KT, OM, GBE, AC, QSO

CASSELL&CO

Cassell & Co
Wellington House, 125 Strand
London WC2R OBB

First published 2000

British Library Cataloguing-in-Publication Data
A catalogue record for this book is available from the British Library

ISBN 0-304-35329-9

Distributed in the USA by
Sterling Publishing Co Inc
387 Park Avenue South, New York
NY 10016-8810

Edited by John Gilbert.
Cartography by MACart, Maidenhead.
Printed and bound in Great Britain.

CONTENTS

It is not given to many people to make an indelible mark on history. Terry Lewin is probably best known as the Admiral who was Chief of the Defence Staff during the Falklands conflict. Less well known is the fact that he was the last person to hold that position who had served throughout the Second World War. In contrast to some other occupations, senior officers in the services only become senior with the passage of time and the exposure to a great deal of experience. It was this experience of a 'hot war' that was to be so valuable during the campaign in the South Atlantic.

This is the biography of a man, whose character and intellect enabled him to introduce imaginative administrative and social reforms, which are so essential to keeping the Royal Navy an effective fighting force in an era of rapidly changing technology. Admiral Lewin is acknowledged to have made a significant contribution to the development of his service, but the climax of his professional career was when he became the principal military advisor to Mrs. Thatcher's Government and found himself master-minding a very difficult confrontation thousands of miles from this country.

The fascination of this book is the mixture of fortuitous events and deliberate decisions that eventually propelled Terry Lewin to the very top of the British military pyramid. I think the author has succeeded in creating an accurate portrait of the person that I first came to know when we were Midshipmen together and then, after his retirement, when we served as fellow Trustees of the National Maritime Museum. I remember him as a man of great simplicity, immense enthusiasm and with a cheerful disposition, which tended to mask the steely resolve of a dedicated and brilliant professional.

INTRODUCTION

When, near the end of his life, Admiral of the Fleet Lord Lewin asked me to write his biography, I agreed without hesitation. I knew him well enough, having worked for him in several appointments, to realise there was nothing tentative about the invitation and one does not refuse a request in such circumstances. His career had spanned over 40 revolutionary years in the history of the Royal Navy and the national defence, and his life almost the last 80 years of the century, so there was no doubt about the scale of the task, and we both knew that. Characteristically, he did a tremendous amount to help in those last few weeks, taping over 50,000 words which were transcribed by a helper in the village, and putting together the more important of his extensive papers with pithy guidance notes on the covers. He also gave me the privilege of two interviews, the first vivid and vigorous and lasting two hours, the second, on a bad day, saddening but still illuminated by his spirit and the fortitude of his family. So all the best of this book comes from him.

We had some discussion over the title. He had long wanted to do a series for the quarterly *Naval Review* called 'Whitehall Warrior', covering his seven posts in the Admiralty and Ministry of Defence. As editor, I was sad that he had never got round to it. But we quickly agreed that it was an inappropriate title for a full biography, because he was so much more than that – what on earth had his war record in HMS *Ashanti* to do with Whitehall, to say nothing of the Far East Station and the Fleet? Eventually we settled on *Lewin of Greenwich*. His taking that title for his peerage was an indication of his deep relationship with the whole of that great complex: Observatory, Museum, Queen's House and College. He had learnt in it, lived in it, presided over it and deplored its fragmentation.

There was a subtext too, which I put to him and he readily agreed. There is a conscious echo in the title of Ruddock Mackay's masterly biography of Jacky Fisher, *Fisher of Kilverstone*. For both men presided over revolutions in Britain's naval forces. Fisher brought them to a great-power zenith; Lewin controlled, in a way that this book will do its best to explain, their transition to a worthy maritime fighting arm of a modern medium power. Paradoxically, Fisher emerged somewhat tarnished, Lewin gleaming. Their styles could scarcely have been more different: Fisher abrasive, flamboyant, temperamental, emphatic to the point of brutality; Lewin calm, rational, studied, often conciliatory. But both were great persuaders, both could charm their way out of a hornets' nest, both were of steely determination and both had the saving grace of humour.

Guided by notes left by Lord Lewin, research followed a rigorous schedule. There must have been over 50 interviews, stretching between Falmouth and the Isle of Skye; one of the pleasures was meeting mutual friends once again. Many correspondents wrote reminiscences in response to appeals in service journals. Official documents, mostly from our great Public Record Office, were essential source material on Lewin's Whitehall work; it was unfortunate that one of his most important Ministry of Defence appointments, that of Vice Chief of Naval Staff from 1971 to 1973, was still barred by the 30-year rule. The papers from those years will be a rich seam to be mined by anyone undertaking a more definitive biography in say twenty years' time. Libraries and archives at colleges and museums were invariably helpful in providing information, often of vital importance.

When compiling a list of individuals who had helped, I found it came to nearly 150 names, and this will appear on another page. It is also the only place in the book where full decorations are given, and I hope they are right; any mistakes are mine. But there are a few names that do not appear there, because they ought to be mentioned separately. They are first Lady Lewin, who has acted throughout with the utmost kindness at a terribly difficult time for her; Emily Roe, their granddaughter, who put together his papers and managed them with such skill; and Tim Lewin, Terry's eldest son, who has kept close touch and provided many endearing memories. Tim has read the whole script and made valuable comments. The rest of the family has been equally supportive: Susie Roe, whose recent OBE for her work for the Woodland Trust would surely have delighted her father as much as any of his own honours; and Jonathan Lewin, who before he fell ill found and provided audio and video tapes that were indispensable source material. His tragically early death in May 2000 at the age of 40 was greatly mourned by all who knew him.

Two of Terry's closest friends have also read the text and made important additions and corrections: Vice Admiral Sir Roderick Macdonald, KBE and Captain Tony Sainsbury, VRD, MA, RNR. Their advice and constant contact has been invaluable and heartening.

Finally, and as always with a new book, I have to thank my wife Patricia: this time particularly for her forbearance in accepting that I would dedicate the best part of a year to an unexpected and exacting (though, for me, exciting) task, and also for her patience in giving me the run of the family computer and the benefit of her superior expertise in its use. Without that kind of support, I don't know how authors get through.

ACKNOWLEDGEMENTS

The following individuals have kindly provided material for this book by interview, telephone call, letter, provision of documents or any other means within their power. It is acknowledged with much gratitude. This is also the only part of the book in which their full titles and decorations appear; every effort has been made to ensure these are accurate on the date of publication. All errors and omissions are mine.

His Royal Highness the Prince Philip, Duke of Edinburgh, KG, KT, OM, GBE, AC, QSO

Admiral Sir Peter Abbott, GCB
Mr Jim Allaway, *Navy News*
Mr R. E. Amory
Admiral of the Fleet Sir Edward Ashmore, GCB, DSC
Captain C. K. S. Aylwin, RN
Vice Admiral Sir Thomas Baird, KCB
Dr P. Baly
Captain A. R. Barnden, RN
Captain D. W. Beadle, CBE, RN
Mr Tony Beasley
Mr J. H. Beattie
Captain C. P. R. Belton, RN
Admiral Sir Jeremy Black, GBE, KCB, DSO
Field Marshal the Lord Bramall, KG, GCB, OBE, MC, JP
Air Vice Marshal D. Brook, CB
Mr David Brown, Naval Historical Branch
Commander I. W. V. Browne, RN
Admiral Sir Lindsay Bryson, KCB
Rear Admiral J. H. Carlill, OBE, DL

Rt. Hon. the Lord Carrington, KG, GCMG, CH, MC, PC
Admiral Sir Simon Cassels, KCB
Commander John Casson, RN
Captain C. J. T. Chamberlen, LVO, RN
Geraldine Charles, National Maritime Museum
Rear Admiral R. A. G. Clare
Commander R. A. Clarkson, LVO, RN
Rt. Hon. Sir Frank Cooper, GCB, CMG
Commander P. S. Cotes, RN
Lieut.-Cdr. M. A. Critchley, RN
Mr J. R. Crole
Rear Admiral T. R. Cruddas, CB
Commander John Davis, RN
Captain Desmond Dickens, Trinity House
Rear Admiral C. C. H. Dunlop, CB, CBE, DL
Lieut.-Cdr. D. C. Eve, RN
Mr J. Ferguson
Mr J. D. Ferguson
Lieut.-Col. Jon Fleming
Captain D. W. Foster, RN
Commander H. L. Foxworthy, OBE, RN
Commander Chris Furse, OBE, RN
Captain R. W. Garson, CBE, RN
Captain D. J. I. Garstin, RN
Rear Admiral J. R. S. Gerard-Pearse, CB
Captain James Goldrick, RAN
Mr R. Gorman
Mr W. M. Graham, VRD
Air Chief Marshal Sir Michael Graydon, GCB, CBE
Rear Admiral Sir Paul Greening, GCVO
Commander P. G. Gregson, RN
Lieut.-Cdr. J. G. Grindle, RN
Captain D. Hart Dyke, CBE, LVO, RN
Captain G. G. W. Hayhoe, CBE, RN
Admiral Sir Peter Herbert, KCB, OBE

Rear Admiral J. B. Hervey, CB, OBE
Rear Admiral W. A. Higgins, CB, CBE
Admiral of the Fleet the Lord Hill-Norton, GCB
Mr J. G. Holcombe
Mr Adrian Holloway
Mr Stephen Howarth
Brigadier Miles Hunt-Davis, CVO, CBE
Commander D. C. V. Isard, RN
Mr A. R. M. Jaffray, CB
Captain N. C. H. James, RN, JP
Mr F. T. Jewett, BA
Commander M. D. Joel, RN
The Judd School, Tonbridge
Vice Admiral Sir James Jungius, KBE
Mr Tony Kearns
Mr S. R. Kennerley
Captain P. R. D. Kimm, OBE, RN
Dr Roger Knight
Captain R. V. Lake, MA, MSc, RN
Mr H. W. Lane
Rear Admiral P. LaNeice, CB
Captain T. J. F. Laurence, LVO, RN
Admiral of the Fleet Sir Henry Leach, GCB
Vice Admiral Sir Louis LeBailly, KBE, CB
Mr Leo Lee
Mr Jon Lewin
Rear Admiral R. J. Lippiett, MBE
Captain P. Lucas, RN
Colonel John Lucken
Commander J. D. B. McCarthy, RN
Captain C. N. MacEacharn, CBE, RN
Vice Admiral Sir Ian McGeoch, KCB, DSO, DSC
Alan McGowan, PhD
Mr Trevor McMullan
Professor P. K. M'Pherson, SM, MA, CEng, FIEE

Mr D. J. Melhuish
Mr John Melia
Rear Admiral L. E. Middleton, CB, DSO
Mr John Montgomery, RUSI
Sir John Moore, KCVO, CB, DSC
Vice Admiral Sir Michael Moore, KBE, LVO
Mr G. Morralee, BEM
Admiral Sir Anthony Morton, GBE, KCB
Sir Richard Mottram, KCB
Rt. Hon. Sir Patrick Nairne, GCB, MC
Rt. Hon. Sir John Nott, KCB
Captain A. J. Oglesby, OBE, RN
Sir David Omand
Mr Richard Ormond, MA, FSA
Admiral of the Fleet Sir Julian Oswald, GCB
Captain C. H. H. Owen, RN
Rt. Hon. Lord Owen, CH, PC
Mr H. C. Page
Rt. Hon. Sir Michael Palliser, GCMG
Commander F. E. R. Phillips, RN
Mr Tom Pocock
Captain M. T. Prest, MBE, RN
Libby Purves, OBE
Mr K. Purvis
Sir Michael Quinlan, GCB
Mr Bob Riley
Rear Admiral Andrew Robertson, RAN
Rear Admiral J. T. F. G. Salt, CB
Mr I. Sanderson
Rear Admiral Sir David Scott, KBE, CB
Captain Richard Sharpe, OBE, RN
Captain P. T. Sheehan, CBE, RN
Admiral Sir Jock Slater, GCB, LVO
Commodore David Smith, RN
The Ven. Graeme Speirs

Mr Rodney Stannard
Dr J. Stevenson
Mr Patrick Tailyour
Mr W. G. Tapley
Lieut.-Cdr. Richard Tarran, RN
Rt. Hon. Baroness Thatcher, LG, OM, PC, FRS
Commander J. P. T. Torr, OBE, RN
Mr H. F. A. Tree
Vice Admiral Sir Anthony Troup, KCB, DSC
Allison Wareham, Royal Naval Museum
Mr P. Warwick
Professor J. W. N. Watkins
Vice Admiral Sir John Webster, KCB
Lieut.-Cdr. P. Wells-Cole, RN
Rear Admiral A. J. Whetstone, CB
Mr R. E. White
Lieut.-Cdr. A. C. Whitton, RN
Admiral Sir David Williams, GCB
Mr S. R. Williams, BEM
Mr B. Wines, MBE
Mr Richard Woodman
Admiral Sir John Woodward, GBE, KCB

A CANDIDATE FOR WAR
1920–1941

All families are unique and most consider themselves in some sense remarkable. But the Lewin family of eastern Kent in the 1920s showed few characteristics that marked it out from the normal run. In its circumstances it seemed to be about as close to the middle of middle England as one could get.

Eric Lewin was the son of a postmaster who had moved from Bedford to Dover around the year 1900.[1] Eric began his career as a telegraph boy and had progressed to Post Office clerk by about 1910. His sister, unusually for a woman in those days, went to university and took a physics degree, subsequently following a teaching career.

Eric, a tall and handsome young man, was active and practical and moreover could see, as could many, the likely road to war. He joined the East Kent Yeomanry, a cavalry regiment of the Territorial Army. Britain's small standing army of the time relied heavily on Territorial units to bring it to a war footing, while those in the TA regarded it as a broadening of experience that would stand them in good stead if war came. Few foresaw the coming carnage of the Western Front.

It may have been the uniform on Eric's six-foot-three frame that first attracted Margaret Falconer. She was the daughter of a Scottish family that had come south from Fochabers and set up a tailoring and outfitting business in Dover, gaining critically the contract to supply the needs of the local garrison. This was the foundation of a substantial business that enabled them to live in Murray House and take a leading part in the commercial community of the town. Margaret was musical; she played the piano well and sang contralto in the local operatic society. It is not known exactly when she and Eric first met, but shortly before the First World War they married. The two families, Lewins and Falconers, remained on good terms for many years.

With the outbreak of the 1914–18 War Eric went off to France with his cavalry regiment, still a trooper. Few survived the war from start to finish, particularly in that theatre, but Eric was lucky: not only that, but he progressed through the ranks until in early 1918 he was quartermaster sergeant. In this capacity he had one day the duty of bringing up supplies by mule train, under fire, to forward units. He showed such effectiveness and courage that he was awarded the Military Cross and promoted captain in the field. It was a crowning achievement for someone who had had, in his son's words 80 years later, 'a good war'.

His wife had stayed in Dover, waiting no doubt for good news or at least the absence of bad, and for the occasional spell of leave. Their first son, Alexander, was born in 1916; and when Eric returned home the family was completed, on 19 November 1920, by the arrival of Terence Thornton Lewin.

Eric's war record had given him a head start in the post-war scramble for secure jobs and he became an executive officer in the Office of Works, a post he held for the rest of his working life. The Falconers, on the other hand, had been hit by retrenchment and the reduction of the Dover garrison; their business was eventually sold and they moved into other fields of commerce. Thus there was little to keep the Lewins in Dover, and much to be said for their moving closer to London where commuting was easier.

They settled on the town of Tonbridge, and moved there in 1921. Their new home was at 3 Quarry Gardens, a three-storey semi-detached house at the west end of the town. The proximity of the Judd School was significant. The Judd was one of two academic foundations of Sir Andrew Judde in the middle of the sixteenth century;[2] the other is Tonbridge School itself. Both were then, as they are now, administered by the Skinners' Company. It is clear that Eric and Margaret were very mindful of their sons' future education, and the Judd was one of the best grammar schools in the country. They almost certainly did not seriously consider Tonbridge School; as one of Britain's great public schools its fees were probably beyond their means and its high social catchment and predominantly boarding emphasis would neither of them fit in easily with the boys' background and upbringing.

So it was to the Judd School that, after initial and rigorous training at a local kindergarten, Alexander and then Terence went for their schooldays. Alex, artistic, musical and sensitive, did not greatly enjoy them. The hurly-burly was not for him. But Terry took to it with gusto. He was an active, athletic boy, good at all games and sports, and a good mixer. He was not outstanding academically, though consistently one of the youngest in his class: since classes were selective, in the old grammar school tradition, this is significant of the school's view of his potential.

No one recognised that potential more acutely than his headmaster, C. Lloyd Morgan. He was something of a war hero himself, having lost a leg at the Front, and was much looked up to by the boys; indeed he was one of the outstanding headmasters of the period. Lloyd Morgan and Eric Lewin had struck up a rapport, due partly to their shared war experience, partly to the proximity of the Lewin home, and partly to Eric's great interest in his own sons' progress and in education generally. It did not extend to favouritism on Lloyd Morgan's part; that would have been foreign to his principles. But it could not have done young Terry any harm.

One sadness of those years was the early death of Margaret Lewin from cancer, when Terry was thirteen. In retrospect[3] he spoke of this with great calm, though he acknowledged that it was 'traumatic' at the time. Shock was rather alleviated by the fact that Mabel, Margaret's younger sister, had for some time been a member of the Lewin household and continued to run it after Margaret's death. Terry, however, was accorded greater freedom than he might have had under Margaret's regime; he later thought this not altogether a bad thing. Independence of action was something to benefit a well-grounded boy.

Responsibility came to him at school in various forms. There was an active League of Nations Union, and he first comes to notice in the school magazine[4] with a report on a debate: 'War, Yes or No?', which may well have mirrored the agonisings of the Oxford Union some years earlier.[5] Lewin reported no conclusion but recorded a 'spirited discussion'. At the same time he was games secretary, a house prefect, in the junior swimming relay team, a committee member of the chess club and treasurer of the badminton club.

By March 1937, he was house captain of Delta House. 'House Notes' appeared over his name in issues of the school magazine for the next eighteen months. They are mostly 'Come-on-Chaps' exhortations in the conventional style of the time,[6] and were probably the target a year later of 'Hints on Writing House Notes' by a wag who produced an all-purpose text in which the writer could strike out whatever was not applicable: 'if we do better / worse / just as well / just as badly, we shall surely keep / win / lose the Shield', and so on.[7] Terry learnt subtler leadership skills later on.

He certainly could not be criticised for not setting an example. He won almost everything in the athletics, he was vice captain and then captain of rugby, he entered the small sixth form and specialised in mathematics and the sciences, and in his last year became head boy. Lloyd Morgan recognised him as 'a boy with splendid possibilities'.[8]

It was this record of achievement that led to one of the most formative events of young Lewin's life. The Public Schools Exploring Society had been founded in 1932 by Surgeon Commander George Murray Levick, who had been a member of Scott's last expedition to the Antarctic in 1910–13.[9] In spite of the society's name, it had from 1934 included in its expeditions a few boys from schools and organisations other than public schools. Lloyd Morgan was of course aware of this and with Eric Lewin's agreement applied to the local education authority to sponsor Terry's participation in the Newfoundland Expedition of 1938. This was duly approved and on 28 July[10] the party left Euston for Liverpool.

There were 30 boys altogether, and of these it appears[11] that 27 came from the great public schools of the day: mostly boarding institutions, charging high fees, that sought to produce the leaders of the nation both intellectually and in the service of the state for succeeding generations. Five of the party were from Rugby, five from Marlborough, four from Radley, and two from the Royal Naval College at Dartmouth. The non-public school boys were Terry Lewin; E. J. Young from Price's School, Fareham; and a late arrival called McCann whose school was not recorded. The party was led by Commander Levick himself, now a fit and active 62. He was always known as 'the

Admiral'. Second in command was 'the Mate', Major Carkeet-Jones, and the senior medical officer was Sir Charles Gordon-Watson.

RMS *Newfoundland* took five days to cross the Atlantic. It was the first time young Lewin had been at sea and like anyone in those circumstances he was apprehensive about seasickness. It took him about 36 hours to become acclimatised and he did not suffer again. In fact, he seems to have taken to sea life with all a healthy boy's enthusiasm and curiosity but, perhaps, no rapture. There was plenty to occupy him: talks from 'the Admiral' on what was to come, films of what previous expeditions had done, competitive games and exploring the ship. They arrived at St John's on 4 August and disembarked on the 5th.

All the boys were issued with a basic kit of expedition clothing; an open-neck shirt, hard-wearing trousers, boots and gaiters and a hat were standard, and a waterbottle the only obligatory shoulder-wear. This allowed scientific gear to be carried, for the stated object of all PSES expeditions was scientific exploration – in this case, survey of a hilly and little-known part of Newfoundland. Personal survival and self-preservation in the wild were, certainly, valuable skills and experience to be acquired, but they were only part of the expedition's objective, and in this they perhaps contrast with the more person-centred aims of most similar operations today – though not those of the British Schools Exploration Society, direct descendant of the PSES, which continues to state 'adventure related to scientific field-work' as a primary objective.[12]

The party made a 19-hour overnight journey in a special train to Deer Lake. They crossed the lake by boat, went up for another hour by logging tram and walked for two more hours to a brief stop at Adie's Pond for lunch; then an advance party under Levick pressed on to establish the base camp while the remainder – including Lewin – bivouacked overnight among the mosquitoes. At 5.30 next morning, says Lewin's notebook, 'Cooked breakfast. Soup voted good by everyone. Porridge would have gone down well with milk and sugar.'

That was the pace that was set. For the next month the party split basically into three. Lewin found himself in the survey party, possibly because he had volunteered but more likely because of his known sixth-form specialisation in mathematics.[13] This entailed setting up marks, mostly on hilltops, and taking angles which would subsequently be used in making a proper triangulation. The entry in Lewin's notebook for Sunday 14 August is typical:

> Up at 6.30 to cook porridge. Then draw lots to see who stays in camp. Pat [probably Colonel Paterson, an assistant leader], Steve, Q [Quartermaine], Sarson and self go out. Carry lunch, sweaters in rucksack. March off to Flat Top Hill ... V. steep ... clear top and take angles all round. Down to river for lunch. Rain after lunch for a bit. Then up Centre Hill. Very bad going indeed. Steep as the side of a house. Move about on top to find best site for theodle [theodolite]. Then take sights all round. Down other side of hill to East River, came unexpectedly on Mate's camp by a pool. Doc squeezed my boil and dressed it. Then home up round Prospect Hill. Home at 7. 10 miles of very hard going. Then bathe and redress boil. Hoosh,[14] biscuits etc. ... up at 11.30 to go down and take an astronomical sight. Go down to Base Line.[15] Go up to far end with torch. Finish about 00.30am. Back to warm up and bed ...

So it went on: unfailingly cheerful acceptance of rigorous conditions both of terrain and weather, occasional dangers, constant irritations from flies and mosquitoes, and not infrequent mishaps to other members of the party. Levick himself, to his chagrin, sprained an ankle early in the expedition.[16] Food was a constant preoccupation. The standard was porridge for breakfast, a snack lunch, frequent replenishment by chocolate bars, biscuits and cheese, and stew for supper. But supplements in the form of freshly caught (or occasionally smoked) fish often appeared, and some of the more enterprising cooks would improvise; Lewin's Welsh rarebits were much admired.

So was his developing leadership. Near the end of the trip, on 1 September, he recorded:

> I set out [on the way to the next camp] for a record. There were three of us altogether. Quartermaine always hums one line of a

tune over and over again when he is marching and I determined to see if I could stop him. We travelled very fast. Half way we had a halt of 2 min, and we nearly ran the last bit. The others were pretty nearly done in by the time I got them there but we broke the record. 1 hr 18 min it took us. As Quartermaine and I were cooks we had to start cooking right away ...

The recipe for fishcakes is then recorded in some detail.

It is not surprising that Levick's report at the end of the expedition was unusually approving. He found something good to say about almost everybody, but on T. T. Lewin the warmth is clear: 'A first class fellow in every way. Very hard working. Unselfish ... will carry any load. Good tempered and nice mannered. Is a really good character.'

Lewin recorded the whole experience in an article in the school magazine,[17] in which he claimed it was 'the most enjoyable time of my life'. The article adds little to what is already known from his and Levick's notebooks, but is particularly engaging in its detailed exposition of the rations, the steady porridge/ snack/ stew routine occasionally varied by a 'glorious gorge' (his phrase) breakfast lasting two and a half hours. He had the priorities right.

What he did not of course refer to in his article was an incident that must have been reported by Levick to the Judd School and was later – no doubt to Lewin's embarrassment – retailed by the headmaster at morning assembly. Another boy in the party had injured a leg and 'TTL immediately and happily shouldered two back kits for the remainder of the long journey.'[18] 'Will carry any load', indeed.

Sixty years later Lord Lewin looked back on that six weeks as one of the most character-building experiences of his life. There is no reason to dispute that. Coming from a different background and milieu, he had more than held his own with a bunch of those thought to be born and bred as the nation's leaders. He had proved his own endurance, resourcefulness and courage. He had seen how academic knowledge can be put to practical use. Most of all perhaps, he had developed to a marked degree the ability to get on with all kinds of people in all circumstances. One final note in his diary is worth quoting:

> A lumberman came [into the tent]. He said he liked our biscuits
> so we swopped some biscuits for bread ... we were soon joined
> by other lumbermen, and Sparks [the naval telegraphist who
> served as rear link to the party] came up. They were all very
> interesting men ...[19]

Back in Britain, the news awaiting Terry Lewin was not so good.
Before leaving for Newfoundland he had taken four Higher School
Certificate examinations, in pure and applied mathematics, physics
and chemistry. He now learned that he had failed two of these. This
was something of a blow. University places were not at all numerous,
scholarships even less so, and probably he had not regarded himself
as a serious contender, but that avenue was now in any case out of
the question. He considered applying for the Police College at
Hendon, which had just instituted an officer entry, but the lowest age
for acceptance was 20. He was quite undecided as to the course his
career might take.

He discussed the future with his father. Eric Lewin's advice was
clear: war was coming (the Munich crisis occurred at the end of
September, and Eric believed not a word about 'peace for our time'[20]),
and he recommended that Terry should join one of the fighting services. The only one that appealed was the Royal Navy. The young
Lewin had been fascinated by sea life; it appeared that he thought the
Navy would give freer scope for his talent than either of the other services; and he had, on his own later admission, been influenced by seeing
the performance on the Newfoundland expedition of two Dartmouth
cadets – who had, in the normal course, entered that college at the age
of thirteen. He thought they were 'wet as scrubbers',[21] and that he
could do a great deal better.

There was no time to lose. The Navy was recruiting officers by
what was then called the 'Special Entry'; this method, catering for
young men who had completed their secondary education, had been
running since 1913[22] but tended to produce a lower proportion of
seaman officers, and more engineers and paymasters, than the Dartmouth entry – which was still regarded by many as the main source for

the Royal Navy's élite. In 1938 the need to recruit was pressing, a larger Special Entry intake was called for, and the prospect of war meant increased interest from high-calibre recruits. Selection was by both examination and interview. The examination was that of the Civil Service Commissioners, unique to applications for certain grades of the public service, with some compulsory subjects including English, general knowledge and mathematics and some options. Most candidates were able under the rules to take four shots at it, if they applied early enough, and it was unusual to pass the first time; recourse would be necessary to a crammer, who would teach the student not any new material so much as how to pass the exam.

That leisurely schedule was not open to TTL. He had left it almost too late; his age meant that he had only one shot, in October 1938. He stated firmly in his application that he wished only to join the Royal Navy in the Executive Branch.[23] It was all or nothing.

He passed well. He was fifth in the order of merit of Executive Cadets. His academic results were creditable, scoring relatively well in English and poorly in pure mathematics,[24] but it was his marks for 'Interview and Record' that put him among the leaders. There, he scored 390 out of a possible 400. Partly this was due to his excellent report from the Judd School, but it also owed much to his record on the Newfoundland expedition and the clarity and modesty with which he told of it. As a matter of interest, two candidates scored 400. One was Roderick Macdonald, who had captained the Scottish Schoolboys at rugby football and arrived at interview with his arm in a sling to prove it. He will appear again in this narrative. The other was a candidate who had on the day of the interview featured in the national Press for apprehending a burglar in his father's London house. The subsequent career of that officer was by no means as bright as those of Lewin or Macdonald[25] – his bubble reputation burst early.

So Terry Lewin became a cadet in the Royal Navy, and he joined HMS *Frobisher* at Portsmouth early in January 1939. *Frobisher* was a stationary training ship; she had served as an operational cruiser in the 1920s and 1930s, but in 1937 her armament had been removed and she was assigned to harbour duties. On the outbreak of war she was to be rearmed and re-mobilised, but at this time her role was to introduce young gentlemen of the Special Entry to the rudiments of life afloat. They slung hammocks, underwent instruction in elementary seamanship and navigation, ran cross-country and played rugby. Lewin unsurprisingly found himself in the First XV and, much more surprisingly, helping to beat the Royal Military Academy at Sandhurst, a shock result that may have caused some bells to ring.

Another member of that team was, naturally, Roddy Macdonald. He and Lewin had met the day they joined *Frobisher*. By one of those alphabetical chances that govern affairs in the best of democracies, they found themselves with adjacent sea chests; and shared interests and complementary characters ensured that they remained friends to the end of Terry's life. Another rugby-playing friend was Ian Browne, who sold Terry his car, 'Tumblebug', for ten pounds.[26] That they remained friends says a lot for Ian Browne, or Terry, or 'Tumblebug', or most likely all three of them.

So it was spring, and time to be off to sea in reality. The training cruiser was HMS *Vindictive*, a near sister ship of the *Frobisher*, still fully mobile although largely demilitarised. She had had a curious career since her launch in 1918; converted to carry aircraft while under construction, she had been re-converted to a 'Hawkins' class cruiser in the mid-1920s, at one time sporting an armament of six 7.5-inch guns. Now, however, she had extra accommodation and working space for the cadets, many more boats than was usual for a ship of her type, and other training equipment. At one time a concession to modernity was included in the provision of two Hornet Moth floatplanes, which were used to give familiarisation trips to air-minded cadets,[27] but these appear not to have been on board for the 1939 cruise.

By now Lewin could have had little cause for apprehension in the prospect of going to sea. But one small incident at the outset of the *Vindictive*'s summer cruise is indicative of his approach to new situations then and throughout his career. Cadet T. R. Cruddas had through illness been back-termed from the winter cruise and had joined *Vindictive* with the 89 Special Entries of Lewin's term, as well as the intake from Dartmouth, in early May. Of all those newcomers, Tom (now

Rear Admiral) Cruddas recalled 60 years later, only one had taken him aside and asked, 'What goes on in *Vindictive*? What's the routine? What do you need to look out for?' The enquirer was Terry Lewin.[28]

In fact the routine in *Vindictive* was active and spartan, designed to inculcate sea sense and self-reliance and an understanding of the conditions in which the sailors of the lower deck then worked. The young officers were in separate messes but these were no different from those of the ratings, and 'broadside mess' routine entailed all the chores including scrubbing out, preparing food and maintaining clothes in presentable condition with a minimum of facilities for doing so. The ship spent a lot of time at sea, and maintaining her efficiency and appearance was a large part of the work on deck; wooden decks would be scrubbed at 6.15 every morning, paintwork carefully freed from rust and painted, brightwork greased in bad weather and polished in good.

Always there was boatwork. *Vindictive* carried a specially large complement of boats, some propelled by power but most having the options of sail or oars only. 'Away seaboats' was the most commonly carried out evolution at sea; Roderick Macdonald's fine picture, the original of which now hangs in the Britannia Royal Naval College at Dartmouth, shows four whalers pulling round a dan buoy, previously dropped without warning. Recovering boats and buoy, all done by hand, involved the whole ship's company and gave further opportunities for cadets to exercise – under supervision – their powers of command. In harbour, cadets ran the power boats for liberty trips and used the sailing and pulling boats for recreation.

The *Vindictive*'s summer cruise had been planned for the Baltic and had been eagerly looked forward to on that account. But Germany had invaded Czechoslovakia that spring; the international situation was steadily worsening. The Baltic was considered imprudent and the cruise was rescheduled for Iceland, the west coast of Scotland and the west coast of France.[29] It lasted from 4 May to 31 July. *Longueurs* were Scapa Flow and Campbeltown but highlights included an unexpectedly effervescent Reykjavik, Oban in glorious weather, Guernsey with its great hospitality, and the French naval college at Brest.

Lewin took his full share of all this activity. He is recorded for special success on two occasions. The first was winning the 880 yards race in the athletics meeting in Campbeltown. That was well within his compass, and to be expected. A new field for competition, however, was a specially organised sailing race at the St Sampson's regatta in Guernsey. This was started with anchors down abreast the committee boat and consisted of four laps round a one-mile course. Fifteen boats took part and the whaler coxed by Cadet Lewin won.[30]

Theoretical training was not neglected in either *Frobisher* or *Vindictive*. Classroom instruction concentrated on professional subjects, principally seamanship and navigation, with introductory material on engineering, electrical and armament matters. Terry Lewin had no difficulty at all with these subjects[31] and the examinations at the end of his term in *Vindictive* showed it: he passed out top of the Special Entry and gained four months' seniority.[32]

Pre-war training patterns included a second term in the seagoing training cruiser, but the coming war made its cancellation almost inevitable. Still, there was summer leave to come, and Lewin, Macdonald, Browne and two others chartered *Madcap*, an ex-Bristol pilot cutter, for sailing in the Channel and western coasts. They were about to leave their homes for Gosport when ordered to report to the Resident Naval Officer, Invergordon.[33] The uneasy peace was over. The world, and the Navy, were never going to be the same again.

Macdonald and Lewin, still linked by the alphabet, were appointed to the brand new cruiser *Belfast*. Launched in March 1938, she was of 13,000 tons, carrying twelve 6-inch guns and a variety of smaller armament; her 80,000 hp steam plant gave her a maximum speed of 32 knots. She was the archetype of the last breed of British cruisers. Happily she was preserved at the end of her service and now graces the Pool of London.

Belfast was assigned to the Northern Patrol whose duties included contraband control and the capture of German vessels attempting to run the blockade in either direction.[34] On 9 October 1939 *Belfast* scored a particular success in taking the liner *Cap Norte*, carrying reservists from South America to Germany. Cadet Lewin (his advancement to midshipman had not yet occurred) was in charge of the cutter carrying the boarding party.

But the good fortune was not to last. On 21 November *Belfast* was proceeding to sea for firing exercises when, in the Firth of Forth, she suffered a massive underwater explosion that broke her back. It was one of the very first magnetic mines, laid by a small German coastal submarine, *U-21*, some days before.[35] *Belfast* was towed back to the dockyard at Rosyth by the tug *Krooman*, which relinquished target-towing for this more pressing duty, and consigned to a long and low-priority refit.

Lewin and Macdonald were appointed the next day to HMS *Valiant*. This was regarded by Lord Lewin in later life as one of the most significant milestones in his career and it is not hard to see why. *Valiant* was in many ways the finest battleship in the navy. Launched in November 1914, one of the highly successful 'Queen Elizabeth' class, she was of 36,500 tons; only 600 feet long but with a beam of over 100 feet, she was a massive and steady platform for her main armament of eight 15-inch guns. She had just completed a two-year modernisation that had much enhanced her anti-aircraft armament among many other improvements, and she was newly fitted with air warning radar – only the second set to become operational in the fleet. Much more than all this, however, she had as her captain and second-in-command two of the most outstanding officers in the Royal Navy, Captain Bernard Rawlings and Commander Peter Reid.

'They did *Valiant* properly,' recorded Lord Lewin nearly 60 years later,[36] and no doubt Rawlings and Reid saw to it that They did. She left Portland for Bermuda on 13 December 1939.[37] The work-up off Bermuda lasted for six weeks and included every kind of warlike exercise, and by the end of it *Valiant* was a confident ship. She returned to home waters with a trooping convoy from Canada and spent the next few months with the Home Fleet in Scapa Flow, carrying out anti-aircraft guardship duties frequently and monotonously. A German air raid on 16 March broke into the routine: Lewin noted that the two-pounder pompom crews were not closed up and 'our own R D/F [radar] watchkeepers could have given 13 minutes' warning': lessons were being learned, and the command took note.

But sterner matters were in hand. On 6 March Grand Admiral Raeder issued his detailed orders to the German Navy for the Norwegian campaign,[38] and exactly a month later they were put into execution. It was an example of extempore use of naval force, coupled with surprise and the rapid establishment of land-based air power, that caught Britain's planners on the hop and in the event was a great German success. *Valiant* was employed with the fleet, acting mainly as a covering force; it was her sister ship *Warspite*, always something of a rival, who took part in the crushing Second Battle of Narvik that avenged the grave damage to the British Second Destroyer Flotilla in the First. Lewin's *Journal* gives an account from the point of view of a junior officer in a ship that was engaged mainly against sporadic air attack; some of his observations show much penetration, if a certain naïvety. On the damage to the cruiser *Suffolk*, bombed close to the Norwegian coast after she had asked for air cover which was not made available, he had some constructive things to say about co-operation between the fleet and the aircraft of RAF Coastal Command.

As the reverses, first in Norway and then in the Low Countries and France, continued, the fleet spent much of its time in the Flow and much of its thought on how best to counter air attack. One of the more lunatic inventions, reportedly sponsored if not concocted by Churchill's scientific adviser Professor Lindemann, was the UP (Unrotating Projectile), which threw up a number of bomblets that then descended by parachute in the path of an oncoming aircraft. Lewin's *Journal* recorded the 'disadvantages': 'length of loading time, large flash on discharge, and difficulty of stowage of the missile, as it is susceptible to dampness'.[39] It certainly was, having phosphorus as one of its main elements, and it made the UP a much distrusted weapon.

At the end of June 1940, *Valiant* was ordered to join Force H at Gibraltar, and in early July took part in the operations off Mers-el-Kébir which resulted in the destruction of several units of the French

Fleet with heavy loss of life. Midshipman Lewin was in no doubt as to the necessity of the action, and that reflected the sentiment of the gunroom and most of the ship's company; the wardroom tended to take a different view.[40]

In August *Valiant* returned to the United Kingdom for a very brief docking and the embarkation of stores for Malta, whose defence was already preoccupying the British authorities. The force seeing her through to Malta was very strong and included two aircraft carriers. The opportunity was taken to mount a raid on Cagliari and conduct several diversionary operations.[41] *Valiant*, with four destroyers, was detached for Malta and entered Grand Harbour to much cheering on 3 September. Stores were unloaded very rapidly. Midshipman Lewin was given complete charge of clearing B gun deck: typical of *Valiant*, he recalled, 'the sort of job which in any ordinary ship would have been given to a lieutenant'.[42] Perhaps, though, it was because he was already regarded as capable of doing a lieutenant's job; certainly some of the junior midshipmen thought so.[43]

Valiant went on to Alexandria to join the Mediterranean Fleet. The next four months were exceptionally active for her and for the fleet generally. Many operations, interlinked and involving intricate plan-ning, were conducted with the object of disrupting Italian movements, luring out their fleet and at the same time keeping Malta supplied.[44] But the crowning achievement was the Fleet Air Arm attack on Taranto on 11 November, which altered the balance of naval power in the Mediterranean for well over a year. *Valiant* was part of the covering force. All this was recorded with accuracy and cool judge-ment by Midshipman Lewin in his *Journal*. That was of course its purpose; any midshipman would be expected to do it. More significant were his forward-looking comments on the use of radar, the plotting of contacts and the transmission of information to other ships of the fleet. These, with Macdonald's equally cogent ones, were carefully studied by the command; they were original, and just the sort of thing young, fresh minds could best manage.

Developing professionalism was not at odds with midshipmen's high spirits. Dismissed from the gunroom table for some misdemeanour or other, Lewin and Macdonald took their loaded plates with them and retired to a remote gunnery control room, with an accompanying rendering of the doings of Ivan Skavinsky Skivar and Abdul Abulbul Amir. The benign and far-sighted sub-lieutenant, Terence Stopford, chose to ignore the incident, with the result that the two felt guilty of their uncivilised behaviour 'for ever after'.[45] And when sport was not available ashore (as it sometimes was in Alexandria), it might be found at sea: the off-watch midshipmen played deck hockey constantly, rushing off to their action stations when the 'alarm to arms' was sounded, but only after carefully marking the position of the puck – a rope grommet – so that the game could be resumed as soon as the air raid had finished.

It was little wonder that Captain E. C. Morgan, who had relieved Rawlings on the latter's promotion, said he could not spare these two midshipmen for the customary 'small ship time' in destroyers; they were too important to the control of the anti-aircraft armament. Lewin allowed himself a firmly worded and well-argued gripe in his *Journal*; it passed without comment. Morgan (nicknamed 'Black' Morgan on account of his saturnine looks and reserved nature) did however take immense interest in the midshipmen's education, and at the seamanship examination for lieutenant, Lewin duly achieved a first-class certificate.

So then, in April 1941, they were to return to the United Kingdom for professional courses. Some 20 midshipmen from the fleet travelled round the Cape – the Mediterranean was already becoming difficult to traverse from end to end – and a week's stopover in Durban was spent by six of them touring the Drakensberg in a Buick Straight 8.[46] They were promoted acting sub-lieutenants in Freetown, and when they arrived back in Britain their courses were conducted in the training establishments round Portsmouth, by then a badly bombed city. Courses were much curtailed – officers were desperately needed in the fleet – and Lewin duly emerged with the coveted full hand of first-class certificates, which would entitle him to accelerated promotion to lieutenant in due course.

He was appointed to HMS *Highlander* on 4 October 1941. She was a destroyer, the type of ship to which he had aspired, but a somewhat unusual one; she and her sisters were known as the Brazilian Hs, since they had been building at Vickers for Brazil and on the outbreak of war had been purchased for the Royal Navy. Their fire control, for whose management Lewin as sub-lieutenant was responsible, was in his words incomprehensible, so that he had to resort to primitive methods to make it work at all. In any event, gunnery was not likely to be the *Highlander*'s main role, since she was escorting Atlantic convoys, and submarines were the chief menace.

It was an arduous and frustrating time: arduous particularly because of the weather which was more often foul than not, and frustrating because the U-boats were at that point in the war gaining the upper hand. Their numbers now allowed pack attacks to be mounted, air cover for convoys was not yet available, and improvements such as H/F D/F (high frequency direction finding) and ahead-throwing weapons were still under development. The United States had not yet entered the war, though the US Navy was beginning to report U-boat movements to the British authorities and provide escorts to the mid-Atlantic meeting point. It was indeed in one of these operations that Lewin saw HMS *Broadwater* sunk and USS *Kearney* torpedoed on 17 October. Although the latter did not sink, the memory of standing by her, with the accompanying reek of fuel oil, remained vividly with him.[47]

Nor was the *Highlander*'s atmosphere congenial. Lewin did not greatly like his messmates and considered the command rather stodgy. It was time for a stroke of luck, and it arrived, as so often happens, in the form of a crisis.

In November 1941, when *Highlander* was in Liverpool for a boiler clean, Lewin contracted diphtheria. Fortunately there was a doctor on board who quickly made a correct diagnosis and had the sub-lieutenant moved to Fazakerly Isolation Hospital. He was extremely ill for several days, but made a complete if slow recovery. He remembered returning just before Christmas to his father's new home in Pinner (Eric Lewin had remarried): with the train four hours late, he spent most of the night wrapped in his greatcoat on the steps of the war memorial at King's Cross Station.[48] It was no way to convalesce, but there was a war on.

The new year brought a turn in fortune, perhaps the greatest of his life. He was appointed to the 'Tribal' class destroyer HMS *Ashanti*, to relieve the sub-lieutenant, who needed treatment in hospital for a hernia.

Sub-lieutenant Lewin had served his apprenticeship, if it could be called that. He had done well; he was ready. He needed to be, for the next three years would present him with every kind of test that modern naval warfare had to offer.

ASHANTI
1942–1945

HMS *Ashanti* was a 'Tribal' Class destroyer, built by Denny Brothers and launched in November 1937. The British 'Tribals' were a class of sixteen ships – several more were built for Commonwealth countries – and they were at that time the biggest and most powerful class of destroyer in the Royal Navy.[1] Their gun armament of eight 4.7-inch was particularly impressive, marred somewhat by the fact that the guns could elevate only to 40 degrees, limiting their performance in anti-aircraft fire. Close-range anti-aircraft guns were steadily modernised and augmented throughout the war. Four torpedo tubes completed the anti-surface ship armament, and the ships had the standard anti-submarine equipment of the day: a relatively short-range asdic (active sonar) set for detection and prosecution, and depth charges for attack. Their steam plant of three boilers and two single reduction turbines generated 44,000 hp and the ships regularly exceeded 30 knots in service. Complement was about 200: a necessary number to steam and fight the ship but entailing cramped accommodation in a ship of 1870 tons designed displacement.

That did not matter greatly to the crews of these ships, particularly those companies that had served in them more or less since the beginning of the war. They were regarded with justification as the crack destroyers of the fleet, able to take on any task and always in the thick of action. In consequence losses were heavy; only four of the British 'Tribals' survived the war.

One of the earlier losses benefited *Ashanti* in a roundabout way. She had suffered severe damage from a high-speed grounding in October 1940 when escorting the new battleship *King George V* up the east coast of England,[2] and repairs in Swan Hunter's yard at Wallsend-on-Tyne took many months. During that time she had only a skeleton crew, but when the time came to recommission in August

1941 it turned out that a ready-made ship's company was available, for the crew of her sister ship *Mashona*, sunk by a U-boat shortly after the *Bismarck* action in May and fortunately nearly all rescued, were available after survivors' leave and formed a knowledgeable and experienced team.

That expertise was more than matched by the *Ashanti*'s new captain and first lieutenant. These were two of the finest destroyer officers in the service. Commander Richard Onslow – 'Dickie', or sometimes 'horse' on account of his profile[3] – came from generations of distinguished naval officers and had already made a great reputation in command. His second-in-command, Tony Bailey, was subsequently described by Lewin as 'madly enthusiastic and very efficient':[4] another, like Onslow, who had determined to make his career in destroyers in preference to the more esoteric crafts of gunnery or torpedoes, which with their talents they could no doubt have mastered with ease.

So it was a confident, exceptionally well-managed ship that Sub-Lieutenant Lewin joined in January 1942. *Ashanti* had, moreover, achieved recent operational success; taking part in a diversion operation connected with the Vaagsö raid further to the south,[5] she had penetrated Vestfjord and captured a German trawler.[6] As the capture had happened on Christmas Day, there had been a certain amount of good humour about the business and no lives were lost.

The wardroom Lewin joined was an almost entirely regular-service one, of a character that became less and less usual as the war went on. There were indeed two sub-lieutenants from the Royal Naval Reserve, but even they were experienced ex-*Mashona*s, and all the other officers were 'straight-stripe', that is to say RN. Lewin's were the traditional sub-lieutenant's tasks: forecastle officer with responsibility for anchor work, correspondence and cash officer in the ship's office, divisional officer for the boys' division and gunnery control officer (on the last of these duties, he found himself being intensively quizzed by Tony Bailey about the spotting rules within half an hour of joining).[7]

The *Ashanti* was regarded as a lucky as well as an efficient ship; some attributed this to the powerful magic of presentations made by the Asantehene, paramount chief of the Ashanti tribe, and spells cast by his witch-doctors, when she visited Takoradi in 1939.[8] 'The juju', mounted on the pompom gun deck, was 'never mentioned in derogatory terms' by any member of the ship's company.[9] But she had an Achilles heel, which was her machinery. It had not been helped by her grounding in 1940 and the hurried repairs thereafter, but it did in fact plague her all her life, and at this particular time leadership in the engineering department was not at its strongest.[10] Lewin found himself involved in the problem quite quickly. The ship was at sea with the fleet when he noticed smoke coming from a hatch next to his cabin, and when this was investigated following his report, it was found that a plummer block (the connection between the drive from the turbine and the propeller shaft) had seized, putting the port shaft out of action. The *Ashanti* was sent to Immingham for the necessary repair, and other remedial work.

Immingham was a somewhat bleak east coast town in those days, and a fortnight's welcome leave was given to each watch. Terry Lewin went on the first leave party and returned to the ship on Easter Monday. His own account, dictated in 1998, best tells what happened next:

There was a party with Wrens in the captain's cabin, the wardroom being out of action for some work and painting. I debated whether to turn in or just poke my nose into this party. It's not much fun joining a party when it's been going for some time. Anyway, I went to the party, opened the door and immediately across the room a very very pretty and attractive Wren attracted my attention and I manoeuvred my way towards her and we struck up a conversation and I discovered her name.

She was Jane Branch-Evans. The *coup de foudre* was almost a cultural cliché of wartime, featured in countless films, books and songs, most memorably as 'Some enchanted evening / You may see a stranger'; but sometimes it was genuine and sometimes it was permanent, and in the case of Jane and Terry it was both. During the next fortnight they saw much of each other and 'as we sailed away to Scapa we started a correspondence which went on for many, many, many years. She wrote to me every day, I wrote every day and of course my letters could only be posted when we were in a place where we could send the mail ashore'.[11] It was a routine that had been followed by naval letter-writers for many centuries.

One of the most touching aspects of the research for this book was the number of people who claimed to have introduced Terry and Jane or in some way influenced their meeting: who had invited her to the party, who had been quartermaster on watch at the time and told him it was going on, who had played mixed hockey with them either after or possibly even before that meeting.[12] It has been thought best to use his own words for events which were still clearly fresh in his mind at the end of his life.

But for the time being, the war went on. For *Ashanti*, it meant a convoy to North Russia. These were by now well-established operations. The first had been in August 1941;[13] it was now May 1942, and convoy PQ16 was in fact the sixteenth to sail, although some of the numberings had been mixed up on the way.

Well-established or not, though, the patterns of the convoys varied, and they varied most between summer and winter. In winter, with very long periods of darkness, the principal enemies – particularly in the earlier years – were wind and temperature. Gales and icing were often extreme, and some ships did indeed capsize owing to the build-up of ice on superstructures, while weather damage was incessant. Wear and tear on ships' companies was in proportion: working outside was both hazardous and extremely difficult, retarded by necessarily heavy clothing and frozen, therefore recalcitrant, gear, while living conditions below were primitive, cold and damp.

In summer it was a different pattern. The almost constant Arctic daylight gave ample opportunities for German forces operating from close by in northern Norway to attack the convoys. Threats were posed from the air, by both dive and torpedo bombers; by submarines, of which up to 20 might at peak be deployed; and by surface forces, the battleship *Tirpitz* being the most potent but by no means the only powerful unit in northern waters. So serious indeed was the summer threat that the Admiralty wished to discontinue the convoys in the summer of 1942, resuming in the autumn,[14] but political considerations made it in the government's view essential that they should continue.

Thus PQ16, which sailed from Reykjavik in Iceland on 21 May, was the most heavily escorted yet, and was also in fact the largest so far, consisting of no less than 36 merchant ships. The ocean escort, which was to see the convoy round the North Cape until relieved by the local escort of Russian destroyers and British minesweepers, consisted of five modern destroyers including *Ashanti*, four corvettes and an auxiliary anti-aircraft ship. There were two layers of heavier cover: a force of four cruisers with destroyer screen operating not far to the westward, and, more distant, most of the rest of the Home Fleet including an aircraft carrier, two battleships and numerous supporting forces.

Terry Lewin's account of this convoy is brief and laconic. He recalled 'fairly heavy attacks' from the air but they were effectively repelled by the escort, helped by the brave pilot of a Hurricane fighter launched on a once-only mission from the specially converted merchant ship *Empire Lawrence*, who duly shot down his target before being picked out of the sea – without his Hurricane, of course. The Russians, whose part in the escort of convoys was by no means as negligible as is sometimes suggested,[15] helped to beat off the attacks from 28 May onwards. In all the convoy lost only six ships, which Lewin 'thought was pretty good'. Much of the credit was due to Richard Onslow himself who, promoted acting captain because of the sickness of his Captain (D), was in command of the ocean escort, and not a little to Sub-Lieutenant Lewin, who as signal officer of the *Ashanti* found himself drafting signals for both the formation and operations of the convoy and escort.

The *Ashanti* was involved in the disastrous following convoy, PQ17, only indirectly as one of the escorting units of the distant covering force. Despite the strength of this, and of the closer covering cruiser force, the threat posed not only by the *Tirpitz* but also the pocket battleship *Lützow*, both in Altenfjord, was deemed by the First

Sea Lord in the Admiralty to be of a scale and nature that demanded an order to the convoy to scatter.[16] The results were catastrophic, as unescorted merchant ships were picked off by aircraft and U-boats; 24 out of 39 were lost.

That was in early July 1942. Requirements for heavily escorted convoys now arose in two widely separated theatres. It was necessary, for political as well as strategic reasons, to send another to North Russia as soon as possible, to re-establish Allied confidence in the system and to discourage any German belief that they could cut off the flow completely. Even more urgent, however, was the need to resupply Malta, whose siege had already been in progress for two years, alleviated only by spasmodic operations that brought in fresh aircraft, fuel and food, generally in that order of priority. The latest of these operations had been in June, a double-pronged plan to send near-simultaneous convoys from Gibraltar in the west and Alexandria in the east, each over a thousand miles of disputed sea. The western effort had got only two ships through out of six; the eastern had been forced to turn back entirely.[17] At the same time, the German *Afrika Korps* under Rommel had advanced to El Alamein, within 60 miles of Alexandria – a success made possible largely by the inability of Malta-based forces, even submarines, to interrupt his supply lines.

The whole Mediterranean situation, let alone that of Malta, was desperate. The island, awarded the George Cross in April for its corporate heroism, needed a minimum of 25,000 tons of supplies a month to survive.[18] A decision was therefore made at the highest level to pass a convoy through from the westward to Malta in August; there was no alternative, except the island's surrender. The priorities between the Mediterranean and the Arctic had resolved themselves; the next Arctic convoy would have to wait until September.

Clearly it was necessary for the Malta convoy to consist of fast, modern merchant ships and to be escorted by the most powerful forces available, for the threat was formidable. The Axis powers occupied all the land to the north of the convoy route, from Sardinia eastwards; from bases along this littoral, German and Italian air forces could mount heavy attacks at very short range, allowing little warning for the defenders and quick refuelling and rearming for the attackers. Moreover, large numbers of submarines could be disposed athwart the convoy route; E-boats would have similar opportunities in the narrow waters of the Malta Channel; and over all loomed the possibility that the Italian surface fleet might atone for its previous lack of success and make a sortie that would give the *coup de grâce* to an already wounded convoy.

While the scale of the operation was unprecedented, the plan was not in essentials different from those of previous convoys approaching Malta from the westward. The convoy would be formed well before passing the Strait of Gibraltar and for the first 600 miles or so of the Mediterranean passage would be escorted by very powerful combatant forces including aircraft carriers. However, these were too valuable to risk as the narrow waters between Sicily and the African coast were approached, and at that point the main escort would turn back, leaving the last few hundred miles to be negotiated by the convoy and a 'through escort' consisting of cruisers and destroyers, with minesweeping units to see it into harbour at last.

Thirteen merchant ships of the convoy were assembled in the Clyde and sailed from there on 1 August, with one joining at sea later. They were the best available: fast, modern and well-manned, their parent companies household names in those days; Blue Star, Blue Funnel, Union Castle, Shaw Savill, Glen Line. The commodore was A. G. Venables, one of those retired Royal Navy officers who had returned to service in this role and gave all their time, sometimes their lives, to it.

The through escort was with the convoy almost from the start. It consisted mainly of Home Fleet units and was under the command of Rear Admiral H. M. Burrough, a seasoned flag officer who had amongst many other distinguished services commanded several Arctic convoy escorting forces and conducted the Vaagsö raid. Burrough flew his flag in the cruiser HMS *Nigeria* and had under command three other cruisers, six fleet destroyers and five lighter 'Hunt' class destroyers. He knew the *Ashanti* well, and must have been glad to have her among his destroyer force; in fact she was the only Tribal in the through escort. But all were seasoned campaigners; and if any of the merchant ships were not up to scratch before they joined Burrough's force, he soon made sure they were: Lord Lewin recalled in later life that all were exercised in emergency turns and changing formation 'until they could manoeuvre like a flotilla of destroyers'.[19]

The heavy escort force was commanded by Vice Admiral E. N. Syfret, and included the battleships *Nelson* and *Rodney*, and no less than three aircraft carriers, *Victorious*, *Indomitable* and *Eagle*. This too met the convoy well to the westward of the strait. But bad weather meant that underway refuelling of the escorts could not take place as planned and they had to be sent into Gibraltar in groups to top up with oil. Axis intelligence, known to be active in Algeciras across the bay, was quick to detect that something was afoot.

The main convoy passed through the strait in thick fog on the night of 9–10 August, in a state of some confidence. There had been no losses on the way south, and that was a good start. A dummy convoy staged from the other end of the Mediterranean was to create a diversion, and that might help. But few were under any illusions about the strength of the challenge to come. It would mean days at action stations, constant air attack by day, E-boat threat by night and submarine threat all the time.

Sub-Lieutenant Lewin's action station was the director from which the gun armament was controlled, and there he stayed for most of the ensuing week, fortified mainly by corned beef sandwiches and comforted by the Mediterranean sunshine, so different from the North Atlantic conditions he had been used to.[20] Indeed, for the first 24 hours a Mediterranean cruise was what it was like.

Soon after noon on the 11th the carrier *Furious*, which had joined the force with the single mission of flying off fighter reinforcements for Malta – necessary, but of little use without the fuel the convoy would bring – had almost completed her operation some miles to the north of the main convoy, when the first casualty of 'Pedestal' occurred. It was a serious one. The German submarine *U-73* penetrated the screen and conducted a classical attack on the old carrier *Eagle*, striking her with four torpedoes. She sank in eight minutes, four-fifths of her company being saved. But nearly all her aircraft went down with her, and this depleted the force's fighter strength by over 20 per cent.

That was particularly serious because the force would soon come within range of the Sardinian airfields where the German *Fliegerkorps II*, as well as numerous Italian *Regia Aeronautica* units, were based. Already it was being shadowed and its position reported. Shortly before sunset on the 11th the air attacks began. Lewin recorded that 'every ship relieved the tension of the day by opening fire at the slightest opportunity': understandable if, in the long run, imprudent, and hazardous to friendly fighters returning to their carriers.[21] In fact only three of the 36 attackers were shot down by gunfire, and the fleet's fighters, hampered by inexperienced radar control and inadequate aircraft performance, scored no successes.

But the good news at nightfall was that the convoy had suffered no more than near-misses: so far so good. The night brought no casualties and there was one success far to the west, where the escort of the *Furious*, returning to Gibraltar to embark more aircraft to be flown off to Malta, encountered, rammed and sank an Italian submarine, the *Dagabur*. The destroyer involved, *Wolverine*, was herself put out of action by the ramming: a usual penalty of that form of attack.

The next day was very different. The night had given opportunities for snatched sleep, and it would prove to be needed as air attacks, from German and Italian formations alternating, went on with almost no respite from 9 am onward. Many of the attacks were from low level, often by torpedo-carrying aircraft, and this gave *Ashanti*'s main armament plenty of opportunity in spite of its limited gun elevation. In the afternoon the convoy passed through an area infested with submarines – the narrowness of the Mediterranean made evasive routeing impossible – and fleeting contacts and torpedo alarms were numerous. Detection of submarines by Asdic was, as always in those waters in summer, difficult because of the temperature layers that have the effect of bending the sonic beam,[22] but the glassy sea at least made it possible to see periscopes unwarily exposed and the wakes of torpedoes when fired, so that many submarine attacks were thwarted by counter-attack from the escorts, and others were ineffective.

The most intense air attacks came not long before sunset and were the heaviest yet, conducted by a combination of German and Italian units, mostly dive- and torpedo-bombers with fighter escort. They were in general well co-ordinated and although met with extremely heavy anti-aircraft fire – including, memorably, low-level barrage from *Rodney*'s huge 16-inch guns – some inevitably found their mark. The destroyer *Foresight* was hit by a torpedo and had later to be sunk, after her crew had been taken off, by British forces. But the most serious casualty was the aircraft carrier *Indomitable*, which suffered two direct hits and three near-misses from dive bombers, and was effectively put out of action although she could still steam. Those of her aircraft that were airborne had to be recovered by the *Victorious*.

In any case it was time for the main covering force to withdraw, as the narrows were approached. Syfret handed over command to Burrough and turned westward with his precious, though wounded, heavy ships and their depleted escort. Meanwhile the convoy – which during all the long day had not lost a single ship, though the *Deucalion* had suffered damage from dive-bombing and was lagging with a single destroyer as escort – steamed on towards the most hazardous part of its voyage.

The first obstacle to be negotiated was the minefield on the Skerki Bank, to the north-west of Cape Bon, which the convoy had to round in order to reach Malta. The ships had to be 'swept through' by a force of only three minesweepers (the fourth, *Foresight*, which was specially fitted for sweeping, was already out of action). A narrow two-column formation therefore had to be adopted and this gave the waiting submarines better chances both of evading the screening destroyers and of firing torpedoes at ships which, because they were perforce not zig-zagging, presented more predictable targets. Lord Lewin's later recollection was also that concentration on the manoeuvres to get into the new formation, as well as weariness after the day's long fight, had 'perhaps temporarily relaxed the watchfulness' of the escort.[23]

One Italian submarine commander rose to the occasion triumphantly. Lieutenant Ferrini in the *Axum* tracked the convoy and escort carefully during his run-in and in the final stages of his attack he had an almost unbelievably favourable situation: a cruiser as his primary target at about 1500 yards, beyond her on the same bearing another smaller cruiser, and beyond that again a merchant ship. He fired all his four bow tubes and awaited results.[24]

They were beyond any submariner's wildest dreams. All four torpedoes scored hits: one on the cruiser *Nigeria*, Burrough's flagship; two on the anti-aircraft cruiser *Cairo;* and one on the tanker *Ohio*, which was the only specialised oil tanker in the convoy and therefore arguably its most important single unit. The situation, so favourable to the British a few moments ago, had, in the words of a lecture given by Lord Lewin 50 years later, been transformed at a stroke.

Nigeria was badly injured. She took on a 15 degree list and began circling to port, her steering gear for the moment jammed. To Burrough it was clear that she could not continue. She must return to Gibraltar, and that meant detaching two of his valuable escorts to protect her on the way. He clearly needed to transfer his flag to continue the operation, and as his flagship he chose the *Ashanti*. Partly the decision was dictated by the operational situation; *Ashanti* was close by, and she was highly manoeuvrable and likely to effect the transfer much more quickly than one of the remaining cruisers. Partly too, perhaps, it was a matter of personalities; Burrough knew Onslow very well and the two men admired each other greatly.[25] So there it was: *Ashanti* was now a flagship. Since some of Burrough's key staff had managed to transfer with him, the ship's officers including Lewin could continue to concentrate on fighting their own ship rather than attempt the duty of conducting the whole operation with their limited manpower.

Other important facilities of the force had been lost with the damage to the *Nigeria* and the even more severe wounds to the *Cairo,* which later in the night had had to be sunk by British forces. These two ships were the only ones equipped to communicate with the most capable fighters on Malta, the RAF's Beaufighters; they were not yet within range of the convoy but lack of effective control of them would be felt next day. Finally, the damage to the tanker *Ohio* was extensive. Her cargo caught fire and only the sea, flooding in through a gaping hole in her port side, put the fire out. After an hour her crew regained control, the engines were restarted and she set off after the convoy, escorted by the 'Hunt' class destroyer *Ledbury*.

All this happened as dusk was falling: the night was still to come. It began badly with the convoy in confusion, though doggedly still making for Malta, and with another air attack as unexpected as it was unwelcome. Nearly 40 German aircraft delivered their attack against the ships silhouetted against the western sky, and now the merchant ships really began to suffer. The *Empire Hope* and *Clan Ferguson* both blew up with shattering explosions: their cargoes included ammunition and high octane fuel (it was with just this sort of casualty in mind that all ships had been loaded with mixed cargoes, so that any getting through would deliver a diversity of stores rather than one particular category). To the subsequent astonishment of all, the great majority of the crews survived and were rescued. Shortly afterwards, the same fate met the lagging *Deucalion*. Meanwhile the *Brisbane Star* had been torpedoed by Italian aircraft, and left the convoy to attempt to reach Malta by an inshore route.

The period from midnight to dawn was one of the most nightmarish experiences faced by any naval force. Lewin recorded:

No intelligence had warned that lying in wait ahead were some 20 Italian and German E-boats. For the next five hours there was an almost non-stop battle – gunfire continuous as the ships tried to engage the difficult and fleeting targets … pitch dark night – dark shore horizon to starboard. Starshell would only have assisted the enemy.

The first ship to be hit was the cruiser *Manchester*. She sustained fatal damage in her engine room and had to be scuttled before morning, many of her crew escaping to be interned by the Vichy French authorities in Tunisia. Before dawn four merchant ships had suffered similar fates: *Wairangi, Almeria Lykes, Glenorchy* and *Santa Elisa*. The convoy was now down to six ships in rather straggling company, with a seventh proceeding independently, while its escort was a relatively weak one of a damaged 6-inch gun cruiser (*Kenya*), an anti-aircraft cruiser (*Charybdis*) with 4.5-inch guns only, and seven destroyers of varying armament. This no longer had to cope with E-boats – they had secured their victory and their place in history – but the air threat was as strong as ever and there was an Italian surface force, consisting of four cruisers and escorting destroyers, assembling to the north of Sicily.

This potential threat never materialised. There was confusion in the Axis high command and disagreement between German and Italian commanders, and the full story may never be fully known; what is beyond doubt is that the Italian surface force was ordered back to harbour before midnight on the 12th.[26] The missed opportunity of annihilating the convoy was the worst part of the outcome for the Axis; an added bitterness was that on their way back to harbour the cruisers *Bolzano* and *Muzio Attendolo* were torpedoed by the British submarine *Unbroken* and sustained damage that put them out of the war.

Air attack was thus the principal threat that the convoy, now only nine hours' steaming from Malta, had to face from dawn on the 13th. It was intense. As Lewin recorded:

> The raids started about 8 o'clock and continued without a break throughout the forenoon: a seemingly never-ending stream of Ju87s, Ju88s, Heinkel and Savoia torpedo bombers ... three Ju88s made a co-ordinated attack on the *Waimarama* – she could not avoid them all. Hit by four bombs, she could not survive.[27]

Some survivors were rescued from a sea of flame by the destroyer *Ledbury*, but 87 were lost, the largest casualty list for any merchant vessel.

Still the remaining ships ploughed on. The *Dorset*, isolated to the north, was caught by six Ju87 Stukas and hit, later to be finished off by a further attack. All of her crew were picked up, including Apprentice Desmond Dickens, who will feature later in this book.[28] Meanwhile *Ashanti* had taken close station on the *Ohio*, which had become the principal target of the air attacks. It was clear to friends and enemies alike that of all those vital cargoes, her oil was the most precious. *Ashanti*, armed with close-range Oerlikon guns now as well as her slower-firing pompoms,[29] shot down at least one Ju87, but this was not a clear winner because the aircraft crashed into the *Ohio*'s side. That, and numerous near-misses, finally brought the tanker to a halt, but she was then tended by the destroyers *Penn* and *Ledbury* and finally, triumphantly, after one of the most epic tows in history, brought into Grand Harbour late the following evening, 14 August.

Twenty-four hours earlier the remaining three ships of the main convoy – *Port Chalmers, Rochester Castle* and *Melbourne Star* – had also entered harbour to a tumultuous welcome; and shortly before the *Ohio*, against all odds, the *Brisbane Star* completed her roundabout voyage to Malta. She had 'survived the unhelpful attentions of French boarding officers during her unpremeditated stay in Tunisian waters'.[30]

Was there any respite for *Ashanti*, roses and kisses from Maltese maidens or at least a night's sleep? There was none. Burrough turned round the ships of the through escort and headed west. They came under air, submarine and E-boat attack but 'this was a different ballgame – hustling along at 25 knots – *Kenya*'s damaged forefoot throwing up a spectacular bow wave ... no ship was more than superficially damaged ... [before we] rejoined Admiral Syfret who had remained at sea'.[31]

Operation Pedestal had been a success, in spite of the enormous cost. It saved Malta from starvation and surrender, and swung the balance in the central Mediterranean against the Axis. Once more Rommel's supply lines could be harried, and the British Eighth Army, reinforced round the Cape, could prepare itself for the coming victory at El Alamein. It was no wonder that, many years later, reunions would be held to recall what was by any standards an epic of maritime warfare in which, indeed, much heroism – and it is by no means too strong a word – was displayed on both sides.

And the *Ashanti*, the lucky *Ashanti*, had been hit by one .303 bullet that broke the Oerlikon call-up buzzer on the bridge.[32]

There was little enough time to relax. *Ashanti* returned to Scapa Flow, to join in preparations for the next convoy to North Russia.

This, PQ 18, was the first after the disastrous PQ 17 and much thought had gone into the best way of getting through a large convoy in conditions which, while no longer high summer, still gave enough light and fair weather to allow massive air, submarine and possibly surface attacks against it.

The solution was not far from the 'Pedestal' pattern. The 44 merchant ships of the convoy would be accompanied by a powerful through escort consisting of three elements:[33] a defensive and close screening section consisting of destroyers, corvettes and anti-aircraft ships; an escort carrier able to operate limited numbers of anti-submarine aircraft and fighters, with her own small destroyer screen; and a 'fighting escort' under Rear Admiral Bob Burnett of one light cruiser and no less than 16 modern destroyers, normally to be stationed around the convoy but able to react swiftly to any surface threat that developed. It was this element that included *Ashanti*, with Onslow still acting Captain (D) of the 6th Destroyer Flotilla. Beyond this formidable escort, there were covering forces: three cruisers deployed to the north of the convoy, and far to the west, distant cover from two battleships with attendant destroyers.[34]

Most of the convoy had sailed from Loch Ewe on the west coast of Scotland on 2 September 1942 and were joined by the remainder off Iceland on 9 September, when the escort in all its elements was also completed. The threat they faced was mainly from the Luftwaffe, which had available over 200 attack aircraft in northern Norway, and submarines, of which twelve were deployed along the expected convoy route. Although some initial dispositions were made by German surface units, they were on Hitler's orders not to be risked unduly and in fact never sailed.

PQ 18's experience in the event was rather like that of 'Pedestal' too, though proportionately, losses were much lighter. For the first few days all went well; *U-88* was sunk ahead of the convoy on the 12th, but two merchant ships were sunk in their turn early on the 13th, an even score for that period. Cloud and rain or snow storms had so far made life difficult for the attackers. But by noon on the 13th shadowing aircraft had appeared and in the afternoon heavy air attacks developed. The aircraft of the escort carrier, *Avenger*, were Sea Hurricanes without sufficient performance to cope with the most concentrated of the attacks, a 'Golden Comb' by 55 Heinkel 111s armed with torpedoes.[35] Six of the eight ships in the two starboard columns of the convoy were sunk.

This, however, was the summit of German success, for the weather once more took a hand and the next day allowed them only one two-hour period during which air attacks could be mounted. Moreover, the presence of the escort carrier had a powerful psychological effect, because attacks were concentrated on her, giving a chance for the ships of the convoy to remain unscathed. In fact the *Avenger* survived, and only one more merchant ship was destroyed by air action, while a U-boat torpedoed and sank the important oil tanker *Atheltemplar*. By 16 September, when the fighting escort parted company, the convoy was in Russian waters and suffered only one more loss, at the entrance to the White Sea on the 18th.

Lewin was aloft in the *Ashanti*'s director amongst all this. He recalled later PQ 18 as on the whole a successful convoy.[36] At each air attack about eight of the destroyers of the 'fighting escort' would take close station on the convoy to give optimum concentration of anti-aircraft fire, and although the attacks were determined they would be met with an intense barrage. After PQ 17 it represented a significant triumph in getting three-quarters of its ships through and, what was more, during the summer. It now remained to escort the homeward-bound, empty convoy QP 14, consisting mainly of the ships of PQ 16 with some survivors of PQ 17 – a total of 20 vessels.

The plan was to go as far north as possible, near the ice edge which was at its least extent in September, and thus minimise, at least, the risk from air attack. This was a correct tactic so far as it went, particularly as the weather was calm and clear. But 'the submarines were evident all around ... I sighted a German submarine on the surface at about seven miles and had the pleasure of loosing off about three salvoes. Of course, none of them fell anywhere near it, but at least the submarine soon disappeared under the surface'.[37] In the subsequent hunt, with extremely difficult water conditions, the submarine could not be successfully attacked.

Luck held until 20 September, which was not a good day. The U-boats scored three successes. The minesweeper *Leda* was sunk by *U-435* astern of the convoy, and the merchantman *Silver Sword* (a survivor of PQ 17) by *U-255*. Finally, in the evening, *Ashanti*'s sister ship *Somali* was torpedoed by *U-703*. She was hit in the engine room on the port side; the explosion was massive, throwing the torpedo tubes mounted directly above the engine room into the air and causing the whole of the port main engine to fall through the bottom of the ship.[38]

Ashanti was close by at the time, and indeed had just exchanged stations with *Somali* (some subsequently ascribed this to 'the luck of the *Ashanti*' again). Onslow initially conducted an anti-submarine hunt with *Eskimo*, another sister ship, in order mainly to keep the submarine down and preclude further attack. That purpose at least was achieved, although, so far as can be discovered, no damage was done to the submarine. The hunt was turned over to *Opportune*, who had joined on the orders of the admiral, and Onslow now turned to the problems of the *Somali*.

Her captain was Lieutenant-Commander Colin Maud, one of the great characters of the Royal Navy, massive, outspoken, bearded, still a lieutenant-commander, said Onslow, 'because Their Lordships had never been quite able to reconcile promotion with his sometimes exaggerated sense of fun'.[39] He advised that the ship was indeed in a bad way, without power except for one very shaky emergency diesel generator, and with all structural integrity on the port side gone, but that the keel seemed intact and the starboard side stringers were holding, and shored-up bulkheads had for the time being contained the flooding.

So Onslow decided to try to save her. It would be a long tow, 700 miles to Akureyri in northern Iceland, and they could not expect to make more than 6 knots; five days, then. If the weather held, and the fuel held out, and the submarines kept off, it might do, just.

The small force around the *Somali*, consisting of *Eskimo* and *Opportune* with *Ashanti* who was to be the towing ship, was augmented by the escort trawler *Lord Middleton*, also detached from the main convoy by Burnett. She was to prove invaluable later.

Meanwhile the convoy pressed on: its safe and timely arrival was the overall objective.

Passing and starting the tow presented every sort of seamanship problem: towing cables too heavy, the *Somali* unmanageable when steering by hand pump (the last-resort emergency method), and the towing wire thrumming ominously in the *Ashanti*'s fairleads even in a flat calm. It was considered essential to remove all possible topweight from the *Somali*, and this became Sub-Lieutenant Lewin's task for the next two days. In the *Ashanti*'s motorboat, generally a most unreliable craft but running sweetly throughout this operation, he shuttled between his parent ship and the *Somali*, helping her small remaining ship's company (most had wisely been disembarked to the surrounding ships) to take down all extraneous gear: in his own words, 'going up the mast unbolting radar aerials and throwing them over the side, disposing of ammunition lockers, anything heavy high up in the ship ...'[40]

During the first night the original towing wire had parted, but this had been foreseen and a new tow was quickly passed, using the *Ashanti*'s gear. This worked better, but the *Somali* still yawed violently and this reduced the speed that could be safely maintained. The torpedo gunner of the *Ashanti*, George Covey, hit upon the idea of connecting an electrical supply between the two ships; this would allow *Somali* to be steered by her primary system, a steering motor working the rudder head. It would mean hanging an electrical cable on to the towing wire by means of shackles at intervals along it, and because the tow was submerged at the low point of its catenary the cable would need to be insulated, but it might be done.

The necessary length of cable was not available in one piece. Lengths had to be collected by the *Lord Middleton* from all the ships of the force: mostly the shore lighting cables that were carried as standard issue. At least six 50-yard lengths were required, each connected to the next by what was hoped to be watertight jointing material. Then, for four hours, Lewin and the motorboat's crew (56 years later he remembered their names: Leading Seaman Payne and 'the absolute rascal' Leading Stoker Wylie) painstakingly shackled the cable at 10-yard intervals along the length of the towing wire, working 'often with arms up to the shoulder in water at 32 degrees Fahrenheit, with hands that soon became bruised and bleeding'.[41] Finally, the cable end was hauled on board *Somali*, connected up and switched on.

It did not work. One of the joints was not watertight, and there was no way of identifying which one, short of hauling the whole cable back on to *Ashanti*'s quarterdeck and testing it. This heartbreaking process was just beginning when *Somali*'s battery-powered Aldis lamp began to flash: 'Reel of insulated cable found in tiller flat. Details follow.' The newly found cable was speedily collected by *Lord Middleton* and brought to *Ashanti*; it was perfect for the job, without the need for any jointing. No one could say where it had come from; probably it had been 'rabbited' from the builder's yard just in case it should come in handy. It certainly came in handy now.

Once more Lewin and his crew were in the motorboat, but this time the task was less arduous and took only an hour, and the electric cable, with even an additional field telephone link, was soon supplying power to the stricken ship. Towing gathered pace, the tanker *Blue Ranger* appeared as if by magic and supplied the force with fuel, and not far from the Greenland coast course was gradually altered to the southward and the comparative safety of Iceland.

But now, after four days of almost flat calm, without which the passing of the tow and all the comings and goings of the motorboat would have been impossible, the weather began to change. When it did, it changed dramatically, as katabatic conditions – caused by very cold air gathering over land masses and then sweeping down towards comparatively warm areas of sea – so often do, with very violent and often unpredictable winds.

Lewin had the middle watch, the 'graveyard watch' between midnight and four in the morning. It was by then blowing a whole gale and snowing:

> About 1 am there was a blue flash and the sentry on the quarterdeck telephoned up to say that the tow had parted. I called the Captain who turned the ship, slipped the towing wire and there was poor *Somali* broken in two with her bow almost

vertical and her stern floating away. The remains of the small ship's company were clustered on the forecastle, finding it increasingly difficult to hold on and dropping one after another into the icy cold water ... I saw coming down close to the ship's side the First Lieutenant of the *Somali*, whom I knew. I put a line round my waist, gave the other end to another of my favourite rogues who I knew I could depend on called Topsy Turner, and told him to hold on to that rope with his life and I went over the side, down the scrambling net to try and save *Somali*'s First Lieutenant. He recognised me and said 'Terry, Terry, help me.' I did my best but being in the water fully clothed, he was extremely heavy. He had his life jacket on and blown up ... I tried to hold him by that, but unfortunately the tapes which secured it parted, he slipped out of my hands and drifted away astern.[42]

Lewin's experience was repeated by many other brave *Ashantis* who did their best at the foot of the scrambling net. Of all the *Somali*'s people along the *Ashanti*'s side, only one was rescued alive. This was Maud himself, to whom a heroic Leading Seaman Goad had actually swum out from the ship and hooked on a line to the torpedo davit, on which the 17-stone Maud was unceremoniously hoisted. According to Lewin, he behaved in character: 'He was absolutely rigid with the cold and was carried along the upper deck singing out "Jolly good show, tra la, tra la", because he had drunk the whole contents of his hip flask – wise chap!' Subsequently he drifted into unconsciousness and hypothermia, and it took twenty minutes' frantic work by the *Ashanti*'s doctor, Surgeon Lieutenant Baly, to revive him. Baly sported a black beard not inferior to Maud's own, and when Maud woke up he feared the worst: 'My God,' he said, 'Mephistopheles!' Maud dined out on this story for years, and many thought it apocryphal; it was a pleasure to have it confirmed by Dr Baly himself.[43] Leading Seaman Goad was awarded the Albert Medal for his exploit: he had the option to change this to a George Cross later in the war, but chose to retain the Albert Medal, which Lewin thought characteristic of him.

When the situation regarding survivors was finally assessed, the story was not as bad as had been feared. The *Lord Middleton*, which had been first on the scene of *Somali*'s sinking (clearing the parted towing wire, which made the *Ashanti* unmanoeuvrable, had taken some time), had picked up over 30 alive, which, considering the very short space of time in those waters before hypothermia set in, was rapid and effective work. But 40 had been lost, and Richard Onslow, years later, was still 'haunted ... by the thought that perhaps I should have foreseen' the worsening weather and the breaking-up of the *Somali*.[44] As for the tow itself, he was 'sure we were right to try'.

Maud was determined that the attempt should not go unremembered. He gave to the *Ashanti*'s wardroom a framed print, with an inscribed silver plaque, of Vermeer's painting of 'the girl with a pearl'. It will reappear later in this narrative.

Sub-Lieutenant Lewin had come through the experience with his already considerable reputation much enhanced. Earlier in 1942 he had been Mentioned in Despatches for 'distinguished services in *Ashanti* in taking convoys to and from Murmansk, through the dangers of ice and heavy seas and in the face of relentless attacks by enemy U-boats, aircraft and surface forces';[45] now he was awarded the Distinguished Service Cross for 'gallantry, skill and resolution in His Majesty's Ships escorting an important convoy to North Russia in face of relentless attacks by enemy aircraft and submarines'.[46] The wording makes no mention of towing the *Somali*, perhaps because this was arguably not in the face of the enemy. In any event, he was now Sub-Lieutenant Lewin DSC, soon to become Lieutenant Lewin DSC with a good deal of backdated seniority. There were not many such: there was, in the folklore at least, a sort of tariff that ensured, for example, a DSO for the captain of any ship that sank a submarine and a DSC for her first lieutenant, with commensurate awards for any particularly distinguished performance by members of the ship's company. A DSC for the 'Sub' had to be well deserved.

Ashanti and her people had had a desperately hard summer. She was due for a boiler clean and went down to Rosyth for eight days:

four days' leave to each watch, including travelling time. Terry
Lewin managed two and a half days in Yorkshire, where Jane was
now stationed:

> We picked up exactly where we had left off and before I left, I
> think we had both decided we were meant for each other ... I
> suggested that when the time came, we might perhaps get
> married ... We had no money and the prospect of marrying on
> a Lieutenant's pay with no money of your own was too much to
> contemplate, but even so we were strong enough to agree that if
> we had to wait until we were 30 [the age at which Marriage
> Allowance became an entitlement pre-war], we would wait until
> we were 30.[47]

The brief respite over, *Ashanti* returned to Scapa, but not for long. She
was soon back in the Mediterranean for the Allied landings in North
Africa, Operation Torch. This massive, brilliantly planned operation
took place on 7–8 November 1942, with overall complete success.[48]

Subsequently *Ashanti*, with some cruisers and fleet destroyers, was
based in Bône, and sorties were carried out from early in December
with the object of finding and destroying Axis convoys seeking to
resupply their troops in North Africa. Most of these forays were made
at night and many of the days back in harbour were occupied in
sporting activities on makeshift pitches; *Ashanti* was a 'very sporting
ship' and the most abiding memory of at least one member of the ship's
company (never mind the war) was 'our rugby team was never beaten'.
Christmas was accordingly celebrated with soccer and rugby matches,
officers against chief and petty officers at soccer in the morning and
rugby against the ship's company in the afternoon which, Lewin
remembered, 'prevented ... anyone getting too drunk'.[49]

Celebration was again in order when on 31 December Richard
Onslow was promoted to captain. He had during 1942 acquired three
DSOs and, with a fourth later, was to become one of a very select
band. But his promotion meant that he almost at once left *Ashanti*,
with Tony Bailey in temporary command and the very young Lewin as

first lieutenant. There was intense speculation as to who might be Onslow's successor. It turned out to that it was to be Lieutenant-Commander John (always for some reason called 'Jimmy') Barnes, an officer of the Physical Training specialisation which had the reputation of being strong on springing but not so hot at thinking. There was some trepidation in consequence; and Bailey and Lewin tried to extend the interregnum by what they called 'Operation Dodge Barnes'. 'Barnes arrived in Gib, we were in Oran. Barnes got a lift down to Oran, we'd gone to Algiers. Barnes got to Algiers, we had gone back to Gib. We managed to evade Barnes for about four weeks ... Tony Bailey revelling in his new command ...':[50] the war was becoming a little more light-hearted.

When Barnes finally arrived, he turned out to be a highly experienced destroyer officer and expert ship handler as well as what the navy calls a 'great player'. He quickly endeared himself to the ship's company; one correspondent thought him 'the best destroyer captain in the second world war'.[51] Bailey, due for his own first command, left for the *Paladin*; and Lewin, at the age of 22, was confirmed in the appointment as first lieutenant of the *Ashanti*.

One of the few 'Tribals' with a lieutenant-commander in command, *Ashanti* found herself a kind of odd-job boy of the fleet, escorting convoys, carrying out more 'club runs' from Bône and doing another tow, this time of a broken-down merchant ship, for 600 miles in the Atlantic, with the merchantman finally making Dakar. Machinery defects were becoming more and more prevalent, and a five-week maintenance period in Malta only partly alleviated them. *Ashanti*, after a final high-speed run from Gibraltar to Malta with a cargo of ban notes,[52] was ordered home for a long refit in Silley and Weir's yard on the Isle of Dogs, London.

A major consequence of this unexpected turn of events was that the ship's company, ex-*Mashona*, which had served *Ashanti* so well for the past two years and more, was broken up. When she recommissioned it was with a very largely 'hostilities only' crew, 80 per cent of whom had never been to sea before. Lewin managed to keep a nucleus of key ratings, including his trusted chief boatswain's mate, CPO Dockwra, but much effort would be needed to make the ship into an efficient fighting unit again. Some new arrivals would clearly be assets: the new doctor was Sub-Lieutenant Stevenson RNVR, who showed true north-country grit in obeying Lewin's very first instruction to him, which was to castrate the ship's cats. 'You need', he observed half a century later, 'to wear thick gloves'.[53]

The other consequence was much more personal. Terry and Jane both managed to get substantial amounts of leave, spent much time in each other's company ('separate rooms I may say', notes his memoir) and finally said, 'To hell with this bloody marriage allowance lark, let's get engaged.' The engagement was announced on 4 August 1943, auspicious for many reasons, not least because Roddy Macdonald's appeared in the selfsame issue of *The Times*.

Recommissioned, still under the command of John Barnes, *Ashanti* sailed for Scapa and arrived there on 15 October 1943. There was little time to work up, and her first lieutenant felt that she was 'far from a fighting unit and I was worried that we might run into some battle'.[54] Taking a convoy through to Murmansk did not greatly harden the new ship's company and Lewin was relieved that *Ashanti* was not one of the destroyers selected to join the *Duke of York* for the action that sank *Scharnhorst* in December 1943: the messdecks leaked, the men were seasick and the ship was not really ready.[55] Much remained to be done.

The ship's material state was not helped by heavy weather encountered when escorting the battleship *King George V*, with Winston Churchill on board, in mid-January 1944.[56] A further three weeks in dock at Devonport was necessary. The first evening in, Terry telephoned Jane: 'By a miracle of telecommunications, I managed to speak to her and said ... how about getting married on Monday week? And without a moment's hesitation she said yes ...'

Preparations in the Branch-Evans household, a country rectory at Sigglesthorne in the East Riding of Yorkshire, were appropriately frantic, and Terry and Jane were married by Jane's father on 14 February 1944. The best man was Surgeon Lieutenant Stevenson; he and Terry had become something of run-ashore 'oppos' and the 'Doc' was keenly interested in every aspect of the ship's life.[57] The honeymoon, only a week, was spent in the Lake District and then 'We each had to go back and fight the war in our respective ways.'

1944 was the year of Operation Overlord, the invasion of German-occupied France by British, American and Canadian forces. Planning for this massive undertaking was already well advanced, and dispositions were being made accordingly. After a brief return to northern waters covering two Arctic convoys, *Ashanti* moved south to Plymouth once more, to become a permanent member of a powerfully armed cruiser and destroyer force whose mission was to deny the western approaches to the Channel to all enemy surface forces, whether these were bent on resupply by coastal convoys or on disrupting invasion preparations.

Operations of this sort had been going on since the middle of 1943, under the overall title of Operation Tunnel. Initially they had been very much *ad hoc*, conducted by units brought together at short notice, and this had on one occasion ended in disaster when the cruiser *Charybdis* and the destroyer *Limbourne* were sunk by a much better-prepared and better co-ordinated German force. Now British forces were to have more cohesion. The 10th Destroyer Flotilla was formed under Commander Basil Jones,[58] consisting of four British ships, *Tartar, Eskimo, Ashanti* and *Javelin*; four Canadian Tribals, *Haida, Huron, Iroquois* and *Athabaskan*; and two Polish ships, *Blyskawica* and *Piorun*.[59] They were rigorously worked up, concentrating on night encounter exercises, often with a light cruiser whose principal duty, according to the destroyers, was to illuminate their targets with starshell[60] while the flotilla attacked with gunfire and torpedoes.

. . ivity became steadily more intense from the beginning of April onw..rd. Many of the sweeps were unproductive. The night of 25–26 April, however, saw some hot action. The Allied force consisted of the cruiser *Black Prince* and the destroyers *Haida, Athabaskan, Huron* and *Ashanti*. Unknown to them, a force of three German destroyers had left St Malo soon after dark.[61] These were 'Elbing' class vessels, classed as torpedo-boats by the German Navy but in fact the equal of many Allied destroyer classes, though inferior in gun-power to the

Tribals. Their mission was twofold: to lay a minefield off the north coast of Brittany, and then to cover the passage of a convoy going down-Channel to Brest.

By that stage of the war, radar was generally fitted in the surface craft of both sides, and shore radars were operated by the Germans on the French coast. What is now known as Electronic Warfare was also practised; not only was Bletchley Park decrypting a great deal of German radio traffic – producing the famous 'Ultra' material – but intercept equipments in ships were in fairly general use. *Ashanti* was fitted with 'Headache', which was able to listen in to German voice radio, and had the added bonus of a Danish rating who spoke German and, listening to this device, was able to give a commentary in real time.[62]

The opposing forces first became aware of each other's presence soon after 1 am on the 26th, and the first thought of the commander of the German destroyers was to protect the convoy which was to the west of him. It soon became clear, however, that his own force and not the convoy was the Allied force's objective, and realising his inferiority he turned east. It was too late; the attackers had superior speed and gained on the Germans, opening fire at about 2.20 am and quickly gaining hits. Starshell was fired by both sides, and the Germans conducted a spirited counter-attack with torpedoes, duly reported by the *Ashanti*'s 'Headache' which helped the British and Canadian ships to comb the tracks.

The *Black Prince* withdrew because of the torpedo threat; it must be presumed that this was part of the doctrine of these operations, since there was no subsequent censure. The destroyers, now under the tactical command of Commander H. C. deWolff RCN in *Haida*, were in any case well superior in fighting power to the Germans, without the cruiser's support. Yet they found it extraordinarily difficult to sink the most heavily hit of the 'Elbings', the *T29*; four outfits of torpedoes were fired without success. The usual *coup de grâce* weapon having failed, she was finally sunk by gunfire at 4.20 am. The other two German ships escaped under cover of smoke.

The 26 April action ended with an unfortunate mishap when *Ashanti* collided with *Huron*. Lewin's recollection of the event (he was on the bridge, though Barnes was handling the ship) was twice recorded during the 1990s; the accounts differ in detail. The earlier one[63] read:

> We were ... leaving the scene of action at 30 knots in the order *Haida, Ashanti, Huron, Athabaskan*. Jimmy Barnes was doing his destroyer commander act, gripping both voice pipes and following the next ahead at two cables [400 yards]. *Haida* signalled on TBS [voice radio] 'Blue Six' (sixty degrees to starboard together), then 'Negative'. There was some doubt by the Yeoman of Signals whether it was 'Negative' or 'Executive' – which was what we said in those days. Everyone was watching *Haida* to see if she started turning, and she did, so Jimmy B. put on starboard twenty [degrees of wheel]. We discovered afterwards that there had been the same mix up on *Haida*'s bridge, and the officer of the watch had turned although the signal had in fact been cancelled and she soon started turning back. We were all still watching *Haida* when someone looked the other way and saw *Huron* about to cross our bows at speed. We went full astern but our bow scraped down her port side, wiping off her boats, the torpedo davit and the depth charge thrower.

Barnes's reaction had been extremely quick and Lewin's later account sums the affair up as 'not really a bad collision ... [it] led to another couple of weeks in dock while our bow, which had been turned round a bit, was straightened out ...'.[64] In another account,[65] *Ashanti*'s damage is given as the bow being split back 19 feet from the stem. War and peace are indeed very different: the reaction of the media to damage of that nature today can be imagined.

Meanwhile Jane Lewin, still in the Operations Branch of the WRNS, had been transferred from Immingham to the operations room near Fort Southwick just north of Portsmouth, augmented to control the invasion forces. There were snatched moments of leave together, but the war's imperatives made them brief. D-day on 6 June found the 10th Destroyer Flotilla working out of Plymouth again, with the task of sealing the Channel approaches against any German incursion from the Brest area. On the night of 9 June all eight operational ships were at sea, alerted according to one account by air reconnaissance[66] though another ascribes the information to Ultra.[67] Four German destroyers were expected to make a sortie from Brest. *Ashanti* was short of fuel, having been recalled to patrol before she could be topped up, but had just enough to stay in company and had added water ballast to give stability.[68]

Jones stationed the more experienced division of his destroyers – *Tartar, Ashanti, Haida* and *Huron* – directly in the expected path of the German force, with the other division – *Blyskawica, Eskimo, Piorun* and *Javelin* – two miles on his seaward quarter. The enemy was detected ten miles ahead at 1.14 am, and Jones manoeuvred his force skilfully to spread the ships across the Germans' front, with all forward guns bearing but at the same time well-disposed to comb torpedo tracks in the face of the expected attack. This duly happened at a range of just over two miles, and all the Allied ships reported seeing the tracks, but none were hit.

The enemy force now split, the leading ship turning north towards the seaward of the Allied divisions. *Blyskawica*, leading this division, turned to fire torpedoes, but then unaccountably carried on to the north and effectively led her division away from the action. This was a most unusual thing for a Polish ship to do – they were generally keen to the point of imprudence to get at the enemy[69] – and can probably be ascribed to confusion as to the true situation.

The battle then developed into a gunfight between four German destroyers and four Tribals. The Germans turned out later to have been a powerful force: two Narvik-class ships, *Z24* and *Z32*, armed with five 5.9-inch guns, an ex-Dutch destroyer, the *Tjerk Hiddes*, now called *ZH1*,[70] which had five 4.7-inch, and the ubiquitous Elbing *T24*. The Tribals gave much better than they got. *Tartar* was hit several times, a fire being started at the base of her funnel from paint irregularly stowed ('an acquisitive first lieutenant', commented Lewin) and *Ashanti* suffered one hit, but *ZH1* was mortally wounded and finally blew up after being hit by two torpedoes from *Ashanti*, while *Z32* was pursued by the Canadian Tribals and finally driven ashore on the Ile de Batz. *Z24* and *T24*, the latter it seemed having a charmed life, escaped, though both were damaged.

As with all night actions at this time, the impression was one of extreme confusion and mayhem. Lewin spent much of the action in the charthouse plot, which was a rudimentary operations room, but made frequent sallies up to the bridge to see what was going on. At one point he was about to remonstrate with his captain for turning to join *Tartar* without finishing off the *ZH1*, when he was told the latter had just blown up.

The subsequent report of these proceedings[71] gives an interesting insight into the developing arrangements for Action Information, a rapidly expanding science. Only the *Tartar* had anything resembling the operations rooms that became standard a few years later, and only *Tartar* and *Eskimo* had Plan Position Indicators, the now-familiar rotating radar displays. It was little wonder that the plots were confused. It is most unlikely that the lessons were not hoisted in by the keen and highly intelligent 24-year-old first lieutenant of the *Ashanti*. He was to make use of them many times, most tellingly of all a whole generation later.

The *Ashanti*'s largely conscript, hostilities-only ship's company had come a long way from the dispirited, seasick, far from battle-ready crew they had been six months before. Leo Lee, able seaman, recalled half a century later how Barnes and Lewin 'soon licked HO ratings into shape. A generally happy "bluenose" crew ...'[72] Lewin would no doubt have given credit too to the hard core of ex-*Mashona* ratings he had managed to retain – particularly Chief Petty Officer Dockwra, who was not only a highly effective chief boatswain's mate but the director layer in action, providing the basic elevation and training data to the guns' fire control systems, and introducing at least one important innovation that greatly helped accuracy in blind fire.[73] But the morale and spirit of a ship must stand or fall by the personality and professionalism of the captain and first lieutenant, and in this the *Ashanti* was, as in all else, lucky.

The results of the Ile de Batz action were far-reaching. In effect, the Germans decided that Allied dominance of the western approaches to the Channel was so complete that major movements along the Brittany coast were no longer feasible.[74] Sporadic enemy activity continued, however, and on 13 June *Ashanti* and *Piorun* made havoc amongst a group of German minesweepers between the Channel Islands and St Malo, sinking three and putting several more out of action. This success was repeated a fortnight later, and by the end of it no less than ten minesweepers and two armed trawlers had been removed from the order of battle.

Now it was time to extend the sea reach of Allied forces to help in eliminating German ground resistance in western France, and *Ashanti* found herself often 'trailing her coat' on the Bay of Biscay coast. Lewin recalled:

I would be sent in with a gang of armed thugs in a motorboat to make contact with the Free French, [giving them] cased sten guns and ammunition ... to stir up trouble with the Germans ... I can remember particularly the enjoyable visit to Sables d'Olonne ... where we were welcomed with open arms, rushed off to the local Free French headquarters, given champagne, and sent off back to the ship with very large baskets of apricots.[75]

More orthodox operations included cruiser and destroyer sweeps against surface forces operating out of St Nazaire, a particularly successful action in early August almost completely annihilating an eight-ship convoy and its minesweeper escort. During this action *Ashanti* suffered her only serious casualty of the war: a rating manning Y gun lost a leg, and some others were more lightly wounded. She was a lucky ship.

But by now she was, materially, a desperately weary ship. Often she returned to harbour with only one boiler working out of three; she regularly ran out of fresh water, her auxiliary machinery was in a parlous state, and constant high-speed running and frequent gunfire had aggravated every mechanical and electrical ill.[76] Early in October 1944, now under the command of Lieutenant-Commander C. R. Purse, she was ordered to Palmers' Yard on the Tyne to refit.

It was time for Lieutenant Lewin to consider his future. He was a seasoned destroyer officer now, much decorated (he had been Mentioned in Despatches twice in 1944, once for the minesweeper action on 13 June and once for the convoy action on 6 August),[77] and reported on in the most glowing terms by captains who were themselves highly regarded sea warriors. But the Channel war, which had given the best prospects of early destroyer command, was clearly coming to an end, and the offer of second-in-command of a 'Ca' class destroyer in the Far East ('three steps down from a Tribal', recalled Lord Lewin with an uncharacteristic sniff) did not appeal – not least because Lieutenant Lewin had been married for nearly a year and had snatched very little of anything that might have been called home life.

So he volunteered to specialise in gunnery. This was then the élite specialisation of the Royal Navy, as it had been at least since the turn of the century; in spite of the dominance of anti-submarine warfare in the all-important Battle of the Atlantic, and the coming emphasis on carrier air operations in the British Pacific Fleet, it had kept its own mystique, its discipline and precision, its durable tribal loyalties. It had traditionally been a road to high rank.[78] Moreover – and in his case this probably weighed more heavily than personal ambition – it was an appropriate specialisation for an officer of Lewin's experience. He had been in turn the gunnery control officer, the gunnery officer, and the first lieutenant responsible for gunnery efficiency, in one of the most heavily gun-armed destroyers of the fleet. He knew a lot about it already. His professional academic qualifications were more than adequate; he had a first-class certificate from his sub-lieutenant's course. So, unsurprisingly, he was selected for the 1945 long gunnery course, and a new phase of his life began.

GUNNERY OFFICER
1945–1951

Gunnery is meant to be an exact science. Its object is to place a projectile in a position where it will cause damage to its target. Given the nature of most projectiles – either solid, or filled with high explosive – that means either hitting the target, or making the projectile explode very close to it indeed. To achieve that with shells fired from guns, the movement of the target, between the time of firing the gun and the time the shell arrives at the target's position, has to be allowed for.

That is the essence of the gunnery control problem. For surface fire, its solution had preoccupied navies since the beginning of the twentieth century.[1] For defence against aircraft, it had engaged their attention somewhat marginally between the wars and then, much more vitally, during the Second World War itself. During that war, much anti-aircraft fire was a matter of loosing off every available shell and bullet in the general direction of the enemy and hoping he would fly into it; nevertheless, the underlying principle was that a system or systems of gun control should produce acceptable accuracy.

The specialist gunnery officer, as a professional, needed to be a master not only of the systems provided but of their underlying principles, in order to keep them at their optimum performance and to help develop improvements. He needed therefore a sound knowledge of the mathematics of the four-dimensional problem of 'target movement during time of flight'; of the ballistic characteristics of his weapons; and of the theory behind the electronic, electrical and mechanical components of all his equipment. With this basis of knowledge, he could then go on to the matters of organisation, training, drill, safety measures and upkeep that would make him competent to be the custodian of the gunnery department of a ship of the fleet.

With this agenda, the Gunnery Long Course took over a year. The first month, which in Lieutenant Lewin's case came at the close

of 1944, was at the Royal Naval College, Greenwich: his first introduction to that great complex, designed by Wren and carried on by
so many other eminent architects, which made an instant impression
on him,[2] and one whose imprint persisted and recurred throughout
his life. This introductory month at Greenwich was to cover the
basic mathematics and physics that would be required for the
gunnery course.

For gunnery specialists were expected to be of high technical attain-
ment. At that time the Electrical Branch of the navy was still in course
of formation; there were a few ordnance engineers, some of them
extremely competent and inventive; but the chief burden of technical
knowledge and development still fell on executive [seaman] officers of
the gunnery specialisation. The technology of the time was neither easy
nor robust: thermionic valves, servomotors, hydraulics, cams and gear-
wheels all had a part to play, sometimes unharmoniously.

This theoretical foundation laid, Lieutenant Lewin joined HMS
Excellent at Whale Island, Portsmouth, in January 1945. Jane was still
in the WRNS, at HMS *Dryad*, the navigation school at Southwick
Park just outside Portsmouth; it had acquired the additional responsibility for training in Action Information,[3] and Jane was part of that
organisation. They set up home in 'a ground floor flat in Stavington
Avenue, Portsmouth which gave us an adequate kitchen, dining room
and bedroom and an outside loo ... Jane picked up her bus out to
Dryad at North End ... We went on my bicycle and I gave her a lift on
my crossbar to North End and proceeded on to Whaley.'[4]

Lewin found congenial company among the long course officers.
They included several who figured in his subsequent career and family
life: Peter LaNeice, Alan Archibald and John Marrack, whose names
will recur in this narrative. From a purely service point of view the
most important may well have been Tony Synnot, an officer of the
Royal Australian Navy who had himself served in a 'Tribal', the
Punjabi. Synnot ('the wives' pin-up boy on the long course'[5]) rose to
be Chief of the Australian Naval Staff and Chief of Defence Staff in
Australia: his career and Lewin's thus marched together, with notable
results for co-operation in the Australasian area.

At the end of the long course, after the examinations and the practical tests that abounded, Lewin was awarded the Egerton Testimonial for the best overall result.[6] In later years he ascribed what he said was a narrow success to his 'shouting, sword drill and gun drill': if so, he soon relinquished shouting except on the parade ground, for 'he never raised his voice' was one of the most general comments made by individuals about his subsequent behaviour.

For the five months after completion of the long course, Lewin remained at Whale Island on the staff. This hiatus was not unconnected with his talent for rugger and the presence at *Excellent*, as appointments commander, of John Willy Forrest who had been an England international just before the Second World War. The United Services Rugby Football Club at Portsmouth was at that time of a very high standard, augmented by officers doing their eighteen months' National Service who tended to gravitate towards the Royal Navy if they were interested in developing their rugby talents. Lewin, modestly starting each season in the Extra A, soon gained a place each time in the First XV. Whale Island's atmosphere was enlivened by the sight of him and Lieutenant Hooke, RNR, rushing up and down the slopes hurling rugby balls at each other.[7]

But winter 1946 came to an end, and in April Lewin was appointed to HMS *Bellona*, a light cruiser of 7350 tons, mounting eight 5.25-inch guns and a heavy secondary anti-aircraft armament. These ships of the 'Dido' and modified 'Dido' classes had been conceived very much as anti-aircraft cruisers. They were fast, their 62,000 hp giving them 32 knots, and many of them, including *Bellona*, had distinguished war records.[8] However, they were designed for war and not for peacetime cruising, and particularly for their ships' companies they were cramped and uncomfortable.

Moreover, it was a bad time for the seagoing fleet. The war was over and retrenchment was in the air. That might not immediately affect the ships and men who would remain, but the massive demobilisation, going on at the same time, certainly would. The peak strength of the Royal Navy, including WRNS, during the Second World War had been 863,500,[9] and by the end of 1946 it was to fall by half a million.[10] This was bound to cause turbulence, aggravated by the need to man seagoing ships with increasing proportions of regular personnel and therefore deprive them, probably, of what they believed to be well-earned time ashore.

For the Royal Navy was weary after six years of war. That did not apply to the service alone, of course; the whole country was; but the malaise did certainly apply to the fleet, and few ships were without some souls who, having suffered (or believed they had suffered) more than most, found what refuge they could in the bottle. It was a lucky wardroom that did not have some of these, and *Bellona*'s was not one of the lucky ones.

The Lewins moved to Chatham where *Bellona* was finishing a refit. The ship did get to sea, and the great excitement of the summer was a visit to Murmansk to collect a cargo of gold bullion, which was in payment for war supplies. Lewin noted that 'as Gunnery Officer I was responsible for loading this on board and stowing it down in the magazine. Everybody was desperate to see what gold bullion looked like so we contrived to burst open one of the boxes ...'[11] With a visit to Narvik on the way back, the bullion was safely delivered to Rosyth where it was stowed in two railway wagons and 'seemed to be completely left for the next two or three days'.

Then came a change in *Bellona*'s programme and the Lewins' fortunes. *Bellona* was to be transferred to the Royal New Zealand Navy and near the end of the summer RNZN personnel arrived to take over. This fitted well with the immediate future for Terry Lewin and for navy rugby, since he was back at Whale Island for the start of the season, and was due to continue in the south of England with a 'dagger' gunnery course at Greenwich after Christmas.

It was not so convenient for Jane, who was pregnant; the baby was expected in April. The manoeuvres leading up to the birth of Tim Lewin in a nursing home at St Leonards, near Hastings in Kent, on 10 April 1947 may not be unfamiliar to those who had anything to do with the navy at that time, though they might appear intricate now; they involved naval friends who had medical relations, and several changes of address during the dreadful winter of 1946–7. The

National Health Service was in process of formation. In any event, Tim, their first child, arrived safely and the Lewins set up home in Mayday Gardens at Blackheath.

In the meantime Terry had contrived to win his first rugby cap for the Navy. Now at Greenwich for the course, he was under the aegis of Commander R. J. L. Hammond, for whom the phrase 'sports fanatic' was appropriate. Cricket, rugby and squash were his specialities and 'get fit quick' his motto.[12] Hammond got, and kept, Lewin fit by playing him at squash, Hammond left (wrong) handed and regularly winning 9-0. The inter-service rugby matches were postponed for months because of the weather; when they finally played the Royal Air Force, Lewin recalled, 'the ground was mostly covered in snow ... I scored a try in the corner ... I've always felt some doubt that I never really got the ball over the line ...'[13]

The 'dagger' gunnery course was for specially selected gunnery officers only, destined to be deep specialists who would lead the material and professional development of the branch, and its equipments, through succeeding generations. It involved a great deal of theoretical work in higher mathematics and physics, and Terry Lewin was not too sure of his abilities in that field, nor certain that 'dagger' gunnery, with its emphasis on experimental work, was a path he wished to follow. That was for the future; the immediate problem was to secure the qualification, because failure would not be well regarded. The only other officer on the course, John Marrack, had a natural bent for the subjects being taught and was certain to cruise through the examinations; he and Lewin persuaded the professors that an exam was not necessary for either of them.[14] They duly qualified as 'Dagger G' at the end of 1947.

An appointment to *Excellent* was a natural sequel, made even more obvious by the continued presence of Forrest as appointing commander. The Lewins moved from Blackheath, where they let their house, to a flat in Hayling Island. This was convenient to Terry's place of work, which was Frazer Gunnery Range at Eastney, quite remote from Whale Island but easily reachable by ferry from Hayling.

Frazer had the dual role of carrying out live firings, over a restricted arc to seaward, and conducting experiments in advanced fire control systems. The gunnery world was opening its eyes to all kinds of new systems of fire control: the old geometric solutions, with their largely mechanical predictors, were beginning to give way to systems that used the observed rate of movement of the target, along and across the line of sight, to predict its future behaviour. These so-called tachometric systems had been developed in the USA, and they could be used for both close-range anti-aircraft fire and for longer-range fire with medium-calibre guns. It was an exciting time: 'The instruction staff were the cream of the instructors from Whale Island, Petty Officers, Gunner's Mates, young, intelligent and enthusiastic and the whole place was absolutely humming.'[15]

No doubt it was to a large extent Lieutenant Lewin who made it hum. The Commander (G), James Farnol, wrote as head of his department in early 1949: 'His professional ability and powers of leadership are exceptional, and he should go far in the Service which he adorns.'[16] Farnol was a hard, tough gunnery officer (it was said that at one Friday divisions he stopped a rainstorm by marching out of the drill shed and inspecting the sky) and did not write such words lightly.

There was a second Navy rugby cap for Terry in 1948, but the summer had its sporting side too. In 1949 the Whaley athletics were, like everything else, fiercely competitive. Lieutenant Andrew Robertson, of the Royal Australian Navy, was detailed to throw the javelin for the Long Course. One day he was at practice in the presence of a star New Zealander, Fred Bland, of the rival Ordnance Engineers' team. Bland, at the far end of the field and in true antipodean fashion, told Robertson he couldn't throw that far – and Robertson for once did:

> Fred, being an ordnance engineer and not a gunnery officer, ran away along the line of flight and not across it ... [the javelin] pinned him to the ground like a moth ... Terry was a tower of strength as we staunched the wound and got Fred to the sick bay. We yarned about the incident for years ... It was a bond between the three of us.[17]

Frazer had been a pleasant 18-month interlude, rewarding professionally, domestically and in the sporting field, but it was time for Lewin
to return to sea. Now a lieutenant-commander, he was appointed in
July 1949 as flotilla gunnery officer to the First Destroyer Flotilla,
based in Malta. The flotilla was composed of ships of the 'Ch' class,
'Emergency' destroyers built towards the end of the Second World
War.[18] While old 'Tribal' men like Lewin believed nothing matched
those ships, others might have said that the 'Emergencies' were the
classical destroyers of all time. They were fast, handy, well-balanced
vessels, their 40,000 hp steam plant giving them over 30 knots. And
although they had not had an easy time since the war – the Palestine
emergency, with its distasteful task of seeking to stop immigrant
ships,[19] had not been kind either to their material state or to their
ships' companies – they had at least not served throughout it, and were
generally reliable mechanically.

The gunnery fit was relatively modern without being innovative.
The ships had been built too early to be fitted with tachometric
systems, but the gunnery radar was an up-to-date set and the four 4.5-
inch single mountings, with remote power control, were well placed
and could develop a high rate of fire, given well-drilled crews. Close-
range armament of Bofors and Oerlikon guns was a useful adjunct,
though for reasons of topweight the most modern Bofors mountings
could not be fitted.

Lieutenant-Commander Lewin could, therefore, consider that he
was going to a crack destroyer flotilla, and the Mediterranean station
had never suffered from post-war malaise in the same way as had the
Home Fleet. Under the guidance of two uncompromising Commanders-in-Chief, Sir Algernon Willis and Sir Arthur John Power, and
given enough operational challenges to keep it sharp[20] as well as a full
exercise programme, the Mediterranean Fleet was maintaining standards of efficiency as well as smartness.

Lewin joined a wardroom of considerable talent in HMS *Chequers*,
the leader, and it was soon to be enhanced. The current first lieutenant
was shortly to be relieved by HRH the Prince Philip, Duke of Edinburgh. By now a senior lieutenant, Philip had been shipmates with

Lewin before; he had joined the *Valiant*'s gunroom as a junior midshipman not long before Lewin and Macdonald left it, and Macdonald told years later the story of how the prince had reasoned, in what the admiring midshipmen thought to be flawless demotic Greek, with the owner of a cinema in Alexandria to reserve the best seats in the house for the gunroom officers.[21] In fact, from 'not knowing what to expect' from Midshipman Prince Philip of Greece,[22] the gunroom had found him an excellent messmate.

Lewin, as senior staff officer of the flotilla, therefore looked forward to the arrival of the new first lieutenant with equanimity and pleasure. It has been said that the equanimity was not entirely shared by his Captain (D), who 'had felt a painful urge to call [Prince Philip] Sir'.[23] But in general, the arrangement worked out extremely well, and the rapport between the two men, senior staff and first lieutenant – not always the easiest in a destroyer leader – was close and cordial. People remarked on it half a century later: one informant, a junior lieutenant at the time, observed that on the hockey pitch, with Lewin at centre half and Philip at centre forward, the understanding between the two was formidable and effective.[24]

The games side of the Navy was, indeed, still there in Malta, and further afield when the fleet went off for its frequent cruises. Rugby remained on the Lewin agenda, and he played for the Navy, still at wing three-quarter, the first winter in the Mediterranean, scoring two tries in a famous victory against the Army on the grass airfield at Ta Qali.[25] In a picture taken of this event, he is seen to be wearing knee coverings: it was a well-known fact that the iron-hard grounds in Malta could be extremely damaging to limb if not life, and it seems likely that shortly after this he stopped playing the game at top level, a sensible move as he entered his thirties. It may well have been on Jane's advice: she had joined him in Malta with an addition to the family, Susie, born on 26 September 1949. Henceforth games were equally strenuous (hockey, played on bald Malta stone, and middle-distance running, again at Navy level) but not quite so risky.

The professional side of fleet life was, however, his chief business, and he made sure the First Destroyer Flotilla (it became a 'Squadron', to bring it into line with NATO nomenclature, in 1951) was a tip-top operational outfit. When the ships were in Malta and not undergoing maintenance, they would go to sea most weekdays to carry out the requirements of the Weekly Practice Programme: testing and tuning of sensors and systems, anti-aircraft tracking and shoots, anti-submarine exercises, line and screening manoeuvres, and diverse burgeoning arts such as electronic warfare, damage control, nuclear, biological and chemical defence, and replenishment at sea. Often the day would culminate in the hurly-burly of a Night Encounter Exercise, with starshell illuminating sometimes the 'enemy', sometimes not. The machinery and organisation for operational control were developing all the time: communications and plotting arrangements were advancing at a rapid rate, the Mediterranean Fleet regarded itself as being in the lead, and the 'Fighting First' reckoned to lead the fleet.

When the fleet went off on a cruise, it did so, in the memorable phrase of one ship's captain, 'fighting its way from place to place'.[26] Exercises of larger scale were then the norm, with ships forming screens on the heavier units, submarines disposed to make dummy attacks, and aircraft conducting sustained sortie rates, the scenario sometimes extending to days or weeks to simulate, as far as possible, the conditions of war. Everything had to be recorded and analysed: extracting the 'lessons learned' was one of the principal functions of a staff officer.

In April 1950 several of the staff changed, the experienced incumbents being relieved by equally talented successors, who included James Pertwee as torpedo and anti-submarine specialist, and David Loram for communications. Many subsequently achieved high rank: the team was a good one, and Lewin ensured it was cohesive. Then in July, Prince Philip himself left, to take up his first command, the frigate *Magpie*, also on the Mediterranean station. By common consent, this period of naval service was probably the happiest time of their lives for Philip and his wife; without yet the cares of monarchy, they were able to enjoy the existence of a naval couple on a congenial station.[27] The new first lieutenant of *Chequers* was Tony Troup, a submariner whose carefree manner hid great drive and uncompromising insistence on high standards.

Command of the flotilla also changed that summer. John McBeath, the previous Captain (D), was a hard-bitten, highly competent destroyer man. He was succeeded by Michael Townsend, another destroyer specialist, more flamboyant and dashing but with much underlying judgement. He quickly sized up his staff gunnery officer and found him 'outstanding in every respect': that was the brief report he wrote fifteen months later,[28] and his trust in and reliance on Lewin's work throughout that time were everywhere apparent.

Tony Troup recounted an episode during the combined fleets' gathering in Gibraltar in the spring of 1951 when he was called to Townsend's cabin shortly before the ship was to sail on a large-scale exercise. Townsend was ill, clearly not capable of going on the bridge:

> He told me to take the squadron to sea and carry out the exercise without him. This I did, me driving the ship and Terry running the squadron, it was the greatest fun for a week and no one ever knew, but it certainly would not have been possible without Terry's masterly understanding of how to do it all.[29]

In the early summer of 1951 the Mediterranean Fleet was returning from a cruise that had included the fleet pulling regatta in Marmarice Bay (Townsend, true to form, had personally led a large team formed to fight a forest fire that broke out on one of the adjacent islands). The grand finale for the First Destroyer Squadron was a spread torpedo attack on the depot ship *Forth*, firing full outfits of 'fish' with blowing heads that could then be recovered by ships' boats. It was a great success and in the Mediterranean dawn the sea was littered with destroyers, boats and the bobbing orange heads of the torpedoes as they were reclaimed by their parent vessels.[30]

The squadron returned to harbour during the forenoon, but instead of the expected leave and relaxation there were further orders. Ships were to fuel, store and top up with ammunition and sail forthwith for a destination that was not immediately made known to ships' companies. All they were told was: 'It is going to be hot ... very hot.'

Mediterranean Fleet destroyers were accustomed to crisis management, much of it at the eastern end of the station where the
Arab–Israeli situation remained tense, with its maritime focus in the
Gulf of Aqaba and the Strait of Tiran.[31] But although the First
Destroyer Squadron went east and through the Suez Canal, they did no
more than make a high-speed pass toward the Tiran Strait, a cover
plan only. They turned south through the Red Sea towards their true
destination, the Persian Gulf, 2000 miles away. On 2 May the Iranian
government, led by Prime Minister Mossadegh, had nationalised the
Anglo-Iranian Oil Company, and this had caused a severe crisis
between Britain and Iran; Iranian oil supplies were still important to
the United Kingdom, even though a greater diversity of sources was
becoming available in Kuwait and Saudi Arabia, and their security was
an important issue. The Shah was at that time in exile and Iran was in
a turbulent state. Iraq was still under a good deal of British influence,
with a small RAF establishment in Shaibah and some British personnel
in the Iraqi armed forces. The only other permanent British presence in
the Gulf was the small naval base at Bahrain, with the Senior Naval
Officer Persian Gulf (SNOPG) and his three 'Bird' class frigates, of
which two were generally on station. These were not considered sufficient on their own to take any initiatives that might prove necessary;
the Iranian Navy was small and thought not to be efficient, but operations in the close-quarters situations that might arise could well
require the use of 'definitive force',[32] and it was this that the destroyers
were expected to provide.

Hot it was. As the four ships, *Chequers, Chieftain, Chevron* and
Chivalrous, steaming at 25 knots through the south-west monsoon,
rounded Ras al-Hadd on the eastern tip of Arabia, heat and humidity
struck at once, and it is fair to say they were the major preoccupation for
the whole of the time the squadron was in the Gulf. It was, some said,
statistically the hottest and dampest summer recorded for years. True or
not, living conditions on board were barely tolerable, difficult enough for
the officers, outrageous for the men. The ships were not air-conditioned;
the only compartment so fitted was the cypher office, and it was extraordinary how many volunteers there were to decrypt top-secret signals.

There were plenty of those. The orders went under the codename Buccaneer, and many of them are closed to this day. But the dispositions of the squadron, which are well known, give plenty of clue as to the outline of the plan. It was very much governed by geography. The Abadan refinery, focus of the Anglo-Iranian Oil Company's operation, was on the Iranian bank some 50 miles up the Shatt-al-Arab, the waterway formed by the confluence of the Tigris and Euphrates rivers debouching into the Gulf. The small Iranian sloop *Palang* lay there as a guardship, covered by the guns of the military ashore. Some miles down the river, at Khorramshahr, lay the larger Iranian frigate *Babr*. Basra, on the Iraqi side, was some miles further upstream.

The British stationed a cruiser, *Euryalus*, during the stay of the First Destroyer Squadron, opposite Abadan with one destroyer normally in attendance. Further destroyers were usually stationed at Basra. Had Buccaneer been ordered, the most likely pattern would have been a cutting-out operation reminiscent of the Napoleonic wars to capture the *Palang*, while the remaining destroyers ferried troops down from Basra to capture and secure the refinery and evacuate the British nationals holed up there. What was to be done with the refinery once it had been captured was never clear. 'Terry', remembered Tony Troup, 'was in his element hatching up daredevil schemes for boarding ... and other schemes for retaking the oil refinery.' Depth charges towed on grass (floating) lines were a favoured option.[33]

None of it happened. The government at home was undecided as to whether this sort of action could have a favourable outcome, and as August drifted on into September the squadron was released in ones and twos to the wider waters of the Gulf, even sometimes to the (relative) fleshpots of Bahrain, Ras at Tannura and Kuwait, where a certain amount of coolth, if very few other amenities, might be found. Ships took every sort of initiative to keep their companies alert and interested: 'sods' operas' (concert parties), banyan parties to land on desolate islets for a few hours, hands to bathe with vigilant shark lookouts, unexpected sorties to keep engineers and watch-keepers sharp. And indeed, morale remained high, considering the conditions and the clear perception that there was no prospect of military action. But, Lord Lewin recorded, of 'the 1000 men we had in our four ships, every single one had prickly heat ... we were no longer fighting efficient ships'.[34]

Relief by the Third Destroyer Squadron, the *Saintes, Vigo, Armada* and *Gravelines*, came not a moment too soon and the prospect of a late-October visit to Istanbul was enticing. On its way the squadron called in to Khor Kuwai, an inlet on the Musandam peninsula where there was a resident small oil tanker and a tiny British shore station manned by a caretaker,[35] to top up with fuel in order to get to Suez, its next refuelling stop.

> While we were alongside the tanker, I got a signal from the C-in-C: 'Regret to inform you that your son is seriously ill with poliomyelitis' ... there was absolutely nothing I could do to get home because we were really in one of the remotest parts of the world. However Captain (D), God bless him, steamed the squadron at 20 knots to Suez where I was popped into an aeroplane and back to Malta. So Jane had to endure the first ten days or a fortnight of our dear son Tim, aged four, being struck down with polio and not knowing how bad it was going to be.[36]

It was not the worst, but bad enough. Tim was then paralysed from the waist down (his subsequent successful battle for recovery, mobility and a full life is a story of determination and fortitude which cannot be done justice in this book) and was in the Naval Hospital at Bighi. Jane was able to visit him daily, being taken across the harbour in the barge of the Flag Officer Malta, Rear Admiral Guy Grantham. When Terry arrived back in Malta he found two pieces of news that lightened the situation. First, his relief having been appointed, he was not required to rejoin *Chequers*. Second, Tim was no longer on the danger list and arrangements could be put in hand to repatriate him and Jane and place him in a suitable hospital in England; the Lord Mayor Treloar Hospital at Alton was chosen.

So Jane and Tim went home by air ambulance ('an RAF York – not all that comfortable'[37]) and Terry and their daughter Susie by an air trooping flight. There were inevitable difficulties caused by the some-what early return to the United Kingdom, and the family had a domes-tically difficult couple of months before they finally resettled in Mayday Gardens.

It had been a sad end to a brilliant two years' service. The sympathy for the Lewins was unbounded: far beyond the support of Captain (D) and the squadron doctor, Bob Askham, it extended throughout the ship and indeed the squadron. The news had circulated like wildfire, and the anxiety was almost palpable.

Naval wives are not a species. All faced then, and face still, similar challenges and risks: separation, the strain of managing family prob-lems alone, money worries particularly in early years, constant changes of home (or worse separation), and most of all perhaps the 'grey mistress' syndrome, the priority that the service takes in the mind of the dedicated spouse. All have their individual ways of coping: the options may have changed over the years, but the diversity of methods has remained constant. Jane Lewin was one of the most individual: forthright, sometimes fierce, always totally loyal to Terry and her family, as he was to her and them. The difficult times, and the end of 1951 was undoubtedly one of them, were surmounted by a relation-ship that never failed.

INTRODUCTION
TO WHITEHALL
1952–1955

In the normal course of events Lieutenant-Commander Lewin, as a specialist gunnery officer, would expect an appointment to HMS *Excellent* after a tour at sea, and in February 1952, after foreign service leave that was much needed in the difficult family circumstances, this duly occurred. He was appointed Staff Officer (Policy), which entailed the development of gunnery tactics and marrying them with the other tactical requirements of a fleet, notably anti-submarine warfare. It was a matter of recognising 'the need to treat the sea battle as a whole',[1] a theme that stayed with Lewin throughout his naval career.

The post was a new one, the task intellectually exciting and rewarding, and an addition to it – the integration of air gunnery into Whale Island's work, a development suggested by Lewin – gave added scope. Ken Lee White, who had moved with the Air Gunnery School from the Royal Naval Air Station at Culdrose, became head of the air gunnery department, and shared an office with Lewin. They became close friends. All in all, it was a harmonious staff at Whale Island; Peter LaNeice, a contemporary gunnery officer, recalled the laughter up and down the corridor, not always to the approval of a serious-minded Commander (G).[2]

Domestically, too, life was more settled. The Lewins had let the house in Blackheath once more and moved to a ground-floor flat in New Town House, Hayling Island. This was fairly convenient for Alton, where Tim was still at the Treloar Hospital, and for the nursery school which Susie was beginning to attend. The family bought its first car ('Tumblebug' had long gone, indeed it was rumoured that Eric Lewin had sold it when Terry contracted diphtheria in 1941), and Tim remembered journeys in this Morris 8 tourer, with his father singing much of the time. 'Ivan Skavinsky Skivar' was heard again, and 'Casey Jones' joined the repertory.[3]

His taste in music may have been simple (in gunroom days it had included repeated gramophone renderings of Judy Garland and Deanna Durbin) but he was no philistine. In the *Valiant* he had introduced Roddy Macdonald to *Burnt Norton*, at that time the only one of T. S. Eliot's *Four Quartets* to have been published. It was an unusual piece of reading for a 20-year-old midshipman. Tim Lewin has his father's copy still.

At the end of 1952, to great delight but to no one's particular surprise, Terry Lewin's name was on the list of half-yearly promotions to commander. In the Royal Navy all promotions before this rank were automatic, after a fixed time in the previous rank. Promotion to commander, however, was on merit, and generally considered the most significant step in an officer's career. It occurred, if and when it did, in a 'zone' of seniority as lieutenant-commander that stretched from three to eight years or thereabouts. Those who were promoted early in the zone clearly had greater chances of achieving the higher ranks later on. Terry Lewin was 'second shot':[4] a good augury for the future.

His next appointment was to the Royal Naval Staff Course at Greenwich, which he joined in March 1953. The course at that time lasted less than six months – the Navy had never taken staff training with quite the same seriousness as the Army or Royal Air Force – and it was not considered worth while to have the upheaval of another family move, so it was a matter of weekend commuting to Hayling Island and some quite intensive work on the 'schemes' during the week.

The director of the staff course was initially Captain Luce and later the redoubtable Tony ('Crap') Miers, VC, well known as one of the most outspoken officers in the service. His report on Commander Lewin at the end of the course was a eulogy, though true to form he found some flaw: 'An outstanding officer who has found the staff course almost too easy ... no praise is too high for him ... if he fails at all it is in public speaking ...'[5] That was to be corrected later.

When his promotion came through, Terry Lewin had expected to be appointed, after the staff course, to one of the posts in the gunnery division of the Admiralty. These were the usual 'slots' for newly promoted specialist commanders, worthy enough but not inspiring unless one could contrive to make it so – and that was not easy, given the power of continuity in Whitehall. However, history and old acquaintance had taken a hand. Captain Mike Townsend had moved on from the command of the First Destroyer Squadron to the post of Naval Assistant to the Second Sea Lord, an odd title which covered one of the most influential jobs in the Admiralty, that of running the executive [seaman] officers' appointments. Townsend telephoned Lewin straight away when the news of his promotion came through, offered him a job on NA2SL's staff, and fought through the change against the expected opposition.[6] So, in September 1953, equipped with the regulation umbrella and bowler hat, Commander Lewin joined the Admiralty for the first time.

The first few months were spent in statistical work of the kind that had always occupied that particular post in the staff of NA2SL – the 'back room boy' who worked out the billets required in the fleet and on shore for officers of various descriptions, compared these with the officers available to fill them, made recommendations as to how the posts were to be filled, and worked out the promotion factors. It was detailed and, in itself, absorbing work. But something more fundamental and exciting was on the way, and it is necessary to go back a little into history to explain how it came about.

Since the end of the war, with retrenchment affecting the size of the seagoing fleet, the Admiralty had been aware of growing difficulty in giving enough time, in command of ships, to seaman officers from the rank of senior lieutenant-commander upwards. As far back as 1949 the Naval Secretary, Rear Admiral Peveril William-Powlett, had put to the Board of Admiralty proposals to limit destroyer and frigate commands to commanders and above,[7] and the principle had reluctantly been accepted. Some went further: the Commander-in-Chief Far East Station, the far-sighted 'Daddy' Brind, had suggested that some seaman officers of captain's rank should not expect sea command at all.[8] This notion gained ground during 1950.

But there, for the time being, it had ended. The Korean War broke out; more pressing appointment problems arose; some officers were even recalled to service; and the staff divisions in any case took up entrenched positions. The problem was only resurrected in October 1952, and even then took six months to wind its way towards the Board.[9] The Board temporised, the First Sea Lord showing particular resistance to change, and its decision in June 1953 to 'increase the sea time of the best captains' (with, presumably, some compensating reduction in the sea time of the less good) did little to resolve the issue.

At the same time, many other problems surrounding officer structure were becoming apparent. They were summed up in a *Naval Review* article[10] once the whole business was over, and the authoritative words of the author of the article cannot be bettered:

> ... incomplete integration of the Fleet Air Arm into the line of command ...
>
> ... wide disparity of opportunity between branches, leading to waste of talent and frustration ...
>
> ... career prospects which are not commensurate with the standard of entry it is desired to recruit ...
>
> ... equivocal status and slow promotion on the Branch [ex-lower deck, previously the warrant officers'] List, leading to frustration and loss of lower deck talent to the shore ...
>
> ... the unknown future size of the Navy, leading to the risk of over-provision of permanent, cadet-entered officers.

Such a plethora of issues meant that the Navy had to put its house in order, and in late 1953, just at the time Commander Lewin was settling in his chair at the Admiralty, the Committee on Officer Structure and Training was formed under Vice Admiral Sir Aubrey Mansergh. The composition of the committee, with two notably sharp rear admirals in John Hughes-Hallett (succeeded in 1955 by Deric Holland-Martin) and M. W. Richmond, and a highly experienced civil servant, B. C. Sendall, as its secretary, reflected its importance, and the terms of reference its radical nature:

> 1. To review the present officer structure of the Navy fundamentally and exhaustively without regard to previous decisions;

to recommend what types of officer will be required in the future, in what numbers ... and how they should be employed in order to gain experience ... and to advise on the most suitable form of training for each type.

2. The Committee should specially address themselves, as soon as they are in a position to do so, to the form of training to be given to officers who join under the new cadet entry at about 18 ...

The committee would clearly require staff support for its work, and this was where Commander Lewin came in. He had all the background and knowledge of the system to provide detailed advice on how the ideas of the committee would work out in practice. But – and this was probably the point at which the committee was most faithful to its radical remit and most far-seeing in its arrangements – he was not to work alone. He was to be joined by officers from the other main branches of the naval service, the engineers and the paymasters; and the selection of the individuals for this work was, as it turned out, critical. They were respectively Commander Louis LeBailly and Commander Colin Dunlop. The triumvirate were collectively known as the Ferrets.[11]

It would be wrong to say, as some have suggested, that Terry Lewin, or the Ferrets as a whole, were the architects of the reforms that followed the Mansergh Committee. The main committee were their own men, senior officers of strong character, great experience and sound intellect, and Mansergh was an exceptionally perceptive and far-sighted chairman. What is for sure is that the Ferrets, as well as providing the detailed staffwork without which the committee would have been fatally short of the evidence necessary to support their proposals, entirely supported the general thrust of the committee's ideas, sometimes moved ahead of them by providing additional evidence when it had not been asked for, and were increasingly called upon as advisers rather than simply as 'assessors' – which was their official title.[12]

The committee's deliberations lasted in all about 18 months[13] and their conclusions – approved of course by the Board of Admiralty –

appeared in three phases. The first, as required by clause 2 of the
Terms of Reference, was the new training pattern for officers. The 16-
year-old entry, introduced in 1945 to replace the previous dual officer
entry at either 13 or 18 and at least partly an attempt at democratisa-
tion, was deemed to have failed to attract or produce an officer corps
of sufficient quality. The decision had already been taken to move to a
single entry at the age of 18 or thereabouts for career officers, and the
committee's recommendations set out the training pattern they
believed to be required.[14]

This was to be a three-phase course lasting two and a half years,
based upon the Royal Naval College at Dartmouth. The principle was
that 'officers should be taught the groundwork of their profession'
during this course: in consequence, it was to replace initial training, the
training cruiser, fleet time as midshipmen, and sub-lieutenants' professional courses. The first phase of two terms was aimed at producing a
common academic base amongst cadets of varying academic background, and teaching basic nautical and leadership skills. The second
phase, also as cadets, was to be a single term in the local training
squadron 'as part of the rating complement', as an introduction to life
at sea. The third phase, now as midshipmen, was to be of five terms in
the college and in the frigates of the Dartmouth Training Squadron
(big brothers, as it were, of the local squadron) and to cover 'all the
principal professional subjects together with the science and mathematics these need'. It would replace both fleet time as midshipmen and
sub-lieutenants' courses at the specialist schools like *Excellent* for
gunnery and *Vernon* for torpedo and anti-submarine warfare. At the
end of this period of training, officers would join the fleet as sub-lieutenants. The 'non-executive branches' (they were still called that), the
paymasters and engineers, would be subject to the same training
pattern with variations appropriate to their specialisation.

It is doubtful if Commander Lewin or the other Ferrets had much
to do with this part of the Mansergh Committee's work. The outline
above has been introduced for two reasons: first, the new training
pattern had a profound effect on the later recommendations of the
committee and indeed formed part of the *one overall concept*

(Mansergh's italics) designed to build a new officer structure;[15] and second, Lewin himself was to deal with its implementation when he commanded the Dartmouth Training Squadron in 1962–3.

The second main plank of the Mansergh Committee's structure was its solution to the problem of sea command. As has been shown, this had bedevilled the Board for years and it was time to grapple with it. The figures were stark. There were some 465 seaman commanders and only about 80 ships that qualified as commanders' commands.[16] If every commander was to be given command when in or near the zone for promotion to captain, each could expect a year at most, and for large chunks of that the ship might be in dock or otherwise unemployed. It was considered deeply detrimental to efficiency to allow such a system: there would be too many inexperienced commanding officers afloat, they would have too little time to establish their authority, ships' companies would inevitably be unsettled and under-confident.

The solution had to be, in the view of all those involved, to 'split the list' into those who could expect sea command and those who could not. Then, those who had been selected to enjoy sea command (the 'post list', derived from the ancient term 'post captain') could expect at least one commission, with eighteen months' seagoing, during their time as commanders, and a similar spell if they were promoted to captain; some might get more than one such commission in each rank. The remainder, rather more than half the seaman commanders in the Navy, could not expect any sea appointment at all; they would fill staff billets and sometimes executive posts ashore, and if they were promoted to captain the same career pattern would apply.

'Doing the arithmetic' for the necessary separation into the two lists – inevitably to be known colloquially as 'wet' and 'dry' – fell to Commander Lewin. The proportions were just as bad as had been feared: under 50 per cent could be 'wet' and the remainder would have to be 'dry'. Random selection was considered out of the question: aptitude must be taken into account, and so must possible progression to the very highest ranks, which was thought of necessity to be the prerogative of those officers who had had command. The final selection was done by Captain Townsend as NA2SL in charge of a small committee that included some distinguished and highly experienced sea officers.[17]

The sensitivity of the whole business was extreme. Officers of the seaman specialisation had been brought up to regard command of their own ship as a principal target point of their careers. Whatever else happened, however many boring jobs were to come before and after, and even however many blasts, difficulties and disasters were to occur during it, it was to be uniquely theirs, the culmination of their training and experience, a test and an expression of their personality and professionalism. To be deprived of even the prospect was desperately hard.

An honest and sincere attempt was made to provide for the 'dry' list a worthwhile career pattern, not least to persuade officers on that list to remain in the Navy. There was at that time no shortage of billets ashore, and many of them offered a good deal of interest and variety. It was also considered imperative to offer a career path to high rank for both lists, and the temptation to reward 'wet' officers who had just missed promotion with a step in rank on the 'dry' list was steadfastly resisted.[18]

There was some difference of opinion as to whether the distinction, for each individual officer, should be overt or covert. It went on for years.[19] Colin Dunlop advised that although officers should be told which list they were on, it should not be made public.[20] Terry Lewin's views are not recorded. In the event, it was decided that no attempt should be made to hide the decisions, and it was Lewin who had to draft the format of the letters to individual commanders and captains, informing them which list they were on. 'The mailing of them was very carefully timed so that they arrived on the morning on which the announcement of the split list was made.' Terry Lewin 'had no idea on which side I was, went into the office that morning and found my letter on my desk and found to my joy I was a post list officer'.[21]

The split list, then, was the second of the reforms made by the Mansergh Committee. The third was the most far-reaching, and to understand its background it is necessary to go back a good deal further into history.

The role and status of the engineer had always been one of some difficulty in the Royal Navy. Before the advent of steam in the 1830s, the propulsion of ships by sail had been managed by the same people who fought them in action, the seaman officers. It was a fully integrated system of command and control. The first engineers often came with the machinery, almost as representatives of the building firm and not under any form of naval engagement. However, as the mobility of the fleet came to depend more and more upon steam and less on sail, engineers entered the naval service proper; they were first given uniforms in 1837, and by the mid-1860s a chief engineer with 15 years' seniority ranked with a commander.[22] Formal professional training at the Royal Naval Engineering College was introduced in 1880.

Nevertheless the relationship with the seaman officers was often an uneasy one. The mobility of the fleet was now largely in the hands of the engineers; by 1895 scarcely any ships had masts and yards capable of carrying sail. Yet the seamen were accustomed to, and trained in, directing ships in battle and handling them at sea. They jealously guarded the prerogative of 'military command'. Moreover, there was a social element. In the last two decades of the nineteenth century, the Navy had become a fashionable service. The seamen officers regarded themselves as an élite, and their engineering colleagues, all too often, as inferiors.[23]

The man who determined to set matters right at the turn of the century was Vice Admiral Sir John Fisher. As Second Sea Lord, with the support of the First Lord of the Admiralty Lord Selborne, he instituted what became known as the Fisher-Selborne scheme. Under this, all officers – whether destined to be seamen, engineers or Royal Marines – would enter the new Naval College at Dartmouth and undergo a common training as cadets and midshipmen. Later, in the ranks of sub- and junior lieutenant, they would be trained according to their specialisations, but from the rank of commander onwards there would be much interchangeability of functions and all would have a chance of promotion to the highest ranks.[24] The objective was, in Fisher's words, 'up to a certain point some community of knowledge and a lifelong community of sentiment'. The first cadets under the Fisher-Selborne scheme joined the Naval College at Osborne (Dartmouth was not ready) in 1903.

For the next 20 years the scheme continued, at least in form. However, it ran into problems. The Royal Marines opted out quite quickly and the scheme for them was formally abandoned in 1912.[25] Worse, selection and training as engineers was not popular with parents; only about one in 20 cadets actually volunteered for that specialisation.[26] It was necessary to supplement the Dartmouth entry with the Special Entry: that under which the young Lewin joined, years later.

Finally, in 1925, came what engineers called 'the great betrayal': in effect, a reversal of the Selborne-Fisher principles and the return of the engineer officer to inferior status. An Order in Council set out what were called 'categories' of naval officer: executive (a new title for seamen), engineer, medical, dental, accountant, instructors and so on. Only the executive officers were to have military command. All other categories were to wear distinguishing cloth between the stripes denoting their rank. 'Military command' embraced a wide range of functions, including discipline; it is said that even after the Second World War, schemes of complement showed seaman chief and petty officers in the chain of command above non-executive officers.[27]

So the position of engineers had remained until the formation of the Mansergh Committee. That of the other main 'coloured-stripe' specialisation, the Supply and Secretariat Branch, was similar although their origins were different. They were descendants of two strands of officer: the purser, who in the sailing navy had been responsible for the victualling, and to some extent the pay, of seagoing ships; and the captain's or admiral's secretary. They had a good deal of power in the first of these duties, and a good deal of influence in the second; but the position of the power behind the throne was seen to be an uneasy one, and they aspired to a more straightforward measure of command.

This situation was that which was described in general terms by Mansergh as 'wide disparity of opportunity between branches, leading to waste of talent and frustration'. He, and his committee, were convinced that it was not only a wrong that should be put right, but that putting it right would set the Navy on a much more effective course. It is clear that he had very early formed in his own mind the direction in which he hoped the committee would go, and that this was the principal reason for the selection of two particularly able commanders, from the 'E' and 'S & S' specialisations, to join Lewin as Ferrets. In fact, both LeBailly and Dunlop had made their own views clear, orally and on paper, when inputs to the Mansergh study had been solicited in its initial stages.[28]

The solution, the 'Grand Design' which was to be the essence of the rebuilt officer structure,[29] was the General List to comprise all cadet-entered officers who were not on the Post List. The institution of the Post List, 'undertaken for quite extraneous reasons, open[ed] the way for the introduction of common status and common command powers' amongst such officers.[30]

Once the Post List had solved the problem of sea command, many of the other issues of differentiation fell away. There was no reason why an engineer or supply officer should not do duty as officer of the day – the captain's representative for the time being – in a shore establishment or a ship in harbour. Nor was there any reason for his disciplinary powers to be different from any other officer of his rank. Bridge watchkeeping in a ship at sea was, to be sure, the natural function of the seaman; but there was no reason why officers of any specialisation, so long as they met the eyesight requirements, should not obtain watchkeeping certificates, and 'plumbers and pussers' were to be encouraged to do so.

Most critically, the prerogative of 'military command' was to be shared by the three branches. The position of the designated second-in-command was of course safeguarded both ashore and afloat; but below that level, in Mansergh's examples:

In a shore establishment, it will be the senior General List officer on the books who will be responsible for putting out the fire ... Similarly in a ship's boat, not only will [the senior General List officer present] give orders for the boat to 'carry on' but, if circumstances necessitate taking over command of the boat from the coxswain or officer of the boat, it will be incumbent on this officer to do so ...[31]

It was envisaged from the start that further up the ladder of seniority, General List officers of commander's and captain's rank would have equal opportunities to become commanding officers and second-in-command of shore establishments. Indeed that was one of the greatest incentives to those branches that had felt themselves unjustly deprived in the past, and was the ultimate symbol of the cession of military command.

In the negotiations leading to this major reform there had been one category full of what can only be called self-doubt, and that was the newly formed Electrical Branch. This had drawn its officers from four main sources: the torpedo officers who had had responsibility before and during the war for electrical matters on board a ship; the warrant electricians, ex-artificers, who had provided practical knowledge during the same period; the officers of the Special Branch, recruited largely from universities during the war, who had handled the new technologies of radar and sonar; and post-war recruits to the branch who had undergone a graduate course at the University of Cambridge. Understandably, the branch was none too sure of itself, and its representative, who joined the Ferrets from time to time, rode to strict and cautious instructions from his chief.[32] At one time, indeed, the head of the Electrical Branch emphatically stated to the main committee that they did not seek military command.[33] However, it is clear that eventually the 'greenies' (the colour of their distinguishing cloth) were persuaded that it was in their interests to become part of the General List. Whether Lewin was instrumental in this change of heart will probably never be known now; what is certain is that then and later, he was wholly in favour of bringing the Electrical Branch, whose future he saw as critical to that of the Navy as a whole, into the mainstream.

Another aspect of the reforms, and one too easy to overlook, was the important part promotion from the lower deck had to play. Since about 1900 this had been a feature of naval life in the warrant officers who had provided such loyal and experienced service during and between the wars, and in more than a scattering of accelerated promotions into the main officer corps through the mate and then upper yardman schemes.[34] The title 'Warrant Officer' had already been changed to 'Branch Officer', but this was mostly cosmetic. The Mansergh Committee consulted widely with the representatives of the branch officers themselves and called for a comprehensive report from the assessors.[35]

The process involved two months' intensive work over November–January 1954–5; the result could scarcely be seen as radical at the time, since its main elements were to accord the ranks of sub-lieutenant and lieutenant (Special Duties) to those who had previously been called branch officers, and to give a limited avenue of promotion to commander on this newly named SD List. In the event, it was more far-reaching than that, since schemes of complement subsequently allowed for more flexibility in appointing as between the General and SD Lists. Lewin, who at least once went on record as advocating somewhat more radical measures,[36] probably foresaw this development from his appointing chair.

The whole of the Mansergh process was periodically submitted to the Board in a series of interim reports at intervals between March 1954 and the summer of 1955,[37] drawn together by the civil service secretariat[38] towards the end of that year and promulgated as a single Admiralty Fleet Order, No. 1/56, in January 1956. It was, and remains, the most far-reaching and basic document on officer structure in the Royal Navy. Its results have since been mulled over, dissected, questioned, with a wealth of anecdote and some statistical evidence, mostly within the confines of the service. It has been modified to a degree: as an instance, the wet/dry system has been replaced by a Sea Appointments Board which reviews each seaman officer's career periodically and decides which individuals should have sea command. But its basic structure has stood for over 40 years, and that alone suggests that it was of durable quality and did most of what it set out to do. It was Dunlop who provided its slogan, quoting Drake's speech (on the occasion of hanging his second-in-command): 'I must have the gentleman to haul and draw with the mariner, and the mariner with the gentleman. *Let us show ourselves to be all of a company*'.[39] Increasingly, over the years, the Royal Navy has been true to that watchword.

It did not happen all at once. Reaction to AFO 1/56 was in some quarters extreme. There are tales, well-authenticated, of the in-tray of the Second Sea Lord – the universally liked and respected Admiral Sir Guy Russell – overflowing with letters from outraged seaman officers accusing him of betraying his cloth. Similar hate mail assailed Mansergh and Townsend; it is possible that some reached Commander Terry Lewin as well, though he does not record it in his memoir.

He, in any case, had moved on to other aspects of his regular appointing job. The most far-reaching of these was a survey of the system of promotion from lieutenant-commander to commander, and commander to captain. The system then current had been invented in the time of Sir Algernon Willis as Second Sea Lord in 1946, and was based on the principle of 'even flow', with a more or less steady trickle of promotions from each seniority batch of officers as they passed through the zone. Lewin's analysis, and comparison with the systems of other navies, validated even flow[40] and it remained the guiding principle to the end of the century.

He did not, therefore, seek change for the sake of change – always a temptation for a junior commander in an Admiralty post. One change he did make, however, and it was almost universally welcomed. This was to announce half-yearly promotions six months in advance of the date they were to take effect. In this way, the lucky officers' future appointments could be discussed without too much time pressure and the necessary adjustments made to the appointments of other officers who had not caught the selectors' eye. The inevitable misgiving, that an officer selected might during his six months' probation commit some unforgivable sin either professional or moral, has not in any recorded case come to pass, and at the time of writing the system has been in force for 45 years.

DESTROYER COMMAND: HMS *CORUNNA* 1955–1957

It was time to move on. Commander Lewin was due for his next appointment in summer 1955, with Admiralty Fleet Order 1/56 still months away from issue; that is the way Whitehall works. In fact, he had been lucky that such a definite outcome to an important matter had been achieved during his time. The experience of those less fortunate was simply of helping along what appeared to be a seamless process. He might well find that himself, later in his career.

Officers on the staff of the Naval Assistant to the Second Sea Lord had the inside track when it came to their next appointments, and in the spring of 1955 Lewin (over sandwiches in St James's Park)[1] had told Commander Bill O'Brien, the commanders' appointer, that he hoped for command of a destroyer. To his dismay he was told a couple of weeks later that he was to go as executive officer and second-in-command of the battleship *Vanguard*, then in reserve and to be recommissioned. This was not a happy prospect: she would be the only battleship in commission, many in the Navy regarded her as a white elephant, her role would be unclear, and getting her going again after some time in reserve would be a nightmare. It was a great relief to Terry that politics and economics (and maybe common sense) intervened and a decision was taken at Prime Ministerial level to scrap the proud and beautiful ship.

No other sea appointment was immediately available and the family settled down to a few weeks of halcyon summer, living in Hayling Island and picnicking frequently on the South Downs. As these things tend to do in the Navy, it did not last as long as had been expected. O'Brien telephoned from the Admiralty and offered Terry the command of HMS *Corunna*. This was what had been hoped for, but there was a snag: the current commanding officer had to leave in a hurry because his wife was seriously ill, and Terry was to join in Rosyth, Scotland, within three days.

It was a classic 'pier head jump': an offer that could not be refused, but severely disruptive of family plans. As always, everyone buckled to and Commander Lewin duly departed for Rosyth to take up his first command.

Corunna was a 'Battle' class destroyer, not the very last class of destroyer built for the Royal Navy but one of the most classical in design. She was built by Swan Hunter, always a good start for a ship, and launched in April 1944: 355 feet long and of 3350 tons displacement, she was heavily armed with five 4.5-inch guns, eight 40 mm Bofors, ten 21-inch torpedo tubes, and the Squid ahead-throwing anti-submarine mortar. The fire control arrangements were such as to gladden a dagger gunnery officer's heart: the main 4.5-inch armament was controlled by the American-designed Mark 37 system which worked on tachometric principles, and the close-range Bofors weapons were on STAAG (Simple Tachometric Anti-Aircraft Gun) mountings which could 'lock on' to targets using their associated radar. The 50,000 hp steam plant could drive the ship at 31 knots.[2] The 'Battles' were in many ways direct descendants of the 'Tribals', but a good deal more sturdy and reliable: all those characteristics would have endeared *Corunna* to her new commanding officer.

Command is, as has already been suggested, something unique. Where Admiralty, and indeed other staff work, involves corporate decision, continuity of policy and management of change responding to a multitude of outside factors, command of the entity that is a warship is singular, wholly responsible, subject certainly to a variety of influences ranging from superior orders to the stresses of wind and sea, but always resting ultimately with the ship's captain. Of course the sensible captain consults, of course he delegates, but command is a unity and it is his.

It is for this reason that, while a change of post in staff appointments often entails a lengthy period of turnover, change of command is rapid to the point of brutality. A couple of hours mustering the Confidential Books, a few words of encouragement over a welcoming glass, a signature or two, and the new captain is on his own. He must make all the arrangements to meet his new officers, speak to his ship's company, and familiarise himself with every aspect of his ship, and he must do all this rapidly so that when he first takes her to sea, he does so with full authority and in safety.

Terry might have felt the need for augury. He found it just across the jetty, for there lay the inert but familiar hulk of a destroyer: the *Ashanti*, no less, waiting for her last journey to the breaker's yard. Lewin took a nostalgic wander round, and found in the wardroom, still screwed to the bulkhead, the Vermeer print that Colin Maud had presented after the epic tow of 1942. It was removed in quick time and transferred to *Corunna*'s captain's cabin. Terry wrote to Richard Onslow, who fully agreed its bestowal; it remains in the Lewin family still.[3]

The first professional test was not long in coming. He had joined *Corunna* on 28 October 1955; on 1 November she left the basin in Rosyth in which she had been lying[4] and proceeded to sea for calibration of her High Frequency Direction Finding equipment. This was not an unusual first sally for a ship coming out of a short period of maintenance, but the initial movement from the confined space of the basin was tricky at dead low water, and Lewin recalled a good deal of caution in getting *Corunna* pointed in the right direction.[5] Perhaps he recalled the old mariners' adage: 'Outward bound, don't run aground'.

Next day *Corunna* sailed in company with *Agincourt*, Captain (D) of the Fourth Destroyer Squadron (Captain Nicholas Copeman) for passage northabout Scotland. The weather that first night was predictably filthy, and Lewin was seasick after so long ashore: 'I managed to keep it to my sea cabin and I trust no one ever knew. By the morning I was better and was not seasick again while I was in *Corunna*.' It was as well; the next day was full of exercises on passage, with massed air attacks out of the Royal Naval Air Station at Lossiemouth, dummy torpedo firings and stopping to exercise seaboats,[6] familiar fare but enough to keep a new, relatively junior commanding officer on his toes.

On 5 November the ships arrived in the Mersey and *Corunna* locked in to the Birkenhead complex, to be welcomed by that hospitable place for a visit that included a very large number of tours

by school parties; the Navy was already conscious of the need to keep itself in the public eye and to improve its recruitment. It could scarcely have had a better advertisement than a destroyer of the Fourth Squadron; the ships were smart and good-looking and the *Corunna* had been kept in admirable order by her first lieutenant, Lieutenant-Commander Alex Mortensen, and his team.

A visit to Belfast, in company with *Agincourt*, followed and on 17 November the ships departed for Londonderry, which at that time was the home of the Joint Anti-Submarine School responsible for advanced training for both Royal Navy and Royal Air Force units. The approach to Londonderry is up the River Foyle, and includes a notorious bend called The Crook. *Corunna* was halfway round this when the coxswain reported the wheel jammed. It was a nasty moment; Lewin stopped engines and was preparing to manoeuvre to keep out of trouble, a very difficult task in such a place with shoal water close on either side. To his relief the wheel came free again and the ship was able to proceed up-river to her berth.

Behind this lay a story that Lewin recalled with relish: there had been two stokers on watch in the tiller flat:

> One, a very young stoker, said, 'What do we do if we have a steering failure then?' and the older stoker said, 'Well, you take this pin out here and put it in there.' With that he took the pin out, the coxswain moved the wheel and the holes went out of line. Frantically he waited until the two came back in line again, popped the pin back and all was well ...[7]

Terry learned all this years later at a reunion when all was confessed. The 'very young stoker' had, long before, left the Navy and now was in the business of manufacturing seals. When Lewin became a peer, the seal-maker presented him with a seal of his coat of arms.

The visit to Londonderry, with the associated exercises at sea, was mainly to give the squadron an introduction to the current anti-submarine scene, now subject to NATO procedures and tactical instructions. On 6 December the ships left for their home ports, and the *Corunna*, manned as she was by the Chatham port division, arrived there on the 8th. The log[8] records that on that day the captain cleared lower deck and addressed the ship's company. It would have been a good opportunity to tell them how he had found the ship in his first six weeks in command, to point the direction in which he wished them to develop, and to wish them a good Christmas leave.

The prospect of a further 18 months in the Chatham-based *Corunna* had encouraged the Lewin family to migrate again, and it was planned to move at Easter to the large if rather run-down Brewster House at Doddington in Kent. Meanwhile, however, the ship was to sail in January for the annual gathering of the Home and Mediterranean Fleets at Gibraltar. This had been a regular feature of naval life since the turn of the century, involving combined exercises and manoeuvres and a good deal of competition on and off the sports field.[9]

The 1956 gathering included a visit to the Spanish enclave of Ceuta across the Gibraltar Strait for two ships of the Fourth Destroyer Squadron, *Barrosa* and *Corunna*. They arrived there on 2 February,[10] and nothing untoward happened until 5 February. Although the log recorded nothing but Force 3 winds all day and the ship was open to visitors from 2 till 6 pm, she was at immediate notice for steam and hurricane hawsers were rigged; clearly a strong wind warning was in force. During the night the wind got up with dramatic suddenness, 45 knots being the maximum recorded. At 1.45 am, libertymen having been recalled, the ship slipped and in the most difficult conditions left harbour stern first, turning on an anchor to point to seaward. Rex Phillips, a young lieutenant and navigator in his first job as such, recalled the tremendous coolness and expertise with which Lewin – still dressed in black tie from a dinner party ashore – handled the ship.[11]

But Phillips had already been given much cause for admiration. Taking over as an inexperienced officer, but one wanting later to specialise in navigation, in January 1956, he had had nothing but help and understanding from his captain. The Fourth Destroyer Squadron was a crack outfit, and the squadron navigator was the needle-sharp

Lieutenant Commander Ian Mackay, with a formidable array of widgets that needed to be mastered in precise manoeuvres using radar; Phillips would manage these in the operations room with confidence, knowing that his captain on the bridge would be following events with an expert eye. In Phillips's words, 'He was always a step ahead but he still made you feel it was you in charge of the operation.'

Later in February, still in Gibraltar, the *Corunna* was berthed along-side the Fleet flagship on a rainy Wednesday. The Commander-in-Chief, Admiral Sir John Eccles, sent a message to Lewin that he would like to walk round *Corunna* before dinner – in other words, at tot time, just after the rum issue. Lord Lewin's own words best tell what happened:

> Things went reasonably well, the chefs in the galley were cheerful and the dinner looked good, until we got as far as the ERAs' [Engine Room Artificers'] Mess ... The Chief ERA, who was an absolute dragon for keeping his mess clean, made sure all his messmates took off their boots before they came into the mess. He welcomed the Commander-in-Chief standing in his stockinged feet, with his big toe sticking through a great hole in one sock ... What I didn't know was that he'd won the last house at tombola [the naval equivalent of Bingo] in the Fleet Club the night before and had duly celebrated and had just had his tot and was well away again. The Commander-in-Chief said, 'Well now, how are things down below Chief?' and the Chief immediately launched into an absolutely glowing description of what a marvellous ship *Corunna* was, how well she ran, how happy everybody was, how good the machinery was and you couldn't stop him. The Commander-in-Chief was really very amused by this and left chuckling to himself.[12]

After the fleets had dispersed and the Fourth Destroyer Squadron had returned to the United Kingdom, it was time for Easter leave and consideration of the final weeks of the current commission. The programme already showed a visit to the Pool of London, always a popular item for a ship's company, but now this was to include a plan brewed up in Gibraltar during the spring gathering. The Governor, Lieutenant-General Sir Harold Redman, was the colonel of the King's Own Yorkshire Light Infantry, the regiment of Sir John Moore who had famously died at Coruña in 1809. Redman was anxious to go to Coruña in this capacity (not, of course, as Governor of Gibraltar, which would have been more than sensitive diplomatically) and had asked that *Corunna* should take him. This was much welcomed by the ship and her captain, and on 2 May, having had a most enjoyable visit to London, she left Portland for the final leg of the commission, cheered out of harbour by *Agincourt* and *Barrosa*.[13]

The general was embarked at Lisbon where the ship made a brief 24-hour call, enough to give some leave to each watch; Portugal had not been on *Corunna*'s previous itineraries. Then an overnight passage brought her to Coruña, where she secured alongside on 7 May.[14]

The visit was conducted in the highest traditions of Spanish and British protocol. Official calls were extensive and prolonged, the general – dressed in full KOYLI uniform and given a great welcome – discussing all details of the forthcoming ceremonies with the captain-general and military governor. The ship's cocktail party that evening was a bumper success: 'About 120 of the 60 invited attended', recorded the Report of Proceedings. Perhaps that was due to the presence of the cruise liner *Reina del Mar* in an adjacent berth.

The next day was the high point of the visit, a ceremony at the tomb of Sir John Moore in the walled garden of the monastery of San Carlos. A small detachment of British soldiers had been embarked specially and were joined by a small naval guard from the ship. Lewin recalled that inevitably, when they marched out, the light infantry set off at their usual rapid pace and left the sedate sailors far, far behind. A luncheon party co-hosted by Lewin and Redman followed – the seating plan had been the subject of 'an hour's intense discussion' with the chief of protocol – and included the production by one of the guests of a Brown Bess musket, picked up from the battlefield long ago, which was presented to the ship.

One possible embarrassment during the visit was quickly solved by the captain himself. Some illicit liquor, mostly Spanish brandy, had been coming inboard from the ship's seaward side and a stoker, having too much taken, obstreperously wanted to go ashore – which could well have spoilt the day, or even the visit. The officer of the day found himself wrestling with this problem when at 3 pm Terry Lewin arrived back from shore.[15] Quickly and without fuss, the lad was persuaded to turn in and possible trouble was averted. Some clue as to how the magic worked is suggested by one of the ship's company, in his own words: 'The gentleman was not a disciplinarian, why? You may ask, because of respect, himself showed it, that's why the crew showed it.'[16]

All the usual accompaniments to a foreign visit were duly observed: the children's party (trips round the harbour in the ship's motorboat disguised as a pirate galleon), the ship open to visitors (9540 in two days), the final luncheon party ashore (complete with speech in Spanish by Terry Lewin), the ship's company dance. He summed up the company's view as 'the best run ashore of the commission'; many friendships had been made:

> At the start of the visit there was a definite feeling of wariness among the local authorities, particularly the military; this was almost certainly due to the presence of the Governor of Gibraltar … when they discovered how genuine was our interest in Sir John Moore and the battle, their attitude changed.[17]

With a full power trial to boost her on her way, the ship returned to Chatham on 14 May to recommission. This was quickly accomplished; she left with her new ship's company on 31 May. Commander Lewin was still in command; the appointers had kept their word. He had established great rapport with his previous ship's company, and was 'flattered that quite a large number volunteered to recommission and I was able more or less to pick the best of them …'[18]

Eulogies can be tedious, and this book will include only a few, but that of Lewin's Captain (D), Nicholas Copeman, on the occasion of recommissioning must figure here partly for its cogency but also because it is a marvellous example of report-writing when the reporter *really* wants to catch the eye of authority:

> Very occasionally one meets a young officer who appears to
> have all the attributes needed to reach the highest posts in the
> Navy – Commander Lewin is one. He is a natural leader, has no
> fear of responsibility, has a good knowledge of tactics, marked
> intelligence and is also a very nice man.[19]

The next commission was to be on a somewhat different pattern from
the last. It had been decided, rather than keep ships on one station for
the whole of their commissions, to split them into two 'legs', to give
everyone some time in home waters. There was a downside to this:
assistance to families to join husbands on foreign stations was abolished. There was no option, therefore, for the Lewin family beyond
staying at Doddington, and Jane and the children were to be on their
own there for the next nine months, while *Corunna* was on her
'Mediterranean leg'. With an English winter to come, that was none
too attractive; Brewster House had a form of central heating, but there
were rats in the coal-hole and Tim, with Napoleon the Alsatian in
company, was firmly put in charge of fetching fuel.

The Fourth Destroyer Squadron now consisted of *Agincourt*,
Corunna, *Barrosa* and *Alamein* and was commanded by Captain D. H.
F. Hetherington. He had been in command of *Cheviot* in the First
Destroyer Flotilla when Terry Lewin was flotilla gunnery officer in
1949, so they knew each other of old. Hetherington was an unusual
officer, given to knitting and playing the clarinet, but he was no slouch.
The exercises carried out on passage to Gibraltar, and then on to
Malta, were intensive and kept all ships alert: manoeuvres conducted
by captains and officers of the watch, gun and mortar functioning
trials, dummy torpedo firings, night encounter exercises with starshell,
and 'away seaboat' every middle watch.[20]

The occasion of joining the Mediterranean Fleet in Malta had for
well over half a century been a commanding officer's dream and nightmare. The fleet regarded itself as the epitome of smartness, precision
and fighting efficiency, and in spite of natural inter-fleet rivalries, that
tended to be the view of the whole of the Navy. The first test was to
produce the ship looking immaculate, without a rope's end out of

place, and with every man correctly dressed and either fallen in or clearly doing something necessary to the conduct of the ship. Pat Stearns, the new commission's first lieutenant, could be relied on under Lewin's guidance to supervise all that.

The commanding officer's chief task was to berth the ship with the mixture of dash and precision for which the Mediterranean Fleet was famous. Destroyers lay at head and stern buoys in Sliema Creek, always with bows pointing to seaward so that they could get out of harbour quickly in emergency. If you berth in a creek facing out, then you have to go backwards to get in. Destroyers are not easy to manage when going astern ('making a sternboard') and the test was to do it quickly and safely. There is a little bay opposite the entrance to Sliema Creek and the technique was to turn sharply into this, with one engine stopped and the other going slow ahead, reverse the inboard engine to help the turn and stop the ship's forward movement, then when pointed (backwards) towards the creek, to put both engines astern at whatever revolutions the captain dared to set and steer (all wheel orders being in reverse, so to speak) towards the allocated berth. Before reaching this, it was necessary to send away the boats to put buoy-jumpers on head and stern buoys ready to receive the first wires from the ship, and, critically, to stop the main engines and put them ahead to arrest the sternway just as the ship came into the berth.

None of this would have been easy in a flat calm with Sliema Creek empty. Generally, there would be enough wind to complicate the manoeuvre and the creek would be nearly full of other destroyers in their own berths, greatly narrowing the path. Moreover, particularly for a newly arrived ship, those destroyers would be full of observers watching to see how the new boy got on. Each captain's style would be entered in the collective memory-bank: how many revolutions astern were used during the sternboard, at what precise point the initial turn was begun, when the boats were released, and whether there was any sign of intervention by the engineer officer, who traditionally sat on a little wooden seat just forward of the torpedo tubes in clear sight of the engine-room hatch and had been known, in moments of perceived crisis, to instruct the engine-room staff to give an extra tweak to the throttles that had not been ordered from the bridge.

Terry Lewin would probably have been mortified to hear of any interference from the 'engineer's bridge'. He had after all been in the Mediterranean Fleet before, under a dashing destroyer captain, and knew the principles. In command, he took to it readily: 'Taking a destroyer into Sliema was one of the great thrills in life and I can still go through all the engine and wheel movements which were necessary …' He only admitted to one poor performance in his time in *Corunna*, when he was allocated an unfamiliar berth far up the creek in shallow water and failed to put the engines ahead soon enough, resulting in an encounter with the stern buoy. This was made worse by the fact that the previous occupant had left the permanent stern wires hanging down from the buoy instead of securing them to it in the approved manner, and the propeller, racing ahead, gathered many turns around it. It took all night to clear, and a high-speed run to sea next day confirmed that no damage had been done. All was forgiven by the Flag Officer Destroyers, Deric Holland-Martin.[21]

Corunna, with the rest of the Fourth Destroyer Squadron, had arrived in Malta on 11 June 1956, and for the next six weeks life on the Mediterranean station followed its accustomed pattern. Most weekdays the ships went to sea for serials in the weekly practice programme. It was a familiar enough routine for Terry Lewin: every sort of warlike and seamanlike exercise to bring him, his officers and his new ship's company to a peak of efficiency.

The routine was varied in July by a brief visit to Tripoli in Libya. King Idris was still on the throne and there was a flourishing British base at El Adem. Then it was time to help develop the still young NATO alliance by a visit to Augusta in Sicily for exercises with the Italian Navy. British forces, brought up with a rather patronising attitude to the Italians due to their perceived under-performance during the Second World War, usually found these experiences salutary: the Italians handled their ships well and knew their way about.

But times were about to change dramatically. On 26 July Colonel Gamal Abdel Nasser, the president of Egypt, nationalised the Suez

Canal. The story of how the situation was handled, or mishandled, has been told in many publications, and the reasons for the cumbersome nature of the action have been well covered, particularly by Eric Grove.[22] It is enough to say here that things were never going to be the same again.

For *Corunna*, for the time being, there was no change to the programme. Her next assignment was the Cyprus patrol. At that time the Greek extremist movement in the island was vigorously promoting Enosis, union with Greece, and Eoka, its para-military arm, was very active. The Royal Navy mounted a continual patrol of two destroyers and four minesweepers, boarding any vessels suspected of gun-running or other clandestine activities. The general pattern was that the ship, usually operating independently under the orders of the Flag Officer Cyprus, would remain at sea all night and anchor for a few hours during the day, landing half the ship's company for recreation on a convenient beach. When at anchor great vigilance was required against the threat of attack by frogmen, but by then the instructions for the necessary surveillance, the so-called Operation Awkward, were well established.

Flag Officer Cyprus was the formidable Miers, VC,[23] and his small staff looked after the patrol ships well. 'Our mail used to come down and be delivered somewhere to us every day, we used to get fresh fruit and veg whenever we wanted it and we really felt they were taking an interest and looking after us'.[24] Miers could be kind too, in spite of his reputation as the rudest man in the Navy, and Lewin recorded many instances of consideration, indeed courtesy.

But the build-up to Suez was going its halting way, and the authorities had to decide what to do with *Agincourt* and *Corunna*. Both were overdue for a six-week refit, and because of the crisis many other ships had been deferred and the Malta dockyard, always politically sensitive, was short of work. It was decided that in spite of the impending Operation Musketeer, which looked as August and September went on to be more and more likely, in spite of the misgivings of many senior officers including Mountbatten the First Sea Lord,[25] the two ships should refit in Malta until almost the end of the year.

Thus, Terry Lewin's part in the Suez adventure was non-operational. In fact for a time he worked as chief censor in the Cable and Wireless office, and found this tedious because in effect the Press managed to by-pass that channel completely. There were other occasions when he helped his Captain (D) to act as rear link in Malta for the Flag Officer Flotillas, who was afloat in the depot ship *Ranpura*. But he would have been exposed, as those in the ships at sea were not in most cases, to the controversy surrounding the conflict in the national and indeed local media, and, as will be seen, it had an effect much later.

In the meantime there was a ship to be refitted. There are few more awful environments than a destroyer in the bottom of a dry dock. Everything is in pieces, all the usual amenities are lacking, disturbance and disruption everywhere. Keeping up the interest and spirit of a ship's company is a real challenge. Lewin was in his element, organising 'teams of officers and ratings to compete with one another in tramping across the landscape and then boarding cutters and whalers, sailing to some other point on the coast, and still more tramping to a final destination which was eventually revealed through a series of "treasure-hunt" type clues'.[26] There was no resentment apparent over this yo-ho-ho treatment, which in other hands could so easily have gone wrong: 'By taking an interest in his crew they would have followed him without a *drip*, we held him in such high esteem.'[27]

Jane was able to come out from England for a fortnight, the children being looked after at home by Pru Archibald, a friend from Whale Island days. The Lewins rented a flat in Floriana overlooking Grand Harbour, and it was a relaxing time for both. After Jane had returned to England, Terry moved in to a flat with his Captain (D) in Valletta for the rest of the refit.

On 6 December *Corunna* began her climb back to operational status with the necessary basin trials, ammunitioning and storing, sea trials and calibrations.[28] By the 20th she was back in Sliema Creek, and Christmas was coming. It came, however, in a somewhat unusual way. Mail at that time came mostly by land via Sicily, and in the run-up to Christmas the mail steamer that brought it across to Malta went on strike. Lewin volunteered the *Corunna* for a mail run to Syracuse, and left at 1 am on 24 December. She picked up hundreds of bags of mail and returned to Malta at 5 pm, going into Grand Harbour with the leading seaman postman dressed as Father Christmas in a prominent position on the bridge. The fleet cheered, and got its Christmas mail.

After that it was a quick return to the operational scene. The Middle East situation was still very volatile after the abortive Suez operation, and *Agincourt, Barrosa* and *Corunna* were ordered to Port Said, leaving Malta on 27 December. Matters subsided and after a week the ships left for a further Cyprus patrol. Lewin was invited by Miers for a couple of days' skiing in the Troodos mountains, but this was cut short by orders for *Corunna* and *Barrosa* to return to Malta; *Corunna*'s captain was hurried down to Paphos to rejoin his ship, which the first lieutenant had brought round from Famagusta.

The new assignment was to escort Admiral Sir John Hamilton, the Commander-in-Chief Mediterranean, in his yacht *Surprise* to Naples where his relief, Admiral Sir Ralph Edwards, would embark. The C-in-C, it was said, 'wanted two good-looking destroyers';[29] and after all, in Italy it is always necessary to *fare la bella figura*. So it was done, and having looked handsome, the *Corunna* and *Barrosa* duly returned to Cyprus patrol. The routine was the same as in summer, the weather and recreation not so pleasant.

Lewin was not yet near the end of his time in command, having been promised that he would go on to the end of the commission, probably November 1957. There are some indications that he was, if not bored, just a little concerned to maintain his cutting edge. An officer who joined as an acting sub-lieutenant in January 1957 recalled that in that month, Terry popped into the wardroom for coffee and said, 'Right, let's change things a bit. Pilot, you take over as guns from tomorrow. TAS, take over navigation. Guns, take over TAS. OK?' And so it was done.[30] Not only would the officers concerned broaden their experience, the captain would need to be extra alert to correct mistakes.

But that was one of his strongest points. The same officer had some days before been officer of the watch during an intensive set of practice serials, and in his inexperience had made many errors. 'Terry was great; in his cabin, he ran through with me all the mistakes I had made, and with a broad grin, said, "Well, I hope you won't make those mistakes again" … every single person on board *Corunna* wanted to do well, *so as not to let Terry down*'.[31]

He need not have been concerned at any staleness in destroyer command, because that was about to change. Soon after Christmas he received a letter from the Flag Officer Royal Yachts, Rear Admiral Sir Connolly Abel Smith, informing him that he was one of three officers short-listed to be executive officer of the Royal Yacht *Britannia*.[32]

Lewin's immediate reaction was dismay. He tended, like many of his contemporaries, to regard Royal Yachtsmen as somewhat effete, spending most of their time in harbour and occasionally going as far as the Solent for Cowes week. He regarded himself as no courtier, but a fighting captain of a going destroyer who wanted to continue that way. After agonising for 36 hours – 24 before, and 12 after, writing – he sent a letter to Abel Smith saying that he wished not to be considered for the appointment. It had no effect; he was ordered to join *Britannia* anyway.

He addressed his splendid ship's company for the last time and was relieved by Commander Godfrey Place, VC, an officer remembered by many as a worthy successor though with a different style. Lewin was pulled ashore in the ship's whaler by his officers, and cheered by the ship, in traditional fashion. He returned to Brewster House at Doddington to start a new and different chapter of his career.

THE ROYAL YACHT
1957–1958

Walter Bagehot divided the elements of the English (*sic*) constitution into two: 'first, those which excite and preserve the reverence of the population – the *dignified* parts, if I may so call them; and next, the *efficient* parts ...'[1]

The Royal Yacht *Britannia* had to be both dignified and efficient. As a floating palace, the temporary home of the monarch and any members of the Royal Family embarked, and as a national symbol, she had to be immaculate in appearance, functioning and conduct; as a ship, she had to cope with every vagary of wind and tide, stress of wind and weather, just like any other ship.

She had been built for the job. Launched at John Brown's yard on the Clyde only four years before Commander Lewin joined her on 11 April 1957, she was of 4700 tons displacement, 360 feet long with a steam plant capable of driving her at 21 knots. She was fitted with stabilisers to help combat a tendency to roll. Her complement was given as 271, but this would vary quite significantly according to whether members of the Royal Household were on board.[2]

As was suggested at the end of the last chapter, Terry Lewin was uncertain what to expect from his new wardroom and ship's company. He knew by now a little about his predecessors: the first Commander of the Yacht had been 'Fish' Dalglish, a rugger-playing gunnery officer whom he had known at Whale Island, and the second, whom Lewin was to relieve, was John Adams, a highly intelligent non-specialist of established reputation. Neither of these squared with Lewin's preconception of the position as a 'sort of courtier job'.[3]

Nor did the ship's company. Some 40 of the crew of the previous Royal Yacht, the *Victoria and Albert*, which had not functioned as such since the Second World War, had indeed transferred to *Britannia* when she first commissioned, but the pace of life in the new vessel had quickly persuaded them that it was not for them, and Lewin's crew was now of an average age not much more than that current in the Navy as a whole. In particular the seaman chief petty officers, his key ratings, were only just turned 30, held acting rate, and were 'desperately keen to do anything'. He recalled their names 40 years later: CPO Goddard the coxswain, Cain the chief boatswain's mate, Hunter the coxswain of the Royal Barge.[4]

The wardroom was of equal quality, but there the atmosphere Lewin found on joining was not so encouraging. The Yacht had just returned from a round-the-world cruise with His Royal Highness Prince Philip that had been dazzling in its impact and had ended with a highly successful state visit to Lisbon. The officers were naturally very pleased with the way it had all gone. Hugh Owen, who joined six weeks before Terry as deputy supply officer and assistant secretary, recalled 'a certain amount of arrogance, perhaps even snobbery, in the wardroom'.[5] The Lewin verdict was: 'very full of themselves ...'[6] and another quote from him spoke of 'smugness'.[7] A number of changes were in train in the ordinary course, and that, combined with Terry Lewin's matter-of-fact and human approach, quickly corrected matters.

The ship was in the course of final preparation for the summer, and departed from Portsmouth for trials and work-up on 28 April. Still in command was Rear Admiral Sir Connolly Abel Smith, who had been Flag Officer Royal Yacht since the ship first entered service. He was one of the great characters of the Navy, a well-connected Scotsman, confident, a delegator-extraordinary, an expert ship-handler, something of a showman, perfect for the job and much loved by all.

The first Royal Duty of the summer, and the most important planned for the year, was a state visit to Copenhagen. Preparations had begun on 8 April, with the ship still at 'H' moorings in Portsmouth harbour, with the arrival on board of the Queen's Equerry.[8] The next day, Mr Venner, Controller of the Household, arrived on board, and for the succeeding week the meticulous process gathered pace: car transporter trials, the embarkation of the sailing yacht *Bluebottle*, hoisting in the Queen's Rolls-Royce with its own transporter, embarkation of the Royal Stores, the arrival of key household staff and the Royal Marine Band.

All this required the personal attention of the new commander; however expert and dedicated his subordinates, and Royal Yachtsmen had a reputation for both qualities, the responsibility was his, as it would be for any executive officer of a normal warship. In the Yacht, however, he had one additional factor to consider: the relationship between the standing officers and crew, and the officials of the house-hold. Their relative duties needed constant redefinition as circum-stances changed. Mostly, the links forged over long experience of working together were enough to ensure full and cordial co-operation, but inevitably questions of demarcation would arise and it was up to the commander, ultimately, to sort them out. Often, the personal touch was needed.

This was early borne in on Commander Lewin when the Yacht went round to Hull to embark Her Majesty on 18 May. *Britannia* anchored in the stream, and the Humber flows fast at that point. Moreover it was a squally, unpleasant day. It was not improved when an RNVR boat made a 'heavy alongside' at the starboard forward accommodation ladder and smashed its main stringer. Soon afterwards further members of the household were attempting to embark at the after ladder from one of the Yacht's boats, and 'a mature lady … with what looked like an expensive jewel case … was dithering about getting out and I shouted out to her "jump". She came up the ladder, gave me a look which went absolutely through me like a knife …'[9] This was the redoubtable 'Bobo' Macdonald, the Queen's personal maid, and the case almost certainly contained Her Majesty's personal jewellery. To cap a day full of interest and variety, the Queen, with the Duke of Edin-burgh, arrived on board at 4.50 pm and as she met the new commander, she 'looked me straight in the eye and said, "Oh yes Commander, you're the chap who didn't want to come to my yacht"'.[10]

But the twinkle in the Queen's eye had assured Terry Lewin that all was well, and Connolly Abel Smith had given him the assurance, born of long experience, that the shipwrights of the Yacht would have repaired the broken ladder by the next morning; and so it was.

With her escort of three destroyers, which included *Corunna* (the ship's company were convinced their erstwhile captain had fixed it), the Yacht sailed for Copenhagen that evening. The weather on passage was unfriendly. By midnight on 19 May the wind had increased to 30 knots and the next day was unpleasant, to the degree indeed that the Queen's dressing table became unshipped from its footings.[11] Again the shipwrights came to the rescue.

The State Visit began on 21 May and a summary of the events that day gives some idea of the precision that was expected, and achieved, on these occasions: it was the fruit of months of extremely careful planning by the palace authorities and the ship, taking in the advice of government departments and the local embassy staff.

At 8 am salutes were exchanged with the Kronborg Battery at the entrance to the Sound. Shortly afterwards the ship stopped to embark the British ambassador, the Danish Royal suite and the pilot, then proceeded towards Copenhagen. Aircraft of the Royal Danish Air Force flew past at 9.45 am and at 10 am precisely the Yacht passed the breakwater – Commander Peter Mitchell, the navigator, was unfailingly accurate in such matters. When the first wire was out to the mooring buoy at 10.12, ship was dressed overall with flags, and all ladders and boats were lowered, simultaneously. It was a form of display, and one in which the whole of the Royal Navy, particularly its bigger ships, excelled, but it was a sight to gladden any seaman's eye and no doubt that of the *Britannia*'s commander, who was responsible for its smooth organisation. At 10.35 the ship's company of the Yacht manned ship, lining the upper deck at precisely spaced intervals, to welcome the King and Queen of Denmark who arrived in their barge at 10.42. Welcomes having been exchanged, both royal parties left the Yacht at 10.55. Ship was unmanned at 11 am and the Yacht prepared to shift berth. *Britannia* slipped at 11.47, the dressing lines coming down as the slip wire came clear of the buoy, and berthed alongside at the Langelinie quay by 12.10 (up dressing lines again).

After that, particularly as the Queen and Duke of Edinburgh stayed at the embassy for most of the State Visit, there could be some relaxation and leave for the ship's company, and indeed the usual adjuncts of a visit to Copenhagen, including visits to the breweries, were enjoyed. One item specific to the Royal Yacht is worth recording. On 23 May the Queen and Prince Philip gave a state dinner party on board for the King and Queen of Denmark. This, since their arrival at that time of year in that latitude would be well before sunset, made it necessary to fulfil standard Royal Yacht protocol by manning ship. In consequence, leave was suspended between 7.50 pm and 9.20 pm, the ship's company took up their man-ship stations, welcomed the royal visitors as tradition demanded, and then the non-duty watch and part of the watch could go ashore again. The 'Yotties' did not turn a hair.

After a State Visit it was usual for the Yacht to have some time in harbour to reorganise and recuperate, but on this occasion there was no respite for either the ship or its royal occupants, for the next event of the summer followed hard upon. This was to be a royal review of the Home Fleet in Scottish waters. On Saturday 25 May the *Britannia* slipped from the Langelinie quay in the early evening, and anchored two hours later off Elsinore to re-embark the Queen and Duke of Edinburgh. Then it was across the North Sea, with the weather again unpleasant, to be joined on Monday afternoon by Her Majesty's Fleet, including three aircraft carriers – *Ark Royal, Albion and Bulwark* – as a prelude to the naval gathering at Invergordon. A fly-past by the carriers' aircraft was followed by the traditional steam-past and cheer ship, and the sight of three carriers manoeuvring at speed and in close company was one to be remembered.[12]

The next two days were eventful for the fleet – which perhaps needed some cheering up after Suez – and even more so for its royal guests, for the tempo never seemed to slacken. Lords of the Admiralty and flag officers were in abundance, there were dinner parties and receptions, a concert party in the *Albion*, ceremonial sunset, a regular jamboree.

In all this the commander of the Yacht would have been a key figure, but not a high-profile one. Two points, neither apparently of great import, nevertheless show the care that has to be put into such occasions. The first was the activity of the Royal Barge. This was necessarily a showpiece boat. Its handling could safely be left to its experienced coxswain and crew, but its appearance had to be constantly under scrutiny; with the whole fleet in harbour, there was bound to be some oil about, and in those days ships did not have internal sullage tanks, so that 'gash' would be floating, however carefully regulated ships might be. In consequence, the barge was hoisted after *every* trip to be carefully wiped down, and lowered in pristine condition just before its next assignment. That was not a procedure undergone by any other boat in the fleet. It entailed turning out the hands required, whenever required, and doing the job swiftly, efficiently and without complaint. It was 'Royal Yacht standard'.

The other point is a more general one. There are few jobs more taxing than producing and maintaining, for very important people, an environment of calm in a busy world. In pursuit of that ideal, quiet was the watchword in *Britannia*; most evolutions were carried out by hand signal rather than spoken commands, and normal footwear for the crew was plimsolls.[13] This was standard routine, and there was no likelihood of disturbance from inside the vessel. And the fleet, at its anchors or moorings nearby, was on its best behaviour. But even in the quiet waters of a Scottish loch, and even in those days before the advent of a rabid Press and lunatic special-interest groups, some intrusion might be expected, and security measures both overt and covert were necessary. The guard boat patrolling round the Yacht, as always when royalty was on board, was symbolic of something more comprehensive.[14] It was up to the commander, with advice from the household, to oversee all these matters.

The fleet gathering came to an end on 29 May, with the Queen and Prince Philip embarked in the great carrier *Ark Royal* accompanied by the Commander-in-Chief, Admiral Sir John Eccles, and the fleet manning and cheering ship. *Britannia* sailed discreetly soon afterwards, anchored some way down the Moray Firth, and re-embarked the royal party for a short time before they, and the other VIP guests, finally left for the shore. She proceeded south that evening, and the log has only one more entry of significance for that day: '2255 Exercised seaboat'. Naval matters had to have the last word.

June and early July was a period more in line with Lewin's preconception of Royal Yacht life. *Britannia* lay at her moorings in the northern reaches of Portsmouth harbour, and the biggest excitement was a Great Rat Chase during the nights of 1 and 2 July. The creature was first sighted during the middle watch and was ineffectually chased, but the next night the opposite watch was occupied between 1 and 3.30 am in a prolonged campaign that ended in the rat's death by broom handle.[15]

The Lewin family took the opportunity to move again. The house at Doddington in Kent was inconvenient for Portsmouth where the Royal Yacht was based, and they took 'the ground floor of a rather grand house called Strangehall in Bosham'.[16] This entailed new schools for the children; Tim was now of preparatory school age and went to Oakwood, not far away, where in spite of a leg still in full-length calliper he took part in cricket and boxing as well as his academic work; Susie went to the primary school in Bosham.

The Yacht's seagoing assignments for the rest of the summer were relatively relaxed, compared with the hectic introduction at the end of May, though they were naturally of considerable significance to the places visited. After the usual preparations during the previous week, *Britannia*, with the First Lord embarked, made her way from Portsmouth to Southampton on 24 July. There Her Majesty and the Duke of Edinburgh embarked, accompanied by Princess Andrew of Greece, and a night passage was made to Jersey. The Yacht anchored at 9.30 am and the royal party left for a very full day ashore, followed by a reception for 200 guests in the evening.[17]

The next day, the pattern was repeated in Guernsey, and the next in the tiny island of Sark. It had been intended to put into Alderney the day after that, but in the weather prevailing even Connolly Abel Smith would not enter that notoriously difficult harbour, and the Yacht returned to St Peter Port, Guernsey, so that the Queen and Prince Philip could go to Alderney by air; the islanders must not be disappointed. At the end of the Channel Islands visit, everyone, including the royals, assembled on the forecastle for a ship's company photograph.

It was not quite the end of the summer programme; there was still Cowes Week to come. This lasted from 2 to 10 August, and Prince

Michael of Kent was joined on 5 August by Prince Philip and the Duke
of Cornwall – Prince Charles, who had not yet been created Prince of
Wales. Lewin confessed:

> I was not a keen sailing man at that time and when everybody
> went off sailing at Cowes in the afternoon, I took my golf
> clubs ashore to a rather nice little nine hole course at Osborne
> House ... I had much pleasure in coming back ... crossing the
> harbour to the castle of the Royal Yacht Squadron, leaving my
> golf clubs in the hall and taking tea in the Squadron.[18]

The Royal Yacht had now been in commission for four years, and it
was time for her first major refit. This lasted for the next five months.
Connolly Abel Smith, who lived in Scotland, was also coming to the
end of his time, and was exercising his powers of delegation to the full:

> He would come down on the night sleeper on Tuesday having
> done his hunting on Tuesday, go to his club and arrive in time
> for dinner on the Wednesday, spend Thursday with us and leave
> on Thursday to catch the night train back to Scotland so that he
> could get his hunting in on the Friday ... we sent all our corre-
> spondence up with a flimsy copy to Connolly and he always sent
> the flimsy back saying 'Signed and despatched' and he never
> altered a single word. We all adored the man ...[19]

During the refit Lewin was able to make significant improvements to
the accommodation of the ship's company. Their quarters had been in
marked contrast to the restrained luxury of the state apartments: still
slinging hammocks, and often in odd corners wherever these could be
found, they were cramped and uncomfortable.[20] It was possible to
redesign them for the better, with bunks for sleeping and improved
messing arrangements.

It was during the period of this refit that one of the might-have-
beens of Terry Lewin's life occurred. The reforms in the wake of
Duncan Sandys's 1957 Defence White Paper,[21] with its abolition of

conscription and reshaping of the regular forces, included plans for a significant number of redundancies among the officers of the armed services. The terms were generous, and the nickname 'golden bowler' was quickly applied. One of those who volunteered was Commander Lewin. He had reason: although he had had a succession of first-class appointments and had done well, he felt absolutely no certainty that he would progress to the highest ranks of the service; and with a disabled son, however bright and determined as Tim was, he believed it only right to give Jane as much respite as possible. There had never been any spare money in the Lewin or Branch-Evans families – neither the civil service nor the clergy are notable for that – and the prospect of a decent lump sum, with entitlement to a pension, was immediately attractive.

Terry's application was refused. There were in fact more volunteers than were required, but even if there had not been, the Navy would probably not have relinquished someone who, whatever he thought of his own prospects, was regarded as one of its brightest coming stars. The news was received with some misgiving. But, as always, the family rallied and life went on.

On 31 December 1957 Terry Lewin was selected for promotion to the rank of captain. This was of course a matter for celebration; even though it might have been expected because commanders of the Yacht had always in the past reached at least the next step up, it had come early and reassuringly. However, it was not to mean an early move. The new Flag Officer, Royal Yacht was about to take up his appointment, and the navigator – a key player who was responsible for much of the forward planning of visits – was due for relief in the next few months. Lewin was, therefore, to remain as executive officer well past the time his promotion was to take effect on 30 June. He decided that on that date he would not ship his fourth stripe: the commander of the Yacht, he believed, should look the part.

The new flag officer was Rear Admiral Peter Dawnay, a very different character from Connolly Abel Smith. He was well-connected, had commanded a destroyer squadron with distinction,[22] and had a reputation as a ship handler. But Lewin thought him a 'twangy and nervous' man,[23] who found delegation difficult and worried inordinately about detail that could have been left to his expert subordinates. However this was not everyone's experience of Dawnay; at least one officer found him to be good company and, once some initial fussiness had been disposed of, easy to deal with.[24]

Sea trials of a ship when she has finished refit often sharpen the senses wonderfully, and in 1958 *Britannia*'s took place in an English February. One of the trials was unusual. Ships have nodes of vibration at certain speeds, and before the refit, in Lewin's words:

> At 16 knots which was the normal cruising speed for the Yacht on passage, there was a vibration which went right across the middle of the Queen's bed so they had to get rid of that vibration. This meant putting stiffeners around the stairwell for the stairs which led up from the state apartments to the royal bedrooms ... the main constructor in charge of the Royal Yacht was a super chap called Harry Harrison ... We went out for trials and Harry and I sat on either side of the Queen's bed and then the ship was taken up through the range of speeds from 12 knots to about 20 to see if the vibration had been cured. Fortunately it had ...[25]

After a further stay in Portsmouth, and an emergency docking caused by damage to a propeller when the Yacht overran a buoy, it was time for the first royal event of the year, a state visit to the Netherlands between 25 and 28 March.[26] This followed the pattern already described, except that it was a two-centre visit to both Amsterdam and Rotterdam, in keeping perhaps with the city-state history of that country, whose capital is in neither city but in The Hague.

The rest of the summer was busy, with royalty embarked much of the time but all around the British Isles without any foreign-going, and not too much pomp and circumstance. Queen Elizabeth the Queen Mother was on board for a week in May, cruising up the west coast and to Northern Ireland, and the Queen and Duke of Edinburgh similarly visited the east coast, including the Firth of Forth, from 27 June to 1 July. There had to be, at every place of call, the same meticulous standard of appearance and conduct as for the most important state visit. It was what the inhabitants of each community had every right to expect, and was what they got.

Late July saw two important events in the royal calendar: a call at Cardiff for the last day of the Empire Games, followed by a visit to the Royal Naval College, Dartmouth for Lord High Admiral's Divisions at the end of the summer term. Unhappily the Queen was unable to attend either ceremony because she was unwell, and Prince Philip took her place. For Terry Lewin, Cardiff was a matter of snatching a quick look at Cardiff Arms Park during the last race, then returning on board to prepare the Yacht for sea. She was joined next day by an escort from the Dartmouth Training Squadron and entered Dartmouth on 28 July. Dawnay had been very concerned about the entry to this tricky harbour in the weather prevailing, and had been persuaded only by a signal from the captain of the college at 3 am saying, 'The flags are hanging lifeless here.'[27] The Yacht and her attendant frigates duly entered harbour, and the programme ashore proceeded, as planned.

It was, however, an instance of Peter Dawnay at his most 'twangy'. At a reception during the day, he complained of the presence of a mooring buoy very close to the fairway in the entrance to the Dart. 'It ought to be removed,' said Dawnay. 'If I stay in command much longer,' observed Peter Branson, captain of the *Roebuck*, who had overrun the buoy on more than one occasion, 'it will be – I'll sink it next time.' Dawnay, recalling probably his own mishap with a buoy in Portsmouth harbour, was not amused.

The first three weeks of August were a period of relaxation for the Royal Family on board the Yacht. After Cowes Week, she departed for an extended cruise up the west coast of Scotland, with calls at Helford River and Holyhead on the way. While she was at Holyhead the Queen and Duke of Edinburgh landed for an official visit, and Terry was left in charge of Prince Charles and Princess Anne. He was playing cricket with them on the verandah deck when a Press boat appeared armed with cameras: an early influx of *paparazzi*. He was particularly impressed with Princess Anne's aplomb – just before her eighth birthday – facing up to the photographers and waving to them. The ship's company presented her with her own camera a few days later.[28]

After an idyllic week among the Western Isles, the family disembarked at Fort William on 18 August, and *Britannia* sailed for Portsmouth, arriving on the 20th. And that was the end of Terry Lewin's seagoing in the Yacht. It had been an interesting and formative time, not simply a stepping-stone to higher rank. He had always had latent diplomatic skills, and to some extent these had been tested, for example at La Coruña, but they had been much developed now, not least in the internal workings of the Yacht with the household on board.

Moreover, he had not said goodbye to the earthier side of the Navy. In August 1958 Commander Robert Clarkson joined as supply officer. On his second day a petty officer arrived in his cabin: the commander's compliments, and would he play rugger against HMS *Collingwood* that afternoon? The bus was to leave in fifteen minutes. Clarkson replied that he had hung up his boots five years before, and would take them down the day the commander decided to play again – and was promptly trumped by the news that Lewin would be playing on the wing, outside Clarkson in the centre. It was a *Boy's Own Paper* finale: Lewin scored a try, Clarkson backing up ended on top of him, and the bearded Able Seaman Ivory (second row) observed that that was the first time he had seen seven stripes fighting over a rugby ball.[29]

BACK TO THE MINISTRY
1959–1961

Captain Lewin was appointed to the Admiralty as Deputy Director of Tactical and Staff Duties on 3 November 1958. The job was as involved as its title; with apologies to the reader, a brief discussion of Whitehall organisation is needed.

The size and shape of the fleet, and its aircraft, were developed in the Admiralty at that time through several different channels that came together at the level of the Admiralty Board. The Vice Chief of Naval Staff (VCNS) had working for him the Plans Division, who formulated naval policy in response to the strategy of government (or, it sometimes seemed, what they thought it ought to be, since governments are not always given to clear statements of strategy) and the Operations Division. He and his divisions were responsible for the numbers and deployment patterns of Her Majesty's Ships and Naval Aircraft. The Deputy Chief of Naval Staff (DCNS), on the other hand, was in charge of the shape of the fleet: the characteristics of ships and associated aircraft, and what their weapon systems would be. To this end, he had charge of the specialist divisions: Gunnery, Torpedo and Anti-Submarine, Navigation and Tactical Control, Communications, and Air Warfare. Because these specialists were bound to be advocates for the systems of their individual specialisations, umpires were required, and these at the end of the 1950s came in two forms: a Weapon Equipment Priority Section, working direct to DCNS but with close links to the nascent central defence staff organisation, and the Tactical and Staff Duties Division, which was meant to be the senior and co-ordinating division, taking the overall view of fleet requirements.[1]

It all made third- and fourth-century Byzantium look pretty streamlined, and when one added the inputs of the Naval Intelligence Division, the civilian divisions which shadowed and advised the Naval Staff Divisions and were in charge of the purse strings, the Second Sea

Lord's department with its manpower requirements and constraints, the Controller's department with its immensely powerful Directors General in charge of ship design and construction,[2] and subjected the whole business to intense Treasury scrutiny and control, it is scarcely any wonder that naval projects were long in gestation and often represented a set of uneasy compromises.

It was clearly going to be a busy time for the deputy director of a co-ordinating division, particularly as in the wake of Suez and the radical tenancy of Duncan Sandys as Secretary of State for Defence,[3] times were changing fast and the future fleet must change with them. The Lewins moved once more, closer to London now. Near Ashurst in Kent, they found Pitfields Cottage and it became the Lewin base for some years; 81 Mayday Gardens, their London house, was sold and Pitfields taken on a long lease. Tim was installed in due course in St Edmund's School, Canterbury and Susie at Hollington Park in Hastings; and an addition to the family arrived in the person of Jonathan, born on 20 May 1959. But Terry and Jane, for the first time, were sentenced by his heavy workload to weekend commuting or something very close to it, with most of Terry's week-nights spent in a mews flat shared with brother Alex, now an architect in the Ancient Monuments section of the Office of Works.

It was very easy for weekend commuters to become remote from their families, particularly if the children were at boarding school. 'Friday-night syndrome', with a weary husband arriving home to a wife with a build-up of a week's problems, many of them demanding solution by Monday morning, was well known. It needed a lot of thought and understanding between partners to make the best of things, but Jane and Terry had plenty of that, and the family was a close and loyal one. He had always been a keen carpenter and now, with a rather superior set of equipment given to him by Connolly Abel Smith, he made all manner of things for the children and for the house. Sometimes his enthusiasms took charge: when Tim left his prep school he was surprised to find his father turning up in a Mark 7 Jaguar, 'the former property of an earl who had become a duke. It was maroon with a little secret safe under the floor in the back, Dad used to tell us it was to keep the coronet in … but Mum thought it was too ostentatious and utterly impractical for going to the village shop.'[4] The Jaguar was replaced by a Triumph Herald, the first brand-new car they had ever bought, and they both loved it.

One of the first things to be done at the Admiralty was to simplify the organisation. It would have been too much to expect a newly promoted captain to take the lead in this, but when the more senior Captain Peter Hill-Norton, the head of the Weapon Equipment Priority section, suggested a merger with the Tactical and Staff Duties Division, Lewin enthusiastically supported him. Thus the Tactical and Weapons Policy Division was created, a more powerful unit than the sum of its constituent parts, with Hill-Norton as director and Lewin as deputy. Hill-Norton had not met Lewin before, though both were gunnery officers, and initially had considered Lewin 'a little suspect' because of his Royal Yacht background[5] (perceptions died hard); but he soon realised how capable his deputy was, and how great was his capacity for effective work.

One of the principal tasks in the post-Suez period was to bring helicopters into operation in the fleet. They were seen as having two main functions: to carry troops from ship to shore, as they had done operationally at Port Said in 1956;[6] and to carry anti-submarine detection equipment and weaponry. Although the same basic helicopter might do for both functions, the fit would vary so much as normally to necessitate two different aircraft, and though the larger ships and especially the aircraft carriers might carry helicopters for both jobs, it would greatly complicate their operation if they tried.

In consequence, plans were put in hand for the conversion of the relatively small and slow carriers *Albion* and *Bulwark*, which would have needed extensive modernisation if they were to operate the next generation of combat aircraft, to the Commando carrier role.[7] Capable of carrying a Royal Marines Commando Group, with two squadrons of troop-carrying helicopters – initially Whirlwinds but later Wessex – they would be a powerful adjunct to the government's 'East of Suez' policy that was emerging as the cornerstone of naval force structure for the early 1960s. The development of this conversion was largely in

Lewin's hands and he had, through the Secretariat, to keep up the pressure on the Cabinet Defence Committee for final approval to be given.[8] This was duly done and the two ships proved themselves highly effective units throughout the 1960s.

That was not, however, the end of the need for specialised amphibious shipping. The concept of a 'Landing Ship Dock', capable of trimming down so that landing craft could swim out from within the ship and either land assault troops over a beach or subsequently ferry heavy equipment ashore, had been about for some years and had already been realised in the United States Navy. The Royal Navy was deemed to need two ships of this type, to carry, in addition to troops, tanks and landing craft, all the communication equipment necessary to a Joint Force Commander conducting an amphibious landing. Lewin was chairman of the committee which drew up the Staff Requirement for these ships,[9] which eventually became *Fearless* and *Intrepid*. During their lives they were often regarded as outdated, even unemployable, yet 20 years after they were finally approved they fulfilled, in the Falklands, precisely the function for which they were designed. The wheel had come full circle; they were there – just.

A further large-ship project also sponsored by Lewin did not, at that time, come to fruition. The problem of providing a seagoing base for anti-submarine helicopters was not to be so readily solved as had the troop-carrying question with the *Albion* and *Bulwark* conversions. The smaller helicopter types, such as the Wasp, might be accommodated in frigates, but they were no more than weapon-carriers; anti-submarine detection equipment could only be carried in larger aircraft of the Whirlwind/Wessex type. The Canadians were known to be experimenting with heavy helicopters operating from frigates, but the margins were very tight. Large helicopters could operate from the big fixed-wing carriers such as *Ark Royal*, but their operations would greatly complicate launch and recovery cycles.[10]

The best solution was considered to be a class of helicopter carriers, eventually called 'Escort cruisers'.[11] The initial bid for these ships, of between 10,000 and 15,000 tons, called for five to be operational at any one time. As always tends to happen to a spartan initial concept, the plans ran away. The complement doubled from its original figure of 366. The Staff Divisions weighed in with their favourite projects: the Gunnery Division wanted the Seaslug air defence missile, and roles beyond anti-submarine warfare were mooted. Even so, it was argued, an escort cruiser was the operational equivalent of two frigates, and therefore might be thought a good buy.

The Board of Admiralty had doubts about whether the project could be justified when the fixed-wing carriers had already been specified as having an anti-submarine role west of Suez, and was deeply worried about the effect on the rest of the Navy of finding enough people to man the escort cruisers. Even a highly perceptive paper by the Director of Plans, in mid-1961, giving the ship 'basic cruiser characteristics ... long range, [capable of] independent operations and the ability to support other forces which are unable to provide entirely for their own defence', was unable to sway the Board and the project was shelved. It was to be taken down and brushed off a few years later, but that is for another chapter.

It was in the field of escort vessels, however, that Captain Lewin probably made his greatest contribution to the future structure of the Royal Navy. The story was, as so often in the evolution of ship design, full of complexities, the interaction of personalities, and some irony.

The Royal Navy saw two distinct operational requirements for escorts.[12] The first was for ships to support the major units of the fleet, the strike aircraft carriers and increasingly the amphibious forces. The former particularly were themselves high-speed vessels and their manoeuvres, connected with their primary business of flying aircraft, meant that their escorts had to be fast and agile to occupy and maintain the optimum screening positions for their protection. Escorts had to have gun and/or missile armament capable of engaging aircraft attacking the fleet; while the carriers' fighter aircraft might impose attrition on an attacking force, some would get through, and the carriers' own self-defence armaments were unlikely to be sufficient to cope on their own. Finally, the fleet escorts were deemed to need a good capacity to detect and attack submarines, for the helicopters embarked in the carriers (and even the putative escort cruisers) would not be able to meet a large-scale submarine threat on their own. All this meant that the fleet escort needed, in the view of the Naval Staff, to be a fast, powerful, versatile unit. Such vessels – generally now designated 'destroyers' – would not come cheap, either in initial cost or manpower.

The other kind of escort was intended mainly for convoy work. These could be slower ships, because the average speed of a convoy was still only about 12 knots and the speed margin needed for changing station, responding to indications of submarine threat, and forming surface attack units, was not of the same order as was required for fleet work. The balance of armament, however, still presented problems of ship design: it was not considered possible, in a single modest hull, to install underwater and above-water weapons and sensors to the full extent that the escort of a convoy required.

At the end of the 1950s the Navy's solution to the escort problem reflected, as given the long life and gestation of ships it always had to, a set of developments, modifications and compromises. Fleet escorts were typified by the 'Daring' class, heavily gun-armed big destroyers, and the emerging 'County' class, even bigger and more heavily manned and mounting the Navy's first anti-aircraft guided missile, the Seaslug, as well as having a medium-calibre gun armament and a hangar housing an anti-submarine helicopter. Supplementing these two classes were frigates converted from destroyer hulls, capable of fleet speed but distinctly specialised in the anti-submarine role.

These 'Type 15 and 16 Conversions' tended to occupy a position between fleet and convoy escort. For the latter task, there remained quite a number of war-built vessels of the 'Loch' and 'Bay' classes, slow and soon to be phased out; and the much more capable post-war construction consisting mainly[13] of the Type 12, 41 and 61 frigates. The hull form of these ships had been designed by Ken Purvis of the Royal Corps of Naval Constructors[14] as early as 1945. They were specialised ships: the Type 12 was an anti-submarine ship with a steam plant to give it the necessary speed margin, while the Types 41 and 61 were both diesel-powered, for air defence and aircraft direction roles respectively.

The Type 12 in particular had proved a considerable success in service, its hull form giving it outstanding capacity to operate at speed in rough weather.[15] Altogether the programme, originally for six ships, was extended to 15 and this was fully on stream when Lewin was DDTWP. But he needed to look ahead to what was needed for the future in the escort field as a whole.

Opportunities for initiating a new type of destroyer looked at that moment to be limited. It would have to be designed round a new anti-aircraft missile; the Seaslug was distinctly first-generation, its mounting and missiles occupied vast amounts of space and its accuracy was suspect.[16] The Sea Dart, its successor, was not ready. In consequence, naval staff thinking turned towards the idea of a general-purpose ship to fill the gap, for 'rolling programmes' of escort construction had great attractions: they were easier to get through the Treasury and they kept the warship building yards employed without too many fits and starts.[17]

Lewin had heard of a frigate building in Southampton for New Zealand. It was basically a Type 12, but the New Zealanders had introduced modifications which appeared to be particularly attractive in the general-purpose context. The designer was none other than Purvis himself, who had returned to the RCNC from Cammell Laird, where he had served for a period up to 1954. Purvis was an unusual naval constructor, with a shipyard (Denny Bros.) rather than a naval dockyard drawing office background, but he showed himself throughout his career to be a master of the art of evolutionary design, and so it proved in this case.

Accounts differ as to the exact sequence of events in what proved to be a seminal decision for the Navy. One authority says the New Zealand frigate was 'dangled before the naval staff' by the constructors[18] and Purvis confirms this version. Lewin's memoir is less exact: 'The New Zealanders had made a number of major alterations ... so I went down [to Southampton] with the naval constructor from Bath, Ken Purvis, and my commander who was the destroyer man Duncan Carson.'[19]

Who took the initiative is immaterial. Like all Admiralty materiel developments, it was a corporate one. What was at once apparent was

the merit of what the New Zealanders were doing: 'They had introduced complete air conditioning for the ship, cafeteria messing, bunk
sleeping, all within a Type 12 hull. So we told Ken Purvis, 'This is what
we want ...' It could not have fallen on readier ears. Purvis virtually
had his pencil poised and swiftly produced a design for a frigate which
became the 'Leander' class.

These were ships of some 2500 tons standard displacement, steam
powered with a conventional but modern and efficient plant that drove
them at a maximum of 28 knots. They had two 4.5-inch guns in a
single turret, the Seacat close-range anti-aircraft missile, the Mark 10
'Limbo' anti-submarine mortar and six anti-submarine torpedo tubes,
an air warning and gunnery and navigation radars, and a hangar that
could accommodate a Wasp or similar-sized helicopter. In fact, they
were all-rounders. There was nothing fancy, but an enormous amount
had been done on the displacement and with a ship's company of 230
or so. When to that was added the improved habitability that Lewin's
memoir describes, and which it is known was very near his heart, the
design was clearly a winner.

Yet, such is the scepticism built into the Whitehall system (and
also, perhaps, the influence of the 'Not Invented Here' or NIH
syndrome), that Lewin had to prepare very carefully the case for this
general-purpose frigate, which could operate as a fleet or convoy
escort as circumstances required. There was some prejudice against
Purvis because of his background, and his evolutionary approach led
to accusations of 'old-fashioned design'.[20] Many members of the Ship
Characteristics Committee hankered after something bigger and
more radical. So, possibly, did the Board. Presenting the Staff
Requirement for the 'Leander' as a 'Modified Type 12', therefore,
Lewin had to put it forward as an interim measure until new
destroyers designed round Sea Dart could begin to be built. He
admitted that the board margin, which was an allowance of spare
displacement and power that would allow modifications during the
lifetime of the ship, scarcely existed in the 'Leander' design; and
suggested that as the end of this design line the class should be
limited to seven.[21] On this basis the Ship Characteristics Committee,

headed by the Controller, Admiral Sir Michael LeFanu, endorsed the design and the Board approved.

In the event, the outcome was quite different and much better. The 'Leander' class eventually amounted in the Royal Navy alone to 26 ships, and the design was adopted by many other navies who acquired, either from British yards or built in their own, a total of 30 more. *Pace* Captain Lewin's disclaimer about the board margin, the design proved itself immensely adaptable. Mid-life modifications, some well-conceived and some not,[22] proved entirely possible and by the end of their service lives some of the ships were armed with surface-to-surface and anti-aircraft guided missiles and carried Lynx helicopters. The 'Leanders' were the well-known workhorses of the fleet and were probably the most successful frigate design in the world during the post-war period.

There were some more mundane matters to be dealt with in the destroyer and frigate field. One of these[23] concerned the Dartmouth Training Squadron. At the time this consisted of Type 15 frigates specially converted for the training role, with an enlarged open bridge and a charthouse aft, but these ships, originating from 1943 and 1944, were wearing out fast and replacements were required. Some of the first of the Type 12s, due in any case for refit, were selected for the task, and the necessary modifications included changes to accommodation and, as in any training ship, more boats. Lewin would in time have closer acquaintance with these conversions, though at present he was unaware of it.

If the successful 'Leander' had grown from modest, evolutionary beginnings, and the Dartmouth Training Squadron conversions been well in the common run, the final project with which Captain Lewin had to do as DDTWP was something else. The Royal Navy's fleet carriers had entered service in 1950 or thereabouts and, such is the lead time for major naval designs, their successors already had to be thought about. Lewin was in the chair for the very first meeting to consider the staff requirement for this ship, CVA 01. It required a specially large conference room.[24] This was clearly to be a key project for the future of the Navy. Its fate belongs to a later chapter.

At the end of two years in the Admiralty a relatively junior captain on the post list could expect either a sea command or some other out-of-London appointment. Lewin got neither, but something different: a year at the Imperial Defence College (IDC). This was the senior defence course in Britain, designed to help fit officers and officials for more responsible appointments, including the highest, both in command and on the staff. It was based at Seaford House in the south-east corner of Belgrave Square, a building of some splendour that was habitually referred to by one Italian-speaking lecturer as *questo palazzo*.[25] The one-year course, initiated in 1923, is still run there in the twenty-first century under the title of Royal College of Defence Studies.

The 1961 course consisted of 66 students, drawn from Britain, the Commonwealth and the United States of America, all of brigadier/colonel or equivalent level. Each of the United Kingdom fighting services provided ten, and there were eleven civilian officials, the remainder representing eleven Commonwealth nations plus the USA. The Royal Naval contingent included several, other than Lewin, who subsequently attained high rank: the non-specialist seaman M. D. Kyrle Pope, the aviator H. R. B. Janvrin, the submariner I. L. M. McGeoch and the distinguished engineer H. G. H. Tracy.[26] They were a singularly lively bunch, and the cross-fertilisation that was such a feature of the IDC course had full scope.

Lewin also felt himself lucky in his commandant. This was Sir Robert Scott, a very senior official of the Commonwealth Office whose colourful career had included escape from Hong Kong as the Japanese invaded in 1941, and subsequently a prominent part in the quelling of the Malayan emergency. He was the author of books on counter-insurgency and this was his greatest interest and strength, most appropriate at the outset of the 1960s. Lewin regarded him as 'an absolutely first class man'.[27]

No one could accuse the IDC of overworking its students. One called the course 'a year's paid leave',[28] and a Commandant, some years later, 'a last twitch of the mind before it ossifies'.[29] The routine at that time was a leisurely one, with a forenoon lecture and question time followed sometimes by syndicate study in the afternoon, and without any requirement for individual research or authorship. The quality of lecturer was very high, and so was the level of questioning; someone once said it was the toughest audience in the world. Friendships and acquaintance made at the IDC often persisted for a lifetime.

Terry Lewin could welcome all this, as he could a more relaxed life style that allowed him to be home in Kent between 3.30 and 4 pm. He recalled building a 7-foot pram dinghy with a £10 kit, set up in the end room at Pitfields and ceremonially launched with the aid of a pork-fat runway on to one of the two ponds in the garden.[30] His carpentry was coming along nicely.

One of the highlights of the IDC course was the foreign tour. About five were run each year, each consisting of about a dozen students led by one of the Senior Directing Staff and with a member of the Junior Directing Staff as bear-leader and (though they would not admit it) emergency bag-carrier. A tour generally visited about five countries in one particular region over a period of five weeks, and it was an ideal opportunity to become familiar at the highest level with an area where one had not been before.

It was natural that Captain Lewin should choose the Far East tour. He was not an Old China Hand; on the contrary, his furthest east so far was the Persian Gulf, and that was unusual for a naval officer. Moreover, he had been enthused by Scott, who was a Far East expert: indeed, it was said subsequently that if the Americans had listened to Scott's advice, the Vietnam conflict would not have taken the course it did. In 1961 the area was fermenting and Lewin recalled trips down the Mekong delta from Saigon, as well as visits to Singapore, Hong Kong and the Philippines – all places where political and economic development was rapid and security implications were profound. There seems little doubt that a good deal of his thinking, in the 1960s and beyond, was much influenced by this tour, reinforced by his subsequent operational experience in the Far East.

Towards the end of the IDC course, students were made aware of their next appointments. Lewin had hoped to be appointed Captain (D) of a crack destroyer squadron,[31] but instead was offered and at once accepted the command of the Dartmouth Training Squadron. This was to be a further widening of his experience in a field he had not expected. But appointers are sometimes further-seeing than those they appoint. Captain Lewin joined his new command, HMS *Urchin*, just before Christmas, as was becoming his wont, on 18 December 1961.

THE DARTMOUTH
TRAINING SQUADRON
1961–1963

The scheme of training for naval officers devised by the Mansergh Committee on Officer Structure and Training (COST)[1] had proved less than satisfactory. Criticisms centred on two aspects: the standard of education and intelligence demanded of entrants was too low, leading to variable quality in officers joining the fleet; and the system of training, attempting to train officers to full professional standard in the college and the squadron before taking up their first fleet appointments as sub-lieutenants, led to a loss of confidence in ships' companies when they realised just how inexperienced these young officers were.

Moreover, as so often happens, low entry standards had not led to any ease of recruiting. On the contrary, the lower the reputation of the entry, the fewer applicants there were. In consequence, a high-level committee was set up in 1958[2] under Sir Keith Murray, then chairman of the University Grants Committee, with Rear Admiral J. D. Luce, the Naval Secretary, Mr Nigel Abercrombie, the Under Secretary (Naval Personnel), Sir Willis Jackson, the research director of English Electric, and Professor Harry Allen, as members. Captain Louis LeBailly, one of the 'Ferrets' of Chapter 4, was the staff officer and Mr David Dell, an Admiralty resident clerk, the secretary.

The committee reported its recommendations after less than six months' intensive work, in which they did a great deal of analysis, including comparison with other nations' training systems, and encountered some stiff opposition (one elderly witness thumped the table and shouted, 'We don't want brains, we want leaders of men') as well as a variety of ideas, some bright, some outlandish. A personal, and supportive, interest was taken by the First Sea Lord, Admiral the Earl Mountbatten. The recommendations were approved by the Board and announced in Parliament on 9 March 1959.[3] In brief, they were:

- Raising educational standards for entry to two 'A' levels and five 'O' levels.
- One entry a year to Dartmouth.
- Two years' practical training, of which the second would be in the fleet as midshipmen.
- Degree courses for all officers of the engineering and electrical specialisations.
- A 'concentrated academic course' in the third year for seaman and supply officers.

As always in such cases, the transition from the COST to the Murray scheme took some years to implement, and when Captain Lewin took command of the Dartmouth Training Squadron at the end of 1961 it was about halfway through and he therefore had to become familiar with two different training patterns for the young officers in his care. Moreover, domestic arrangements in the ships were to cause difficulty; juggling midshipmen from the old scheme and cadets from the new, in the limited gunroom space available, was a tricky task for first lieutenants and training officers.[4]

None of this was likely to cause too much anxiety to Terry Lewin. Nor, as a seasoned small-ship captain, was his new command. *Urchin* was originally an Emergency class destroyer, launched at Vickers's yard in March 1943. Her first conversion to Type 15 frigate had been in the early 1950s and her second, to training frigate, late in that decade. While this conversion had given her specialised accommodation and facilities for officers under training,[5] she was by no means completely disarmed, retaining her twin 4-inch guns, her close-range Bofors, her sonar equipment and Mark 10 'Limbo' anti-submarine mortars as well as a full suite of above-water sensors. All these were regarded as useful introductory training for both midshipmen and cadets, and indeed were also necessary in case the ship was ever recalled for war service, since although they did not take part in fleet exercises the squadron were all earmarked for NATO.

The rest of the squadron were similarly modified Type 15s. *Vigilant, Roebuck* and *Wizard*, all, like *Urchin*, based upon Plymouth, generally formed the First Division which took part in the extended cruises, while *Venus* and *Virago* as the Second Division were occupied in day running from Plymouth, sometimes for first term Dartmouth cadets ('seasick cruises') but mainly for junior seamen under training. Though the Second Division were under Captain (F)'s administration, they were more or less an independent command.

The west-country base meant a further move for the Lewin family. They let Pitfields and moved to Old Thatch, a cottage close to the post office and stores of the Devon village of South Milton. Tim and Susie were now both boarders at schools in Kent; Jon, now three, remained with the family. The whole pattern was typical of the compromises and devices that naval families have to go through if family life is to be sustained, and reflected the relative financial stringency even of four stripes and a certain status: few naval families now had any private means to call upon.

Ships of the First Division did three cruises each year, of about twelve weeks each. So it had been in the training cruiser before the Second World War, and so it still was; and even the regions visited during each cruise had not changed. But there was a very good reason for that. What was needed for training was a mixture of optimum weather for navigation and boatwork, interesting places to visit, enough but not excessive seatime, and both ocean and pilotage waters. The right blend was found to be a cruise to the Caribbean in spring, to the Baltic and its approaches in the summer, and the Mediterranean in the autumn.

So it was across the Atlantic to the Caribbean that the *Urchin, Wizard, Vigilant* and *Roebuck* were bound in January 1962. A mixed training complement of some 60 midshipmen and cadets formed about a third of each ship's crew. The remainder were the regular ship's company, sailors, petty officers and chief petty officers, some specially selected for their ability as trainers but mostly as normal ship's complement. It was, after all, important that the officers under training should live and work with a cross-section of the men they would ultimately command. The officers of the squadron, on the other hand, were specially selected, at least to the extent that any officer who showed second-rate abilities could not expect to remain in the ship for long. They contained, moreover, a high proportion of the seaman sub-specialisations, since professional instruction was a part of the cruise syllabus. Thus, for

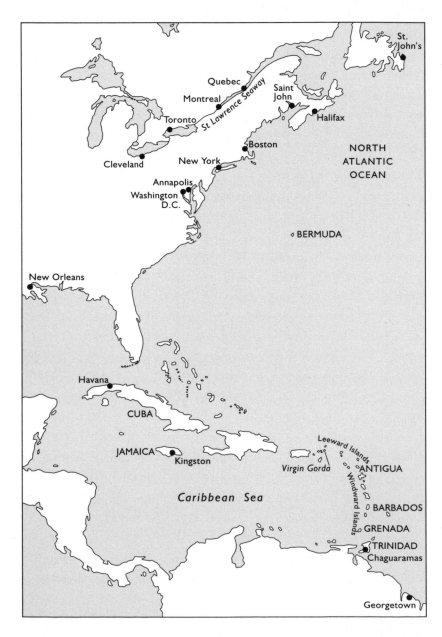

example, each ship would carry a navigation specialist, to give instruction to the young gentlemen in that art.

The material state of these ageing ships always caused concern. A split in an oil tank in the *Urchin* delayed her in Gibraltar while the rest of the squadron sailed on to the Cape Verde Islands.[6] She caught them up there, and they had set course westwards after fuelling at Sao Vicente when something more serious happened. Almost inevitably, it involved HMS *Roebuck*.

The *Roebuck* was an interesting ship. On the ways in Scott's yard on the Clyde in 1943, she had been launched prematurely by a bomb that exploded nearby,[7] had lain on the bottom for the next six months, and had never been quite the same since. She was known generally as 'The Rustbucket', though in 1958 a ruder community called her 'the Floating Scrapheap' and in moments of stress were known to omit the initial 's'.[8] She could behave charmingly, but power and equipment failures were endemic.

On 4 February, after an afternoon and evening full of the usual manoeuvres and transfers for the edification of the young officers, *Roebuck*, true to form, suffered a total steam failure.[9] She lay stopped and dark. It is fair to say that in such circumstances most Captains (F) would, if not actually fussing around, have at least stopped the squadron and prepared to offer assistance, if not a tow. Lieutenant-Commander Simon Cassels, in command of *Roebuck*, recalled that there was certainly no sense of fuss,[10] indeed the only signal he remembered Lewin's making was 'See you in Barbados' as *Urchin* with the rest of the squadron disappeared over the horizon.

From *Urchin*'s log it was not quite like that. In fact she proceeded at only 10 knots for the next one and a half hours, and it was with much relief that *Roebuck* was detected coming up astern at 1.23 am, apparently fully restored, and back in station an hour later. But Cassels was in no doubt as to how much he and his people were trusted by their Captain (F), and what is more it is certain they trusted his judgement; there was absolutely no sense that they had gone unsupported.

Days at sea in the Dartmouth Training Squadron had but one purpose: to give maximum training value to midshipmen and cadets.

The criterion for every activity was whether it was Good for Training (G for T). The up-side of that was, of course, that every moment spent under way was G for T, because by its nature it could not fail to acclimatise young men to life in a warship; but a good deal more structure was needed than that. Thus every duty connected with the conduct and life of the ship was either done under supervision by, or observed by, an officer under training. There was a cadet of the watch on the bridge, a cadet navigator, cadets in the operations room, cadet lookouts and seaboat's crew, cadets working 'part of ship', cadets in the engine and boiler rooms and auxiliary machinery spaces, cadets scrubbing out their messdecks. Duties were rotated so that, so far as possible, all officers under training did every job. That was the 'work ship' phase of training; those not employed on these duties were in training classes under more formal instruction, awaiting or having done their work-ship time.

It may be worth describing a typical DTS day at sea.[11] It started at midnight. Ships at sea do not sleep, though the off-watch parts of their companies do. The squadron would be in a night formation ordered by Captain (F), usually with ships a mile or so apart. The Guide – the ship detailed to maintain a steady speed and prescribed course, on which the other ships had to keep their appointed stations – would change hourly, so that the bridge watchkeepers in all ships would have practice in adjusting course and engine revolutions to keep station on the Guide. Often, a zig-zag plan would be introduced to keep bridge staffs alert and practise them in what was, after all, standard wartime procedure. Social exchanges would be improved by frequent brews of 'kye' (naval cocoa) prepared by the cadet of the watch – definitely a G for T experience.

Half an hour before dawn, the navigation training class would be seen around the charthouse armed with sextants and deck watches, preparing to take morning star sights from which they would hope to work out the ship's position. The hands would be turned out at 6.30 am; pre-breakfast 'scrub decks' was no longer appropriate, since frigates have no wooden decks to scrub. After the 8 am muster, with hands – including officers under training – told off for their duties, the day would start in earnest. The squadron would be ordered into close formation for an hour or more of line manoeuvres; however these might be regarded by some as relics of bygone wars, there is nothing that trains a seaman's eye more surely or gives so much confidence once mastered. Lewin himself was a noted ship-handler and got a great thrill out of it.[12] It would be idle to suppose that a cadet or midshipman confronted with the complex dynamics for the first time would feel much more than freezing terror, but with the calm assurance of his captain and training officer behind him, he would gradually get the hang.

The next serial might well be towing. Lewin was particularly keen on this evolution, recalling inevitably the *Ashanti/Somali* episode.[13] He saw to it that officers were trained in the standard method, using a sequence of light line fired by rifle, floating rope ('grass line') messenger, wire rope and then chain cable passed between towing and towed vessel; but he also showed himself abreast of the latest developments by acquiring a nylon rope issued for trials and demonstrated that it could be used to make the operation simpler and quicker. On one occasion he managed to get the speed of tow (the towed ship was, unsurprisingly, the *Roebuck*) up to 18 knots.[14]

Once the tows had been disconnected it might be time for 4-inch gun firings. The gunnery control system in Type 15 frigates was rudimentary, since the guns were fitted partly to engage submarines that had been forced to the surface and partly to frighten unruly persons on shore, neither of them demanding sophisticated range and rate calculations. The cadets' firings were, in the words of a squadron training officer some years before, an 'introduction to the bang',[15] but none the less important for that. Again, it was a first exposure to another aspect of naval life.

The afternoon could well be occupied by jackstay transfers between pairs of ships. This entailed steaming on parallel courses some 60 or 80 yards apart while loads or people were transferred along a high line rigged between the ships. Tension on the line was maintained by men heaving on it, through a leading block, in one of the ships, the other end being fixed to a highpoint in the other. This was a standard evolution throughout the Navy, and it was important that officers emerging from training should be familiar with it, because next time they did it, they might be in charge.

At 4 pm, the Navy when at sea had for nearly a century gone to 'evening quarters'. This in the DTS was the usual occasion for exercising seaboats. Pulling whalers, and sometimes motor whalers as well, would be lowered – always with cadet crews – to recover lifebuoys or other objects dropped a few minutes before. On return to the ship, boats were hoisted by hand: a corporate operation involving the greater part of the ships' companies, with plenty of bellowing from the cadets in charge. There was an element of competitiveness in most of the things the Dartmouth Training Squadron did, and certainly with seaboats there was pride in being the first ship to report 'Ready to Proceed'. It was one of the advantages of having a squadron rather than a single training cruiser, and Lewin welcomed it.

Recreation was also on his agenda, and it could happen at sea as well as in harbour, given the right conditions. 'Hands to Bathe' was a favourite pipe immediately evening quarters had secured, but the proper caveats had to be observed. One day in the tropics, his first lieutenant had remonstrated that there might be a few sharks about, to be gently pooh-poohed by Lewin.

> Around 1.30 pm I was on the forecastle checking the arrangements for *Urchin* to be taken in tow ... with the ship lying dead in the water. Attempts to signal the bridge that the forecastle was ready were of no avail, as the Captain and all were looking down into the water alongside. There was an enormous shark, with attendant pilot fish, basking calmly ...[16]

'Hands to Bathe' was not mentioned again that day.

The day would end as it began, in reverse order: the navigation class mustering for its evening star sights, the disposition of the squadron for the night, the orders for changing the Guide at hourly intervals, the ordering of a zig-zag diagram. The individuals in the work-ship watches would be different: those that had had 'quiet numbers' the night before might find themselves with something more responsible this time. Everything was new, everything was unique, for those who experienced it: G for T.

So the DTS wended its way across the Atlantic to Bridgetown, Barbados. The subsequent spell in harbour gave many opportunities for boatwork, including races to test prototype Bosun dinghies, soon to become standard navy issue.[17] On 16 February the squadron was about to split up to visit individual islands when orders were received to proceed with all despatch to Trinidad and stand by to give aid to the civil power in Georgetown, British Guiana, where serious riots had broken out. The squadron departed at 1.30 am on the 17th, fuelled in Trinidad and left individually for Georgetown as soon as fuelling was completed.

This left *Urchin* as the last in the queue, since she had been in the inboard fuelling berth in Trinidad. She arrived off Georgetown in mid-afternoon to see the other three ships of the squadron, with *Troubridge*, the West Indies guardship, inside the harbour and a great deal of smoke rising over the town. No sort of communication could be established with anyone.

Worse and worse, the bar across the mouth of the harbour at Georgetown was negotiable only at certain states of the tide, and this according to Lewin's navigator was not one of them. He formally warned his captain, as was his duty, that to attempt the channel would be hazardous. Lewin said:

> I note your advice and we'll enter it in the log and in we go ...
> Everybody holding their breath on the bridge in the hope that
> we would lift the ship about six inches further out of the water.
> Fortunately we made it ...[18]

As he had predicted, the bottom was soft and the liquid mud did no permanent damage to the machinery.

Georgetown was in a bad state but the worst of the rioting was over. Commander David Farquharson in the *Wizard* had taken charge on arrival. Indeed, Lewin's memory was that it was a 24-hour affair, and that the reason no one had answered the radio calls was that they were all watching a football match that had been arranged between the early arrivals of the squadron and a local team. Nevertheless, Lewin's first lieutenant at the time[19] recalled walking with him around the ruins that first evening, with the atmosphere still tense, and reports of what amounted to an assault by fireships: charcoal barges set alight and allowed to drift down-river towards the squadron, and towed away from their path by boats manned by midshipmen and cadets.[20]

There were still, in any case, armed parties to be landed and the situation was monitored carefully for the next few days, before army contingents arrived from the Hampshire and East Anglian regiments. In general, cadets did not form part of these groups,[21] but an exception was made of some Royal Marine Young Officers embarked for sea experience, who had already completed their professional training and were in consequence a little full of themselves. They were somewhat chagrined when they managed to overturn a jeep in the main street of Georgetown.[22]

As the situation subsided and compromises were found between the various parties ashore, the squadron prepared to leave and finally resumed its cruise on 22 February,[23] splitting up between the islands for visits as planned. *Urchin* arrived at Grenada on 23 February, and it quickly became Lewin's favourite island in the whole of the West Indies. He spent some nights in the administrator's house, leaving the ship in the more than competent hands of his first lieutenant Paul Greening, and became firm friends not only there but with a retired Scottish construction engineer who lived close by. Lewin provided him with a Scottish flag to fly and he never forgot it. During one conversation among the local community, Terry discovered that only one person had ever run around the island in less than 24 hours. Since the round distance was 67 miles, this was quite an endurance feat in itself, but he felt it could be bettered.

He had a ready instrument to hand. The Royal Marine Young Officers had quickly recovered from their reverse in Georgetown and were still fairly stroppy. Captain (F) sent for the RM Young Officers and said:

> Look, the record for running round this island is just under 24 hours, what about it? And they took it on and the local fire brigade and police found out about it and so they too decided to enter teams. I was extremely fortunate that the Squadron Physical Training Instructor who lived on board *Urchin* was a marathon champion who didn't let on ...[24]

The race was a great success, ended with a win for the Royal Naval team in under sixteen hours, and established a precedent, of which more later.

Urchin sailed on 28 February and that day carried out no less than 25 dummy anchorages, each conducted by a different midshipman.[25] Bringing a ship to anchor in a specified place requires a variety of skills in precise navigation: the identification of marks, the initial determination of her position by cross-bearings, swinging her on to the preplanned anchoring course using a knowledge of her turning characteristics, keeping her on that planned track in spite of cross winds and currents, adjusting speed so that she is going gently ahead when the anchor is due to be let go, and finally announcing that critical moment; while all the time keeping the command informed in clear terms of what is going on. It is usually a young officer's first introduction to the pilotage art, and there were few who approached it with less than trepidation. But most would feel a good deal more confident when they had finished it, even though many mistakes would inevitably have been picked up.

The squadron gathered again at Virgin Gorda, an anchorage that had accommodated larger groups in its time and would again.[26] This was a place for boatwork and sailing races, and a memorable session of General Drill: competitive evolutions based upon facing ships' companies with unexpected tasks that would foster agility of mind, hand and eye and develop power of command. These had progressed some way since the more stereotyped, and much more cut-throat, drills of the Mediterranean Fleet a hundred years before, when the Commander-in-Chief, 'Pincher' Martin, would customarily hoist the signal 'Bury your Dead' on completion.[27] There were no casualties in the Dartmouth Training Squadron, and a planned expedition to a neighbouring island was cancelled when it was found to be covered with cactus and gorse, the beaches littered with poisonous sea-eggs and the surrounding water full of barracuda. More relaxed banyan parties were substituted.

After a short stay in Bermuda, passage across the Atlantic and some anti-submarine training in the Portland exercise areas, the squadron returned to Dartmouth where the midshipmen and cadets were disembarked, and then went round to Plymouth for Easter leave. It was quite usual for ships' officers, and officers under training alike, to look around with surprise after a cruise and realise that they had been working on average sixteen hours a day for the last twelve weeks. The training programme was absorbing not only of time but of interest. Leave periods were the more prized, and Lewin, as a benign Captain (F), made sure that full use was made of them for rest and relaxation.[28]

The summer cruise was always one of the most popular among cadets and ships' companies alike, since it went to Scandinavia, with its natural beauty and friendly people. In 1962 it began with some pomp, not always a feature of DTS programmes, with a visit to Copenhagen under the gaze of the Commander-in-Chief, Admiral Sir Wilfrid Woods, flying his flag in the destroyer *Jutland* (not part of the Dartmouth Squadron). The five-day visit was marked by some ceremony – a cadet guard marching to a wreath-laying at the Nyhavn Memorial made a marked impression[29] – and tremendous hospitality. Not least, it was an opportunity for close liaison with the Danish Royal Naval College, with social and sporting events intermingled: one of those times when, if all goes well, the foundations of alliances are strengthened from the base up.

Sailing on 21 May, the squadron went on to Bergen on the west coast of Norway, having first done some pilotage training in the lovely Hardanger Fjord. Bergen too was a home of naval officers' training, the Norwegian Royal Naval College having moved from Oslo some years before, and again many friendships were forged. After a two-day visit the ships journeyed deep into the Sogne Fjord, even more dramatic than the Hardanger. Lewin recalled that having already been to the head of this 100-mile inlet, he decided to take *Urchin* up a particularly narrow side fjord which 'narrows down to something like 3 cables [600 yards] with mountains 1000 metres high on either side. It winds along ... then opens out into an open space ... with just enough room to turn the ship round and take her back down again ...'[30]

The squadron gathered and went south again, splitting up for individual ship visits. *Urchin* went to Aabenraa in Denmark for a couple of days, followed after rendezvous by two days' seatime in the Skagerrak and Kattegat areas.[31] One of the limitations of the Baltic cruise was apparent during these passages: opportunities for weapon training were constricted, particularly by the prescribed 'Nemedri' routes that still existed through the wartime minefields. Some attempt was made to minimise this, at least in the field of anti-submarine warfare, by a new device, the Towed Asdic Repeater Target (TART), which was meant to simulate echoes from a submarine when 'pinged' from a neighbouring ship's sonar. It had not been at all successful in the fjords, and water conditions in the Skagerrak were unhelpful, but it was better than nothing.

The final visit of the Scandinavian cruise was to Göteborg in Sweden, and for the cadets and ships' companies of the squadron it was a fitting climax. Hospitality and friendliness were everywhere, and the vice president of the city council is said to have summed it up by quoting an old Swedish folk-song 'which describes the arrival of the English ships at the Bar of Göteborg. The local maidens adorn themselves to greet the sailors while their menfolk sulk in jealousy ...'[32] Then it was a fast passage back to Devonport, going northabout Scotland and arriving on 12 June.

There was a second leg to the summer cruise, with a change-round of midshipmen; the cadets remained on board for the whole twelve weeks. The second leg was to French west coast ports and was just as intensive in its activities, possibly with a little more specifically training activity and a little less of the bright lights.

It was during the autumn cruise that the change-over from the COST to the Murray scheme of training bit with most force. There were now no midshipmen, only cadets, and the 'Murray' intake warranted only two ships. These were *Urchin* and *Vigilant*, the latter now under the command of Lieutenant-Commander Jeremy Grindle.[33] He was a relatively junior officer to be in command and, to boot, an observer by specialisation. 'Observer' is the most misleading officer title in the Royal, and possibly any, Navy. It describes, or misdescribes, the officer who sits in the back of a multi-seat aircraft and acts as its tactical controller. He is responsible for its navigation, the direction of its sensors and the deployment of its weapons, and he has to be capable of doing about five things at once for the whole of the time the machine is in the air. In spite of this set of attributes, observers were generally considered to be somewhat below pilots in the pecking order of the Fleet Air Arm of those days.

Grindle, therefore, had to tread a delicate line between being a picked man (which, being an officer with an outstanding record, he was) and a picked-upon man. It was a measure of Terry Lewin's kindness and understanding that he treated *Vigilant* with a mixture of firmness and courtesy throughout what was, by his own admission, the least enjoyable of all his cruises, partly because the weather in the Mediterranean autumn was 'fairly universally depressing'.[34]

It took them to Gibraltar, Malta, Barcelona and Valencia, with a final call at Huelva, where Lewin's principal recollection was visiting the grave of 'Major Martin', the 'Man Who Never Was', recounted so vividly in Ewen Montagu's book of that name. The work at sea was as unremitting as ever, on the patterns already described (though it appears the TART was in better shape) and was enlivened by exchanges of quotations between *Urchin* and *Vigilant* that became something of a squadron game.

It was by no means new, and has been chronicled in several books of naval lore.[35] But it can reach a certain pitch, and when accounts of it are included in obituaries, as they were in Lewin's case,[36] some more needs to be said. Grindle is the best witness. Bible quotations, giving chapter and verse for brevity, were the most frequent, and that was not an unusual practice, but the use of the *Oxford Dictionary of Quotations* was less common. It became a bridge book in the Dartmouth Training Squadron. It solved at a stroke the difficulty with Shakespeare, where quotations from the *Collected Works* giving act, scene and line number might get back a mystified signal asking 'Which edition are you using?'; and if it slightly reduced the scope for erudition, it at least stopped the erudite from too much display of learning.

Grindle remembers particularly two passages between him and Lewin (quite apart from the quotation from the Scottish Play which was noted in the obituaries and might have been thought by old troupers to be asking for trouble). The first was when *Vigilant*, chronically short of fresh water as many of those old ships were, was taking an underway suck from *Urchin*. Rather cheekily, Grindle signalled Pooh-Bah's line from *The Mikado*: 'I accept refreshment at any hands, however lowly.' Lewin came back at once, from the same source, with 'It revolts me, but I do it.'

The second was much later, when Grindle had just assumed command of a Naval Air Squadron. Lewin, still in command of the DTS, made a signal to him that simply said 'Boatrope'. The boatrope is a line secured inboard in a ship and led into the bow of the seaboat kept for instant use in emergency at sea; Lewin as a Captain (F) had always demanded particular precision in the catenary of this rope in all ships of the squadron. It was a gentle reminder to Grindle that such points of detail do matter. Grindle replied with a quotation from Washington Irving: 'There is a certain relief in change, even though it be from bad to worse; as I have found in travelling in a stage-coach, that it is often a comfort to shift one's position and be bruised in a new place.'[37]

The winter of 1962–3 was the worst of the century in and round Britain. It started snowing, and blowing, just after Christmas and froze, blowing intermittently, for the next ten weeks. The squadron was due to go to the West Indies as usual at the end of January and that was no problem for them, though for the wives – many of them marooned, like Jane, at the end of nigh impassable lanes – it certainly was.

Terry had planned to embark Tim in *Urchin* for a few hours while the ship did post-maintenance sea trials on Friday 18 January, before he went back to boarding school on the Sunday. Land transport was just manageable and Tim duly came on board. The ship was in White-sand Bay when shortly before noon she was ordered to go to the assistance of a tanker which was in trouble off Ushant. *Urchin* duly turned downwind and was within 15 miles of the tanker when she was told that the ship was now in tow by commercial tugs, and the Navy's help was no longer required.

It remained only to turn *Urchin* round and go back to Devonport. By now, however, the wind had increased to 65 knots from east-north-east,[38] with the air temperature recorded as 27 degrees Fahrenheit. With their high freeboard the Type 15s were not easy to turn in such conditions. Lewin eventually got her round:

> When we got her into the sea she hit one at the top, the next one halfway down and the next one right at the bottom, and a solid mass of green water came rushing across the forecastle towards the bridge and smashed in all the bridge windows, flooded the bridge to a depth of about two feet and water descended through the ship down below. Tim ... was sitting in my bridge chair in his school uniform and received the whole lot of water and broken glass in his chest. He thought it was quite amusing ...'[39]

It took them eighteen hours to claw their way back to Devonport through a shrieking night, with Tim by now installed in a cot in the sick bay though undamaged and still smiling, and the wind was still blowing 35 knots when they berthed next morning. Then it was necessary to get Tim home, dry off his clothes, and to cap it all, 'On the Sunday the snow had started [again] and we had a fairly hazardous journey to Exeter to put him on the train back to Canterbury.'

The weather was not much better for the whole of the squadron's passage south to Santa Cruz de Tenerife, but after that, predictably, it improved. The first call the other side of the Atlantic this time was the US base at Chaguaramas in Trinidad,[40] but after that the cruise went by and large on its planned and accustomed way, the ships separating for weekend visits and making rendezvous (also G for T, sharpening lookouts, navigators and cadets of the watch) early in the week for multi-ship exercises.

There were two excursions from the norm. The first was when *Urchin* was at Montserrat: this was Jane's birthplace and naturally of interest to Terry, particularly as it was 14 February and their wedding anniversary. A party ashore had been arranged and was about to begin when a signal was received ordering Captain (F) to detail a ship to proceed at once to Grenada, where Lord Avon (previously the Prime Minister Sir Anthony Eden) had suffered a heart attack, and take him and Lady Avon to Barbados where he could receive specialist treatment. *Urchin* was the most conveniently placed ship, so steam began to be raised immediately, but as this would take some three hours the party went ahead,[41] a more benign version of Drake's game of bowls before setting sail against the Spanish Armada.

Urchin made an overnight passage at 28 knots to Grenada and arrived at 8 am, somewhat surprising the Avons since they had not been told a ship was being sent to embark them. However, they duly arrived on board just before noon[42] and passage was made to Barbados at a more sedate ambulance speed. The invalid duly and successfully disembarked, *Urchin* returned to Grenada which was her next place of call anyway.

It was here that the other departure from normal West Indies routine occurred. The round-the-island race the previous spring had been a great success and helpful to relations between the Navy and the local authorities, but Lewin had been interested during the summer to hear that the islanders' *amour-propre* had been stimulated to the extent of organising an interim event during which the record had once again been broken, and by a very considerable margin. It is clear that he pulled a string or two with the drafting offices, for in January 1963 Petty Officer George Morralee joined *Urchin*.

Morralee was an underwater weapons rating and was made captain of the quarterdeck,[43] and a good one too, but Terry Lewin's exceptional interest in him was quickly apparent when he sent for Morralee, who was the Navy's champion steeplechaser and a marathon runner of note, and said, 'I need you to break a record for me.' Terry continued, 'This is probably my last ship', and went on to explain the history of the round-the-island event. Morralee looked at the problem and concluded that he could probably manage a time of under ten hours: the latest record stood at twelve hours thirty-seven minutes.[44]

On arrival at Grenada, having had the morning watch from 4 to 8 am, Morralee was a little put out when told the race was to be that night. It left hardly any time for reconnaissance or preparation, much less sleep. Nevertheless the teams, including two from the island, started at 8 pm sharp, and Morralee fulfilled all expectations. Fortified by (non-alcoholic) refreshment at every police station on the route, and in spite of reportedly going four extra miles through an unscheduled detour, he came home in nine hours and five minutes.[45] Instructor Lieutenant Onyett was second, an hour and three quarters behind, and the Royal Marines Young Officers all finished in good times.

For a Captain (F) who had himself been a noted athlete, it was the high point of a second and, for all he knew, last West Indies excursion. It had been a more orthodox cruise than that of 1962, and it continued its planned and accustomed way with general drills, dummy anchorages, and all kinds of underway exercises, via Trinidad, Barbados and Bermuda, to arrive back in the United Kingdom before the end of March.

The shape of the Dartmouth Training Squadron was about to change. The plans laid in DTWP four years before[46] were now being realised, and the Type 15 frigates were gradually to be replaced by Type 12s specially converted in Devonport dockyard. Some of the Type 15s were to continue in service for a year or two, though the *Roebuck* among others had gone into merciful retirement. But it was thought that the first change-over to the new class should be the prerogative of the Captain (F), and in consequence Lewin and the majority of the *Urchin*'s company transferred to HMS *Tenby*.

If they thought they were moving into a shiny ship, almost as good as new, they were in for a shock. Partly no doubt as a result of the dreadful winter (one must be charitable to dockyards, though naval officers and ratings at the time certainly were not), the ship was in a very poor material state, dirty and unkempt. Lewin's ship's company without the cadets was woefully short of working hands, and on the brief shakedown cruise he augmented the crew with any volunteer sons of the ship's company who wanted to come along. One of the most enthusiastic was Tim, none the worse for his encounter with the green sea of January.[47]

The summer cruise programme was to be different too. During the 1962 spring cruise's final days, while the squadron was at Bermuda, Commodore Gervase Cook had visited Lewin, partly to see his son who was one of the cadets under training and partly as a representative of the Commander of the British Naval Staff in Washington. They had discussed the possibility of a squadron visit in 1963 to the US Naval Academy at Annapolis for June Week, the end of the academic year. This plan had come to fruition, so it was westward across the Atlantic, rather than east to Scandinavia, that the DTS sailed. Exercises on passage followed the usual squadron pattern.

It was a source of great worry to Lewin that his ship, which as leader of the squadron ought to set an example, and on such a diplomatically important visit was expected to show the highest standards, was not looking as well as she should. Above all, she needed painting, but thereafter there was much clearing up to be done. Three days in Bermuda were unhelpful because it rained almost throughout, and it was only in a secluded part of Chesapeake Bay that they finally found weather, and just enough time, to do the painting.[48] Lewin is not often, up to that point, recorded as addressing the ship's company – probably he did so no less, and no more, often than most commanding officers – but on this occasion he did,[49] no doubt to impress on them the tempo of the cruise ahead and the standards that would need to be set.

They could be left in little doubt when the squadron arrived in Annapolis on 1 June, with two German training ships (named *Hipper* and *Graf Spee*) already present and all eyes probably on the British.

The cadets were at once introduced into a social programme of a scale that matched the size and complexity of the academy,[50] with grand balls every night, sporting and sailing fixtures and the parades inevitable to graduation ceremonies. Each ship of the squadron had embarked a Land Rover – an innovation which, with the Gemini dinghy that also became a feature of the ships, can probably be ascribed to Lewin – and expeditionary parties tracked the ships in their subsequent advance to the north.

However, for Captain (F) there was still the question of the *Tenby*'s material state. In the middle of the Annapolis visit appeared the daunting figure of Vice Admiral Sir John Bush, the Commander of the British Naval Staff in Washington. He was sometimes known as The Burning Bush, and he was not pleased with what he saw. 'He said to me, Terry, this is terrible, the ship looks appalling, look at this, look at that … I explained to him what had happened and I said, you come back and see us in about three or four weeks' time and we will look a bit different.'[51]

One thing was for sure, the necessary cleaning and tidying up would have to be fitted into a very crowded programme. By diverting through the Chesapeake–Delaware Canal they managed to gain a few hours on the way to Boston, but in the case of the *Tenby* this did not help much: an anxious engineer officer 'appeared on the bridge and said we'd got an oil leak in the boiler room, we'd got to stop. I said, Jim I can't stop, I'm in the middle of a bloody canal … hang a sheet in front of it, I'll anchor as soon as I can.'[52] Once in the Delaware River, this was done and the pinhole leak, which had been spraying hot oil all over the boiler fronts, was repaired. *Tenby* caught up the squadron and there followed a magical passage through New York harbour in the clear of the morning, with a US Navy liaison officer giving a commentary from the bridge on all aspects of the great city.

There was a brief period at anchor on the way to Boston, though it did not give any respite to Captain (F) who embarked in *Torquay*, the other converted Type 12, for passage exercises. The three ships (the third was *Wizard*) arrived at Boston for another hectic visit over a long weekend and then split up for Canadian ports, *Tenby* visiting St John,

New Brunswick. Reunited, the squadron made its way up the St Lawrence and entered the Seaway on 18 June.

The St Lawrence Seaway presented all commanding officers – though not the cadets – with interesting ship-handling problems and it is noticeable that the ship's log for those days[53] contains every course steered and every engine movement: nothing seems to have been left to chance. A brief visit to Montreal was followed by a longer one to Toronto; Canadian hospitality was warm and friendly. Ships then dispersed to Great Lakes ports in the USA, *Tenby* going to Cleveland.

Some shadow was cast over this phase of the cruise by news of the death of Terry's father. It was not unexpected, since he had been suffering from cancer for some time, but they had been close since his earliest days and his counsel had set Terry on his career. 'It didn't come as a surprise,' he recorded 35 years later, 'but nevertheless quite something to think about' – a laconic comment from someone in his situation at the time.

In Cleveland, Lewin was confronted with a new challenge. He had already handled Press conferences enough, but now he had to make a Fourth of July speech in the United States and, what was more, near the scene of one of the US Navy's greatest victories over the Royal Navy in 1813; and, to boot, in competition with a baseball double-header between the Cleveland Indians and the Boston Red Sox followed by the New York Yankees. The audience, addressed through a loudspeaker system, was estimated at a quarter of a million. It was some measure of the success of the speech that the ship was later in danger of capsizing from the weight of visitors on board. Gangway sentries just managed to control the flow.

The squadron reassembled and resumed some seamanlike exercises before retracing its track towards the open sea.[54] By now Sir John Bush had made good his promise to 'see us in three or four weeks' time' and was embarked for passage, and he was joined by the even more exalted Admiral Sir Charles Madden, Commander-in-Chief of the Home Fleet. Bush, who had seen the ship in her far from perfect state earlier in the cruise, was now satisfied with the attention to detail above and below decks; the ship's company had turned to with a will for their Captain (F).

One admiral or the other, and sometimes both, remained on board for the St Lawrence Seaway passage and down river to Quebec, where Lewin was confronted with a difficult if classical berthing problem, involving a 180 degree turn not far downstream of the berth and then bringing the ship alongside against the run of a fairly strong current. He was by now well used to the *Tenby*'s handling characteristics, the Seaway and Welland Canal having given plenty of practice, and was clearly proud of this particular manoeuvre, as well he might be: the log records a mere three minutes elapsing between the first line going across to the shore and the order 'Finished with Main Engines'. 'With John Bush on board and my Commander-in-Chief on the jetty watching us come in. What a fluke!'[55]

The one-night stay in Quebec soon over, and a fuelling stop at St John's, Newfoundland, intervening, the squadron fought and exercised its way back to the United Kingdom. It had been the most exhausting of Terry Lewin's cruises in the DTS. A final flourish was a visit to Dart-mouth escorting the Royal Yacht with Her Majesty the Queen embarked, making good her promise to conduct the Lord High Admiral's Divisions that she had been unable through illness to carry out in 1958. This was followed by an excursion to Morgat in Brittany for a squadron pulling and sailing regatta, with cadets from the Combined Cadet Force embarked this time.

He arrived for his farewell party ashore by Gemini dinghy, a craft to which he had become much attached. A chromium-plated chair had been improvised for him to sit in, in rather monarchical fashion, and when he was 'wearing his pendant' afloat as captains do on occasion, the bowman of the boat was said to crouch in the forepeak holding it aloft.[56] At the party his officers presented him with a salver on which were inscribed the usual compliments on the front, and on the back the simple initials 'RHIP'. It had its significance: 'When I detailed someone off for a dirty job, I used to add at the bottom "RHIP" (Rank Has Its Privileges) so they felt a little better about it.'[57]

Terry Lewin was now 42 years old, in the middle of his captain's time and, as it turned out, in the middle of his naval career. It is worth attempting some description of the man at this stage, before he embarked on the greater tasks and responsibilities that were to come. It so happens that his time in the DTS is unusually rich in anecdote from those who were there, and this may help to fill in the picture.

The first quality that emerges is Lewin's essential goodwill and his conscious desire for the best for all his people. 'There were never any "buts" when it came to Terry. Everybody liked him; everybody spoke positively.'[58] 'He made few changes to the detailed running of the Squadron. It was his incredibly engaging personality which made the largest impact on everyone.'[59] 'Leaving the ship one wet winter's evening, a car stopped and picked me up: it was our Captain who was able to take me not only to the [Dockyard] Gate but to my home as well, which was on the other side of Plymouth.'[60]

Secondly, he made sure that this spirit extended right through the ship and indeed the squadron. All were to be involved. His care for the chiefs and petty officers was apparent: he suggested that 'the wardroom might like to invite the CPOs' Mess to drinks after the Admiral's Inspection':[61]

> The assessment of the young officers at the end of cruise was made at a meeting with the Captain when all the opinions of all those who faced these young men were sought and noted. These meetings were innovated by the Captain and were very thorough.[62]

An official reception for CPOs and POs was held in *Tenby* during the visit to Cleveland, on the forecastle which is the normal venue for wardroom parties.[63] People remembered that 'he could name every man on board from the youngest sailor'.[64]

None of this was at the expense of the proper exercise of authority. At defaulters:

> He could and frequently did look incredibly stern ... a sort of cross between a disappointed father and a benevolent and understanding housemaster. He was firm and took no nonsense ... The majority, I think, left the Table feeling embarrassed that they had let down themselves, their captain and their ship.[65]

It could be laced with humour: on one occasion a rating was charged with 'an act to the prejudice of good order and naval discipline in that he did urinate in a waste paper basket in the cabin of [an officer] at 0230', and the captain asked whether the basket was metal or wicker. It was metal, said the officer. 'Well,' said Terry with a look from beneath his eyebrows, 'That explains why you woke up.'[66]

But then humour was never far away, often, when in the training role, blended with humanity and consideration. When *Urchin* was at Greenwich, Midshipman Michael Moore was coxswain of the motor cutter taking Captain (F) ashore, in full fig, to meet Princess Margaret. Moore accomplished the business of coming alongside well enough, but on leaving found himself incapable of getting the boat away from the jetty in the strong tidal stream. Without a word Lewin took the tiller, 'made a few simple engine orders to my colleague who was having more fun at my predicament than he had had for years, and we were away. When we were straight and level he silently handed back the tiller. By this time I was a gibbering wreck.' On return to the ship, Moore tried to bring the motor cutter alongside going down-tide. That, as mild-mannered sailors might say, is not a recommended manoeuvre, and once again T. T. Lewin silently took the tiller and brought the boat alongside head to tide in the proper manner. Fifteen years later, Commander Moore of HMS *Tartar* greeted Sir Terence Lewin, Commander-in-Chief Fleet, for an official call, to be asked with a smile, 'Have you learned to drive a motor cutter yet?'[67]

Breakfasts with midshipmen, two or three a day, were a feature of life on cruise. This was not a Lewin innovation – it had been a custom in the prewar Navy – but he certainly insisted on it throughout the squadron,[68] to a varied reception from the captains, at least one of whom is said to have invited the midshipmen to get on with their breakfasts and disappeared behind a newspaper. It is a fair bet that breakfasts with Lewin were not like that. He was concerned to know and assess all the cadets and midshipmen to the maximum extent that their limited time on board allowed, and the other captains in the Squadron knew that if any of their young officers presented problems, Captain (F) wished to know and to be involved.[69]

So, over the years, but particularly during this time in the Dartmouth Squadron, a distinctive Lewin style had emerged. It was human, humane, humorous but at the same time deeply professional and disciplined. Above all, it was based on the involvement of all in the common good of ship and service: 'All to be of a company' was to apply vertically as well as horizontally. Few will be found to say it was not the best sort of leadership. Some will maintain that Lewin was the innovator in this style; that if he had not led the Navy towards it, it would never have happened. That must be a matter for speculation; it is worth pointing out only that others, more informal and individual, had preceded Lewin, the most prominent being Michael LeFanu.[70] It was probably Lewin's great contribution to set the style within the boundaries of naval orthodoxy, so that future commanding and senior officers could adopt the pattern without eccentricity.

Were there any weaknesses apparent in what was undoubtedly an impressive performance? There is a toenail of clay, perhaps: some traces of self-indulgence peep out. The Mark 7 Jaguar, the Gemini chair, were little bits of flamboyance that were not entirely in character, a tendency he subsequently checked. The North American cruise of 1963, which was very much Terry Lewin's brainchild, shows similar traces. At one stage he diverted a long way from the planned track to look at a reported iceberg, throwing many careful training plans into confusion.[71] Moreover, the Seaway and canal passages, 'tedious' even to the *Britannia Magazine*,[72] were scarcely G for T. No doubt the visits were vastly successful in diplomatic terms, and the cadets saw a great deal of American life in a few crowded weeks, but it is noticeable that opportunities for more orthodox training simply could not occur; for example, the logs show no record of cadets carrying out dummy anchorages. It may be that they were no longer in the syllabus, on the introduction of the Murray scheme; but if they were deleted, one wonders when the young officers would have had that first introduction to the haven-finding art.

At any event, Captain Lewin's masters were well pleased with his performance as Captain (F). In a report of November 1962, Admiral Sir Charles Madden, then Commander-in-Chief Plymouth, had

expressed reservations: 'I have noticed certain indications of inexperience ... At present I estimate his chances of promotion [to flag rank]
as "Fair", but he may well improve on this.' He did; as Commander-
in-Chief Home Fleet, in September 1963, Madden thought him 'a very
good officer and inspiring leader' with good chances of promotion.
There had been moments, earlier on, when he was feeling his way and
allowed his natural modesty to circumscribe that warm humanity and
professional zeal; and later, he may have over-corrected a little as confidence returned. Both those phases were behind him now. An identifi-
able Lewin style had developed, and it was good.

TACTICAL AND
WEAPONS POLICY
1964–1966

Considering the success of his time in command of the Dartmouth Training Squadron, the appointment for which Terry Lewin was originally destined at the end of 1963 was a curious one. It was the command of HMS *Cambridge*, the gunnery firing range at Wembury in South Devon, something of a backwater and not at all the sort of job to which an up-and-coming officer in the middle of his captain's time would aspire. There was some indication that Admiral Sir Nigel Henderson, the Commander-in-Chief Plymouth, who thought highly of Lewin, had asked for him to stay in his command; and it could well be that the less than glowing report from Madden, his predecessor, the previous November[1] had influenced the authorities in planning to send Lewin to the relative obscurity of *Cambridge*.

In the event, it did not happen. The Lewins looked over the Captain's House, an old vicarage that would have been their first married quarter, and were planning the move when weightier matters intervened. Illness in the senior ranks of the Admiralty had caused premature retirements and the early promotion of Captain Richard Janvrin, the Director of Tactical and Weapons Policy (DTWP), to rear admiral.[2] With his experience in the deputy director's chair three years before, Lewin was an obvious choice as Janvrin's replacement, and it is also likely that some in high places had been surprised that an officer of proved ability in Whitehall was being put out to grass at the other end of Devon. So Captain Lewin was to be DTWP, from 19 December 1963.

A three-month period of unemployment was not something Their Lordships generally tolerated, so Terry was detailed to study the future of the Joint Anti-Submarine School at Londonderry in the interim. By then, the working-up organisation at Portland under the Flag Officer Sea Training was in full swing, and in spite of the advantages of the Londonderry area for advanced anti-submarine training – deep water, the proximity of RAF Ballykelly and a school with developed training patterns and doctrine – there was serious doubt whether the defence budget could sensibly sustain both establishments. Lewin, with an RAF group captain and a principal from the civil service as secretary, listened carefully to all concerned[3] and produced a report recommending closure. Regrettably, no trace can be found among the public records.

It had been a turbulent time domestically. On the assumption that the *Cambridge* appointment would happen, arrangements had been made for Jane to have an operation for an enlarged thyroid. When all changed, it was decided to go ahead with this, but Terry was greatly chagrined at his inability to give the support he had hoped and planned for. It was, as he recalled, 'typical of the naval officer's wife's hard life'.[4] It was also necessary, of course, to move back closer to London; the Lewins were relatively lucky to be able to repossess Pitfields without fuss.

For this ministry tour, Terry determinedly set his face against weekend commuting. He generally caught the local train from Ashurst, driven to the station by Tim who was now the owner of a 1932 Austin 10/4, bought for £5 from a local gardener (it was still in use in 1999, bearing out Tim's description of the Lewins as 'a family of hoarders'). The car's first arrival had been a 'cold move', dragged and pushed into the dark recesses of the Pitfields garage, with four-year-old Jon at the wheel. 'Under Dad's directions,' remembered Tim, 'he neatly poked out both its headlamps on the mower handles.' Tim wore a John Lennon cap in those early days of the Beatles. One of the grander Lewin neighbours, who turned up at the station in a chauffeur-driven Alvis, once asked Terry if Tim was 'his man'. The reply is not recorded.[5]

The Whitehall scene into which the new DTWP stepped was a fast-moving one. Admiral of the Fleet Earl Mountbatten had been Chief of Defence Staff, nominally the top uniformed post, since June 1959 and had chafed almost throughout his tenure at his limited powers. He had a small staff, no control over programmes and no right to tender independent advice to government. Mountbatten, who had been a Supreme

Commander with joint-service responsibility during the Second World War, was convinced that much more power should reside in 'The Centre',[6] and from 1962 onward had steadily lobbied to this end.

The single-service Chiefs of Staff were equally convinced of the need, as they saw it, to protect and promote their own services in the interests of the national defence as a whole, and personally suspicious of what they regarded as Mountbatten's ambition. They had vigorously opposed radical proposals for reorganisation put forward by Mountbatten in 1962[7] and this had led to an independent study by Lord Ismay and Sir Ian Jacob. Their report, of February 1963, had suggested three options[8]:

- To leave the basic system unchanged.
- To extend the Ministry of Defence to include as subordinate departments the three service ministries, the latter to be 'radically changed by a geographical redistribution', but the three services to remain intact.
- To institute a completely integrated, functionally organised Ministry of Defence, with the three services retaining their identity at unit and formation level but fused in their higher organisation.

Unsurprisingly, the government had chosen the second of the options (in spite of Ismay-Jacob's strong pointer to the third as the optimum[9]), and when Lewin arrived at the Admiralty preparations were already being made for the 'geographical redistribution' that was a key element of that option. It involved a move from the west to the east side of Whitehall, to the building that had long housed the Air Ministry and the Board of Trade and was now to be the colocated (but not fully integrated) Ministry of Defence. The Board of Trade moved out from the north end, leaving behind its two colossal nudes over the door,[10] the Naval Staff took up the very north and the General Staff the middle. Vesting day was on 1 April 1964.

Work in the Tactical and Weapons Policy Division was never likely to be less than hectic. It had to lead on every staff requirement for ships and weapon systems: each must be justified, worked out in detail, costed and impeccably presented to the Weapon Development Committee where it would come under scrutiny not only from the other services and the chief scientific adviser, but also the Treasury. The papers, even in their distilled form, occupy massive amounts of space in the Public Record Office.[11]

Sir Roderick Macdonald recalled many years later the atmosphere in the 'engine room' of DTWP.[12] There were four desk officers, all of commander's rank: one to deal with CVA 01, the project for a new fixed-wing aircraft carrier; one to supervise command, control and communication systems, already burgeoning with the computer age; one dealing with submarines and minesweepers; and Macdonald himself, who handled cruisers, destroyers, frigates and patrol vessels. They worked in a five-desk room; the fifth desk was occupied by the deputy director, Captain James Jungius. 'All were mad keen to progress ship and weapon improvement. Most projects were inherited from their desks' predecessors, such was the time between conception and hardware.'[13] Over the whole of this team presided the director, Captain Lewin, answering in his turn to the Deputy Chief of Naval Staff.

To be justified, projects had to be related to overall government defence policy. That of the early 1960s has been characterised by some writers[14] as 'East of Suez'. This is something of a shorthand. The Sandys defence policy in 1957 had put much stress on nuclear deterrence to cope with the threat to Europe, and included the well-known phrase, 'The role of naval forces in total war is uncertain.' But it always accepted that there was a world elsewhere, and that in the limited operations that might occur there, a role for naval forces certainly did exist. That was the principal justification for the Navy's general purpose forces, including the carriers, although earmarking for NATO purposes was always regarded as a political plus. In the intervening years, however, another role for the Navy had appeared, in the shape of the Polaris submarine force, agreed with the USA at the Nassau summit of 1962 and now a-building. That had somewhat increased the naval share of the defence budget, but it brought in its train a number of commitments, for high-quality manpower, training and operational support, that had not been apparent in cost terms at the start.[15]

The problem, then, was to juggle all these requirements, in a world that was rapidly changing technologically, in a way that would not outrun the limited resources available. In early 1964 the conundrums did not look completely insoluble. CVA 01, after any number of design modifications,[16] had been approved in principle the year before and the Navy had celebrated accordingly; but they would have been less jubilant had they known, as a few did,[17] that the long lead items had not yet been ordered and that, moreover, in pleading for them, the Secretary of State for Defence, Peter Thorneycroft, had written that CVA 01 would be 'the first and only ship of her class'.[18] This was a hostage on which much ransom might be demanded.

Another was the mix of surface forces that were to escort the carrier as well as doing all the other jobs that the smaller ships of the Navy do: patrol, convoy escort, surface action, as well as the tasks of uneasy peace and quasi-war. In 1963 much attention was paid to 'The Escort Mix', to which as well as the well-established 'Leanders' and older destroyers and frigates was now to be added a class of specialised air defence destroyers, the Type 82s, large, expensive and heavily manned, sporting the new Sea Dart anti-aircraft and Ikara anti-submarine missiles but with no provision for a helicopter. Macdonald could see the financial problems looming here and suggested a small and simple escort, manned by about 100, to make up numbers, and this found favour with some Board members,[19] but the staff requirement came to nothing because the seaman specialist tribes opposed it. It is not at all certain that Lewin's heart was in it either; when it came to a battle between Quality and Quantity, he nearly always came down in favour of Quality.

A third conundrum concerned the aircraft to be operated in the East of Suez role. The Royal Navy and Royal Air Force had stalked round each other for years discussing, often with a soldier as umpire,[20] whether they could make use of a common aircraft or even a common airframe. Projects as different as the vertical take-off P1154 and the naval Buccaneer, and many variations, all came under consideration but eventually foundered on differences of requirement and procedure. They were not helped by naval aviators who looked for nothing but the best in the new generation of carrier-borne aircraft, nor by the Air Staff who regarded naval aircraft as a marginal asset and were fully preoccupied with their long-range, frontiers-of-technology, immensely expensive strike and reconnaissance aircraft, the TSR2, which had no conceivable shipborne application.

Into this cauldron of competing claims to scarce resources came a new and decisive ingredient. In October 1964 a Labour government came into power, the election having gone narrowly in favour of an administration led by Harold Wilson. The new Secretary of State for Defence was Denis Healey, who had for years taken the closest interest in the whole business of defence and was a natural choice for the post. He was, moreover, well known for his incisive and brilliantly intellectual approach, tempered by a very hard-headed attitude to finance. Since one of the Ismay–Jacob reforms was to give much increased budgetary control to the Centre and specifically the Permanent Under Secretary, who answered directly to him, Healey was by far the most powerful holder yet of the defence portfolio.

Healey almost at once initiated a full-scale Defence Review, which lasted until February 1966. It turned essentially into a battle between the Naval and Air Staffs as to how the East of Suez requirement for combat aircraft strength should be met.[21] The first casualty was the TSR2; its costs were escalating exponentially and Healey made a quick interim decision, in April 1965, that it should not be proceeded with. At this point the real possibility of a revived joint RN/RAF project based on the Buccaneer aircraft – the P1154 having been finally abandoned[22] – was offered. The Air Staff rejected this because the navigation system of the Buccaneer 2 was optimised for long passage over the sea and they considered that extensive modification would be needed to meet their requirement for overland work. Lewin was disappointed by this outcome, and observed 35 years later the irony of the RAF's Buccaneer 2s, taken over from the Navy, operating satisfactorily in the Gulf War of 1991.[23]

Instead of a British-made solution to the gap caused by cancellation of the TSR2, the Air Staff put its faith in the swing-wing F-111 made in the USA, and this became the centrepiece of their argument ably conducted by Air Chief Marshal Sir Charles Elworthy, the Chief of the Air Staff, and Air Vice Marshal Peter Fletcher, the Assistant Chief of Air Staff (Policy). Both legally trained, they are acknowledged to have been exceptionally effective advocates for the RAF's cause, and to have been more than a match for the Naval Staff headed by Admiral Sir David Luce, the First Sea Lord, and Vice Admiral Sir Frank Hopkins, the Deputy Chief of Naval Staff (a professional naval aviator, and Lewin's direct boss).

How central a part Terry Lewin played in the 'Carrier Battle' is not entirely clear. The doctrinal and policy side was handled by the Director of Naval Plans, Captain Peter Ashmore, while Lewin covered the more technical issues – though not, of course, the detailed design matters, which lay even further downstream and largely in the Controller's department in Bath. The Directorate of Naval Air Warfare, a critical player, was not always inclined to work through DTWP at Lewin's level, particularly as Hopkins was an aviator. It needs to be recalled that there were differences of view in the Naval Staff about the wisdom of pursuing CVA 01: some thought the project would cripple the rest of the Navy if proceeded with, others that the whole future of the Navy depended on it, and many in between wished it could cost less and allow more space for the many other developments that were so highly desirable. These included the nuclear-powered 'fleet' submarine force that was to follow the Polaris boats now building, the development of amphibious forces, escorts and minesweepers in sufficient numbers, and the necessary weapon, command, control and communication systems to go with all these things, to give a balanced force that could respond to national needs, above all the unexpected contingencies that the Navy knew from experience were those most likely to happen.[24]

It was a fair question whether CVA 01 was a political runner at all. Its cost was a natural target for the Treasury: like a large handbag, it could be lifted out by the handles and taken away. The TSR2 had been a similar project, and that had already gone. The narrow justification for both systems, in the East of Suez role, made them more attractive for the axe. Other projects, even the F 111, did have a greater variety of roles, at least as advertised. It is apparent from the documents now available that from the middle of 1965, Healey's thinking was running strongly against CVA 01. His private secretary, Patrick Nairne, assumed in a minute of 1 July that the Secretary of State would 'decide to go ahead – without final commitment – with the steps necessary to reach a final decision against the carrier programme'.[25]

It may very well be that Lewin reached a similar conclusion about the same time. The existing carriers were always a factor in the minds of DN Plans and DTWP; *Eagle, Ark Royal,* the newly modernised *Victorious* and the about-to-be modernised *Hermes*, were subject to every sort of permutation to show that, with CVA 01 coming into service as 'the bottom dropped out of the *Ark*',[26] they could just squeeze one carrier permanently East of Suez with another at fifteen days' notice.[27] But it all looked desperately tight; there was a clear implication that if CVA 01 was approved, her sisters would logically follow, with more expense; and the downstream effect on other naval projects, and on technical manpower, was predictably nasty.

In August 1965 the Air Staff weighed in with a paper called outright 'The Case for Dropping Carriers'.[28] This rehearsed all the expected objections including the small number of shipborne aircraft deployable under the latest carrier plan, the carriers' own slow speed of deployment, their limited operational endurance, their vulnerability and their need for escort. However, it ended even more strongly with the assertions that there was, east of Suez, no need to control the military situation at sea because there was no significant threat posed from the sea to Britain's vital interests; that a carrier's contribution to deterrence against limited aggression was unproven; and, most tellingly of all because it chimed closely with Healey's thinking as it was emerging, that the use of carriers in intervention operations was limited to rare cases, and 'the UK cannot afford resources to cater for every conceivable situation'.

Looked at in hindsight, it is strange that the Naval Staff did not counter by pointing out that in the confrontation with Indonesia, then at its height, the carriers with their mobile strike capability were the essential deterrent underpinning of the British position; they might have been pre-empted by the Chief of General Staff's support for CAS when he minuted, 'The Army has learnt to place greater reliance [for air support] on the RAF than on strike carriers.'[29] And there were, indeed, considerable RAF resources in the Far East at the time.

That in any case was Plans' business, not DTWP's. DTWP were about to be involved in a more desperate throw. The US Department of Defense had expressed concern at the possibility of the Royal Navy's relinquishing its carrier force, partly because British carrier technology such as the angled deck, the mirror landing sight and the steam catapult had been a world leader, adopted in each case by the US Navy.[30] Consequently the Pentagon had made an offer to transfer one or more carriers of the 'Essex' class to Britain. Hopkins led a small team, including Lewin, to Washington at the end of August.

A full day's discussion told the team a great deal about the ships, three of which in varying states of maintenance might become available. The most attractive part of the possible deal was the price, which was $50 million for one and, rather surprisingly, $150 million for two;[31] the logic was impeccable because the two-ship deal included a lot more spares and logistic support. There had been an enormous amount of detail packed into the negotiation, and Lewin had probably never needed to show his grasp of a brief more fully than when he wrote the 44-paragraph paper over the night flight home.[32]

The preliminary judgement was that 'there [are] many problems associated with modernising, maintaining and supporting these ships, but there is no factor that would make the project unworkable'.[33] The most difficult stumbling block looked like being habitability; in particular, US petty officers messed with the junior rates, and to accommodate the British system of separate messing arrangements, extensive internal changes would be needed. On the technical side, arresting gear and operations room arrangements were the chief matters for concern. Various options were offered for replacement and subsequent deployment programmes.

Healey did not at all reject these initiatives. In fact, it is probable that he kept them in play deliberately, in the near certainty that they would run into practical difficulties, as well as doctrinal objections that were bound to come from the technical establishment, which had a vested interest in British equipment and construction. It was not until the end of October that the Assistant Chief of Naval Staff (Warfare), who had taken over the project, reported that 'cost will certainly be greater than previously thought, and some of the risks formidable'.[34] Cook, the ACNS(W), was regarded by some as an arch-pessimist,[35] but it is not certain that in his heart Lewin was any less sceptical about the American carriers. His own recollection was that the spares, stores and logistic support for a single or even two ships, all to totally different patterns from those in the British fleet, would have imposed an impossible burden, and not only he but other authorities thought the accommodation problem a killer.[36] After October, the proposal ran steadily into the sand.

Meanwhile, under pressure from Healey, the Naval Staff had reluctantly embarked upon a paper entitled 'The Navy Without Carriers'.[37] This made a cardinal mistake in basing itself on a three-year-old strategy paper, COS (62)1, when Ministry of Defence thinking, prompted by Healey's fertile mind and constant probing of assumptions and prejudices, had moved meanwhile into a style of much freer thought and attention to first principles. The paper did, however, get better when it grappled with questions of size and shape, probably reflecting DTWP input. Notably, it postulated reintroducing 'a class similar to the escort cruiser'[38] with anti-submarine helicopters, Sea Dart, Ikara, good command and communication facilities, and an emerging commando-carrying role. Six of these cruisers would be in addition to the existing specialised amphibious ships, 15 destroyers, 69 frigates, 4 Polaris submarines, 15 nuclear powered fleet submarines, 21 conventional submarines, 56 mine countermeasures vessels, and 5 Royal Marines Commandos.

There were not many more casts of the dice. The underlying assumption of the Defence Review, that Britain would not embark alone on military action against serious opposition, was increasingly firm, and the carrier case was almost powerless against it. It was in vain for the Navy Minister Christopher Mayhew to argue, as he did on 7 January 1966, that 'by abandoning carriers we should sacrifice the element of self-sufficiency East of Suez which is vital to any scheme of inter-dependence'.[39] That was a fair point of principle, but by then it was the figures that were counting, and they stacked up inexorably against the naval case. The Cabinet discussed the Defence Review on 14 February 1966,[40] and the review itself was issued a few days later.[41]

It was clear from the first paragraphs of the review that it was finance-driven. The Government's financial target for defence spending was 'a stable level of 6 per cent of Gross National Product by 1969–70' which meant £2 billion at 1964 prices, or a reduction of 16 per cent on the plans of the previous government. Having set this out frankly, the review then discussed how the defence coat could be cut according to the reduced cloth. It acknowledged that the North Atlantic Alliance was vital to the survival of the United Kingdom, but implicitly accepted the then NATO 'strategy' which was based on an early recourse to nuclear weapons if deterrence failed, and so discounted preparations for a long conventional war in Europe. However, it was not here that the scope for big-money reductions lay. That was in the area 'Outside Europe', the arena for the Whitehall battles of the past seventeen months.

After a *tour d'horizon* of British commitments and responsibilities, which concluded that 'It is in the Far East and Southern Asia that the greatest danger to peace may lie in the next decade' (confrontation was just ending), the review turned to the way in which Britain might cope with the variety of threats to stability, given the assumption that she would not attempt, without allies, to land or withdraw troops against sophisticated opposition outside the range of land-based air cover. While accepting that the present carrier force would continue well into the 1970s, it rejected the requirement for CVA 01; by the time she might be ready, in 1973, 'Our remaining commitments will not require her, and the functions for which we might otherwise need a carrier will be performed in another way', namely:

> Aircraft operating from land bases should take over the strike-reconnaissance and air-defence functions of the carrier ... Close anti-submarine protection of the naval force will be given by helicopters operating from ships other than carriers. Airborne

> Early Warning aircraft will continue to be operated from existing carriers, and subsequently from land bases. Strike capability against enemy ships will be provided by ... surface to surface guided missile[s] ...

The 'aircraft operating from land bases' were by implication to be F 111As, a purchase of 50 being mentioned later in the review. They were eventually to be succeeded by the Anglo-French Variable Geometry Aircraft, which was stated to be 'the core of our long-term aircraft programme'. Curiously, there was no mention in the White Paper (which actually was bound in a rather sombre shade of purple, found richly symbolic by some) of the 'Island Base Strategy' which was well known to have been the key element of the Air Staff's case during the Carrier Battle. There was no mention of the airfields projected to be built on the atolls of Aldabra and Diego Garcia.

The immediate outcome of the review was the resignation of the Minister for the Navy, Christopher Mayhew, and of the First Sea Lord, Admiral Sir David Luce. The reasons they gave were different: Luce's were based on the cancellation of the carrier and the operational penalties that would flow from that, while Mayhew's were more strategic in arguing that without carriers, the British East of Suez posture was untenable and commitments there should be relinquished straight away.[42] Hopkins accepted the post of Commander-in-Chief Portsmouth, and Captain George Baldwin, the Director of Naval Air Warfare, sought no further naval employment. There were no other overt resignations or early retirements.

Reaction in the Royal Navy as a whole was extremely sharp. Thirty-two years later, Terry Lewin could reflect that 'With hindsight, nobody was going to win in the Healey Defence Review',[43] but at the time, the sense that the service had been singled out for emasculation was widespread. Some of the articles written for *The Naval Review* in the rest of 1966 are quite remarkable in their intensity:

> Satan is cackling in Hell ... We have in charge of our country men of low calibre ... In the air is a smell of decadence, too

much welfare, ease, gambling, corruption, crime, homosexuality and a preoccupation with sex ... No longer is it enough to be the world's finest naval officers ...[44]

But a more considered view was emerging already: 'a junior aviator', while deploring the phasing out of the carriers, and pointing out deficiencies in the arguments of both sides, amongst them the Naval Staff's inflexibility over carrier design, wrote: 'If the government's policy really is to scuttle our forces East of Suez, then the decision not to build carriers is justifiable.'[45] Another article predicted that 'the island bases will never be built and the F 111 never be bought',[46] words that turned out to be prophetic two years later. Finally, thought was turning already to the feasibility of operating Vertical Take-off Aircraft from carriers much smaller than CVA 01; the work of Lieutenant-Commander (retired) F. P. U. Croker, originally for the Royal United Services Institute, was reprinted and studied.

For Terry Lewin, however, all these things had for the time being yielded place to more practical matters. Towards the end of 1965 he had been sent for by Rear Admiral William O'Brien the Naval Secretary, who was in charge of the appointments of senior captains, and told that he would be invited to command HMS *Hermes*. As one of the four remaining carriers in the Navy, in process of refit to enable her to take the latest naval aircraft, she was a greatly prized appointment. She had, moreover, been O'Brien's previous command, and that in some way seemed to add to the honour. Lewin was, in his own words, flabbergasted; he had not in all modesty expected such a plum. There were ironies in plenty to come, but for the time all were put aside; he joined *Hermes* almost exactly on the day the Defence Review was announced.

CARRIER COMMAND
1966–1967

Command of an aircraft carrier is a daunting task for anyone. It is all the more so for an officer whose speciality is not the skilled and arduous business of flying from, and to, that very small piece of deck in the middle of a large expanse of ocean. Indeed the United States Navy for many years restricted carrier command to officers who had that qualification. The Royal Navy had never made that a policy, and on the whole its wider catchment of carrier commanding officers had worked, although there had been at least one spectacular failure in the command and subsequent loss of HMS *Glorious* in the Second World War.[1] So, though Captain Lewin's appointment to command *Hermes* set no precedent, it was still a test of the utmost rigour.

Nor was it any consolation that as carriers go, the *Hermes* was only a little one. To the contrary, if she was to carry the latest and most capable aircraft of the Fleet Air Arm, as she was destined to do, she would have to work to the absolute limits of her design. Bigger and more powerful carriers like *Eagle* and *Ark Royal* might have some margin when operating such aircraft; *Hermes* was to have almost none.

She was of the same basic design as the *Albion*, *Bulwark* and *Centaur*, one grade up from the light fleet carriers of the *Ocean* class that had been hurriedly built at the end of the 1939–45 War and had given good service particularly off Korea in the early 1950s. Laid down in 1944 by Vickers, she was not launched until 1953, but had been well cared for in the interim, and after completion she had done only two commissions before being taken in hand for her long refit in 1964. Of some 28,000 tons and 650 feet long, with two shafts driven by a steam plant delivering 76,000 hp, she could do a maximum of 28 knots with a clean bottom and everything working perfectly. After refit, she had a 6.5 degree angled deck to facilitate aircraft operations, and important innovations such as the mirror landing sight to keep incoming aircraft on the right approach path, steam catapults to boost them into the air on take-off, a widened flight deck with deck-edge lift to help the ranging and stowage of aircraft, and the 984 three-dimensional radar to give the ship the best possible ability to control them once they were in the air.

These were all the most modern devices that were then available, but every one was absolutely necessary if the ship was to operate the aircraft planned for her. The fast combat aircraft were to be a squadron each of the Buccaneer 2, its main mission striking at targets either at sea or ashore, and the Sea Vixen 2, an all-weather fighter. Both were very heavy – it was commonly said that the Buccaneer fuselage was hewn out of the solid metal – and put massive stresses on the deck, the catapults that launched the aircraft and the arrester wires that restrained them on landing. O'Brien, the last captain of the *Hermes* before her long refit, had expressed deep concern about the prospect of the Sea Vixen 2s being operated from the ship.[2] 'I am already demanding the maximum from my pilots [flying the lighter Sea Vixen 1],' he wrote, and added words to the effect that he was also already demanding the maximum from the ship. The Admiralty had replied in soothing terms, citing improvements that were being planned, but the file must have been known to Lewin and was not encouraging.

Two other types of aircraft were to be embarked in *Hermes*, and although neither was so materially critical as the fast jets, they would carry their own problems. These were a flight of Gannet Airborne Early Warning aircraft, propeller-driven, with the role of detecting hostile raids flying below the carrier's own radar cover, directing fighters to intercept, and controlling strikes against surface targets; and a squadron of Wessex anti-submarine helicopters equipped with dipping sonars and anti-submarine torpedoes, which were an essential adjunct to surface ships, always in short supply for screening and in some conditions not so effective as the helicopters at detecting submarines. Flying these two types on and off a carrier was relatively simple, but hustling them about the deck and hangar, so that they would allow other operations to go unhindered, was not, and neither was their control once they were in the air.

'The purpose of an aircraft carrier is to fly aircraft.' That is a maxim that is engraved on the heart of every carrier captain, and it was quickly carved on Terry Lewin's. He was lucky in one sense: he had taken the ship over in the middle of a long refit, and trials would not start for some months. He was given a few days to observe operations on board *Eagle* in the Channel by her kindly captain, Derek Empson (who was a specialist aviator), and was able to absorb much information; but he was not too proud to seek advice and knowledge from others. Lieutenant-Commander (Flying) Bill Whitton – always known as 'little F' – was sent for very early in 1966 and quizzed about how flying and deck operations were done, and what the parameters were; and Whitton, answering honestly that he had had a 'pier head jump' and needed to do a lot of homework himself, was in no doubt that they could and would learn together and in harmony.[3]

Before the carrier learning curve got too steep, however, there was something more urgent to be done, and that was to ensure, in the immediate wake of the decisions of the Defence Review, that the morale of the ship's company should not suffer unduly and that the ship should be set on course for a successful commission. At that time, still deep in the refit, *Hermes* had only a nucleus ship's company, but Lewin judged that it was necessary to set the right tone from the start:

> I cleared Lower Deck and explained the Review and was able to give them all the background because I had lived through it and said but don't worry, carriers are going on for five years or more and *Hermes'* commission is going to be the best of the lot. I don't suppose they believed me but I think two years later they probably did.[4]

The same message was transmitted to every new group that joined, as the ship's company built up. Just as importantly, it was taken by Lewin himself to the squadrons that would form the *Hermes* Air Group: 809 (Buccaneers, commanded by Lieutenant-Commander Lin Middleton),

892 (Sea Vixens, Lieutenant-Commander J. N. S. Anderdon), 826 (Wessex, Lieutenant-Commander Ray Duxbury) and 849 'B' Flight (Gannet AEW). They were still forming and doing training from shore, but he visited all of them in their bases at Lossiemouth, Brawdy, Yeovilton and Culdrose, and attended every commissioning ceremony. In doing so he stressed to all of them that they were 'a part of *Hermes*'s ship's company and not just a group which came and lodged as rather unwelcome lodgers'.[5]

It really was, then, to be 'all of a company', as was becoming an abiding Lewin principle. In this he was immensely helped by his heads of department, and in particular at this stage by the Commander (Air), 'Paddy' McKeown. McKeown was himself a pilot of the highest calibre, with much operational experience including service as senior pilot of a squadron at Suez in 1956. He was universally respected in the Fleet Air Arm, and was wholeheartedly with his captain in his desire to integrate the squadrons in the life of the ship. The other key figure in this enterprise would be the executive officer and second-in-command, Commander John Fieldhouse, a submariner whose reputation in his own field was as high as McKeown's in his: cheerful, calm and immensely able.

But first, the ship must be got to sea and set to work. The first trials took place in the Channel in late spring, when the ship's company was still very thin and matters almost entirely in the hands of the dockyard officers and workmen. The programme entailed several nights at sea, not likely to be popular with the 'mateys'. Lewin's approach was typical:

> We decided to make them really comfortable ... each was allocated a bunk, given a little card when he joined, the bunk was made up with sheets and pillows and pillowcases ... the galley laid on the most fantastic meals for the whole of the time they were on board.[6]

It was no wonder that the trials went well, and that they ended, at the request of the trials party, with a group photograph of the whole 500-strong team, Lewin seated in the middle.

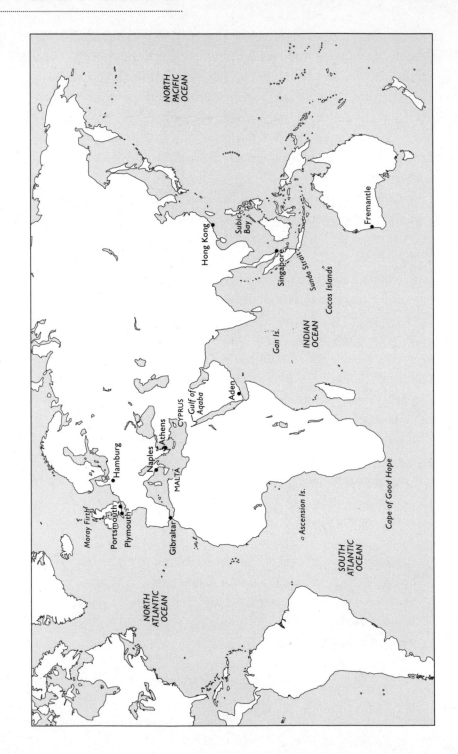

The ship commissioned in Devonport on 16 May 1966.[7] The hangar was specially decorated, Rear Admiral O'Brien (now Flag Officer Aircraft Carriers) and the Commander-in-Chief Plymouth attended, and so notably did a great many officers' and ratings' wives. Jane and the wife of the master at arms collaborated in cutting the commissioning cake.[8] It was an impressive send-off, and two days later the ship left for shakedown and further trials, culminating in a full power trial on the Arran measured mile on 26 June.

Now it was time to reintroduce the ship to her primary function. A helicopter or two touched down; Vixens were seen approaching from astern, but they were only doing a 'beat-up' in passing. McKeown was determined that the first deck landing should be in style, and borrowed a Tiger Moth biplane to do it himself. Since it was the Channel in early July, the wind was strong, and the normal carrier pattern, steaming hell-for-leather into the wind to get the right ground-speed for aircraft landing-on, had almost to be reversed to get the Tiger down. Eventually McKeown settled on the deck, his wings restrained by flight deck crew in the style of the very earliest deck landings near the end of the First World War.

There was a sense of due deliberation about the whole pre-deployment programme, though the Tiger Moth episode might be thought over-symbolic. The first arrested deck-landing was by a Gannet, and it was with a small complement of Gannets and helicopters that the ship made her first foreign visit, to Gibraltar in early September. The operational squadrons had been detailed for the Farnborough Air Show, and *Hermes*'s was a scratch outfit of aeroplanes. That did not mean that anyone was idle. The flight deck organisation had to be perfected to meet the bigger challenges ahead; so did the flying control, operations room, air traffic control, communications and meteorology sections, not to mention the essential support of the supply, engineering, air engineering and electrical departments. A complex of over 2000 people, all trained in their own skills, had to be brought together into a coherent whole, to fulfil that function: the purpose of an aircraft carrier is to fly aircraft.

There were to be three work-up phases. At that time aircraft carriers did not come under the organisation of the Flag Officer Sea Training at

Portland for this activity; they conducted their own work-ups under the overall scrutiny of the Flag Officer Aircraft Carriers. Geographical considerations came into it as well as staff expertise, because the Portland exercise areas were small and crowded with merchant shipping, and a much clearer area existed off eastern Scotland, where there was moreover a convenient naval air station close by at Lossiemouth.

Consequently, after embarking some of her aircraft from the Royal Naval Air Station at Brawdy, west Wales, on the way north, *Hermes* appeared off the Moray Firth on 24 September.[9] Thereafter, for ten intensive days, with no Sunday or any other day off, flying was conducted at steadily increasing tempo, interleaved with replenishment at sea and anti-submarine manoeuvres. The Buccaneer had had some problems with pitching-up on landing in *Victorious*,[10] and the performance of this aircraft was watched with particular care. But all went well, and on 5 October the Flag Officer Aircraft Carriers embarked for the ship's informal visit to Hamburg.

'Informal' might not be regarded as meriting that word in civil life. 'Formal' means full fig, all possible pomp and circumstance, generally to do with state occasions; 'routine' means a welcome break after perhaps a long exercise period, or a short visit to some friendly place that indicated it would welcome a call with little fuss; 'informal' is between the two, and involves a certain amount of ceremonial and official entertainment but also opportunity for relaxation. Aircraft carriers, being large and populated entities, are not easily accommodated in small communities, but Hamburg had no difficulty in absorbing the *Hermes* ship's company and the record[11] suggests that the visit was a friendly one at a time when NATO links were exceptionally important.[12]

Then it was back to the Moray Firth, and here the commission suffered a blow that was to test the *Hermes*'s captain severely. Commander McKeown's wife was diagnosed with terminal cancer and it was not possible for him to carry on as Commander (Air). Lewin was faced with a dilemma at a critical time. He did not want to change what was turning out to be a highly effective team in the air department, and his solution was to promote Whitton, his 'Little F', to acting rank as Commander (Air), and bring in Middleton, the CO of 809 squadron, in Whitton's place – to be christened, in Lewin style, 'Baby F'.[13] After the work-up, the situation would be reviewed and a more permanent arrangement made.

This was not in any way a bizarre proposal. Certainly the roles of Commander (Air) and Little F were not precisely one-over-one; the Commander (Air) planned the whole flying programme, taking into account the training requirements of the squadrons, any operational or exercise directives, and all the geographical and weather parameters, while Little F worked on the detail of each sortie down to the take-off and landing weights and the required wind over the deck, the oomph needed on the catapult to get aircraft into the air and the tension on the arrester wires to catch them when they returned. Even so, both were professionals in the same field and the transition from one job to the other was not far-fetched.

However, the arrangement did not meet the approval of the authorities ashore and it was not long before a relief for McKeown was appointed. He flew in to *Hermes* by helicopter before the end of the second work-up. This was Commander Stan Leonard, who was already well known to Lewin. He was a hero of the Korean War. Hit by gunfire, he had crash-landed his aircraft in enemy territory, breaking both legs, and held off an approaching North Korean patrol with a revolver long enough for a helicopter, complete with doctor, to come and rescue him.

He had since served with distinction, including a spell in a previous *Hermes* commission as Little F. But he still wore full callipers on both legs, and Lewin was in serious doubt as to whether he could manage the ladders that he would need to negotiate between, for example, the briefing rooms well down in the ship and the flying control position next to the bridge. This was not a problem that Leonard would have experienced as Little F, because that job involved being in flying control all the time when the ship was at flying stations. However, his appointment was a *fait accompli*; he was provided with a sea cabin in the bridge structure, and the work-up went on.

The second phase ended with a full-scale exercise in the North-West Approaches and Irish Sea, with an anti-submarine setting and in vile weather. Exercise Roedean was remembered vividly by many, but flying generally continued[14] and the ship's limits were fully tested. On arrival at Portsmouth, she was returned to dock for a propeller change 'to see', as the record wryly put it, 'if the new one would crack in the same place as the first'.[15] Then it was Christmas, and in January 1967 the deployment started in earnest.

The plan was that *Hermes* would spend the next nine months away from the United Kingdom, which was now the maximum time allowed for separation of ships' companies from wives and families: a considerable alleviation from previous patterns when eighteen-month foreign tours, without any entitlement to help in reuniting families during that time, were not unusual. *Hermes* was due to spend the first four months of the nine in the Mediterranean and the remaining five East of Suez. The political situation in neither area was entirely stable, but in general (and contrary to predictions as little as two years before) the Far East was becoming more settled while the Middle East remained turbulent. An aircraft carrier was, whatever might have been argued in the Ministry of Defence, an important counter in any politico-military game that might be played.

There were many matters, from the broadest of international considerations to the narrowest technical detail, to preoccupy *Hermes*'s captain before the ship sailed for Gibraltar on Monday 16 January.[16] It may have been this plethora of concerns that caused a young submarine commanding officer who called on Lewin on Friday 13 January to be less than impressed:

> The submarine had been programmed for a four month Med deployment, the first part of which interacted with *Hermes* in a series of exercises from Gibraltar to Malta ... [I found Lewin] a man of great presence and charm, who clearly had no idea what the exercise programme was about ... [subsequently] *Hermes* proved the easiest of targets.[17]

The submarine commanding officer concerned had not himself served in a carrier, and was probably unaware of the priorities as seen from a carrier's bridge. Those put first the safe despatch and recovery of aircraft and their control once in the air; the protection of the carrier against submarines must be taken into account, and her helicopters will be able to help with that, but it is in any balanced unit the business of the escort force commander, who controls all the available assets. It is understandable that there was no full meeting of minds.

The hammering home of the point about the safe despatch of aircraft was, unhappily, not long in coming. *Hermes* arrived off Gibraltar on 23 January and embarked the Governor and the Flag Officer Gibraltar to witness flying operations.[18] They had been on board a bare half hour when a Sea Vixen rose almost vertically from the catapult, inevitably stalled and fell into the sea fine on the carrier's starboard bow. The ship had been going at 24 knots to give sufficient wind over the deck, and engines were instantly stopped and put full astern. Meanwhile the planeguard helicopter, reacting extremely quickly, had moved out from its station on the ship's quarter and was going into the hover over the ditched Vixen. The momentum of the ship, still going ahead in spite of the braking effect of the propellers, took her into the tail rotor of the helicopter and that, too, fell into the sea.

Other helicopters were airborne and quickly came to the scene, and picked up survivors; but the helicopter pilot and one member of the crew were lost, and one of the two Sea Vixen crew. The origin of the accident was almost bizarre: the instrument panel of the Vixen had not been fully secured, and with the kick from the catapult on launch had flown backwards into the pilot's lap, forcing back the joystick and causing an almost vertical climb. The commendable speed with which the planeguard helicopter had rushed in to help had its own ironic, and tragic, outcome.

It was a desperate indoctrination into the realities of carrier life for *Hermes*'s captain. He must, of course, have steeled himself to the possibility of accidents during aircraft operations: since the introduction of modern measures and devices they had become much safer than in the early 1950s, but it was a rare commission that passed without a fatality, and the brave young officers that flew deserved all their flying pay. Nevertheless, even a seasoned and war-experienced commanding officer was bound to be affected by such an event, and the elements of tragedy that surrounded this particular mishap certainly sharpened Lewin's sadness.

He was, indeed, inclined to blame himself for the extent of the accident, even though things had happened so fast and all the correct actions had been taken. It was fortunate that Lin Middleton, who had been airborne in his Buccaneer at the time and had seen the whole affair from that vantage point, was able to reassure his captain that in his view there was nothing more the ship could have done.[19] Middleton's initiative in giving this opinion was an example of the whole-ship philosophy that Lewin had been so careful to foster, and must have been of the utmost comfort to him.

As always in an operating carrier, there was little room in the programme for introspection. *Hermes* continued on her way towards Malta, refuelling underway from an oiler, carrying out damage control exercises, and flying, flying. She was due to enter Malta on 28 January and was approaching Grand Harbour when a signal was received from the Queen's Harbourmaster saying that all the tugs had gone on strike.

Lewin had set some store on this brief weekend visit to Malta. Later in the Mediterranean leg of the deployment, *Hermes* was due for a fortnight's maintenance period there and arrangements were already being made to charter two aircraft to bring out up to 250 wives and families from the United Kingdom. This was an initiative of the kind for which *Hermes* was becoming well known, and for which her recently formed Families' Association – another innovation of Terry Lewin's – was responsible. He was keen to give the ship's company a chance to book accommodation for the maintenance period in plenty of time, and the brief stay in Malta in January was the best chance to do this.

The prospect, then, of enforced anchorage in some relatively remote spot like Marsa Xlokk, rather than going into Grand Harbour, did not appeal. But a carrier is a big heavy floating object, and Grand Harbour is very restricted; manoeuvring *Hermes* into her berth between head and stern buoys, without tugs to push and pull, would be an exacting and possibly hazardous business. On the bridge they played for time, carrying out a 360 degree turn 'while we discussed what to do. We decided that as it was such a beautiful calm windless day we'd have a shot at going in ... We were very lucky.'[20]

Few watchers would have thought there was much luck about it. There was a little help, from one tiny tug, manned by the Queen's Harbourmaster and his officer staff, shifted from bow to stern as the ship swung through a full 180 degrees abreast the berth; but it was almost entirely the work of the captain, with the advice of his navigator, Lieutenant-Commander Michael Prest – although the latter always maintained that having lined up the ship for any berthing manoeuvre he, unlike some carrier navigators, relinquished the conn to the captain: 'He would take over the ship and give the final orders.'[21] In any event, 25 minutes after passing St Elmo breakwater the main engines were rung off,[22] and that would have been a slick manoeuvre with the help of all the tugs in Malta.

The weekend over, *Hermes* sailed for more flying exercises, this time with the Flag Officer Aircraft Carriers embarked. Natural wind remained light and the ship was flogged unmercifully to maintain enough wind over the deck. All went well until 3 February, when flying was due to cease before the ship began passage back to Gibraltar for a brief water-wash of the boilers and bilge cleaning.[23] It was almost the final flying serial of the day when Sea Vixen No. 306 made an erratic approach, was ordered to go round again (a 'bolter'), applied power too late and caught the angle, turning over and ditching on the port bow.[24]

This time there was no question of the rescue helicopter being menaced, as the ship had already passed the scene of the ditching, and the pilot, who had ejected, was quickly picked up, though he suffered two broken legs. Because of the aircraft's design, the observer in a Vixen had almost no chance of getting out of the aircraft in such circumstances and, sadly, Lieutenant Brodie was dead when his body was recovered.

So it was a chastened carrier that set course for Gibraltar. Customarily, burial services for aircrew killed in accidents during flying operations are held quickly on the theory that morale suffers less if it is done that way, and the committal of Lieutenant Brodie to the deep was at 5 pm that day. But the squadrons, and in particular their commanding officers, were not happy with the state of affairs.

When there are three fatal accidents in the space of ten days, it is natural for those most at risk to question the competence of the management. No one had anything but admiration for Lewin himself. He had shown himself a self-reliant, caring and immensely capable all-round carrier captain. But so far as flying operations were concerned, he had to be reliant on the ship's air department, and in particular on the Commander (Air). It was natural, therefore, that criticism should focus on Stan Leonard.

It was not a matter of the Commander (Air)'s physical disability. All agreed that he had fought that nobly and made every effort to minimise it, and had largely been successful. It was rather the up-to-dateness of his professional knowledge, and what was thought to be his inability to grasp the implications of the extremely narrow margins to which the modern aircraft were operating from their small, under-powered ship. As an example, Middleton quoted the stark fact that a Buccaneer 2 was committed to a single landing pass, between the time it achieved its maximum landing weight and the time it effectively ran out of fuel.[25]

In consequence, the COs of the fast jet squadrons had formed the habit of 'shadowing' Stan Leonard in flying control, with one or the other generally up there when Buccaneers or Vixens were flying and they were not in the air themselves. It is doubtful if this helped to make relations any sweeter, but they felt they owed it to their people whose lives, after all, depended on the sensitive handling of the flying operation.

Precisely how the matter came to a head, in what manner and with what timing, is debatable since there are different accounts from the protagonists. The captain's secretary of the *Hermes* commission recalled that an approach was made through him by the squadron commanders as a body,[26] and this accords fairly closely with Lewin's own recollection, which is that they 'asked to come and see me'.[27]

Middleton, on the other hand, recalls that he and Anderdon sought separate interviews with the captain. Two things are certain: the COs insisted that they were not intending to be mutinous; and they had lost confidence in the Commander (Air).

It was one of the most difficult situations that can face a carrier captain, particularly one who is not himself an aviator. It is clear that Lewin himself regarded it as one of the crisis points in his career, and the fact that not only he but others concerned volunteered information to the author, and emphasised it in interviews, indicates that it was an extremely serious matter, even though of course it was at the time carefully restricted to an inner circle of officers. The alternatives were stark and neither was risk free. Either Lewin accepted the views of the COs, all of whom were highly proficient aviators and strong characters – indeed Middleton and Anderdon had already been selected for promotion to commander – and applied for a relief for Leonard, or he put his faith in Leonard with inevitable consequent reservations on the part of the COs, and the overhanging risk that just one more flying accident would decisively undermine confidence for the rest of the commission.

Lewin handled it in a firm, courageous and, as it turned out, successful way. He reasoned that none of the accidents that had occurred were the fault of the air department's senior management: one had been a failure of maintenance, one the tragic result of misplaced heroism, and one of pilot error:

> It would have broken Stan for life if we had suggested these accidents were his responsibility which clearly they were not, and so I told them I heard what they said but that they were going to have to live with it and give the Commander (Air) all the support that he needed.[28]

If it was not totally lanced,[29] the boil never came to a head again.

After her spell at Gibraltar, the ship sailed for Malta again, with a less intense flying programme, and at the end of February visited Naples wearing the flag of the Commander-in-Chief Mediterranean. This was very much a standard carrier's four-day visit, with in this case powerful NATO overtones. During *Hermes*'s stay, the Commander-in-Chief disembarked and his flag was replaced by that of the new Flag Officer Aircraft Carriers, Rear Admiral Derek Empson. For Terry Lewin, the change of FOACs was a matter of replacing one friendly boss with another: like O'Brien, Empson was an old and valued acquaintance.[30]

On leaving Naples, the ship was at once involved in NATO exercise 'Poker Hand' in the Tyrrhenian Sea.[31] This was by now pretty standard fare, although it was enlivened by a first encounter with monster carriers in the shape of USS *America*, by replenishment from unfamiliar vessels and by an incident when a fork-lift truck was driven off the flight deck into the sea.[32] This definitely was not a flying accident, although Lieutenant Porter who was driving the truck might have been forgiven for thinking it was one, as he went in from 70 feet. He was picked up in quick time by the planeguard helicopter and the affair was a matter for hilarity rather than anything else. A further mishap to a Vixen, this time on the flight deck when an aircraft fell into a catwalk with some structural damage but no casualties,[33] could well have been a matter for reassurance rather than foreboding: that was the third, it had not been serious, and perhaps the luck had turned.

The Flag Officer Aircraft Carriers' Operational Readiness Inspection was held off Tobruk in early March and was passed with flying colours. Empson addressed the ship's company on 9 March, disembarking on the 10th. Confidence was high as the ship embarked on further Buccaneer trials, to ensure that all problems connected with this new mark of aircraft had been solved, and in three days over a working weekend they were successfully completed; indeed, 809 Squadron went on to become the first fixed-wing squadron to operate for three years without a single accident.[34]

The two-week maintenance period in Malta in the second half of March did, as planned, see the arrival of substantial numbers of families for a brief stay. Jane and Terry took a flat in Sliema, hired a car, picnicked around the island – only beginning then to develop its tourist industry – and met many of the *Hermes* families both on board and ashore.[35] The air group was disembarked to Hal Far.

One evening, 'the Commander and Commander (Air) rang up ... and asked to come and see me about 9 pm. I said yeah, sure come round. They arrived and I opened the door, they both looked very serious and I said what is it, rape or murder? They looked absolutely taken aback because it was in fact rape.'[36] It was an after-a-party incident in the mess at Hal Far involving an officer from *Hermes* and a female officer from the air station, and after the intervention of the Commander-in-Chief's staff and a preliminary investigation, the charges were dropped.

Discipline in a big ship has always been a peculiar art, requiring firmness, fairness and above all consistency, so that all on board believe they are justly treated but equally are unlikely to get away with transgression. That kind of atmosphere must be generated from the top, but is also a prime responsibility of the executive officer, and with John Fieldhouse, Terry Lewin could have no doubts on that score; he could, moreover, be sure that heads of departments, including the Air and the squadrons, would follow consistent policies. A fair indication of the state of discipline on board is given by the number of warrants issued for the punishment of the more serious or aggravated offences; it is of some interest that in *Hermes*, fifteen months into the commission, the number had reached 50.[37] The statistic is not outstandingly high nor low, and speaks neither of a ship run by 'Popularity Jacks', nor by the spiritual descendants of flogging captains.

After the maintenance period was over and the wives had departed, the ship sailed for NATO exercise 'Dawn Clear'. This involved the United States Navy in force, with participation from the carrier *Shangri-La* – one of the ships the Royal Navy was tentatively in the market for two years before. The Vixens were particularly pleased with their operational performance,[38] and morale had certainly been fully restored.

A visit to Athens followed, with the ship anchored in Phaleron Bay. It gave ample opportunity for the ship's company to tour all kinds of ruin and there were the usual accompaniments of children's parties, the ceremony of Beat Retreat on the jetty, sport and sailing races. But much was going on in Greece; and the very day the *Hermes* sailed, 18 April 1967, the colonels carried out their *coup d'état* and took over the government.

It was the ship's first introduction to a politico-military role, as an instrument of government in dealing with a set of increasingly complex situations which continued over the next three months. The first concern in the eastern Mediterranean had to be Cyprus. The island was still under British administration, and the colonels' preoccupation could well be the establishment of further Greek-Cypriot influence. At the same time, British nationals in Greece itself might be affected. *Hermes*'s orders were therefore to remain within 24 hours' steaming of Athens in case emergency evacuation was necessary.[39] It appeared prudent for all sorts of reasons to operate off Cyprus, which was just on the 24-hour limit at full speed.

For the next fortnight *Hermes* took the opportunity to conduct a solid programme of flying,[40] consolidating skills, qualifying the less experienced pilots in night flying, and in the process fully restoring confidence in the management of the Air department. It was one of those occasions, which quite often happen in the naval service, when orders to hang around, in case a situation gets serious, give a chance to do worthwhile *ad hoc* activity.

The opportunity was not confined to flying training. The large, well-equipped and lavishly manned Royal Air Force base at Akrotiri was close at hand, and *Hermes* established a close liaison: 'Every day we brought out two chopper loads of RAF chaps to watch the flying and they all came, from the Air Officer Commanding down to the lowest rank.'[41] Hospitality was reciprocated at weekends, when the ship anchored off and the facilities at Akrotiri were much appreciated.

On 1 May the immediate crisis caused by the colonels' coup was deemed to have passed and *Hermes* was released to resume her planned transit to the Far East Station. She arrived at Port Said on 2 May and passed through the Suez Canal on the 3rd. She made a fast passage through the Gulf of Suez and Red Sea; it is notable that the Log[42] records every sighting of a Russian ship, merchant, fishing or auxiliary.

The area into which *Hermes* was steaming was, in fact, more volatile than either the eastern Mediterranean or the Far East. All around the Red Sea and Arabian peninsula, political, military and propaganda machines were stirring. In Egypt, the regime of President Nasser was strongly anti-western, naturally anti-Israeli and in rivalry with Saudi Arabia. In the Gulf of Aqaba, four regimes – Egyptian, Israeli, Jordanian and Saudi – jostled uneasily, as indeed they had fifteen years before, but since 1957 there had been a United Nations presence at the entrance to the Gulf that had allowed traffic to, and consequent expansion of, the Israeli port of Eilat at its head.[43] And in the Aden Colony and Protectorate, at the southern end of the Red Sea, the forthcoming British withdrawal, announced as taking place some time in 1968, had led to violent jockeying for position amongst rival contenders for power: violence that fell mainly upon the security forces still maintained in considerable numbers by the British in the area.

On arrival off Aden on 6 May, therefore, the captain of the *Hermes* found himself involved in a good deal of intensive briefing on a fast-moving situation. The British High Commissioner was Sir Humphrey Trevelyan, the joint Commander-in-Chief Middle East Admiral Sir Michael LeFanu, the Land Force Commander Lieutenant-General Sir Philip Tower and the Air Officer Commanding Air Vice Marshal Andrew Humphrey. This was an exceptionally able and effective team and Lewin, who already knew both LeFanu and Humphrey, was quickly able to establish good working relations with them all.

The situation was also a busy one on the water. The modernised carrier *Victorious* was already present, with a number of destroyers and frigates, and the opportunity was taken to mount an exercise between the two forces under the control of the Flag Officer Second in Command Far East Fleet, Rear Admiral Edward Ashmore.[44] But the main business was twofold: support of the forces up-country, where the Royal Air Force was fully stretched in its efforts to contain rebels in the Radfan and surrounding areas, and demonstrations of power to give confidence to those elements of the local leadership who wished to support the constitutional position.

Both these requirements were fully met over the next two weeks. Tribute was generously paid by LeFanu in a signal to the Ministry of Defence on 19 May,[45] outlining the achievements of *Victorious* and

Hermes during that time: over 200 sorties up-country including sector reconnaissance, Border Air Defence Patrols, Air Defence Exercises, live firing exercises controlled by Forward Air Controllers, Airborne Early Warning trials and exercises, with in addition two highly impressive demonstration operations and fly-pasts on 12 and 17 May.

Meanwhile, the Gulf of Aqaba situation was sharpening appreciably. On 16 May the Chief of Staff of the Egyptian Army, General Fawzi, demanded the withdrawal of the United Nations Emergency Force (UNEF) from its post at Sharm el Shaikh at the mouth of the Gulf.[46] For various legal and political reasons U Thant, the UN Secretary General, found it necessary to instruct General Rikhye, the UNEF commander, to accede to this 'request'.[47] The stage was now set for Nasser to increase the confrontation with Israel and on 23 May he made a speech saying that under no circumstances would Egypt allow the Israeli flag to pass through the Gulf of Aqaba.[48]

In spite of the worsening situation across the whole Middle Eastern area, *Hermes* had sailed on 18 May eastward, in the hope of resuming her much-delayed passage to Singapore. But by the time she reached Gan, the British airhead in the middle of the Indian Ocean, on 23 May Her Majesty's Government clearly were already beginning to consider her presence closer to the centre of violence to be necessary, particularly as *Victorious* was on her way back to the United Kingdom. A few days of indecision allowed *Hermes*'s sports parties a little time ashore at Gan, and on 26 May she was still in the anchorage there. That evening saw an incident that illustrated the spirit in the ship.

A young steward suffered a brain haemorrhage and the *Hermes*'s surgeon commander advised that it would be fatal to try to move him ashore for the necessary operation. This must be carried out on board, and it would be necessary for the whole ship to be as still as possible. The ship's company was informed, the ship remained at anchor and all unnecessary machinery was switched off. Eyewitnesses say that scarcely a sound was heard throughout the ship for two hours.[49] It was, sadly, to no avail as the rating died after the operation, but the ready sympathy and co-operation of everyone on board was one more indication of the way the *Hermes*'s people were 'all of a company'.

On 27 May *Hermes* sailed again, and her course was westerly for Aden.[50] In fact, two days previously the British Government's Defence and Overseas Policy Committee had considered the possibility of sending a ship through the Strait of Tiran as a demonstration of right in international law.[51] The presence of *Hermes* at Gan had been noted, and her availability to provide air cover calculated. Clearly it would take time to mount such an operation, and in the event it was just one more of many abortive schemes.

Naturally this was not known to Terry Lewin, but he was doing his best to second-guess the next developments in the confused situation. He made a point of broadcasting to the ship's company every night to keep them informed of the international position, the latest orders under which the ship was working and his predictions as to what might happen next.[52] During those high-speed passages with no flying he also encouraged every sort of diversion, from deck hockey, through all those deck games using outsize dice that are beloved of sailors, to impromptu concert parties.[53]

In these activities he was vastly supported by officers and ship's company. As he himself said, an aircraft carrier with its 2000 skilled souls contains a formidable array of talent, and harnessing it is part of the art of command. As one example from many, the ship's daily newspaper *The Hermes Herald* was edited by Captain Pickard of the Prince of Wales's Own Regiment of Yorkshire, second in command of the five-strong Carrier Borne Ground Liaison Section,[54] embarked for Forward Air Control of aircraft in the ground attack mode. At sea, he may well have found himself at a loose end, but editing a daily paper in a way that would satisfy and entertain a diverse ship's company, with the limited facilities available on board (Banda duplicators were probably the limit of technology), must have ensured he was fully employed.

All this unscheduled high-speed steaming, without any opportunity for the planned maintenance on which the efficient running of the ship depended, posed problems for the technical departments. Their resourcefulness was impressive. On the way to Gan the almost worn-out piston of one of the catapults was changed, and on the way back the other;[55] both jobs would normally have been done in harbour. Similarly, on the passage back to Aden one of the machinery units was shut down and the boilers water-washed under way. It was a precedent stored away in Terry Lewin's memory, and came in handy later on.

On arrival at Aden, they found a steadily worsening situation. Unrest had been building up for months; for the British government the dilemma of balancing the need for early withdrawal with the desire to leave behind a stable administration was an exceptionally difficult one.[56] Now, on top of that, the situation over the Strait of Tiran was at boiling point and modern communications, well handled by the Egyptian propaganda machine, ensured that the Aden population was fully informed of the Arab side of the argument.

Hermes and the consorts she found already at Aden, *Nubian, Ashanti, Brighton* and *Leopard*, spent an uneasy five days, exercising spasmodically and steadily increasing their vigilance against saboteurs when in harbour.[57] Diplomatic efforts to resolve the Tiran crisis continued, but in the absence of a firm lead from any of the major powers, they came to nothing. On 5 June, Israeli aircraft conducted pre-emptive strikes against the air forces of Egypt, Jordan and Syria and the Six-day War had begun.

One of the early claims by the Arab states during this conflict was that British help, and specifically help from British carriers, had been used to reinforce the Israeli air strikes. *Hermes* was generally in the offing, a safer place to be than in harbour at or near Aden, so it was necessary to demonstrate that she was still in the area and she was ordered to 'show herself off the port' each afternoon.[58] Her Ship's Log and flying programme were specially flown home in order to convince diplomats of the countries concerned that there had been no intervention.[59]

By 10 June it was clear that the war would result in victory for Israel and her occupation of the whole of the west bank of the Jordan, the Sinai Peninsula and the Golan Heights. A general strike had been called in Aden as soon as the war broke out and there were numerous terrorist incidents,[60] but the situation had since returned to what appeared to be an uneasy calm. It was agreed with the shore authorities that no further purpose was to be served by the retention of *Hermes*, and the ships were allowed to disperse.

At last *Hermes* managed to get beyond Gan without being turned round again, and even the outbreak of renewed violence in Aden – the Crater incidents of 20 June being the worst day of all in the history of the colony[61] – did not affect her; she was by then nearing the Malacca Strait, and on 22 June she secured in the naval base at Singapore. All night leave was given to the watch and non-duty part of watch, three-quarters of the ship's company: the first since 17 April.[62]

A three-week maintenance period was more than welcome, it was essential, and restoration of the ship and her company went on apace. Sport became endemic. The ship's teams had varying success but enjoyment was what mattered; it must have been a particular delight to the captain that the rugby team was the star outfit, winning the Big Ships' Shield and losing only one match in the entire commission. He had a personal success too: he was so far ahead in the veterans' race at the athletics meeting that he practically had time to drink the proffered champagne before the next man came home. 'TT the terror of the track', said the commission book.[63]

Everything was on a large scale and the likening of a carrier to a town, with every kind of activity buzzing, has seldom seemed more appropriate. The church, under the padre Arthur Nunnerley, was a real parish: during the commission no less than 56 children were baptised in *Hermes*, and 35 sets of banns of marriage published.[64] It was singular and memorable for the officers and ratings concerned: at least one thought it worth getting in touch with the author and sending him a photocopy of his own banns.[65] Arrangements were made for the BBC's 'Sunday Half-hour' of community hymn-singing to be recorded in *Hermes* while the ship was in Singapore, and the programme went out on 6 August 1967. Letters of appreciation were received from all over the world.

But 'the purpose of an aircraft carrier is to fly aircraft', and on 17 July *Hermes* left her berth in Singapore for the local exercise areas, where the squadrons were re-embarked and worked-up again after their time ashore at RAF Changi. They provided support to the amphibious forces in the later stages of Exercise 'Firm Stride', held in the Kuantan area.[66] Then it was on to the Philippines, where an intensive week's flying made use of the US facilities in the Subic Bay area. Altogether 300 fixed-wing and 290 helicopter sorties were flown, by both day and night. It was a strong reintroduction to operational imperatives.

For most of this period, and for the subsequent passage to Hong Kong, *Hermes* wore the flag of Rear Admiral Edward Ashmore, Flag Officer Second in Command of the Far East Fleet and the senior seagoing commander on the station. He and Lewin had great admiration for each other, but it had been somewhat tested earlier on, off Aden, when there had been differences of opinion with the flag officer's staff.[67] Indeed it is said that at one point Lewin ordered one of the staff officers to leave the bridge. But Ashmore acknowledged that he was not at this stage served as well as he might have been by his staff,[68] and that situation had long been rectified. Now, after a prolonged period on board, it was clear that mutual confidence was complete.

While the ship was in Hong Kong an unusual mission served to reinforce the high opinions that *Hermes* had earned. There was some unrest in the colony and it was reported that three buildings had been occupied by communists who were building up a base and cache of arms there. A raid by 826 Squadron helicopters, to deploy units from the Hong Kong Police and the Welch Regiment, was planned in secrecy and with elaborate cover stories. Emplaning, deplaning and roping practice was given at Lei Mun Barracks, and the raid was carried out early next day, 4 August. It was entirely successful, resulting in several arrests and the capture of illicit equipment.[69]

On leaving Hong Kong *Hermes* was due for three weeks' intensive work at sea that would take her to the Philippines, then through the Sunda Strait to the Cocos Islands in the Indian Ocean, then to Fremantle on the west coast of Australia. It certainly fulfilled Edward Ashmore's motto, adopted when he took up the flag officer's job, of 'Never in Singapore'.[70] But Lewin was thinking ahead, to the latter end of the commission. This was bedevilled by the plans for withdrawal from Aden.

It had been decided that this should be brought forward to the end of November 1967. Hopes of leaving behind a stable regime or set of regimes friendly to Britain had long evaporated, and the objective now was to withdraw with as little loss of life and as much dignity as possible. In consequence, an impressive naval force was to be deployed for the final phases of the withdrawal, including all the specialised amphibious ships.[71] It was planned that, as the RAF presence ashore was wound up, fixed-wing air support should be provided by two carriers, of which *Hermes* would be one. It was clearly necessary that she should be in tip-top condition, and therefore the authorities decreed that she would have to remain on the Far East Station in the meantime. Worse, she would have to remain in the area over the Christmas period, for the post-withdrawal phase.

Lewin appreciated that to a ship's company that had expected a nine-month deployment, returning to the United Kingdom in October, this would be a devastating blow to morale:

> Captain Tony Morton [Captain of the Fleet, Home Fleet] came out on a visit ... I made a very convincing case that I could steam the ship home on one shaft doing planned maintenance on the other set of engines, changing over halfway and doing planned maintenance on the other half, so that I would arrive back in the UK 120 per cent in date for planned maintenance, the chaps could have their leave and then turn round and get out well in time for [the] withdrawal ... I wrote about a three page letter explaining how this could be done and asked Tony to go back to John Bush [Commander-in-Chief, Home Fleet] and persuade him that this was the right thing to do.[72]

To Lewin's great joy the plan was approved. He had not allowed any of the discussion to percolate in any way through the ship, and almost no one was aware that their return to the United Kingdom had been in jeopardy.

There was emphasis, in this final exercise period for *Hermes* in the Far East, on anti-submarine work; the submarine *Auriga*, as well as two 'Leander' class frigates and a Royal Fleet Auxiliary, was in company. For the period off the Cocos Islands the problem of a diversion airfield, always a preoccupation for fixed-wing carrier aviation in such a far-flung station, was solved by landing a party from *Hermes* at the rudimentary airfield on the island.

It was the helicopters, however, that presented the technical problems; they were bedevilled, in the hot and humid conditions, by a succession of unexplained power failures that culminated during a night anti-submarine exercise with the ditching of a Wessex. By then these aircraft had been fitted with flotation bags and not only were the crew rescued without difficulty, but the aircraft itself was recovered by the ship's crane. Lewin's seamanship and ship handling were commended by Ashmore, who was still embarked in the force, as 'most creditable'.[73]

25 August was the last day of fixed-wing flying on the station for *Hermes*. Ashmore signed her off with a gracious tribute: '*Hermes* has achieved a very high standard in the operation of her aircraft and a professionalism that has been a pleasure to watch whilst my flag has been flown in the ship.'[74] She left Cocos for Fremantle with the frigate *Minerva* and RFA *Olna* in company, arriving on 29 August.

The visit to Fremantle was a fitting climax to the Far East tour. Western Australia had warm and friendly feelings for the Royal Navy and only occasional opportunities to express them, and the level of hospitality matched the scale of the visit. When the ship was open to visitors on 2 September, 5500 people came on board;[75] a ship's company dance found a thousand partners.

Lewin was invited to the races one afternoon but was detained over a long lunch party on board:

> I'd taken the precaution of telling my PO Steward, Fred West, who was a great racing man, to back his selection on each race for me. I got away in time for the [last] race ... dear old Fred had backed a winner in every single race so I made a few bob. I said, 'How on earth do you do it Fred?' And he said, 'All these chaps go round the Far East and you don't back the horse, you back the jockey.'[76]

The ship was ready to leave harbour on 4 September, homeward bound, in good spirits. Lewin would have liked this, his last exit from harbour in command, to be in his usual efficient style. It would in his view have been sensible to ask the head and stern tugs to pull the ship bodily out from the jetty and then steam straight out of harbour. The pilot, however, disagreed because of the strength of the current, and recommended canting the stern out before leaving the berth going astern. Deferring to local knowledge, Lewin agreed; the *Hermes*'s overhanging bow leaned on the jetty; the jetty gave way; a local Press photographer took a picture; and it was not the best of send-offs. It was not often that Lewin confessed to being annoyed, but on this occasion he did. The mandatory Form S232, *Report of Collision or Grounding*, was rendered: it was probably the first and only one of Lewin's career, and no more was heard of it.[77]

By then, in any case, his next step was assured. News of his forthcoming promotion to rear admiral had been received during the passage to Fremantle, to general delight. The next job would undoubtedly be in the Ministry of Defence – the Royal Navy could not forego the Whitehall expertise he had built up in three previous appointments – but the business in hand was to get the ship and her aircraft back in good health and heart.

So the *Hermes* set off across the Indian Ocean for home. The Suez Canal was still closed in the aftermath of the June war, and her course had to take her round the Cape. She was accompanied by a Royal Fleet Auxiliary oiler, at first the *Olna* and then the *Oleander*, to keep her topped up with fuel, and on leaving Fremantle she had also replenished with solid stores from RFA *Reliant*.[78] Indeed, during the whole of her deployment replenishments at sea had been numerous and essential; the diminishing number of shore bases, and the immense operational advantage of independence from them for fuelling and storing, were lessons that had been learnt well (if, compared with the US Navy, a little late) by the Royal Navy of the 'Fifties and 'Sixties. A 'six-ship RAS' [Replenishment at Sea], conducted in late August with three warships including *Hermes* and three RFAs all steaming alongside each other, and faithfully recorded in the commission book, was a bit of showmanship, but it was a token of the importance of the system.

There was no fixed-wing flying on the way home, apart from mail runs for a single Gannet first to Mauritius, then to Capetown. Terry Lewin knew, as any commanding officer does, the importance of mail to a ship's company and took every opportunity of sending and receiving it. It had been part of the naval system for hundreds of years, as had the serial letter to those at home. Terry still wrote to Jane every day.

The technical departments were fully occupied in getting the ship in perfect shape for her return to operations once the Portsmouth turn-round was completed with, necessarily, a large number of personnel changes as well as the captain's. The voyage was begun on the star-board shaft only, with one boiler room shut down, and when work on that unit was completed after a week, the port engine and the other boiler room took over, 19 knots being maintained throughout. They passed Ascension Island, flying some personnel ashore by helicopter for onward passage by air to the United Kingdom; without any claim to second sight, Lewin did not record how handy the base might be in later years. On 27 September, with both units fully restored and connected, they passed the Canaries.

Although the ship and particularly the technical departments had been busy during the passage, tempo had naturally dropped because of the lack of intensive flying, and there was time for recreational activity of all sorts. A full-scale concert party was organised – carriers' hangars, even when occupied by aircraft, make good theatres – eighteen giant 'oggies' (Cornish pasties) were consumed, deck games of all sorts were played, and there was even a session of compulsory PT, lower deck being cleared for the occasion. The captain got around; it had always been his habit to visit remote parts of the ship during the middle watch at sea, and he was known to have his own enamel mug in 'B' boiler room where the best cocoa was brewed.[79] Someone said he knew every man in the ship by name; his memory was legendary.

So the *Hermes* came home. She flew off her jet squadrons to their various naval air stations on 29 September, the Gannets and a stray

Buccaneer on the 30th, and late on 1 October anchored in Spithead. Then came the tiresome business of clearing customs, with everyone anxious to get ashore. Lewin's approach was typical: 'The Customs men came off at 7.30 am and ... we sat them down in the Wardroom and gave them a whacking good breakfast ... I don't know if it made any difference ...'[80] – but the principle of goodwill, followed throughout the commission, was fully honoured.

There was ten days' leave for each watch: for those who were to continue the commission, it might not have been as much as they had hoped for at its outset, but it was incomparably better than staying east of Suez with the Aden withdrawal commitment approaching. Lewin's plan, of which he was justly proud to the end of his life, had worked.

He turned over command to Captain Doug Parker, an experienced aviator who was much looking forward to the *Hermes*. Lewin himself left in style by helicopter from the ship at South Railway Jetty, Portsmouth, to the parade ground at HMS *Vernon*. His car was pre-positioned for the drive back to Pitfields:

> Having got home I said to Jane, 'There you are, that's it. I'm now a rear admiral, there are only two seagoing jobs for a rear admiral and I won't get either of those so I shall never go to sea again and I shall always be home' – famous last words ...[81]

Command of a big ship, for those lucky enough to achieve it, must be one of the high points of a naval career and no apologies are necessary for the length of narrative in this chapter. But the wealth of evidence volunteered by those who served in this commission, and the amount of space devoted to it in Lewin's personal memoir, deserve a few closing remarks.

You do not get sailors referring to their ship as the 'Happy *Hermes*' without good reason. That phrase occurred several times in correspondence. Even more telling was the expression 'dream team' applied to the Lewin–Fieldhouse combination.[82] The word 'inspiring' was used by more than one correspondent, and a frequent comment was, 'You felt you could not let him down.'

But the loyalty was two-way. His consideration for his whole company was well known. He fought, in his measured and reasoned way, for their welfare throughout the commission: the maintenance period in Malta, brief but welcome breaks even for a few hours in Cyprus and Aden and Gan, the long-delayed sojourn in Singapore with careful arrangements for leave parties, and above all the return to the United Kingdom, were all on his initiative, though fully backed and implemented by the administration beneath him.

He was most concerned about the links with families at home. He personally founded the *Hermes* Families' Association which finished with some 600 members – only a very few opted out – and provided not only contacts that were useful when families flew out to join the ship during her brief respites from operations, but a *Hermes Families' Herald* that, probably a good deal less rumbustious than the daily on-board paper, kept wives and families in touch with happenings on board.

He adopted an entirely sensible approach to the rum issue which, at that time, was still made in the Royal Navy.[83] Normally it was made at noon and, at one-eighth of a pint of strong spirits – even though diluted in the issue to junior ratings – was not a recommended diet for someone who might have the delicate job of preparing a complex aircraft for flying that afternoon. Lewin instituted a later issue when flying had finished for the day, with the option of beer instead. In this he was years ahead of his time and it is still something of a mystery how his supply officer, the immensely able Commander Tom Bradbury, swung it past the authorities.

Humour was never far away. Carriers have always had strong photographic sections, and it was well known that the captain enjoyed seeing pictures with the potential for captions. The most famous was probably the photograph of *Hermes* doing a full-circle turn on trials: this was a perfect commentary on her gyrations during the Middle East crises. A picture of a lugubrious sailor greeted the incoming flag officer's staff on arrival off Aden with the legend, 'Welcome to Happy *Hermes*'. When LeFanu inspected the rum and beer issue, a picture appeared of the issuing officer of the day, a large and daunting figure, apparently demanding, 'Forgotten your beer card then?' And when the ship returned to the United Kingdom, it had already been noted that, in the wake of the 1967 devaluation and national gloom, some patriots had begun a campaign with the slogan, 'I'm backing Britain' – so *Hermes* sent out a postcard, appropriately featuring the Union flag as well as a picture of the ship, that said simply, 'I'm Back in Britain'.

It had not been all wine and roses. There had been sadnesses and crises, and Lewin's straightforward Christian faith had been tested more than once. But the sheer spirit and buoyancy of the man, his vitality and above all his interest in and commitment to his people, had overcome all the difficulties and produced something that was remembered with joy and gratitude by very many. When he cleared lower deck at the start of the commission, with the gloom of the Defence Review all around, he had said, '"*Hermes*'s commission is going to be the best of the lot". I don't suppose they believed me but I think two years later they probably did …' They did.

A NON-JOB RESTORED:
ASSISTANT CHIEF OF NAVAL STAFF
(POLICY), 1968–1969

Terry Lewin joined the Ministry of Defence as Assistant Chief of Naval Staff (Policy) early in January 1968. He was, as was customary, in plain clothes; officers in the ministry wore uniform only rarely, so he was not immediately able to put up the one broad and one narrower stripe of a rear-admiral. But the word was around: one messenger was heard saying to another, 'Who's that new bloke then?' 'Oh, he's one of them new sub-lieutenant admirals.' 'Puts you in your place,' muttered Lewin.[1]

A lot had been going on while he was away in *Hermes*. The 'Sixties were in full swing; for the West it was a time of great social and domestic volatility, with every assumption questioned, every attitude challenged, specially by the younger generation. Extremes of personal freedom were fashionable, institutions – including the fighting services – deeply unfashionable. The increasing American involvement in Vietnam caused great resentment, not only in America. Successful defences of freedom, such as Britain's confrontation with Indonesia and the consequent survival of Malaysia and Singapore as independent states, were not mentioned.

Britain's foreign policy increasingly reflected disillusion with empire and the residue of empire. The 1966 Defence Review had planned for withdrawal from East of Suez in the late 1970s;[2] the 1967 Supplementary Statement on Defence Policy[3] had accelerated this programme, with complete withdrawal from the Singapore naval base and head-quarters by the mid-'70s. There was some reference to a generalised East of Suez presence, though just how it was to be achieved was not spelt out. More specific commitments such as Hong Kong had more precise military provision, but at reduced levels.

Against this shifting background the Royal Navy had been attempting to restructure itself in the wake of the Defence Review's decision to phase out the fixed-wing aircraft carriers. Admiral Sir Varyl Begg had replaced Luce as First Sea Lord after the latter's resignation. A tough and determined man, he had the reputation of holding no preconceived brief for aircraft carriers, and neither did his Vice Chief, Vice Admiral Sir John Bush. On the other hand, both were realists with a firm grasp of what sea power could and should do, and of what might and might not run politically in Whitehall, and that went too for Bush's successor in late 1967, Vice Admiral Sir Peter Hill-Norton.

The staff work of producing plans for a restructured fleet had been put in the hands of the Assistant Chief of Naval Staff (Policy), Rear Admiral John Adams. This was a new post, created principally for this purpose, though parallelism with the Air Staff organisation may also have had something to do with it. A Future Fleet Working Party, with Adams as chairman and a very broad remit, was formed with instructions to report within six months.[4] Many of its recommendations were uncontroversial: continuation of the nuclear-powered submarine programme, destroyers of relatively austere character but with good air defence weapons, general purpose frigates which, like the destroyers, would have embarked helicopters, and the retention of the newly acquired or converted amphibious vessels. It still saw the need, though, for some large air-capable ships and, controversially as it turned out, recommended 'a cruiser' capable of operating both helicopters and Vertical or Short Take Off and Landing (V/STOL) aircraft.

Whether Begg was intellectually convinced that sooner or later the Navy would need such a class of ship, or not, is still a matter of doubt. What is certain is that he thought it would be disastrously premature to put it before the government at that stage – it was then, around Easter 1967, not much more than a year after the carrier decision had been announced. The maximum that might be acceptable would be something on the lines of the escort cruiser, thought of in DTWP nearly ten years before,[5] with a complement of anti-submarine helicopters. The possibility of V/STOL aircraft could perhaps be reconsidered when the time was right. Hill-Norton, more warm towards the notion of V/STOL, went fully along with Begg's view on timing, while remaining poised to raise the stakes when it was opportune to do so.[6]

Adams had been extremely disappointed by the rejection of his Future Fleet package, which he regarded as a coherent whole. He was not consoled by the announcement in the 1967 Supplementary Statement that the Type 82 fleet escort vessel – large, expensive, and now inappropriate because there would be no fleet carriers for it to escort – would be developed in two ways: expanded as a cruiser (of unspecified shape) to carry numbers of anti-submarine helicopters and command and control facilities, and downsized to an austere destroyer with a good air defence capability. This was a curious formulation because both new designs were to be of all gas turbine propulsion while the Type 82 was steam and gas, and were to have helicopters as essential elements of their armament while the Type 82 had none; but political and presentational acceptability was what counted. In fact, many of the recommendations of the Future Fleet Working Party were translated into action and stood the test of time;[7] but Adams did not seek further employment.

Thus, when Terry Lewin joined the Ministry of Defence in January 1968, he was effectively walking into a non-job. The Future Fleet Working Party had been and gone; some subsequent work by Adams, on the reorganisation of the Home Commands, had been put in the hands of the formidable Admiral Sir John Frewen for implementation as the first Commander-in-Chief, Naval Home Command, and he was not likely to seek much advice from the ministry; and Lewin was not in the direct line of command which ran from the First Sea Lord, through the Vice Chief of Naval Staff, to the Operations and Plans Directorates.

But he was also walking into the first breath of a financial and policy typhoon. The economic position of the country had radically worsened in the second half of 1967, culminating in the devaluation of November that year.[8] Deflationary measures and budgetary cuts were essential, and defence could not be immune. Some relief was given by the early retirement of *Victorious* who suffered a serious fire in late 1967,[9] but much more 'red meat' (in Healey's expressive phrase) was required.

All came to a head on 15–16 January 1968, a few days after Terry Lewin joined the Ministry of Defence. The 16th was called 'Black

Tuesday' by many. By the end of it, according to the historians of the Chiefs of Staff, each service had endured its 'own Calvary':

> Grandy, the CAS, was forced to accept the cancellation of the F111 to save dollars, and cuts in the RAF transport force to save pounds. Baker, the CGS, was faced with the loss of a further nine fighting units, and with the halving of the Brigade of Gurkhas. And LeFanu, the [incoming] First Sea Lord, was presented with the daunting task of reshaping the Navy for a primarily North Atlantic role without carriers ...'[10]

The bald fact was that henceforth NATO was to be the sole justification for British defence provision. Withdrawal from the Far East bases would be accelerated to 1971–2; the fixed-wing carriers would go in the same time-scale; residual commitments outside the NATO area would be cut to the bone.

As a shift in strategic priorities, the decision of mid-January 1968 stands far and away ahead of any comparable post-war British development. It was highly palatable to the Treasury, who now had a simple stick by which defence expenditure could be measured (or beaten). It was less so to the Foreign Office, though the more European wing could see advantage in it. It was not mortal to the Army or the Royal Air Force, who had large forces already dedicated to the NATO role. But it posed grave risks to the Royal Navy as a balanced force capable of exerting sea power in a way it was accustomed to doing.[11]

There were some factors helpful to the Navy. First, NATO strategy had undergone an important change in the late 1960s. The previous strategy[12] based upon a fairly thin trip-wire of conventional forces in place in central Europe, with the prospect of massive nuclear retaliation in case of Soviet aggression, was increasingly suspect because of doubts that the USA would embark on such retaliation when threatened with a Soviet counter-strike. It had been replaced by the doctrine of Flexible Response,[13] which with its assumption of a more prolonged phase of conventional warfare gave scope for naval activity in reinforcement and resupply, as well as more diverse scenarios in which sea power in various forms could be applied.

Secondly, the Threat could be brought in as evidence. The Soviet Navy was an increasingly numerous and effective force, with strong emphasis on submarines.[14] The Royal Navy had much expertise and experience in warfare at the higher levels but particularly in the anti-submarine field. The United States Navy was preoccupied with Vietnam, and could be expected to welcome a strong British naval contribution to NATO as highly desirable if not essential.

Thirdly, the flanks of NATO, in Turkey and north Norway, were vulnerable, politically sensitive and possible arenas for Soviet incursion, either as isolated and limited acts or as part of a more general aggression. British amphibious forces were well placed and could readily be adapted to support the northern flank in particular.

All these plus points had been taken into account by a prescient Director of Naval Plans, Captain David Williams, during the previous year. A Concept of Operations West of Suez had been prepared, NATO earmarkings of ships and auxiliaries had been subtly increased, commitments to the NATO Standing Naval Force Atlantic had been fully honoured, and contributions to its new On Call Force in the Mediterranean had been volunteered.[15] The Naval Staff was as prepared as it could be, though formidable problems remained.

One was presentational. Having for years justified its major force on a strategy that put such emphasis on East of Suez presence and operations, the Royal Navy had very quickly to formulate and declare a new outlook. Begg was shortly to hand over to LeFanu, and Hill-Norton was exceptionally busy, in close collaboration with the Plans Directorate, driving the new concepts through the ministry itself. But the Navy's change of direction had to be taken to as many influential elements in the country at large as possible. To groups of defence professionals, particularly, a high level of presentation was required. Lewin was known to be an able communicator, and was considered ideal to take on this task.

His most testing assignment was before a meeting of the Royal United Services Institution[16] on 14 February – his wedding anniversary, which he might have thought a good augury. The audience included many officers serving and retired, some of them considerably senior to Lewin, and representatives of the Press. Both speech and question period were on the record. Opening the meeting, the chairman, the retired Admiral Sir Deric Holland-Martin, said 'Rear-Admiral Lewin … is not giving the lecture at an easy time.'

Lewin began by a survey of the pattern of conflict as it had emerged during the nuclear age. From British and other nations' experience, he derived the view that for the non-superpowers, 'war as an instrument of policy can only be used at a very low level and therefore at a level relatively safe from nuclear escalation; for wars of the higher and more dangerous levels only a very short period of time will be available to achieve the aim before the superpowers will combine for their own safety to bring it to an end'.

He acknowledged that the deterrent effect of this pattern had served to stop many conflicts reaching the shooting stage at all, and then linked these principles to the European theatre which was now the primary concern of all British forces. After paying his respects to the 'land shield forces', their prime task 'meeting aggression at every stage', he went on to the naval 'concept of operations both in Europe and outside it which can be likened to that of the chess board, with the deployment of lightly armed frigates, the pawns which are the symbol of our interest, backed when necessary by ships and air power of high capability to provide the whole spectrum of maritime deterrence against air, surface or submarine threat.'

The next section of his speech dealt with Soviet sea power in its broadest sense: not only the Soviet Navy but the oceanographic, merchant, fishing and intelligence-gathering fleets. This was a relatively easy bogeyman to raise – it was well known that Fleet Admiral Gorshkov had recently published his *Sea Power of the State*, the culmination of his challenge to western sea supremacy – but Lewin used moderate language:

This many-sided Soviet initiative with its diffuse and possibly devious aims is far too complex to be faced with rigid formations and pre-conceived tactical ideas ... we must be prepared to match the Russians in *quality* though, of course, we cannot hope ... to match it in *quantity* ... there really is a threat at sea which, in the absence of any international enforcement, we cannot ignore.

Lewin then turned to 'the stake that western Europe has at sea'. He produced telling statistics about dependence on sea traffic, including sea traffic beyond the NATO area that ended in the Atlantic at the Tropic of Cancer, and suggested that 'NATO ... will look to Britain as the most powerful maritime nation of the alliance in Europe to give the lead'. He paid tribute to the newly formed Standing Naval Force Atlantic, and then made one of the more startling statements of the lecture: 'It is not too fanciful to suppose that the concept will spread ... into an altogether larger organisation which could become a European Navy keeping pace with political developments.'

He moved on to discuss the shape of the future fleet, which covered already familiar ground, though he began 'without apology' with the fixed-wing carrier and what it provided, 'defensive versatility and some commanding offensive power ... that was why we liked it so much'. Now the Navy would have to re-provide these qualities, the defensive versatility by the cruiser-destroyer-frigate mix and the offensive power by the nuclear-powered fleet submarines. 'Lord Fisher,' he said, '50 years ago had this concept. Then, he hadn't the means, now we have.'

He acknowledged the necessity to continue development of the mine counter-measures force in both the European and outside-Europe theatres – the latter was still respectable in this context because the British were helping to clear the Suez Canal at the time, in the wake of the Six-day War. He paid attention to the utility on the flanks of NATO of the amphibious forces, and the need to maintain a full spectrum of afloat support to 'ensure the fleet remains self-contained and truly mobile'. His reference to the Polaris force was brief – 'a separate entity though not a private navy' – although he found time for a tribute to the way the project had been managed.

No lecture on naval concepts, at that time or any other, was likely to end without some observation such as:

> It is nearly always the unexpected that happens. Ships last a long time ... the strategic background against which a ship is conceived, designed and built is usually changed beyond recognition by the time that ship has reached the mid-point of its operational life. This puts the premium on flexibility of outlook and flexibility of purpose ... Whatever task our ships may be called upon to carry out in the future ... I am sure that the ships we plan, and the men who man them, will still be able to produce this flexibility of response whenever they may be called upon to do so.

Lewin was subjected to some fairly probing questions from the floor, including some pressure about how nuclear-powered submarines could be directed as offensive weapon systems when, as one questioner put it, they were 'blind, cannot communicate very well, and ... cannot distinguish between friend and foe.' He contented himself with saying that there were such problems, but they 'must be and are being overcome'. (In the event, it was to take some time).

There was one hostage to fortune: in answer to a question about V/STOL aircraft he replied that 'We have at present no plans for operating the Harrier ... from our ships. We have studied it, and we have found that it has no useful application in the shape of Navy we can afford in the future.' That was indeed the party line at the time; only a few months later, with LeFanu installed as First Sea Lord, the answer would have been a very different one. The episode does indicate, however, that Lewin was not prepared, after only five weeks in the job, to step out of line on the issue. 'At present' was a qualifying phrase, but not a strong one, and the rest of the answer left few options open. Technically he was quite right; the Harrier, *in its then specification*, was not a useful vehicle for shipborne operation. But the party line took too little account of its potential.

Clearly the speech was regarded as an important one, for it was reprinted (without any account of the question period) by the Navy's

Directorate of Public Relations[17] later that year. To some extent, of course, it was a distillation of current naval staff doctrine; even sub-lieutenant admirals have people to draft their speeches, and there is no doubt that some of the wording was not originally Lewin's. But it is equally certain that he would have given a strong steer to the drafters, would not have allowed to pass anything with which he did not funda-mentally agree, and applied his own gloss to the phraseology as well as putting it over in his direct, persuasive way.

Curiously, during his tenure as ACNS (Policy) this was about the one truly 'policy' matter with which he was directly charged. But it informed the whole of the rest of his work, which was much more to do with the organisation and supporting structure of the Navy.

Hill-Norton, realising that there was no ready-made remit for the new ACNS(P) but knowing Terry Lewin's abilities from previous appointments, sent for him early on and instructed him to 'sniff around' in several areas.[18] Finance was desperately tight, and Hill-Norton was convinced that many of the supporting arms were being run in an uneconomic way. He was particularly suspicious of the director-generals' empires in the personnel and materiel departments; of the dockyards, which had been favourite targets of cost-cutters since the days of Samuel Pepys; and of the training world, still ruled by the separate schools that taught Gunnery, Torpedo, Anti-Submarine Warfare, Navigation and Tactical Control, and Communications.

The machinery that was set up to help Lewin grapple with these questions was a throwback to an earlier organisation set up by Mount-batten in the mid-1950s, the Way Ahead Committee.[19] Then it had been at Board level and had done much work in rationalising and stream-lining a diffuse set of institutions, many of which were relics of the Second World War. The cuts in operational units during the 'Sixties clearly gave the opportunity for a further round in reducing the admin-istrative and logistic support structure. However, this time the investiga-tion was to be conducted at a lower level, and the Way Ahead Executive Sub-Committee (WAESC) was constituted with Lewin in the chair.

The first area to tackle was the store and ammunition depots, a task in which Lewin was helped by Captain Frank Hearn, a Supply and

Secretariat officer of great experience. Most of the opportunities for savings came from the shut-down of naval fixed-wing flying; sensibly, the Royal Navy took over many of the helicopter deep maintenance and repair tasks for all the services at Fleetlands, Hampshire, while the store depot at Perth and workshops at Llangennech in South Wales were closed.[20] These closures appear to have attracted remarkably little controversy, perhaps because they involved only 1300 savings in civilian posts.

It was a different matter with the Royal Dockyards. The Royal Navy employed altogether at that time 48,500 industrial civil servants, the great majority in the dockyards, and this was a matter of the greatest concern to the 30-year-old, newly appointed Minister for the Navy, David Owen – particularly as his Parliamentary constituency was Plymouth (Sutton).[21] There were four yards: Portsmouth, Devonport, Chatham and Rosyth. Lewin instituted a major study on whether a Navy without carriers needed all of them.

In the view of his committee it clearly did not; three were all that were necessary. The front-runner for closure was Chatham, because if it was closed many other useful savings would come in its wake: the barracks there could be closed, and the Supply and Secretariat School relocated.[22] But refitting facilities for nuclear-powered submarines were a critical problem. The Polaris submarines were destined for refit in Rosyth where a suitable facility had been built up. Rosyth might also have spare capacity to handle the occasional nuclear-powered fleet submarine. But years before, it had been decided to locate the necessary second stream of nuclear refits at, of all places, Chatham. The only rationale for this, in the view of most people in the Ministry of Defence, was that a far-sighted Director of Dockyards intent on keeping his empire intact had persuaded the authorities that it was the right place to put it. The obvious place to have the plant was Devonport, with its deep-water access and very large skilled work-force. But the Chatham facility was under construction in 1968, nearing the point of no return, and industrial difficulties as well as a lot of egg on faces were threatened. The Admiralty Board was not disposed to change the plans.

Nevertheless Lewin, with the support of Commander Derek Satow, an engineer officer with dockyard experience, persisted in his recommendation that Chatham should close. He enlisted the help of David Owen, who had some explaining of his own to do if he was not to be accused of shameless support of his own constituency to the detriment of Kent. Owen was convinced of the essential good sense of the Way Ahead recommendation for the long term, as well as its benefits for Plymouth (Sutton). The difficulty then was to produce a rationale, as well as a plan for an expensive new facility at Devonport, that would satisfy Healey – still Secretary of State for Defence – and the Treasury. Owen finally managed to convince Healey, well after Lewin had left the post of ACNS(P), that it made sense.[23] The third refitting stream at Devonport had to be presented as a technical necessity related to the increasing number of nuclear-powered submarines joining the fleet and then coming up for their first refits; when the time was opportune, it could be said that the hump had been negotiated, the need for a third stream no longer existed, and Chatham could be closed down. Thus the need for 'presentation' (a word of growing vogue in the Ministry of Defence) could be met.

The question of the training establishments was equally complicated. The new-entry training schools, for both officers and ratings, were excluded from the WAESC's remit; but even then there were vested interests in plenty, no less formidable than the dockyards with their well entrenched officers and trade unions. In training, the obstacles were the specialist 'tribes' with potentially powerful backers among senior officers of their respective specialisations, and local constituencies, many of significant influence, that liked having a naval establishment on their doorstep. For this study Lewin had the help of Captain Peter LaNeice, a fellow gunnery specialist and old friend, who had been seconded to the WAESC for the detailed work.[24]

Once again old acquaintance, formed long ago at Whale Island, helped in thrashing out policy. Captain John Marrack, well known to both Lewin and LaNeice, held a key post in the Naval Personnel Department as the Director of Naval Manpower Planning. His acute mind was well tuned to likely developments in the training field. He foresaw that the rigid demarcations between specialisations, both in officers and ratings, would be broken down in a way that made both maintenance and operation of weapon systems more flexible and efficient. It would, therefore, make sense to concentrate training in fewer schools, those that had the most up-to-date facilities; these were the Electrical School HMS *Collingwood*, the Engineering School HMS *Sultan* and the Navigation and Action Information School HMS *Dryad*, all in the Portsmouth area.[25]

It is interesting to take a look, from the vantage point of 30 years, and see how all the various currents in this area were flowing in the same direction. Vice Admiral Edward Ashmore, soon to relieve Hill-Norton as Vice Chief of Naval Staff, had become convinced that the specialist system should be radically overhauled 'with a view to producing people who were tactically or warfare qualified'[26] and had written a powerful paper on the subject. Lewin himself was to put that notion into effect in the operations rooms of the fleet within the next year, as the next chapter will show. And in what might be regarded as the bastion of specialist training, the Portsmouth Command, the Commander-in-Chief Sir John Frewen had 'instructed the staff that they should not obstruct but co-operate'.[27]

So the plan, appropriately named Constrain, was formulated. Probably because it was seen by so many as an inevitable consequence of the way the tide was flowing, it was accepted without too much outcry. There were anomalies: the Signals School, HMS *Mercury* near Petersfield, survived as a separate entity, largely it is said through the influence of Earl Mountbatten.[28] And, as such things inevitably do, it took many years to implement; this book will revisit the scheme as its effects reverberated through Lewin's career. But it did happen, and its main provisions were summarised in the Defence White Paper of 1970:[29]

The rearrangement of general naval training establishments in four ... centres devoted to:

- Weapon engineering training at HMS *Collingwood*;
- Marine engineering training at HMS *Sultan*;

- Tactical/operations training at HMS *Dryad*;
- Ship fighting and management training at HMS *Excellent*.

The new plan involves the eventual closure of the following establishments, their tasks being centralised in the establishments listed ... above:

- RN Tactical School, Woolwich;
- HMS *Dauntless* (WRNS new entry training [at Burghfield, Reading]);
- HMS *Vernon* (torpedo and anti-submarine training [at Gunwharf, Portsmouth]);
- HMS *Pembroke* (supply and secretariat training [at Chatham]);
- HMS *Royal Arthur* (petty officers' training [at Corsham, Wilts]).

The White Paper appears to have been modest in its claim that the savings would amount to 250 naval and 200 civilian posts, and running costs of £1 million a year, for a capital cost outlay of £6.4 million. It is very hard to review such figures in retrospect, because it is so hard to speculate on what might have happened if things had remained as they were. Nevertheless there is no doubt that the Constrain exercise, even if parts of it were substantially modified and others took a long time to mature, did turn out successfully to the benefit of the Navy and the Exchequer.

One other task given to Terry Lewin as ACNS(P) was, according to him, accomplished with extraordinary ease. This was a reorganisation of the Naval Staff as a result of a directive from the Secretary of State which ordered that the posts of the Deputy Chiefs of Staff were to be abolished. It was in fact a godsend for the Navy in Whitehall, whose complex and top-heavy organisation has many times been apparent in this book. Lewin, harnessing the same tides that had been operating in the Constrain studies, recommended the retention of the Directorates of Naval Plans, Operations and Naval Air Warfare, but the abolition of those of Gunnery, Underwater Warfare, Navigation and Tactical Control, Communications and the overarching Tactical and Weapons Policy, and their replacement by Directorates of Naval Warfare and Operational Requirements. There was to be an Assistant Chief of Naval Staff (Operational Requirements) and the whole staff would answer to the Vice Chief.

This rearrangement was so evidently sensible, in tune with the times and compatible with the other services' staff organisation, as well as the emerging central staff structure, that it went through the Board with scarcely a murmur and remained in place for the rest of Lewin's career, suffering substantial modification only as a result of the Heseltine restructuring in the mid-1980s.[30]

Not far into 1969, Lewin had been informed by LeFanu that he was to be sent to be Flag Officer Second in Command, Far East Fleet, the appointment to take effect in August of that year. 'So all that jazz about telling Jane that I would never go to sea again was wrong and I was going abroad for at least 15 months, maybe 18 months without coming home.'[31] But of course it would have been professionally senseless to refuse such an appointment. Even though the Far East Fleet was beginning to run down as a result of government plans, it was still a highly attractive job, with a great deal of independence; while the Flag Officer was subordinate to the Commander of the Far East Fleet, based ashore in Singapore, who himself came under the unified Commander-in-Chief Far East, the station was so widespread that there was ample opportunity for initiative and a considerable challenge to leadership.

It was, without doubt, a sign of the Board's confidence in him that this post was offered. His time in the non-job had turned out very well; the opportunity had been seized, as Hill-Norton had expected it would be, and Lewin had enhanced his reputation as a thinker, an organiser and a persuader. His abilities at sea in charge of a single ship or small group had been amply proved; now he had a larger formation to command.

There was time for some leave before he flew out to Singapore. There was a family occasion: Susie was married to Pete Roe in

Tunbridge Wells, a happy time recalled by Terry with great affection. The closeness of the Lewin family has been apparent no doubt throughout this book, and his joy in this event is clear from his memoir. It is also demonstrated by the fact that his granddaughter Emily Roe acted as dedicated secretary and helper during the last months of his life, and grandson Cosmo spoke so movingly at the Service of Thanksgiving. Love and loyalty, as always, worked in both directions.

THE FAR EAST FLEET
1969–1970

The Far East Fleet might be running down, but it was by no means a negligible force. In July 1969, under the previous Flag Officer Second in Command, Vice Admiral Anthony Griffin, it had taken part in the fifteen-day Exercise 'Julex 69' with participation from the navies of Australia, Malaysia and New Zealand and air forces from all these countries and the United States Navy as well. Altogether 5500 men had been involved, and the Royal Navy's participation had included eleven surface warships, three submarines and six auxiliaries.[1]

It was, therefore, a substantial outfit that Rear Admiral Lewin was to take over in August 1969. He knew Griffin well and was in no doubt that it would be an efficient force as well as powerful on paper. Equally, though, having served on the station before, he was conscious of the sapping effect of being 'too long in the sun',[2] the extended periods at sea caused by the great distances between one port and another, and the relative scarcity of facilities for weapon training. It would be up to him to keep the fleet up to the mark operationally. The programme and major items of administration, including all provision for docking and maintenance, would be handled by the Fleet Commander (Vice Admiral Sir William O'Brien, another old friend) and his staff in Singapore.

To help him in his task Terry Lewin had a small staff: six officers including his secretary, Commander Paddy Sheehan, and his Staff Officer (Operations), Commander Neil MacEacharn, seven chief or petty officers and fifteen junior rates. Some of these were his retinue of cooks and stewards, essential for the amount of entertaining expected of him as a flag officer, and the rest concerned with communications, tactical control and secretarial work. It was very much an itinerant staff, with no permanent home except for a small rear link office in Singapore; when it moved from flagship to flagship, it transferred its gear in a set of laundry baskets, often slung between ship and ship on a jackstay. During his time as FO2, sixteen months, gear was shifted thirty times and the whole office twelve times.[3]

He was given little enough time to catch his breath after arriving in Singapore in the steamy heat of early August. He embarked almost at once in HMS *London*, Captain Loasby, which was to be his flagship for the rest of the year (it was not until 1970 that the multitude of flag shifts really began). She was a destroyer of the 'County' class, big and comfortable ships that before the Second World War would have been called light cruisers and were said to have been classed as destroyers only to get the design past the Treasury.[4] They were powered by a mixture of steam plant and gas turbines and deployed four 4.5-inch guns and the relatively new first-generation Seaslug surface-to-air missile system.

London made her way to Hong Kong by way of Subic Bay for missile firings, which were not successful, and in Hong Kong embarked on a 'hearts-and-minds' project, building a jetty for a remote community, which was.[5] Hong Kong was by now well known to Terry Lewin and a standard port of call for the Far East Fleet. The next commitment was to be more singular: attendance at the bicentenary of Captain Cook's first landing in New Zealand on 9 October 1769. It was to be held at the small community of Gisborne, where the landing took place, with participation from the navies of Australia, Canada, France, New Zealand and the United States as well as three British vessels. Lewin, who subsequently became a considerable expert on Cook, admitted that at that time he knew little about the great navigator and surveyor. The staff acquired the necessary books (including the early work of Beaglehole, whom Lewin met soon afterwards) and FO2 made good use of the long passage south, steaming as he said through those very waters in which Cook sailed.

There was a well-managed formation anchorage on 8 October for the ships of all five participating nations (New Zealand, Australia, Canada, UK, USA) in Poverty Bay on 8 October, and the celebrations next day were memorable.[6] The Hydrographer of the Navy, Rear Admiral G. S. Ritchie, himself a past director of the New Zealand hydrographic service and a maker of modern charts of Gisborne – most of which bore out the accuracy of Cook's original work – added professional and historic lustre. The Governor General was present, and there were ceremonies of royal guards, fly-past and Beat Retreat, accompanied by three combined bands, varied and enlivened by Maori challenge, Powhiri and Haka. But it was the warmth and genuineness of the welcome and hospitality in this quite small community that touched all in the ships that were there: as one example of many, it was said that one sailor was invited to a Maori home where a sheep was ceremonially roasted, and festivities went on until 4 am when he was escorted back to the *London* by the whole community who sang farewell from the jetty.

After that, further port visits in New Zealand might have been expected to be an anticlimax, but both Wellington in North Island and Lyttelton, the port of Christchurch in South Island, were full of hospitality and goodwill. The Tasman Sea was not, and by the time the *London* reached Tasmania, her next place of call, 'the ship was covered from masthead to waterline in salt water so we really needed to stop somewhere and have a fresh water wash down so that the ship looked gleaming for arrival in Hobart'.[7] They consulted the charts and decided on Adventure Bay, which appeared suitable:

> I went down to my cabin, took out one of my Cook books and discovered that this was where Cook himself had anchored when he was looking for somewhere to repair his rigging after crossing the Southern Ocean. Nothing ever changes.[8]

The stay in Hobart was restful compared with the rest of the cruise, and was notable for a joyful reunion with Alan 'Tassie' Richmond,[9] who had served with Terry in *Ashanti*, had been to his and Jane's wedding and had taken a cine film of it. Now he was editor of a newspaper in northern Tasmania and drove down to collect Terry for a tour and weekend at home. It was a welcome break, for the next visit was to the bustling city of Melbourne, and it was the time of the Melbourne Cup.

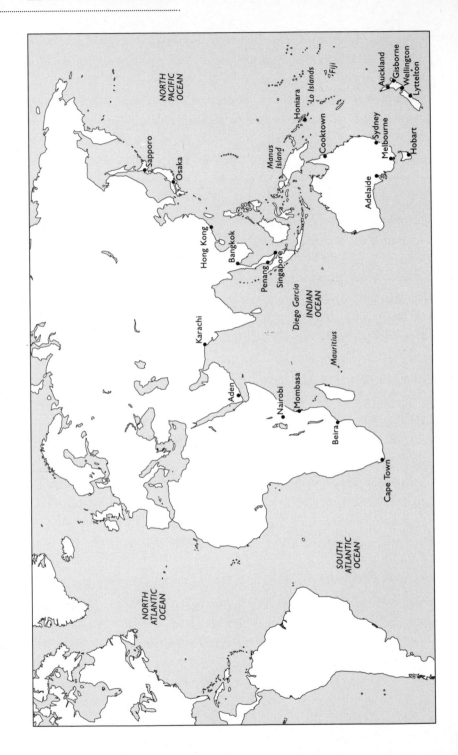

Lewin was not a racing man, and eagerly seized on the proximity of the range at Woomera, and the fact that missile trials were going on there – though they probably stopped for the Melbourne Cup, as everything else in Australia does. In any case, he went to Woomera instead of the races and was most impressed with the potential of the systems then under trial, the Sea Dart (about to come into service) and the Sea Wolf, in its early experimental stages.

The Melbourne visit was followed by a weapon training period involving ships of the old Commonwealth navies including that of Canada. The Flag Officer Second in Command was beginning to think about his next moves in the working of the fleet, a good deal more advanced than straightforward weapon training. But before he could start on these developments in the organisation of his fleet for battle – which was, after all, his aim in this job, however delightful visiting down-under might be – there were visits to Sydney and Brisbane, which were greatly enjoyed by ships' companies. It was now early summer in Australia, and everyone made the most of their time, though – as is usual for flag officers – Lewin found himself in high-level discussions with both senior naval officers and politicians, to say nothing of the Press.

The fleet units were due to arrive back at Singapore on 9 December, about a week after leaving Brisbane. Now came the opportunity Lewin sought: 'exercises on passage' that would not delay the force too much, and would give the first chance of putting into practice concepts of command and tactical control that were beginning to take shape throughout the Navy, and which Lewin had undertaken to study at sea.

It was all linked to the matter of sub-specialisation of seaman officers that was mentioned in Chapter 11, and was part of the rationale for Lewin's work on the Constrain plan, and his reorganisation of the Naval Staff on more functional and less specialist lines, when he was ACNS(P). Exactly the same problems and tensions were being met at sea. In fact it had been at sea, quite understandably, that the revolution – for that was what it turned out to be – had begun. When he was Flag Officer Second in Command Far East Fleet, in 1968, Vice Admiral

Edward Ashmore had found that, although perhaps superior in efficiency to American Combat Information Centres:

> Our own operations rooms were still not functioning properly. For example, I would ask a question of some perfectly competent officer, who would feel that he had to send for the specialist ... in that particular discipline in order to answer my question fully or at all ... Added to this, it seemed to me that we had far more intelligent ratings than we used to have, and that they were very often underused ... I formed the conclusion that there was something wrong in the way that we were training our officers.[10]

In the guided missile destroyers, moreover, 'air defence systems seemed to be operated in quite different ways depending ... on the approach of the commanding officer of each to the advice he was being given'.[11]

The projected revolution, then, was to have two main thrusts. First, the majority of seaman officers were to be trained in sea warfare as a whole, rather than in one or other specialist arm such as gunnery or underwater weaponry. Secondly, procedures in ships' operations rooms, that handled the information flow and the control of the armament, were to be standardised so that tactical doctrine and operation were common throughout the fleet; that reaction to the ever more time-critical threats posed by fast aircraft, faster missiles, agile submarines and intelligent torpedoes could be instant and effective; and that offensive action could be boldly planned and swiftly executed.

The question, as ever in such interlinked schemes, was where the process should start. Lewin had confronted chicken-and-egg problems like this from his earliest days in Whitehall if not earlier, and so had Ashmore and other supporters of the concept. The solution, as usual, was to advance on several fronts at once, choosing anomalies that were obvious to everyone as points of weakness to be probed and reformed, until the whole plan fell into place. In the Ministry of Defence, a start had already been made with the Constrain plan and the reorganisation of the Naval Staff; Ashmore, now Vice Chief of Naval Staff, had placed further developments there in the hands of the Director of

Right: Eric Lewin, father of Terence Lewin, in the uniform of the East Kent Yeomanry, 1913. *(Tim Lewin).*

Below: A formative experience at 18: Terry Lewin, centre, in a surveying party of the Public Schools Exploring Society's Newfoundland Expedition, 1938. *(British Schools Exploring Society).*

Left: Introduction to life at sea: the training cruiser HMS *Vindictive*, 1939. *(Painting by Vice Admiral Sir Roderick Macdonald, at the Britannia Royal Naval College, Dartmouth).*

Above: HMS *Valiant,* in which Midshipman Lewin served under outstanding commanding and executive officers, 1939–41. *(Crown Copyright).*

Below left: First car, 'Tumblebug', T. T. Lewin up. *(Commander I. W. V. Browne).*

Below centre: A try for the Royal Navy against the Army at Ta Qali, Malta, 1950. *(J. H. Beattie).*

Below: Jane Branch-Evans photographed as a Wren, 1943. She and Lieutenant Lewin married on St Valentine's Day, 1944. *(Lady Lewin's collection).*

HMS *Hermes* after her first modernisation, 1966, under the command of Captain Lewin.
Buccaneers, Sea Vixens and a Gannet on deck. *(Crown Copyright)*.

Top left: First Command: HMS *Corunna, 1955*.
(Crown Copyright).

Left: Squadron Command: HMS *Tenby,* leader of the
Dartmouth Training Squadron, 1963. *(Crown
Copyright)*.

This photograph of HMS *Hermes*, under the command of Captain Lewin, describing a full circle was accompanied by the following piece in a Sunday newspaper of 1967, much prized by the Lewin family:

East of Suez: *The Observer*, 28 May 1967
An abstract from the log of HMS *Ubiquitous*, on passage in the Indian Ocean

C in C Singapore to Ubiquitous:
Urgent amendment sailing orders. Courtesy call South African ports cancelled. Re-embark all coloured personnel and Chinese cooks debarked in anticipation SA visit and alter course for Aden. Render all necessary assistance required by local civil and military authorities to maintain order during disturbances. Report position and estimated time of arrival Aden.
Ubiquitous to C in C Singapore:
Your signal received and understood. Wilco. My position 3.15N 79.44E. ETA Aden – early June.
C in C Singapore to U:
Cancel my last signal. Re-debark Chinese cooks and proceed with all possible speed Hong Kong. Make show of strength during civil disturbances. Equip shore patrols with anti-riot weapons. Stand by to take over Hong Kong–Kowloon ferry service from strikers. Report position and ETA Hong Kong.
U to C in C Singapore:
Wilco. Have fetched around to take up easterly course and my position is again 3.15N 79.44E. ETA Hong Kong – Tuesday week.
C in C to U:
Most urgent. Abandon course for Hong Kong and make all possible speed Gulf of Aqaba. Stand by southern approaches to Strait of Tiran outside territorial waters establishing British presence but in view of delicate situation in area establish it with maximum circumspection. Report position and ETA Tiran.
U to C in C:

Wilco. Have come round to westerly course again and am back at 3.15N 79.44E. ETA Tiran – mid June.
C in C to U:
Note amendment to previous signal. In view local customs and feelings debark Jewish personnel before proceeding Tiran.
U to C in C:
Wilco. In view possible Papal pronouncement on situation advise whether should keep RC's below decks.
C in C to U:
Urgent amendment previous signals. Re-embark forthwith all Jewish personnel debark coloured personnel and proceed with maximum despatch Macao. Establish British presence outside territorial waters in support British Consul. Report ETA Macao
U to C in C:
Wilco. ETA Macao uncertain but expect to be back at 3.15N 79.44E in approximately 10 minutes.
C in C to U:
Urgent re-amendment to amended orders. Political situation United Nations re Aqaba question makes immediate courtesy call African port essential. Debark all white personnel and proceed forthwith Mombasa.
U to C in C:
Wilco. Advise whether Chinese cooks classified white or coloured in Mombasa.
C in C to U:
Correction. Proceed Shanghai establish discreet British presence in support two British diplomats being glued by crowd. In view local sensibilities re defectors re-debark Chinese cooks again.
U to C in C:
Wilco.
C in C to U:
Cancel last signal. Proceed at once Gibraltar make discreet show of strength outside territorial waters of Algeciras.
U to C in C:
Show of strength impossible without full complement Chinese cooks.

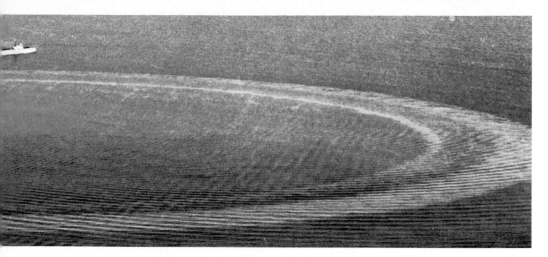

C in C to U:
Re-re-embark Chinese cooks forthwith. Astonished not re-embarked already.
U to C in C:
Wilco. Advise whether should circumnavigate world eastabout or westabout.
C in C to U:
Westabout calling at Malta for major refit. Imperative you reassure local population HM Government still using base.
U to C in C:
Wilco. Have kept helm hard over and am nearly back at 3.15N 79.44E again.
C in C to U:
Correction. Proceed eastabout via North-West passage so as to pass Iceland protect British trawlers suffering harassment Icelandic gunboats.

U to C in C:
Wilco.
C in C to U:
Your signal very faint.
U to C in C:
My signalman very dizzy. But British presence at 3.15N 79.44E almost overpowering. Situation here entirely under control.
C in C to U:
Well done *Ubiquitous.* But in view general world feeling debark all personnel with British nationality before proceeding further.

Copyright © Michael Frayn, 1967 from The Observer *(28 May 1967).*

Reproduced by permission of Greene & Heaton Ltd

Above: Michael Frayn's commentary on the gyrations of HMS *Hermes* in the Indian Ocean, 1967: from *The Observer,* 28 May 1967.

Right: The first deck landing in *Hermes* after refit: a Tiger Moth piloted by Commander D. T. McKeown, the Commander (Air). *(Crown Copyright).*

Left: A Flag Officer enjoying his command: Rear Admiral Terence Lewin as Flag Officer Second in Command Far East Fleet. *(Captain M. Appleton).*

Right: Inspecting the Guard as Commander in Chief Naval Home Command, 1976. *(Navv News).*

Left: Near the beginning of a lifelong interest in Captain James Cook: Lewin ashore at Possession Island, off the east coast of Australia. *(Captain M. Appleton).*

Right: Commander-in-Chief, Fleet: at Admiralty House, Northwood, with Lady Lewin. (*Lady Lewin's collection*)

First Sea Lord and Principal Naval Aide de Camp to Her Majesty the Queen, 1977. *(Crown Copyright).*

Right: Admiral (later Admiral of the Fleet) Sir Henry Leach, who initiated the formation of the Falklands Task Force before the return of Sir Terence Lewin to the United Kingdom in early April 1982. *(Crown Copyright).*

Below: A crucial element of seaborne air power: a Sea Harrier takes off from HMS *Invincible.* *(Crown Copyright).*

Right: San Carlos, May 1982: a Royal Marine mans a machine gun awaiting air attack. As Lewin frequently pointed out, 'the safest place to be was ashore'. *(Press Association).*

Below: 21 May 1982: part of the price. HMS *Ardent,* a prime target of Argentine bombers, burning in San Carlos Water. *(Crown Copyright).*

Above: Royal Marines of 42 Commando disembarking from a helicopter on Mount Kent. *(Crown Copyright).*

Below: The merchant navy's contribution to the Falklands campaign was crucial: the P&O liner *Canberra*, 'the great white whale', fortunately remained unscathed throughout. *(Crown Copyright).*

Above: Installation of Admiral of the Fleet Lord Fieldhouse in the House of Lords, 1988. His supporters are Field Marshal Lord Bramall (right) and Admiral of the Fleet Lord Lewin (right centre). *(Navy News).*

Left: Unveiling by His Royal Highness Prince Philip of the portrait of Lord Lewin in Garter robes, by Michael Noakes, at the Britannia Royal Naval College, Dartmouth. *(J. H. Beattie).*

Left: Inaugurating the Special Entry Book of Remembrance at BRNC Dartmouth. *(J. H. Beattie).*

Right: With Captain Desmond Dickens (left) of Trinity House, at a reunion of Operation 'Pedestal', 1992. *(Captain Desmond Dickens).*

Naval Warfare, Captain Lance Bell Davies, a submariner who had no tribal loyalties to the old specialisations.[12] Lewin was one of those who were to make the initial moves at sea.

He had help from Whitehall. Bell Davies had found that the United States Navy (which did not in any case have such specialised officers as the RN) was also thinking along the lines of 'pre-planned responses' to rapidly developing tactical threats, to be triggered by war-cries that would resound through operations rooms or combat information centres. The British at first used 'Bingo', but this meant something else in American so it was changed to 'Zippo',[13] followed by a numerical suffix indicating the kind of attack that was imminent and setting in train the sequence of appropriate actions; and this was to be introduced to both navies as standard, with subsequent extension to the whole of NATO.

It was these procedures, which were patently necessary and indeed overdue for introduction, that Lewin pioneered in the Far East Fleet. The corollary, and it was self-evident to all but the most diehard, was that all officers, and many senior rates, concerned with tactical and weapon control, should be trained to grasp the whole of the operational situation and not just part of it. That was important not only so that everyone should know his own part in the scheme of things, but that he could if necessary take on the job of his mate next door. Moreover, if everyone was to a degree cross-trained in this way, it would be possible for the ship to be at an acceptable state of readiness for action with only half the crew on watch at a time. 'Defence watches', rather than prolonged periods at action stations with all the ship's company closed up, were to become the norm for periods of tension or even conflict.

The 'passage exercises' during the return to Singapore in December 1969 were the beginning of a steady process that went on throughout Lewin's time in the Far East Fleet, to prove the concept and, just as important, to persuade commanding and other officers that it made sense. The next step, and it was an obvious one, was that seaman officers should no longer be trained in narrow and quasi-technical specialisations but in maritime warfare as a whole. They would henceforth be

'Principal Warfare Officers', no longer gunnery, torpedo, navigation or communications specialists. However, although that was no doubt known to Lewin and he was entirely in tune with it, it would have been premature to stress the idea in the fleet. Instead, he concentrated on the operational questions.

He could, in this field, be very tough with ships that hung back on the new developments. In such a far-flung fleet one of his principal means of keeping ships up to the mark was by inspection, either formal or informal, when he did have them in company,[14] and 'he always went straight for the operations room'.[15] Ships whose organisation for war was slipshod could expect severe correction.

But credit was always given where it was due. He had a day in the submarine *Finwhale*, a conventional boat with a brand-new commanding officer, Lieutenant-Commander Sam Salt. It coincided with Sam's very first dummy attack since passing the submarine commanding officers' course, the 'Perisher', and he had chosen to carry out (or perhaps circumstances had imposed it on him) an extremely ambitious and difficult form of attack that entailed ducking under not one surface escort, but two, in order to get into firing position on his target, which was one of the bigger ships of the fleet. Lewin watched, saying nothing. When the attack was successfully completed, with Salt sweating slightly, Lewin said to him, 'Well done, Sam – I couldn't have done that.'[16]

Nor was he without sympathy for wrong action taken in the heat of the moment. When in command of HMS *Whitby*, Commander Lin Middleton – known to Terry from *Hermes* days – was involved in a snarl-up of frigates featuring a good deal of full-astern manoeuvring, puffs of black smoke and confusion among the ships of the Second Frigate Squadron, but fortunately without any actual collision. Inevitably, FO2 transmitted the well-known signal group that means 'The circumstances of the preceding incident are to be noted with a view to subsequent discussion in harbour' – one better than '*Whitby* wait upon the Admiral with sword and medals', but not much. But in the event the discussion began, 'Did you learn any lessons on Tuesday night?' and ended, after brief and understanding analysis, 'You won't do that again, will you?'[17]

Christmas 1969 and New Year 1970 were a somewhat lonely time for Terry. There had been no plans for Jane to join him at this stage, and he spent the turn of the year at the rest centre at Fraser's Hill, with his flag lieutenant Charles Hunter and his wife to keep him company. While it was cooler, and pleasant, he was professionally anxious to get back to sea. January was traditionally a time for fleet training in the South China Sea, and his new flagship was to be the Assault Ship *Fearless*, commanded by Captain Roger Gerard-Pearse.

Fearless was one of the two 'Landing Ships, Dock' conceived in Lewin's time at the Admiralty in the late 1950s, and had proved her versatility in several operations and exercises since her first commissioning in 1965, notably in the withdrawal from Aden at the beginning of 1968. Of 12,000 tons, she could carry some 400 soldiers – double that number in emergency – and heavy vehicles including tanks, which could be ferried ashore in the four landing craft she carried. With a top speed of 20 knots this specialised amphibious ship was certainly no ocean greyhound and did not look like most people's idea of a flagship, but she was a vessel of great worth and Lewin regarded her as such.

Gerard-Pearse and his ship's company had been on the station well over a year, and it was intended to be a two-and-a-half-year commission – the very last that had been countenanced by the Navy department. Some alleviation had been allowed by the fleet staff: the equivalent of one watch of the ship's company was flown back to the United Kingdom for Christmas 1969, and most of the others had been granted station leave. Nevertheless, in Gerard-Pearse's words:

Terry Lewin was very concerned that we did all that we could for the ship's company and one day he said, 'Roger, why do you call the hands in harbour on a Sunday?' I trooped out the importance of cleaning ship before giving leave again at noon, but this was not good enough! To cut a long story short, we did not call the hands next Sunday and everyone was happy! ... What he got me to do was to challenge 'why' one did many of the routine things and other activities, and to evaluate whether the standard practices being used were necessary or not.[18]

Their first cruise took them up the Malacca Strait to Penang, just beginning to wake out of its elegant sleep as the gateway to the spicy east, and Port Swettenham further down the coast. Then it was through Singapore Strait, with a brief visit to the naval base, and the January exercise with as much of the fleet as could be mustered, traditionally centred on Pulo Tioman in the South China Sea. This was within reach of Royal Air Force bases on the mainland, and there were still submarines on the station, so weapon training and appropriate emphasis on operations rooms was the order of the 'Janex' fortnight. At that time no British nuclear-powered submarines could be spared for operation east of Suez, but the United States Navy provided one to help evaluate the 'Zippo' procedures.[19]

The next major commitment was a visit to Australia to commemorate the bicentenary of the arrival of Cook at Botany Bay in April 1770. This was to be an even bigger event than that in New Zealand the year before, this time with royal participation. However, before that there was time to go to the other side of the Indian Ocean, where the Beira Patrol had been in progress for some four years.

This commitment had arisen as a result of the unilateral declaration of independence by the government of Southern Rhodesia in November 1965, and subsequent resolutions of the United Nations Security Council imposing an oil embargo on the illegal Rhodesian regime.[20] Beginning with something of a flourish when the carrier HMS *Eagle* spent some 60 days at sea in early 1966 to inhibit traffic into the port of Beira in Mozambique, whence oil could flow into the landlocked country of Rhodesia, the Beira Patrol had settled down into a steady slog by two frigates with afloat support from a Royal Fleet Auxiliary (RFA) and an advanced base in Mombasa, Kenya. By mid-1966 the UN Security Council Resolutions had been strengthened sufficiently to allow quite robust rules of engagement against tankers seeking to break the embargo.[21]

Before joining RFA *Stromness* in Mombasa, Lewin made a flying visit to the naval attachés in Bangkok, Karachi and Nairobi. He took passage in *Stromness* to the patrol area to join *Phoebe*, Captain Gwyn Pritchard, and later *Rothesay*, and found them lively and in good heart.[22] He spent much time talking informally to ships' companies, as was his habit, and was quick to report any grounds for complaint or disappointment that emerged. With such a clearly sympathetic listener, no one felt inhibited, though his buoyant good humour stopped conversations from turning into simple 'drip sessions'.

His flagship for the Australian visit was to be HMS *Blake*. She was a curious hybrid. One of the three 'Tiger' class which were the last classical cruisers to be built by Britain, she had lain idle for years after launch and had been completed in 1961 with a gun armament of four 6-inch and six 3-inch. Both systems had taken a long time to develop, neither proved satisfactory in service, and for a 12,000 ton ship with a complement of 600 it was a poor return in terms of fighting power.[23] Thoughts in the ministry quickly turned towards her conversion to some role more in tune with the times.

The solution was one that to some extent hedged against possible cancellation of the escort cruiser, projected in the late 1950s when Lewin was DDTWP. In partial substitution, the 'Tiger' hull could be reconstructed at its after end to accommodate a hangar with a flight deck abaft it, able to operate four Wessex or, later, Sea King helicopters – aircraft that with their dipping sonar and torpedo armament[24] could give a valuable extra dimension to the anti-submarine effort, but were too heavy to fly from frigates. The outcome of the Healey Defence Review had reinforced the perceived need to go ahead with this major reconstruction, and the *Blake* had been taken in hand accordingly.

The result was one of the oddest-looking ships of the Royal or any other Navy. From the stem to the mainmast she looked like a conventional, rather outdated, gun cruiser. From there aft she looked more like an aircraft carrier than anything else, with a massive hangar extending from one beam to the other and abaft that a flight deck with two landing spots. These new pieces of construction overlay a semi-enclosed quarterdeck, for all the world like those of all carriers since the genre began.

Unfortunately the expensive reconstruction had not extended to *Blake*'s machinery. When she came out of the yard she had severe problems that set back her deployment by several months,[25] and she was only now joining the station, with already the reputation of being an unlucky ship. This was borne out almost at once when Lewin, who had gone to Mauritius in RFA *Stromness* to meet *Blake* and transfer to her with his staff, heard that the cruiser had burnt out two boilers. He directed her by signal to proceed on her remaining two boilers directly from Capetown to Adelaide; he would rendezvous with her in *Stromness* in mid-ocean and he and the staff would transfer by jackstay.

There were three complicating factors. The first was that another RFA, *Tarbatness*, had essential stores for the *Blake* and this entailed further staff planning and another rendezvous in or near the Roaring Forties. That was relatively easily planned in. The second was that on leaving Mauritius, the local pilot put *Stromness* aground. That could have been extremely serious, but within two hours she had been floated off undamaged.[26]

The third complicating factor was by far the most menacing. This was cyclone Louise. Tropical storms in the Indian Ocean are generally not so intense as those in the Pacific, but they follow the same general pattern of very high winds revolving round a low pressure centre which is, itself, moving in a generally westerly direction.[27] In the southern hemisphere, which is where the *Stromness* was, the rotation is clockwise and the usual track south-westerly. But a storm can 'recurve', turning to the south-east, and this is an extremely difficult movement to predict.

Cyclone Louise was already blowing strongly when *Stromness* left Mauritius, and it was likely to get worse. There are less and more dangerous courses to steer in the track of a tropical storm; in what is called the dangerous quadrant, the speed of the wind is added to that of the storm itself, and that is where a ship is in most peril. However, the course of the *Stromness* was dictated by the need to rendezvous with *Blake* (who was well clear of the storm zone to the south) and it was judged that so long as the storm did not recurve, the risk of steering a less than optimum course was justified.

The storm recurved. There were in fact two RFA captains on board, one of them the commodore of the RFA himself, as well as Lewin:

Between us we had about 120 years of sea experience and none of us had seen anything like it. The wind got up to 120 knots; we don't know if it got any higher because the anemometer at the top of the mast was blown off at that speed. I was glad I was in *Stromness* which was an excellent sea boat and very steady. We went through the eye of the storm, absolutely typical, with a circle of blue sky above us, then out the other side.[28]

The barometric pressure in the eye was 947 millibars, not the lowest ever recorded but not far off.

After that, the transfer to *Blake* might have seemed almost humdrum, but once on board Lewin encountered problems of a different kind. The ship's material state was as poor as had been predicted, and confidence was not high.[29] It would not have been impossible for Lewin to fly his flag for the Sydney visit, high profile and indeed royal though it was, in one of the frigates that had been escorting the Royal Yacht, but characteristically he thought of the *Blake*'s ship's company: they 'had had such an appalling disappointing run, it was essential that she continued with the programme [for Adelaide and Sydney] ... and then as soon as that was over we could send her back to Singapore for repairs'.[30]

There ensued a 'fairly savage argument' with the fleet staff in Singapore, who took the opposite view. Lewin won, and was sure he was right in retrospect; the ship's company enjoyed Adelaide, a solo port visit, and were then well set up for the grander events in Sydney. Meanwhile, 'to show willing' they were beavering away down below on the defective boilers, replacing the tubes with a limited number of spares held on board, and Lewin himself 'did his share' in the steam drum; indeed one of his signals during the argument with Singapore began: 'From where I am standing inside B2 boiler of HMS *Blake* ...'[31]

The festivities in Sydney were on a grander scale than those in New Zealand, and perhaps for that reason Lewin did not record them in anything like so much detail. He renewed old friendships in the Royal Yacht; it was over a decade since he had been commander, but continuity is one of the characteristics of the Royal Yacht service.

On the day of the bicentenary itself, *Britannia* steamed round to Botany Bay and ceremonies were numerous and colourful; Lewin was on board for lunch, returning to *Blake* in the evening for the spectacular firework display that, in the incomparable setting of Sydney harbour, concluded the day.

When the assembled ships dispersed, *Blake* was released to proceed independently to Singapore. She did not get there without incident; contaminated fuel held her up for 24 hours inside the Barrier Reef, without steam or air conditioning, while the filters were cleaned. It was not the end of her troubles, as we shall see. Meanwhile FO2 had shifted his flag to one of the frigates and took the opportunity, going up the east coast of Australia, to visit places associated with Cook, in whom he was becoming more and more interested. At Cooktown, he landed by helicopter to see the small museum; it was closed, but they found the key under the mat.[32] Further north, he landed by Gemini dinghy at Possession Island where Cook in the name of King George III had taken possession of the whole coast. At the monument that is there, Lewin 'left a message in a bottle and fired three volleys just as Cook had fired three from his Marines' rifles'.[33]

May and early June were a relatively relaxed time. Jane was able to fly out to join him for the first extended foreign break they had known since the early 1950s, and Jon came too. He was twelve at the time and came under the wing of Ben Fisher, the admiral's driver, who was a naval airman by trade. This was another Lewin innovation, ensuring that his driver was not perceived as an idler when the ship was at sea but could join up with the air department and lend a much-needed hand. Ben taught Jon to fish, which he took up with enthusiasm, and the family remained in touch with him after retirement. It was perhaps the start of the Lewin 'following' (to use the eighteenth-century term),[34] of which more later.

The British government, conscious of the sensitivity of the nations of South-east Asia over the accelerated pace of withdrawal from the Far East, had planned a large-scale exercise called Bersatu Padu, to take place in late June 1970. It included the combined forces of Australia, Malaysia, New Zealand, Singapore and the United Kingdom

– all those states that eventually formed the Five Power Defence Agreement – and involved over 20,000 people.[35] The exercise was planned in London, presumably because of its political overtones.[36]

According to eyewitness accounts, all did not go according to plan. The setting was an assault on the Malaysian east coast by a fictitious enemy country 'Ganasia'; the Royal Marines featured on both sides, 42 Cdo as the enemy and 40 Cdo in HMS *Bulwark* representing the home team, who also had a force of fifteen ships at sea, including the fixed-wing Australian aircraft carrier *Melbourne*. These came under intensive mock attacks from shore-based aircraft, from conventional submarines and from fast craft of the Royal Malaysian Navy. Tactical command and control rotated, as is usual in such exercises, between the various allied senior officers involved.

Plans for such exercises are always in danger of erring either too much towards a set-piece demonstration which looks, and in tactical terms is, artificial, or allowing too much 'free play' where encounters are limited and sometimes non-existent because of the fog of quasi-war. From some accounts Bersatu Padu managed both. It was not helped in the case of FO2FEF by the fact that *Blake* broke down again and could not take part; Lewin shifted his flag to the guided missile destroyer *Fife*.

Two incidents stuck in the minds of the staff officers concerned. One was a piece of unrehearsed free play when the Royal Marines attacked an airstrip, occupied by the RAF Regiment, at breakfast time and 'blew up' the stores. This would have been good fun had it not been that it was scheduled to happen an hour later, in front of a large assembly of VIPs.[37] It was subsequently made much of by the naval publicity machine,[38] but probably was regarded as unproductive cheating.

The other had occurred the night before, and was a case of excess of zeal *against* the naval forces. A planned night encounter between the fleet and the Malaysian fast craft duly happened, and that should have been the end of that serial, with the landing force then proceeding towards the beach. However, towards dawn the Royal Malaysian Navy attacked again, throwing the amphibious approach into considerable, and possibly dangerous, confusion. Lewin was in tactical command at the time, and his staff drafted a stiff and severe signal.[39]

He sent for Volume 4 of the Bersatu Padu orders. The staff were mystified; these were the orders for land forces; what on earth did they have to do with an unscheduled attack by fast patrol craft? Lewin tore up the drafted signal and dictated another: 'With reference to attack which has just taken place, attention is drawn to Bersatu Padu Volume 4, Chapter 6 Para 4.' They looked it up, as no doubt the staff ashore would: it read simply:

If chased by an elephant, run downhill.

It was not a bad way of avoiding sense of humour failure.

Bersatu Padu was at least as much a political as a military exercise. During the course of it, a general election took place in Britain, and to the surprise of some a Conservative government was elected under the premiership of Edward Heath.[40] Lewin, now fully sensitive to sentiment in the region as well as to the future of the Royal Navy, asked himself: 'Was I [now] to demonstrate how easy it was [to support friendly regimes in the area with a reduced British maritime presence] or how difficult it was?'[41] It was a conundrum that remained with him, in many forms and contexts, for the rest of his career.

For the time being, however, there was a fleet programme to be completed before the end of his time in command in October. He had them more or less where he wanted now. The new operational concepts and procedures were well on the way to being proved, backsliders had been brought into line, and whatever its shortcomings Bersatu Padu had pulled the amphibious side of the fleet into the general picture once again, after a time-lapse of nearly a year since Julex in 1969.

There were still some problems of motivation. Between them, the Defence Review and the Swinging 'Sixties had some impact on the Navy, and it was likely to be as severe in the Far East as anywhere, with the lack of a fixed-wing carrier in that far-flung station where carrier air power was such an obvious asset, with the general knowledge that fleet strength was running down, and where climate and routine might conspire with a libertarian atmosphere at home to depress standards of conduct and discipline.

The fleshpots of Singapore, and their effect on young ratings, were of particular concern to the Flag Officer Second in Command. Drugs, drink and every form of sex were available, particularly in the notorious area of Bugis Street. Terry Lewin's reaction was typical. In civilian clothes, accompanied only by his secretary (but with prudent backing from the Naval Provost Marshal's Land Rover and patrol) he toured the area one night. His interview with the Chief Catamite, who was in jubilant mood having recently defaced, by glassing, his/her chief rival, was not recorded in detail but is vividly recalled by at least one participant.[42] Lewin's worries were not diminished, but he had a better understanding of the risks to which his sailors were exposed, and it strengthened his determination to keep the fleet occupied in happier and healthier ways.

There were more trivial matters of the same sort. The length of hair was allowed to assume disproportionate importance. Lewin tuned in to that concern. A concession was made throughout the Navy that the regulation length for sideboards (sideburns) might be extended to the bottom of the ear. Lewin, who disliked the very idea, nevertheless grew his sideboards to the lower limit, to demonstrate how far one could go and that it could still look militarily smart.[43]

He was always concerned to bring in the chief and petty officers and junior rates when it was appropriate – and when stuffier senior officers might have thought it inappropriate, too. Admiral Sir Michael LeFanu, the First Sea Lord and a kindred spirit although a man of different and more flamboyant style, paid a visit to the fleet, saying characteristically that he wanted to see the ships and meet the men rather than spend too much time with the fleet staff in Singapore. He had three days with Lewin and the fleet, not only in the usual walk-rounds that senior commanders have done since the Navy recovered from the more absurd authoritarian posturings of the late Victorian era, but in relaxed picnic parties on the beaches of Pulo Tioman and a final evening in *Fearless*, then Lewin's flagship:

We had a sort of general fancy dress party with people from the ships' companies of all the ships, mixed around and talked to the chaps, something you always liked to do and something which they enormously enjoyed. LeF was the most popular and much loved First Sea Lord that I can remember.[44]

Sadly, LeFanu was not to reach the summit of a service career as Chief of Defence Staff, an appointment for which he was clearly destined and which had indeed been announced. He was already suffering from leukaemia, for which he required increasingly frequent transfusions.[45] In July 1970 it was announced that he would retire. The signal was received during the post-exercise discussion on Bersatu Padu. Lewin 'went up on the stage and read the signal to the chaps and there was a general air of gloom'.[46] There were repercussions in appointments right through the senior ranks of the Navy, and they personally affected Lewin, as will be discussed later in this chapter.

Meanwhile, there was the *Blake*. She was still his flagship, when she was working, and he was due to go to Japan in her in early August, to visit the International Exposition in Osaka. They left Singapore, and at 3 am the following morning Lewin was shaken and told that *Blake* had once more broken down and would have to return to the dockyard.[47]

This time there was no chance of shifting the flag to another warship; the fleet was fully dispersed on other essential tasks. The best that could be done was to fly to northern Japan by civil airline, join there a Royal Fleet Auxiliary that happened to be in the area, hoist his flag in her, and proceed to Fukuoka. MacEacharn and Sheehan were fully occupied in re-booting the programme, and it is not surprising that accounts of the next few days are confused. What is certain is that at one moment MacEacharn put forward a plan that would almost, but not quite, meet the requirement and got an unusually curt reply saying 'Try harder'.[48] That he remembered it bears witness to Terry Lewin's normal trust in and courtesy to his staff.

The other anecdote is lighter: on arrival at Sapporo, Japanese customs were unusually officious and there was a problem about Lewin's dress sword, which he would need for official calls. This was a weapon, and import into Japan was not permitted. 'Who do you work for?' enquired the official. Paddy Sheehan was quicker than Terry on this occasion: fixing the man with a steely Irish glare, he replied, 'The Queen of England.'[49] The sword was allowed through.

Entry to a foreign port for a major visit flying the flag of a rear admiral is not the lot of every Royal Fleet Auxiliary, and the *Tarbatness* was delighted to accept it. It was not the first time Terry Lewin had flown his flag thus as FO2, and his trust in and admiration for the RFA was enhanced on every occasion he did it and, indeed, every time they took part in an operation or exercise. The British fleet had come a long way since 1945, when in the Pacific they had been so far behind the Americans in the art of afloat support.

The programme in Osaka was full and varied, with a good deal of double-booking, and the staff officers found themselves representing the admiral on numerous occasions. That was by now no real problem for the close-knit outfit that Terry's staff had become. As early as the Sydney visit in April, he had emphasised the 'family' nature of the job and said, 'We must all stick together.'[50] There are, as a commanding officer was heard to say on another occasion, 'visits for heroes': the Far East was not short of them.

The final run was to be something completely different. It was something after Lewin's own heart and it may be guessed that he had something to do with the planning of it. Its centrepiece, certainly, was a fixed commitment, a naval presence at the independence celebrations of Fiji which were to be attended by the Prince of Wales in early October; but surrounding this was a tour of the islands of the south-west Pacific, including another visit to New Zealand. He took with him two frigates, *Charybdis* and *Minerva*, but his flag was worn for most of the cruise in the RFA *Olmeda*.

Sheehan had, as he often did, flown on for a few days' preliminary reconnaissance and programme discussion some months before,[51] but this had necessarily been only to Fiji and did not take in the numerous islands at which the force was to touch on the way there. These were in the Admiralty, Solomons and New Hebrides groups, all to the east of Papua New Guinea, places that had often been major theatres of the Second World War yet, as Lewin found, touched by it less profoundly than might have been thought. Programmes were necessarily informal and *ad hoc*, with a premium on nimble-footedness on the part of the ships: it was just the sort of thing Terry Lewin enjoyed.[52]

Visits began in Manus in the Admiralty Islands, which had been an advanced base for the British Pacific Fleet 25 years before. Here the Australian administration made them welcome in an area where British presence was clearly going to be thinner and thinner in the future. Two days later they arrived in Gizo in the New Georgia group of the Solomons, and here it really was the South Seas at last, with an escort of war canoes and launches, one sporting a silver band. In true Cook fashion, Lewin was carried ashore by four befeathered warriors. It had been a different kind of landing for John Fitzgerald Kennedy in 1942, when he swam ashore here from his PT boat after it had been sunk in action with the Japanese.

Second World War echoes were louder at the next place of call, Honiara in Guadalcanal. The friendship and hospitality were again overwhelming; sport and dancing were intermingled. It was the same at Lo Island in the Torres group, though necesarily on a smaller scale since the population was only 55. The dictum of 'Trust in God and an Admiralty Chart' was tested: some of the surveys dated from the middle of the nineteenth century, and although accuracy of what had been covered was assured by the standards set by Cook, there were bound to be gaps. Coral pinnacles may go undetected even with more modern methods, and coral reefs can grow. The frigates' helicopters were valuable hydrographic scouts. A final visit to Port Patteson in the New Hebrides (now Vanuatu) set the seal on a memorable week, and the squadron sailed for New Zealand with many vivid memories.[53]

A week in Auckland gave Lewin the opportunity to renew acquaintance in New Zealand, and to shift his flag to HMS *Charybdis*, Captain Denis Foster, for the festivities in Fiji. Suva was reached on 9 October in company with the other ships of the British force, HMAS *Swan* and HMNZS *Blackpool*. Ships' companies were well entertained and enjoyed the visit, which pleased Lewin greatly. He was particularly proud of the performance of the Royal Marine band, which excelled itself in the ceremonies. There was a domestic tale underlying this: suitable service accommodation was not available ashore for the band, so Sheehan had arranged for them to be put up in private houses that had volunteered. At first the Royal Marines bandsmen had been unhappy at the prospect, but when the time came to leave there were tears – it is said, although the Royals would not admit it, on both sides.[54]

The Prince of Wales was embarked on 12 October for passage to the offlying island of Levuka. It was only some 40 miles from Suva, but the programme had run late and it was necessary to make up time, so the flagship went at 20 knots through an unpleasant sea. Prince Charles spent most of the passage, nevertheless, on the upper bridge: 'I think by the time we arrived ... he was fairly damp,' Terry recalled.[55]

The celebrations over, the ships dispersed and Lewin arrived in Sydney on 19 October. Here he handed over the command on 22 October to Rear Admiral David Williams. The actual turnover took place in a rotating-tower restaurant overlooking the city, since as Williams observed 'there was no peace on board'.[56] They were very old friends, having been together in the training cruiser and returned from the Mediterranean in the same troopship in 1941, taking time off in South Africa to tour the Drakensberg together with four other midshipmen. Both had later specialised in gunnery. As is sometimes the way in naval appointing, their paths had scarcely coincided since, but they thought highly of each other and Williams was in no doubt that he would be taking over an operationally up-to-date fleet. 'Terry got the best out of people',[57] whatever the problems of rundown atmosphere, poorly refitted ships and enervating climate.

Lewin already knew his next appointment. The plans had gone through some changes since the announcement of LeFanu's illness and early retirement. Before this, he had been earmarked for the post of Deputy Chief of Defence Staff (Operational Requirements). This had been at the instance of Admiral Sir Peter Hill-Norton, who was due to take over as First Sea Lord from LeFanu; Hill-Norton believed that Lewin, whom he already saw as occupying the highest posts in due time, would benefit from some experience in 'the Centre', whose influence in the Ministry of Defence was steadily growing. It was not a prospect that appealed to Terry, who regarded it as 'an absolute non-job'.

However, with the news of LeFanu's retirement, everything had changed. Hill-Norton would now be First Sea Lord for a short time only, moving on to the top job of all, Chief of Defence Staff. Admiral Sir Michael Pollock, then Third Sea Lord and Controller, in charge of naval materiel development, would become First Sea Lord; Vice Admiral Anthony Griffin, who had been in line to be Vice Chief of Naval Staff, would relieve Pollock as Controller; and Lewin would become Vice Chief of Naval Staff. It was the most challenging of all jobs for a naval officer in Whitehall: unremitting toil, heavy responsibility, constant and rapid changes of topic, a premium on forensic, diplomatic and leadership skills. Lewin's reaction, recalled years later, was one word: 'Hooray!'[58]

THE HEAT OF THE DAY:
VICE CHIEF OF NAVAL STAFF
1971–1974

It is doubtful if anyone ever tried to write a job description for the Vice Chief of Naval Staff. Either it would have been of book length, or it would have been a single statement: 'You are responsible for everything that happens in or affects the Navy'. Neither would have been particularly helpful. John Bush once said to Edward Ashmore (both were VCNS in their time), 'You will find it much easier than being Director of Plans', and Ashmore agreed.[1] There would have been many who took an opposite view.

Certainly the First Sea Lord, the Vice Chief's boss, was the man with whom the responsibility ultimately lay; it was he who was accountable to Her Majesty's Government for the efficiency of the naval service. But the First Sea Lord had many representational duties; the Navy, the public, and foreign diplomats and naval staffs, would all look to him to provide a broad and positive exposition of what the Navy was for and about. It was up to his Vice Chief to provide the basis for all that. The Commander in Chief of the Fleet answered to VCNS; the Commandant General of the Royal Marines answered to him; and all the Naval Staff Directorates, now that the Deputy Chief of Naval Staff was no more, answered to him. He was a full member of the Admiralty Board. Of the other naval members, the Second Sea Lord dealt with personnel, the Third with materiel development, and the Fourth with Fleet Support, all matters of high responsibility, but the Vice Chief was where it all came together, in the plans for the future and the operations of the day.

It was, then, a hugely responsible and varied job that faced the newly promoted Vice Admiral Lewin at the beginning of 1971. Moreover, nothing ran in a simple sequence. That is to say, each stream of business was linked to several other streams, all going at different speeds and often eddying back on one another. It was quite hard to find a source for each stream and an issue to any of them, and only too easy to discover that dams had been built across them by circumstance, or design from inside or outside the service, or by financial restrictions. Thus if, in the course of this chapter, developments turn and twist round upon themselves and constantly find themselves cross-referred to other aspects of the many matters in hand, that is a reflection of how it was.

Lewin had been away from the ministry for only two years, but quite a lot had happened in that time. Under the leadership of Michael LeFanu and with Edward Ashmore as VCNS, a course had been set for the Naval Staff[2] to cope with a future that was based upon the NATO commitment and would feature no fixed-wing carriers. The elements were becoming clear, with a ballistic missile submarine force, a class of 'through-deck cruisers', a mix of air defence and general-purpose escorts, nuclear-powered fleet submarines and a Royal Marines force mainly for Arctic warfare.[3] In fact, it was the foundation for a maritime force for the 'Seventies and 'Eighties, not entirely to the taste of the Navy Minister from 1968 to 1970, David Owen, who thought 'We should put the balance of the Navy underwater'.[4] Those with experience of what navies did in peace, tension and war had less radical views about balance.

The other major development, though its effects were not so far-reaching as might have been thought, was the arrival in office of a Conservative government in mid-1970. The new Secretary of State for Defence was Lord Carrington, whose service to the state for the next 25 years is a matter of history. However, if the Navy had expected a revolutionary shift in policy, a reversal perhaps of the 'irreducible' NATO commitment and a return to an East of Suez policy with all that followed from that, it was disappointed. The 1971 Defence White Paper[5] put forward as defence objectives first, that Britain should 'resume, *within her resources* [italics added], a proper share of respon-sibility for the preservation of peace and stability in the world'; second, to improve the capabilities of the armed forces in certain areas; third, to 'establish and maintain a sound financial basis' for defence provi-sion. But it went on to state that 'It is to NATO that by far the greater part of Britain's military forces is committed', even though it made reference to other existing alliances and specifically to the new Five Power Defence Agreement in the Far East. So, in effect, all new developments would still have to be justified on a NATO ticket.

There were palliatives, though. *Ark Royal* was to be run on to the late 1970s; some six destroyers or frigates were to be maintained East of Suez and some RAF bases in the area would continue in service; there were provisions for continuing presence in the Mediterranean, the Caribbean and the South Atlantic.[6] In fact, it looked rather like the 'pawns on the chessboard' pattern predicted by Lewin in his RUSI speech in 1968.[7] That was not far from a classical naval deployment, an instrument for the use of the sea's surface – which, when all was said and done, was the main purpose of sea power for the foreseeable future. But where was the main striking force, the backing for the pawns and the protection for the users of the surface of the sea? Was it to be nuclear-powered submarines (SSNs) on the Owen model – and indeed as foreseen, at least in outline, by Lewin when he was ACNS(P)?

The Naval Staff had no doubt that SSNs were part of the answer. They were a striking force of great potency. But the problems of tactical control, pointed out by members of that RUSI audience in 1968, were still there: put bluntly, the problem with a submarine was that sometimes it didn't know and you couldn't tell it. It was still by its nature a solitary, and overwhelmingly offensive, weapon system. Some more teeth for surface forces were needed, which would give a reliable counter to the air, surface and missile attack that might be expected from the Soviet naval forces, or from forces supplied by Soviet arms.

As early as 1969, an unsung commander in the Directorate of Naval Plans, John David, had written in consultation with the Directorate of Naval Air Warfare a paper entitled 'The Missile Gap'.[8] Its burden had been that the Soviet long-range anti-ship missiles depended on aerial shadowing for their targeting, and that a combat aircraft, even of limited character, operating from British ships would be critical in seeing such aircraft off in a timely way; it would also have a useful role in probing surface contacts and conducting limited strikes against hostile vessels. Such an aircraft would, necessarily, have to be a short or vertical take-off machine: a Sea Harrier.

This was the first, tentative, in-house effort to justify V/STOL aircraft in the NATO context. By the time Lewin returned to Whitehall as VCNS, it was still something to be spoken of in the most speculative tones. LeFanu had indeed taken some soundings, with a carrot to be dangled before the Royal Air Force in the form of opportunities for RAF pilots to operate from ships; and Ashmore's final injunction to Lewin, when turning over the job of VCNS, had been 'to keep the Harrier in his sights come what may'.[9]

One technical development gave added hope that a Sea Harrier could eventually be justified. Early marks of the Harrier had been underpowered to the extent that getting off and back on to a carrier deck would be about the limit of their operation; useful range and payload were lacking. This had been one of the principal reasons for the caution of Begg, Hill-Norton and indeed Lewin in the late 1960s, although the Directorate of Naval Air Warfare and Hawker Siddeley hinted at significant development even then. Now, in 1970, a radically uprated Pegasus engine gave the prospect of turning the Harrier from what was arguably a toy into a real fighting machine.[10]

Lewin's part in the process that led to the eventual approval of the Sea Harrier in 1975, some time after he had left the Ministry of Defence, is unlikely to be capable of reasoned assessment until 2006 when all the papers become available, and quite probably not fully even then, since so much depended on personal contact and unrecorded negotiation. However, it is clear that he took the closest interest in it and, as will be shown, his contribution must have been a critical one.

The timing of the process is fairly plain. It had to begin with a Naval Staff Target, stemming from the engine development outlined above. Then a Naval Staff Requirement would have been raised, drawing on the operational justification for the aircraft – in the terms of the 'Missile Gap' paper, greatly refined and expanded, but encapsulated in Naval Staff-speak as 'Hack the Shad – probe – strike'. These papers would have gone through the whole central structure of Operational Requirements and Weapon Development Committees, with the Treasury and the other services ever watchful and questioning. After submissions and resubmissions, many of which would have been piloted through by the Vice Chief himself, ministerial approval would be sought and, it was hoped, obtained.

As always, the difficulty would lie in convincing doubters and neutralising outright opponents. Here Lewin was confronted with an unusually difficult situation. He had rejoined the ministry at a time when relations between Naval and Air Staffs were at a singularly low ebb. The Air Staff was led by Air Chief Marshal Sir Denis Spotswood,[11] a proponent of the indivisibility of air power in the Trenchard mould, not inclined to give an inch back to organic naval air capability in the wake of the carrier decision of 1966. This view percolated down through the Air Staff, particularly to the Air Staff briefers who had always regarded themselves as guardians of the faith in any case, and to the Directorate of Air Plans. The Naval Staff were no less uncompromising in their position, and every paper emanating from the south (Air) end of the Ministry of Defence building was scrutinised minutely and suspiciously, as was anything from the north (Navy) end by the Air Staff.

It was no way to get a major, and controversial, project through to completion. Ministers would be scarcely likely to approve any proposal that had only equivocal support from the Chiefs of Staff as a body. Much less would they countenance any project that had outright opposition from one service.

Lewin's task was therefore both to argue and to cajole. The argument was helped by the results of an exercise held in December 1971. Called High Wood, this was avowedly to test the ability of shore-based aircraft of the Royal Air Force to support the fleet against air attack. It was said that it was the result of 'nearly two years' hard bargaining'[12] between the Royal Navy and Royal Air Force, at the highest level.[13] Although in the NATO area and in a NATO setting, it was a national exercise. It lasted a week.

The consensus of opinion on High Wood, both at the time and later, was that it 'resulted in a less than adequate performance'[14] by shore-based aircraft. Their reaction time, against the old but fast Type 15 frigate *Rapid* representing a missile-armed 'Orange' surface force, was inadequate to prevent the simulated firing of missiles on numerous occasions, and this even with the assistance of 'Blue' reconnaissance aircraft.[15] While it may be said that the public reports and assessments all emanated from those who were *parti pris* on behalf of the Royal Navy and the Sea Harrier,[16] and indeed there was some concern that a well-known naval journalist and advocate of carrier aircraft was on board the *Rapid*,[17] it is notable that no disclaimers appear to have come from the Air Force Department; the 1972 Defence White Paper contains no claim of a successful exercise; and one of the principal proponents of shore-based air power in the maritime role made no reference to it in a book published ten years later.[18] Even the fact that the shore airfields were fogbound for one or two critical days of the exercise,[19] which might have been a mitigating factor, proved double-edged, since the ships at sea were in clear conditions where shipborne aircraft could have operated with ease.

That, then, was one piece of evidence that Terry Lewin could deploy discreetly and without too much labouring. Another lever, more positive and more to the liking of the Treasury, was American interest in the Harrier. The United States had no comparable design and there were two fields in which a V/STOL aircraft might be useful to the US maritime forces. The first was as a prime component of the 'Sea Control Ship' (SCS) envisaged as the 'low' end of the 'Hi-Lo Mix' put forward by the then Chief of Naval Operations (CNO), Admiral Bud Zumwalt.[20] But although the Harrier's versatility made it ideal for use in low-intensity conflicts of the sort for which the SCS was projected,[21] Zumwalt's whole project collapsed against the opposition of the big-carrier establishment of the US Navy.

The other US taker turned out to be more durable, and that was the United States Marine Corps. They needed a close support aircraft, and the ability of the Harrier to operate from the flat tops of the 'Iwo Jima' class and their successors filled the bill admirably. In the event, the US Marine Corps bought the aircraft and its inventory still amounted to 180 Harriers (the US designation is AV-8B) in the late 1990s.[22] In this way, the US Marine Corps' interest in the Sea Harrier helped to further its cause in its parent country.

The final lever that Lewin was able to deploy was probably the most effective, and was the most characteristic of Lewin. The Vice Chief of the Air Staff was Air Marshal 'Splinters' Smallwood, a man of great charm and goodwill whose loyalty to the RAF was unquestioned but was allied to fairness of mind. Lewin suggested to Admiral Sir Michael Pollock, the First Sea Lord, that since communications at the top were likely to be no help, he should initiate regular discussions with Smallwood. These duly began, and became regular one-hour meetings followed by a *tête à tête* lunch. The only others attending were the respective secretaries and the ground rule was 'Let's talk about what we can agree on.'[23]

It was a winning formula. There were sure to be many areas where Naval and Air Staffs were in conflict, notably anything that had to do with the allocation of resources; but on matters where there might be opposition on doctrinal grounds, the essential pragmatism and commonsense of the two men could make progress. The Sea Harrier was a prime example. Lewin suggested that if the aircraft was approved, joint training should make use of RAF facilities and some RAF pilots should be included in Sea Harrier squadrons. This was not a new idea; it had been floated by LeFanu in 1969. But it was made more attractive through being put forward 'Vice Chief to Vice Chief', and the fact that the Fleet Air Arm were known not to be too happy about it was something that, perversely, might endear it to the RAF. The results were first seen in the 1972 Defence White Paper: this was much more forthcoming than previous official documents about the prospects for a Sea Harrier, stating several options which were to be studied;[24] and its final fruits were apparent in the agreement two years later, at top level, that the Chief of the Air Staff (then Air Chief Marshal Sir Andrew Humphrey) would not object to the Sea Harrier project when this was put to ministers.[25]

Probably the Sea Harrier was the project above all others that needed the most detailed work and delicate touch in the whole of Lewin's time as VCNS. There were many others almost as critical. One that needed a combination of military and political acumen was the question of Group Deployments.

Lewin's time in the Far East had convinced him that, however current policy might emphasise the NATO role for British defence forces, it was both necessary for the country and beneficial for the Navy to go further afield than the Tropic of Cancer, which was NATO's southern boundary in the Atlantic.[26] This was in line with the sentiments of the new government and not unwelcome to most officials of the Foreign Office, but the question was how it should be done.

The Foreign Office's instinct was for stationed forces. They gave continuity on the station, were able to liaise with British representatives on a firm basis and their presence would become familiar to local populations. They would be readily available, within the limits of their mobility, for assistance in cases of natural disaster, and local knowledge acquired through experience on the station would be valuable in this role. They could provide a contribution to the exercises of other navies and give overt support to alliances: Britain was a member not only of NATO but of the South-East Asia Treaty Organisation (SEATO), the Five Power Defence Agreement (FPDA) and the Central Treaty Organisation (CENTO, comprising the USA, UK, Iran, Pakistan and Turkey). It was noted that the French Navy operated on this pattern, particularly in the Indian Ocean and South Pacific.

While acknowledging these virtues of stationed forces, Lewin took a different view. If a substantial naval force could be despatched say once a year on a widespread deployment, it would have more impact than what were in effect maritime garrisons in penny numbers. The arrival of a visiting group consisting of some five or six warships, with a few auxiliaries for afloat support, would be a memorable event, quite different from the routine visit of a single ship, generating far more publicity and demonstrating that Britain still had significant naval power which could, in the event, be deployed to help friendly states in time of need (or, conversely it must be said, to oppose threats to British interests, since it demonstrated that such a force would be a formidable opponent to tackle). Moreover, a group of this kind would carry a wide variety of naval equipments, some of the most modern kind, and could be used as a platform for defence sales effort to the benefit of foreign exchange – something stationed forces were unlikely to be able to do except in a minimal way.

Also, the operational advantages for the Navy were a most powerful incentive for the group method of operating. A force of several warships, particularly if accompanied by a submarine, could exercise on passage in an almost self-contained way, in order to maintain and enhance its fighting efficiency. Moreover, careful programming and liaison, through naval attachés and advisers, with foreign naval authorities could introduce Royal Naval groups into the exercises of friendly countries or alliances, with an impact that a single on-station ship could not match. A Group Deployment would be largely self-sufficient in stores and fuel because it would be replenished at sea by its accompanying Royal Fleet Auxiliaries, and these too would be valuable adjuncts to exercises particularly with navies that were not so advanced in their techniques or facilities as the Royal Navy had become.

Most importantly, Group Deployments would give the Royal Navy continued self-confidence in its ability to operate wherever and whenever required. Government policy might decree that NATO was to be the focus of defence effort, but history had taught that the unexpected operation in the unplanned place was quite as likely to happen as the set scenario[27] and the capacity to deploy a significant force that could actually do warlike things, rather than simply be around, was immensely important. The spin-offs for the Navy's domestic arrangements were not negligible, either; the 'harmony rules', which had been evolved during Lewin's time in the ministry,[28] laid down maximum periods of separation from homes and families, and these would be best served by well-programmed deployments away from and back to the United Kingdom, rather than the somewhat haphazard arrangements that had been in force on the Far East Station during his time as FO2FEF.[29] At the same time, the attractiveness of visits to far-off places had always been an incentive to the more adventurous youth of the country to join and stay in the Navy, and a relatively large group of ships would give the opportunity to more sailors to see the world than would a garrison force.

In consequence of all these arguments, Lewin was convinced that Group Deployments were the right way for the Navy to go, and he took a great deal of care to persuade the Foreign Office to his opinion. Captain David Brown, the Director of Naval Operations and Trade, and Peter England, the Assistant Under Secretary (Naval Staff), worked out in conjunction with the fleet staff at the Northwood headquarters the details of how it might be done and an evening meeting was arranged at the Foreign Office.[30] Lewin opened by quoting Nelson on the value of frigates and went on to expound the virtues of the group system. The Foreign Office officials were convinced, and their support was critical in carrying the proposals forward. The point should perhaps be made that there would remain, in all the plans, some element of stationed forces; the West Indies would require a ship on call, as would Gibraltar where the situation with Spain remained touchy, the Beira Patrol at that time demanded two frigates, Hong Kong required a guardship, and the Falklands patrol ship was needed in the southern summer. The Foreign Office could thus console itself with the thought that, on the maritime chessboard, some stationed pawns still existed.

It was necessary then to put the case to the Admiralty Board and to NATO. This was another chicken-and-egg process: the Board would not approve without knowing that NATO would countenance lowering the readiness category of several important units while they were deployed east of Suez, while NATO would not give its approval without some intimation that the British were pretty determined to do it. It is likely that Lewin adopted a step-by-step approach on both fronts, with help from some particularly close NATO friends including the Dutch. Finally, these hurdles having been cleared, ministers had to be convinced; but as has been said, the government at that time was not averse to a higher British profile beyond the NATO area and approval was quite readily obtained.

The first group accordingly sailed in May 1973 for a six-month deployment.[31] It was under the command of the Flag Officer First Flotilla, Rear Admiral Richard Clayton; this demonstrated a further bonus of the scheme, experience in independent operating for junior flag officers. A feature of the largely surface force was that it was accompanied by HMS *Dreadnought*, Britain's first nuclear-powered fleet submarine, and a Dutch frigate for part of its time. It worked hard – it was said that it went into defence watches, that is to say four hours on and four hours off, soon after leaving the United Kingdom and only came out of them just before arrival in harbour. Nevertheless it was an immensely successful, and much enjoyed, deployment and set a pattern for the programming and operation of the fleet that persisted to the turn of the century.[32] It was indeed an example of success breeding success, for it survived political, structural and financial vicissitudes in a quite remarkable way, and if a single tribute to Terry Lewin's combination of vision and commonsense is needed, Group Deployments must rank high among the candidates.

Closer to home, the VCNS was confronted by an entirely different, and novel, set of national maritime problems. The first was oil. North Sea oil was not yet on stream, but the number of strikes made by the oil and gas companies allowed no doubt that Britain's fuel needs from about 1980 onwards would be largely met from this national resource.[33] The informed public was beginning to question whether sufficient attention was being paid to the protection of these economic assets, many of which were remote from the practical reach of the law even though international law clearly put them under national jurisdiction.[34] Sabotage by disaffected individuals or groups, terrorist raids, 'sleeping' minefields laid by foreign agencies to be used either for blackmail or escalation, and overt acts of destruction as part of a wider war, were all suggested as threats.

Secondly, fisheries remained a sensitive and developing issue, with the assertion of fishing rights, notably by Iceland, affecting British distant water fleets. The 'First Cod War' had ended in 1961 in compromise although it represented a retreat from Britain's assertion of a claim to fish up to three miles from the Icelandic coast.[35] Now a far wider claim to exclusive rights by Iceland threatened a second. The situation closer to home was complicated by the fact that Britain in 1972 joined the European Common Market and thereby acceded to the Common Fisheries Policy. New questions of jurisdiction, regulation and enforcement were emerging, and the Royal Navy, through its Fishery Protection commitment in both coastal and distant waters, could not but be closely involved.

Thirdly, pollution of the sea by oil had been a live issue for many years; even though pollution by tankers amounted to only a quarter of the total, its public profile was very high because of the visibility of slicks and the great publicity given to disasters such as the stranding of the *Torrey Canyon* off Scilly in 1967 and the *Pacific Glory/Allegro* collision in the Channel in 1970.[36] The institution of a traffic separation scheme in the Strait of Dover in 1967, whereby eastbound ships kept to the southern side of the strait while westbound ones took the northern track, with a safety zone in between, had been generally welcomed by shipmasters (somewhat to the surprise of its initiators).[37] It was in fact the forerunner of hundreds of such schemes that have since been put in operation worldwide and have been most beneficial in cutting down collisions, but it had had its teething troubles, notably in a multiple collision in 1971. There was a general perception that closer control was required.

Finally, the recreational use of the waters around the British Isles was sharply increasing and, curiously for a maritime nation, it was largely unregulated by any form of licensing. There were surprisingly few cases of the irresponsible use of this freedom, but inexperience on the part of sea users was bound to lead to accidents, as was the stress of weather and navigational hazards. In consequence the search and rescue services, which included the lifeboats, the coastguard and the helicopter units at air stations around the coast, frequently found themselves called upon.

All these concerns were linked in Lewin's mind and one Monday morning he said to his Secretary, Captain Don Beadle, 'I've been thinking ...' Such a statement from a senior officer often makes juniors run for cover, but from Terry Lewin it tended to act as a stimulus. At 'Morning Prayers', attended by the Assistant Chiefs and Directors of the Naval Staff later that day, he announced that it was time to look again at the Navy's vision of itself as a purely blue-water, fighting force, and to study the interwoven requirements that were emerging with regard to Britain's coastal waters. The remit was handed to Captain David Macey, an Assistant Director of Naval Plans.

It is not certain whether it was Macey, or Lewin himself, who coined the phrase 'Offshore Tapestry'. Whoever did, the expression was evocative, and it stuck. The study produced by Macey addressed two principal questions: the material resources available at the present time and necessary in the future, and the organisation needed to make best use of the resources.

So far as materiel was concerned, the Royal Navy had a squadron of Coastal Minesweepers (CMS), built in the 1950s, earmarked for fishery protection duties and numerous helicopters for search and rescue work at coastal airfields. The Royal Naval Reserve ran a number of CMS as well, though these were trained for a wartime not a constabulary role. The Royal Air Force had maritime reconnaissance aircraft, principally for anti-submarine work in cold and hot war, but available for some offshore surveillance. Her Majesty's Coastguard had an extensive shore network but no ships, and the Royal National Lifeboat Institution its well-tried and much trusted craft with their willing and able crews. It was not a negligible inventory of assets.

But there were gaps and potentially they were growing. From the Navy's point of view, some new specialised vessels were needed to augment and eventually replace the CMS. It was proposed, and quickly approved, that the Navy should lease the Scottish Office's patrol vessel *Jura*, which would undergo evaluation to see whether a class based upon the design should be acquired by the RN. This duly happened and led to the building of the 'Island' class offshore patrol vessels in the mid-1970s.[38] Another off-the-shelf acquisition was the hydrofoil *Speedy*: in spite of her mobility in calm conditions, the weather factors around the British Isles precluded the production of a follow-on class.

Oil rig security was clearly a matter for the civil power in the first instance, but military back-up was needed to counter serious threats if these arose. The Offshore Tapestry proposals led to the formation of Comacchio Group Royal Marines, based at Arbroath, 400 strong and specially trained in rapid reaction to terrorist or other threats to the rigs.[39] The Royal Air Force willingly took on the widening of its maritime patrol task to include sorties over the oil rigs from time to time. It also, in course of time, assumed a good deal of the helicopter Search and Rescue task, a logical development as Naval Air Stations around the coast dwindled in number, some indeed such as Brawdy and Lossiemouth being taken over by the RAF.

Just as important as the question of resources was that of organisation. The Offshore Tapestry paper found an untidy and uncoordinated picture. There were indeed Rescue Co-ordination centres and networks of communication, but these were not always easy to activate rapidly and were primarily to do with life-saving rather than threats to the environment, maritime traffic safety or salvage. It was tempting to propose a root-and-branch reorganisation, with a centralised service on the lines of the United States Coast Guard which has overall responsibility for all 'Tapestry' matters in and around the USA.[40] This was rejected by Macey's paper. In an article in 1973 he explained:

> If we were starting from scratch … the present amalgam of authorities would not recommend itself as the best answer, but having grown up piecemeal over many years it would require a major upheaval to replace it. Provided co-ordination and co-operation between the responsible authorities is maintained at a high level and certain vacuums are filled an adequate service can be provided.[41]

It is right to say that, to a large extent as a result of Lewin's Offshore Tapestry initiative, the necessary co-ordination has been progressed steadily for the rest of the century. The pattern has not been tidied up completely, and gaps still appear from time to time, as the aftermath of disasters even during the 1990s shows.[42] The number of agencies involved is still considerable, and communications are not always perfect by any means, but there is much better machinery in place, it is constantly being improved, and the need for resources is acknowledged.

In 1972, that acknowledgement was not obtained without reaction
from the naval establishment. There were some who thought any
diversion of naval effort towards constabulary tasks was harmful to
the Royal Navy's function as a fighting organisation, both in materiel
terms and those of naval ethos. Some, too, saw it as the thin end of a
wedge that led to a 'coast defence navy'. Most, however, recognised
that the commitment was an entirely logical and honourable one, and
Admiralty Board approval for the policy was quickly achieved.[43]

One factor that would affect the Offshore Tapestry, and naval operations generally, was the emerging international law of the sea. This
had last been codified in a series of United Nations Conventions in
1958, but events had moved rapidly since. The most dramatic was the
speech of Ambassador Pardo of Malta in the United Nations in 1967,
when he proposed that the area of the seabed beyond the limits of
national jurisdiction should be regarded as the common heritage of
mankind. In parallel with this, and equally reflecting the aspirations of
the newly emerging Third World states, was a plethora of claims to
national jurisdiction over waters far from their coast – either over
resources, or to full sovereignty.[44] It was clear that a further United
Nations Conference on the Law of the Sea was in the offing.

Lewin's chief concern was with the ability of naval forces to move
as freely as possible about the world, though given the multiplicity of
Britain's own offshore interests he recognised that a balance had to be
struck between the rights of coastal and maritime states. He ensured
that the Navy was represented on the negotiating team and took care
to be fully briefed on the preliminaries, which involved some unac-
customed bedfellows since the interests of the United States, the
United Kingdom and the Soviet Union coincided at many points, and
were perceived to be at some odds with, for example, Canada. It was,
as he realised, going to be a long haul. The Law of the Sea Convention was not signed until 1 December 1982, by which time he had
finally left office; but rights of passage for naval forces had, in
essence, been safeguarded.[45]

It was, indeed, a great time in the Ministry of Defence for conferences, committees and working parties. Denis Healey, when Secretary

of State for Defence, had encouraged exchanges between academics and officials, both serving officers and civilians, and these had proved stimulating and productive, if not of hard policy at least of thought and vision. Defence fellowships were instituted for the deep study of issues that might be of importance in the future, and the Imperial Defence College, renamed the Royal College of Defence Studies, assumed an altogether sharper look, with students enjoined to complete a short individual thesis during their year.

All these were largely welcome moves to Lewin and the military establishment generally. Less so were the investigations, into what had been regarded as strictly service preserves, by predominantly academic groups supported by a civil service secretariat and attended, generally in the role of observers or witnesses, by staff officers. One such was the Rotherham Committee which in the early 1970s looked at the long term structure of the fleet. Their chief contact on the Naval Staff was the ACNS(P), Rear Admiral Henry Leach. He found himself profoundly at odds with the views expressed in the committee's report, which advocated what the Navy would think of as a 'mosquito fleet', whose surface units would be able to make rapid and frequent attacks within a limited range from their bases, but whose staying power and ability to control necessary areas of sea would be in grave doubt. Lewin's notebook for early 1972 suggests that he went to see the Deputy Under Secretary (Policy), the powerful civil servant in the central staff who exerted much influence with ministers, about it. But subsequent entries, or lack of them, indicate a fairly relaxed view of the report; it is probable that Lewin assessed it to be so far from the traditional, and to him self-evident, wisdom of a balanced, sea-control force that it would not be taken seriously by ministers. Judging from the absence of follow-up, this assessment was correct.

Another working party was headed by Sir William Hawthorne, an eminent Cambridge mathematician, and included Sir Edward Bullard and Professor Mair. This was to look into the future of Maritime Air, in its broadest sense. Lewin showed himself sensitive to the potential importance of this working party[46] and required to be kept informed of its progress. There were one or two occasions, including the appearance of a controversial first draft, when his backing was sought and readily given, and there may have been other interventions behind the scenes, because Sir William made the decision at a fairly early stage that the vexed question of shipborne V/STOL would not be addressed, and this was a great relief to those in the Navy most closely concerned. Another important judgement, again made by Hawthorne, was that anti-submarine warfare required 'all systems operating' if it was to have any chance of being effective.[47] It is not certain if this pithy phrase got into the final report. In any event, Lewin ensured that the effects of the Hawthorne working party were largely neutral.

A further piece of machinery for investigating the plans of the military was the Defence Operational Analysis Establishment at West Byfleet. This was inhabited by bright, predominantly young, civil servants whose task was to apply computer techniques to military problems. These could be as simple as evaluation of a single projected weapon system, or as complex as a full-scale war game. In the Ministry of Defence, the acronym GIGO (garbage in, garbage out) was freely used about West Byfleet. In other words, the results of the studies could not be more accurate than the assumptions fed into them, and those assumptions were all too often questionable.

Lewin's attitude to such studies was that it was necessary to probe their weaknesses, and in particular the validity of the assumptions, but that they might have valuable things to say and should not be ignored. The same cautious but co-operative attitude was apparent in his relations with the increasingly influential scientific establishment: his notebook is full of references to the Defence Scientific Advisory Council, the Maritime Warfare Advisory Board, meetings with the Chief Scientific Adviser and his subordinates. Networking was an essential part of the business.

So, naturally, given the emphasis upon it since 1968, was NATO. Lewin conducted most of his relationships with the structural side of NATO – the two great headquarters at Norfolk, Virginia and Mons, Belgium – through the senior British officers who held the key appointments of Deputy Supreme Allied Commander Atlantic (DEPSACLANT) and SACLANT's Representative in Europe

(SACLANTREPEUR) respectively. He also had access to the overall NATO headquarters near Brussels, and to its powerful Military Committee, through the UK's Military Representative, another British admiral. He was in no doubt about the necessity of the Navy's showing maximum willingness to take part in all NATO activities and exercises, and ensured that the alliance was mentioned as the 'main beneficiary' of the accelerated shipbuilding programme in the early 1970s.[48]

There were some areas where he could make little progress. NATO's attempt to look ahead to the 1970s and beyond, a document called AD 70, recognised that the Soviet Navy had since the mid-'Sixties expanded its operational scope well beyond the 'fleet areas' in which it had traditionally operated.[49] However, there was no significant follow-up in terms of a change in NATO strategy or the extent of the NATO area, and Lewin's efforts to interest NATO in such basic precautionary measures as establishing dormant machinery for the Naval Control of Shipping, beyond the NATO boundaries, met with little success.[50]

A particularly close relationship was established with the Royal Netherlands Navy. Collaboration between the Royal Marines and the highly regarded Korps Mariniers had been at a high level for some years, with a company of the latter stationed at Arbroath and Arctic-trained. This was useful not only in operational but public relations terms, as a unique arrangement between NATO partners. The Royal Marines, though great survivors, certainly needed at that time all the support they could get, and Lewin was at pains to provide it. At one meeting he sought a telling quotation that could be used in answer to a Parliamentary question, and it was provided by a RNR captain, who volunteered a little-known saying of Earl St Vincent: 'If I had my way, I would (apart from the Household troops and the two scientific corps) turn all the British Army into Royal Marines.'[51] It was the first time Lewin had met Captain Tony Sainsbury; they remained close friends for the rest of his life.

Admiral Maas, Lewin's counterpart in the Netherlands, was keen to extend the Marines' relationship to the two navies and was said at one time to be advocating an actual merger. This was scarcely a political starter, but there is no doubt from Lewin's notebook kept at the time that co-operation in both organisational and materiel matters was unusually close. Unhappily, it never resulted in a truly collaborative project that maximised the industrial and scientific potential of both nations, although both anti-air missiles and mine counter-measures seemed at one time to be promising areas, and British sales of gas turbines and helicopters to the Netherlands were considerable.

On the build-up of the Royal Navy during his time as VCNS, Lewin could in retrospect have had few qualms, although no doubt there were plenty at the time. The 'through deck cruiser', as it was still called, had passed through the most dangerous stages of its journey through Whitehall; the first of the class, *Invincible*, was ordered in April 1973[52] and its Sea King anti-submarine helicopters were in production, even though the V/STOL to be embarked in it remained on a knife edge. The nuclear-powered submarine programme maintained momentum, partly because it was running on such well-oiled wheels and to such an established programme that no one dared slow it down.[53] For the surface forces, no less than six Type 42 guided missile (Sea Dart) destroyers were under construction in 1973, and (to the chagrin of the Royal Corps of Naval Constructors, who had not designed them and therefore were suspicious of their integrity) seven of the stylish Type 21s. Furthermore, a new design of frigate was well past the staff requirement stage. Designated the Type 22, this was to be a more sophisticated and expensive ship than either the Type 42 or 21, with a predominantly anti-submarine role but good self-defence against missiles and aircraft. It would carry no medium-calibre gun, and indeed such guns were beginning to look rather sparsely dispersed among the fleet, since many of the ageing 'Leander' class were losing their 4.5-inch turrets on modernisation.

This flurry of building was to some extent a result of the 'Barber Boom' of 1971–2, when in a dash for growth the Chancellor of the Exchequer Anthony Barber had attempted to reduce unemployment and reflate the economy.[54] It proved a chimaera, and was already on the way to extinction when the Yom Kippur War between Egypt and Israel broke out in 1973 and an oil crisis loomed, throwing Western economies into recession. Some time before this, the naval staff had begun to study whether a more economical frigate than the Type 22 would be sensible, either to supplement it or as an alternative.

Lewin was not drawn deeply into this discussion. It is probable that, with his instinctive feeling for quality rather than quantity, he would have backed the more robust, but more expensive, solution. In any event, the Type 22 was built, but the second batch remained in considerable doubt until an intervention by Admiral Sir Edward Ashmore, by then First Sea Lord. Ashmore had been told of 'a development in American ships that seemed of the highest importance ... the Americans had told us of this 18 months before, but neither the Director involved nor the VCNS [who was then Lewin] had recognised its significance'.[55] It is now certain that this equipment was Classic Outboard, a sophisticated electronic-warfare system designed to provide both technical and tactical data for over-the-horizon detection and identification of surface ships for targeting purposes.[56] Ashmore regarded this as eminently justifying the second batch of Type 22s and it was eventually fitted in them. Lewin's failure to recognise its importance must be regarded as a sin of omission, even though he had a thousand other things to consider.

So far as above-water weaponry was concerned, the situation was in the process of being transformed from that of the mid-'Sixties. Then, the Royal Navy's chief instruments had been the combat aircraft operating from its carriers. They could operate as fighters to protect the fleet against air attack, strike opposing surface forces and mount attacks against shore installations within their range. Air defence missiles and guns carried by the ships themselves were a final layer of defence against threats that had managed to penetrate the combat air patrols; and there had been no provision at all for ships to carry a dedicated anti-ship missile, although some of the air defence systems had a secondary anti-surface mode.

Now, with the fixed-wing carriers phasing out, fighter cover from shore-based aircraft uncertain, and shore-based strike against threatening surface forces even more questionable, much more emphasis would have to be put on the surface ships' own resources in anti-air and anti-surface roles. In neither was the situation as black as it might have been without the foresight of the staff divisions – including Lewin's DTWP – ten years and more before.

Two kinds of air defence missile were becoming available. The Sea Dart was already at sea and undergoing trials in HMS *Bristol*, the only survivor of the Type 82 programme, commanded as it happened by Roddy Macdonald, who expressed his surprise and delight that the missile worked perfectly first time out.[57] With its range, speed and agility, Sea Dart could engage targets crossing its line of sight. It was thus regarded, rightly, as an area defence missile, capable of defending other ships in a force as well as its parent vessel.[58] The Sea Dart's abilities were still apparent two decades later, when in the 1991 Gulf War HMS *Gloucester* shot down an Iraqi Silkworm missile that was approaching the US battleship *Missouri*.[59]

Some five years later in the development cycle was the Sea Wolf, a point defence missile, of much shorter range than the Sea Dart with a great deal of automation built in, so that the swiftest possible reaction was in theory obtainable. It was basically a device to defend only its parent ship, but it could do so against not only incoming aircraft but missiles. During Lewin's time as VCNS the frigate *Penelope* was designated as Sea Wolf trials ship, and trials began in mid-1973.[60] It was planned that the Type 22 frigates would be fitted with the system and that a number of 'Leanders' would be converted also to carry it.

One of the problems with these all-British developments, which were eventually good systems in their own right and a great improvement on their forerunners, the Sea Slug and Sea Cat respectively, was that they proved largely unsaleable abroad.[61] This was due partly to their very long gestation period – the Sea Dart took about seventeen years from its first conception to its appearance in service – partly to their high specifications that all too often meant the theoretical best was the enemy of the practical good, and partly to the unwillingness of British operational requirements staffs, defence scientific establishments and industry to consider modifications that would satisfy overseas customers. All these conspired to make unit production costs high compared with, for example, the American Standard and Sea Sparrow missiles; potential foreign buyers were discouraged, and that in turn put even more pressure on the naval budget. Lewin, with his background in the operational requirements field, could help to find no way out of this dilemma, and it seems doubtful that he ever seriously thought of taking on the immensely powerful captains of the British defence industry or the defence scientific establishment. He would have had no assistance from the politicians, who were always anxious to safeguard jobs in their own constituencies.

In one of the above-water areas, indeed, it proved possible to procure a non-British system without much opposition. Since in the 'Sixties nobody had raised an operational requirement for a ship-mounted anti-ship missile, no British project existed. But the French had one. This was the Exocet, a sea-skimming missile that went at just under supersonic speed and homed on its target by its own built-in radar.[62] It was readily available, it needed little extra on-board equipment, it could be fitted to ships without much structural modification, and it was relatively cheap. The incoming government in 1970 put impetus into a purchase[63] and the guided missile destroyer *Norfolk* became the lead ship for an extensive fit that included all the Type 21 and 22 frigates.

This was not a difficult programme for Lewin to implement, although there was some residual perfectionism among the naval staff that regarded Exocet as a bit of a toy. It seemed all too easy, somehow. They were to be disabused, painfully, later.[64]

There remained a burning question surrounding all aspects of above water warfare: how was sufficient operational warning of developing threats to be obtained by the fleet? In the days of fixed-wing carriers this had been supplied by airborne early warning (AEW) aircraft flying from the carriers themselves; Lewin knew all about that from his days in the *Hermes*.[65] But propeller-driven AEW aircraft could not fly from the 'through-deck cruisers', even if V/STOL Harriers could, and it was debatable whether a helicopter, even of the latest Sea King type, could lift an existing AEW radar set for long enough, and high enough, to give reasonable cover. No lightweight equipment had been designed.

In the north-east Atlantic, the sea area in which – in the NATO scenario – the fleet was most likely to operate, shore-based AEW support was available from Royal Air Force Shackletons. These were ancient aircraft but, modified as they had been to carry the necessary radar, they did the job to the best of their ability. Replacement would eventually be required, and it was not certain what priority it would have, since the RAF was moving towards a very expensive time in buying its Multi-Role Combat Aircraft, the Tornado.

It is clear from Lewin's notebooks that the question of AEW, to be deployed in a helicopter, surfaced again and again during his time as VCNS. The ACNS (Operations and Air), Rear Admiral Peter Austin, and the Directorate of Naval Air Warfare were acutely aware of the deficiency, and the limitations this might put on the fleet's operational capacity. But the difficulty of justification before the operational requirements committees and the Treasury was extreme. If the NATO ticket was the only one that would admit an operational requirement, then it could and would be argued that shore-based aircraft could do the job. Thus, it appears that it was judged simply impossible to commission even a feasibility study under official auspices, although no doubt some unofficial work went on behind the scenes as in the early days of the Harrier. Indeed, even three years later, when the Sea Harrier had at last been approved and the possibility of further organic air capability gleamed, the then First Sea Lord, Admiral Sir Edward Ashmore, had to weigh AEW against competing demands, including that of a replacement for the vital Sea King anti-submarine helicopter. Reluctantly, he did not feel he 'could approve any approach which might jeopardise [the] replacement and therefore told the staff that the AEW radar must wait'.[66]

In the field of underwater warfare, always murkier than in the atmosphere on and above the sea's surface, fundamental developments were taking place. The Soviet Navy was known to have a very numerous and modern submarine force,[67] which included convention-ally- and nuclear-powered boats deploying a variety of ballistic and aerodynamic missiles as well as torpedoes. Most of the armaments were nuclear-capable. The threat was regarded as multiple and diverse:

to the homelands of the NATO nations, to their combatant forces, and to the shipping that would supply them in time of tension or war. It was a primary function of NATO maritime forces to be able to counter these threats.

The first and most critical factor in countering the threat was the ability to detect submerged submarines. As it always had been, sound was the key; other sorts of wave, including light and radar, travel badly through water. There are two basic systems using sound: it can be transmitted in a pulse in the hope of getting an echo back from the submarine (active sonar), or listening devices can be used to pick up sounds made by the submarine itself (passive sonar). Active sonar is more accurate because it can provide a range; passive sonar has the potential to detect targets, particularly noisy ones, further off because sound dispersal ('propagation loss') is much less.[68]

In the 1950s most navies' anti-submarine equipment and procedures followed on from experience in the Second World War, when the work was mostly a matter of protecting naval forces and convoys. In order to attack, submarines – still predominantly of the conventional type with diesel and electric propulsion – had to close with these escorted groups. Active sonar was the principal instrument because of the short-range encounters involved.

But already, the difficulty of keeping enough surface escorts in service to counter the numerous Soviet submarine forces was apparent, and the United States instituted a programme whereby more distant measures, employing passive sonar installations on the seabed with follow-up reaction from long-range maritime patrol aircraft and surface forces, were to be employed. This was the genesis of the SOSUS (Sound Surveillance System).[69] The US authorities calculated that the system, including the remaining escort forces, would impose acceptable attrition rates on the Soviet submarine force in the event of an Atlantic shipping campaign.[70]

In the 1960s, several factors complicated this picture. First, nuclear-powered submarines were appearing in numbers in the navies of the superpowers, with a few in those of Britain and France. These were expected to be very difficult to counter by surface escorts, even if supported by helicopters with dunking sonars and shore-based maritime patrol aircraft. In particular, active sonar contacts on these fast, manoeuvrable targets were likely to be fleeting and the attack solution would be difficult.

Secondly, Western submarines themselves, including the nuclear-powered ones, were considered to have an anti-submarine role. Their stealth; their own hydrophone equipment that could be taken below the thermal layers that so bedevilled surface sonar detections; and their ability to deploy anti-submarine torpedoes with heavy explosive warheads, all made them potentially important parts of the anti-submarine complex, provided they could be deployed in areas of high Soviet activity or 'cued' in the direction of it.

Finally, Soviet submarines turned out to be gratifyingly noisy.[71] This had been expected with the early nuclear boats, but the second generation, all entering service during Lewin's time as VCNS, were not much quieter. Thus the West believed it would have 'sonar advantage' for at least the next decade, because its own submarines were designed for maximum silence and stealth by a combination of many different construction, machinery and operating techniques.[72]

A consequence was that emphasis on passive sonar detection methods was further increased. Indeed, in Ministry of Defence circles the 'Seventies were called 'the decade of the passive' and it was assumed that that would go on into the 'Eighties. Sonobuoys dropped from aircraft, in use since the 1950s, acquired a new importance. Not only the long-range maritime patrol aircraft that had previously carried them, but anti-submarine helicopters operating from ships, would increasingly use them to detect or, more likely, classify, localise and track opposing submarines. Active sets were downgraded in importance, and in some helicopters were regarded very much as a secondary system if not discarded entirely.[73] Development of the sonobuoys themselves, and of equipment to analyse the data they transmitted to their parent units, was stepped up, on both sides of the Atlantic and also in Australia.[74]

This might have meant a severe downgrading of the role of the surface ship in anti-submarine warfare, had it not been for another development in the passive-sonar field. This was the towed array.[75] These were trains of hydrophones towed at a distance from the parent vessel, therefore in water where the ambient noise was much less, and transmitting their data back to the parent through an umbilical attached to the towing wire. Only a bearing would be obtainable, and even this might be subject to ambiguities, but it was a great deal better than nothing. Research was in progress on both sides of the Atlantic on towed arrays, and a frigate was designated during Lewin's time for the early trials.

Finally, increased emphasis on passive methods of submarine detection meant further development of the SOSUS chain. In those days this subject was spoken of, if at all, in whispers and it was not until the early 1980s that NATO issued a remarkably frank account of its capabilities.[76] During Lewin's time as VCNS he was in close contact with Admiral Hal Shear USN, who occupied the OP-95 desk in the Pentagon. It is clear[77] that he concluded with Shear an agreement or agreements that made a British contribution to SOSUS, probably in the form of shore facilities, a reality. There was also a great deal of interchange on all other aspects of passive detection; British defence scientists, notably those at the Admiralty Underwater Warfare Establishment, had long been studying and developing sophisticated techniques in this area, sometimes in advance of America's own.

The relatively rapid production of British nuclear-powered submarines gave other opportunities for US/UK collaboration. While clandestine surveillance operations by Western submarines are rightly highly classified,[78] it is fair to assume that the US Navy would have welcomed British participation in any such operations it undertook on a regular basis, and there are strong indications from a recently published and apparently well-researched book that such participation occurred.[79] It is probable that the Lewin/Shear relationship was the link at policy level, although the British Flag Officer (Submarines) remained the operating authority so far as British boats were concerned.[80]

On operations generally, the VCNS was in a central but not always comfortable position. Day-to-day programmes and control were handled by the Fleet Headquarters at Northwood under the Commander-in-Chief Fleet, and Whitehall's part in that process was to feed in requirements that stemmed from ministerial policy – either continuing, such as the need for the Beira Patrol, or shorter-term when a new confrontation or crisis arose, as in the requirement to provide frigates for protection of the fishing fleet off Iceland during the 'Second Cod War' in 1973.[81] Iceland was a member of NATO just as Britain was, and provided essential facilities to the alliance through its strategic position. In the event, both Iceland and Britain acted with enough restraint to divorce a national confrontation from the much wider, shared NATO interest, but it showed that there was no such thing as a purely military reaction to an international situation – it would always be a politico-military affair, and so Whitehall would always, and rightly, be involved. The Navy was an instrument of government: Lewin never lost sight of this.

Yet he also never lost sight of the need to keep the Navy in good heart. Recruitment and, even more importantly, retention in the Navy was a constant preoccupation, and one of the factors that worked against a healthy situation was the problem of overstretch at sea. Fleet planning in the past had not always paid enough attention to minimising turbulence – he had come across cases when he was FO2FEF where ships had had a 'bad run' that careful planning could have avoided. When plans were disrupted for operational reasons, that made it worse. The effect on morale and retention could quickly be felt. Lewin instituted studies by the Assistant Chief of Naval Staff (Operations) and the newly promoted Rear Admiral Tony Troup, known from *Chequers* days, into the problem, resulting in the 'Harmony' rules, setting limits to time away from home and family.[82]

A singular aspect of the operational scene was the deployment of the Polaris ballistic missile submarine force. Its design, building and support organisation had been the great naval success story – possibly the great British success story – of the 1960s.[83] Continuous deterrent patrol had been established in 1969,[84] with at least one submarine of the four-boat force always on station. The business of control was so detailed and sensitive that it was wisely put into a separate cell at the

Northwood headquarters with which others, including Lewin, did not interfere. He was, according to his notebook, involved in the arrangements for nuclear release procedures – the machinery for obtaining political approval to press the button *in extremis* – but there are, rightly, no further details on this most classified of all subjects.

Already, however, Ministry of Defence involvement was needed in the future of the Polaris force, and this was a matter for the Naval Staff as well as the Central Staff and the scientific establishment. In the arcane world of nuclear deterrence nothing stood still for long, and the British Polaris programme had only been a-building for a couple of years when the Soviet Union showed at its 1964 Red Square parade an anti-ballistic missile nicknamed by NATO 'Galosh'.[85] Its potential was judged to be none too great against a massive attack of the sort the Americans could launch against the Soviet Union, but the British Polaris force normally deployed only sixteen missiles at sea, and each missile dispensed only three warheads in a fairly dense cluster; it might be possible for the Russian Galoshes, when fully deployed, to destroy enough of the missiles, or warheads, to render a British strike ineffective. While British missiles would normally be assigned to NATO,[86] there was always to be a last-resort option in the case of imperative national need, and it was the integrity of this that the Soviet anti-ballistic capability was thought to threaten.

The Wilson government deliberated for some years about the problem. In 1967 staff discussions came to a head and the debate moved on to Prime Ministerial level.[87] It involved the deepest questioning of fundamental doctrine, as well as technical analysis, by Denis Healey, who after a long meeting on 14 June[88] professed himself satisfied that he could now argue in support of a programme to provide a counter to the anti-ballistic missile threat.

The counter fell into two parts. The first was to harden Polaris warheads against the explosion of the Galosh missiles, which was itself expected to be nuclear. This was a relatively cheap and easy operation, but it would only safeguard the warheads against distant explosions. If the Galosh really could 'hit a fly in space', as Khrushchev had boasted, or anything like it, it would have to be seduced away from the warheads by a system of decoys, and that was a more difficult business.

The Americans had been working on a way of doing this, a project called 'Antelope', for their own Polaris, but had discarded it in favour of their new Poseidon missile which dispensed multiple, widely dispersed warheads.[89] The British, however, decided to investigate the decoy option further. The reason was at least as much political as technical; in a minute of 24 July 1967 the Prime Minister, Harold Wilson, said the UK should 'start from the point that we have decided not to develop (or to purchase) a new generation of nuclear weapons to succeed Polaris but that it is implicit in our latest Defence White Paper that the Polaris boats will be retained into the 1970s'. Later in the note, this seemed to be modified to 'as long as the system itself remains viable', which implied a much longer timescale.[90] The Secretary of the Cabinet was instructed to institute a study of Polaris improvements by the Defence and Overseas Policy Committee at official level.

The Chiefs of Staff contributed to this study with a paper[91] that distinguished between hardening of re-entry bodies, which cost little and was quickly approved, and a programme of penetration aids which at the time was called Super Antelope.[92] This was estimated to cost £40 million. Work then proceeded in the technical establishments, and was approaching the stage of a formal feasibility study when the Heath government came to power in 1970. That study was duly approved, and was still in progress, deep in the scientific establishments, when Lewin became VCNS in 1971.

The Polaris Executive, which had been so brilliantly successful in managing the design and building project, was deemed to have done its work by 1968 and was succeeded by a slimmed-down team under the Assistant Controller (Polaris), which answered to the Controller of the Navy.[93] Naval Staff input was still necessary on policy, and like anything else of the kind, it was in VCNS's court. However it appears that Lewin foresaw the amount of detail and negotiation that might be involved, and believed it better to delegate as much as possible to a trusted high-level subordinate. One was ready to hand in the new ACNS(P), Rear Admiral Henry Leach.

The two men were fully aware of each other's exceptional qualities.[94] Leach had been Director of Naval Plans when Lewin himself was ACNS(P) in 1968–9, and his tremendous capacity for detailed work and straight thinking had been impressive. Lewin, who had not immersed himself in the detail of nuclear deterrence – indeed, one acquaintance at that time said he 'never talked nuclear'[95] – was happy for Leach to take on the naval staff input to the Polaris Improvement Programme and the Polaris Planning Group.

The first thing it did was revisit the Poseidon option. From a technical point of view, this was attractive. It would fit into the existing tubes of the Polaris boats, it would obviate an already expensive home-grown decoy programme,[96] and it would give a much more certain counter to the Galosh system if fitted with its numerous MIRV (Multiple Independently-manoeuvring Re-entry Vehicle) warheads. Leach was in favour of this solution,[97] and it is said that joint studies by the naval staff of the UK and USA in 1972 recommended it.[98]

However, there were snags. The first was initial cost. Poseidon would make a deeper hole in the defence budget in certain years than would the slower drip of Super Antelope (renamed Chevaline in 1973). The second was political. It was by no means certain that the US Congress would approve the transfer of Poseidon technology, either with or without the MIRVs, to the UK,[99] and even less certain that Britain's Labour Party would go on with such a project if it returned to government. The third was a matter of internal Whitehall politics. Ministry of Defence scientists in the nuclear field had been working on the decoy system for years, were deeply dedicated to it and in many cases saw their careers bound up with it. Led by Victor Macklen, an astute operator of the Whitehall machinery, they argued cogently for the home-grown solution.

In the end, Leach allowed himself to be persuaded against Poseidon and the Chevaline project went ahead.[100] As has been suggested, this did not at the time occupy a very large part of Lewin's attention. It is necessary to tell the story thus far, however, because problems connected with it arose, in acute form, during his time as First Sea Lord.[101]

Polaris improvements were not by any means the only concern of Henry Leach as ACNS(P). He was acknowledged as the master of the Long-term Costings, the machinery by which the funding of the country's defences for the next ten years was managed. It was typical of the flexible nature of the naval staff organisation that this particular talent, honed during his time as Director of Naval Plans in 1968–70, was utilised in this way; the remit had changed completely since Terry Lewin had held the post of ACNS(P).

Although a master of the arcane arts of Wedging, Pain and Grief Exercises, Shadow Cuts and all the other devices with which staffs sought to alleviate the constant Treasury raids on defence finances, Leach always sought to play it straight. A story is told by Admiral Sandy Woodward, an Assistant Director of Plans at the time.[102] Henry Leach, sick at last of manoeuvring, suggested at a meeting with Terry – 'Why can't we be absolutely honest?' – and then embarked on a half-hour narrative of the Navy's aspirations and problems, warts and all, which by implication he suggested should be put baldly to ministers. According to Woodward, Terry looked at him under his eyebrows, twinkled and said, 'Well, Henry, that's fine: but do you really believe we can afford to be the only honest department in government?'

Yet it is no paradox to say that the honest presentation of the Royal Navy, as an armed service doing a worthwhile job for the security of the nation, was a principal concern of Lewin during his time as VCNS. Public perception of the services had hit a nadir in about 1968, when younger members of the Navy became quite accustomed to being asked by civilian contemporaries how they liked being hired assassins of the capitalist state. Counter-currents soon became apparent. Partly as a result of the more intellectual approach initiated by Healey, and aided by the balanced and thoughtful observations of eminent commentators like Michael Howard, 'the profession of arms' (Howard's phrase) was on the way to re-establishing its reputation by 1971.

There was still much to be done. Lewin's arrival in office coincided with the formation of a Royal Naval Presentation Team to tour the country and present 'the naval case'. It was to be headed by Captain

Raymond Lygo, fresh from command of HMS *Ark Royal* and a receiver at first hand of unwelcome Soviet naval attention when the *Ark* collided with a shadowing 'Kotlin' class destroyer in 1970. Much attention was paid by the naval staff, from the First Sea Lord on down, to the progress of Lygo's team.[103] The presentation was on lines that subsequently became familiar: the importance of the sea to Britain, the NATO alliance, the Soviet threat and British naval provision and plans.[104] The presentation team became a permanent feature of naval public relations and did valuable work in reminding people of what the Navy was for and what it did.

Television provided a much less selective and wider audience, and here Lewin was more actively involved. A bright Assistant Secretary in his office, Lieutenant-Commander Ian Mackintosh, conceived an idea for a drama series centred on a frigate of the Royal Navy. This was accepted by the BBC, approved by the Admiralty Board, and the 'Warship' series was instituted, with BBC editorial control and Mackintosh providing naval advice and writing some of the scripts.[105] It was a brave move by all the organisations concerned and owed much to Lewin's support. There was inevitably some sniping from those who thought the Navy ought to remain the Silent Service, but the effect of the series was overwhelmingly positive and it led to a more open attitude to the media generally, which was on balance beneficial to the services.

There were more direct attempts to improve public awareness of what the Royal Navy was about. A *Financial Times* survey in 1973 provided a comprehensive reference, with a covering article by the Defence Correspondent Michael Donne and substantial pieces by all the Sea Lords and the Vice Chief of Naval Staff. Lewin's contribution was on 'The Concept of Operations' and showed many similarities to his 1968 speech to the RUSI.[106] The underlying principle of deterrence, operating at all levels of confrontation or conflict, was stressed, as was the 'manifest ability to reinforce'. The need for each element of the fleet and its support, in a multiplicity of possible situations, was carefully pointed out, without recourse to scenarios that might be hostages to fortune. V/STOL was mentioned in guarded terms: 'A study is being made.' NATO was stated to be 'the first priority in the conduct of naval operations' – but the Navy's part in the protection of national interests was not discarded. The whole of this carefully crafted exercise reads rather well a generation later.

A wider look at 'Britain and the Sea' was provided by a conference at Greenwich to commemorate the centenary of the foundation of the Royal Naval College in those historic buildings. This had the enthusiastic support of Lewin – the Offshore Tapestry was highly relevant – and attracted a most distinguished battery of speakers.[107] The interdependence of many aspects of 'the sea affair', with all the developments that were taking place in the use of the sea, led many to look for a more co-ordinated government policy. This never came to pass in structural terms – there never was a British Ministry for the Sea – but the conference led to the foundation of the Greenwich Forum, which has been active in promoting British interest in the sea, through networking and conferences, ever since.

This has been the longest chapter in the life of Terry Lewin, not only because it was one of his longest periods of service – the appointment lasted very nearly three years – but because it was the busiest. Those who worked with him had often marvelled at his capacity for sustained and concentrated work. It was never more fully shown than in his time as VCNS.[108] Yet no one ever heard him raise his voice; no one ever found him less than courteous, even when he was being firm as he often had to be. He worked from 9 am to 7 pm and went home every night, shunning the naval staff fashion of keeping late hours at his desk and then retiring to a flat or bedsitter near the centre of town.

Home was initially Kent, but the Lewins moved to Nutley in Sussex in 1973. Tim, who had married in 1972, spent the first few months of marriage with Carolyn ('Woody') Lewin near this village and told his parents of a small house available there, and Limes Cottage became the home of the senior Lewins for the next ten years.

Terry's care for his staff was meticulous in practical terms as well as in manner. When, early in his time, one of his directors, who had not served in the Ministry of Defence before, found himself unable to cope and had to be relieved, Lewin was not only personally sympathetic but instituted an inquiry into how such a situation should be avoided. It was quickly agreed with the appointers that in future all directors and deputy directors should have served in the Ministry of Defence before, so that they knew what they were in for.

But above all, the whole approach was encapsulated in something he said to his incoming Secretary, Captain Don Beadle, when the latter joined in December 1971. 'Don't forget, Don, it is all done by good-will.' All the other attributes and activities – diligent enquiry, assembling and memorising the important facts, applying the necessary vision and imagination, mastery of the brief, selecting and maintaining achievable aims, choosing the right arguments – were to be informed by that unique combination of warmth and energy that he radiated.

It had for some time been generally recognised that he possessed the qualities needed to take him to the highest appointments. In fact, consideration had been given in 1970, when the crisis caused by LeFanu's illness became acute, to promoting him directly to the post of First Sea Lord, over the heads of dozens of admirals, to exercise a long tenure of the top job.[109] This had been opposed by Admiral Sir Peter Hill-Norton, about to become Chief of the Defence Staff, on the grounds that Lewin needed more time and experience, and that the services 'would get more out of him' if they waited for him to come into his own in due course.[110] Lewin himself, when he knew about this much later, was thankful it had not happened: 'Sanity prevailed,' he wrote.[111]

After his time as VCNS, however, no one could have doubted his star quality. It was that which he took to the command of the fleet in December 1973.

FLEET COMMAND
1974–1975

Newly promoted to the rank of full admiral, Sir Terence Lewin (he had been made a Knight Commander of the Bath in January) took over command of the Fleet in December 1973. It was the only fleet Britain had left; the overseas commands, Far East, Mediterranean, and further into history South Atlantic, China and West Indies, had all gone the way of Empire. But there was still a good deal of British sea power about, and no one had done more than Lewin himself to ensure that its influence would still be felt not only in the NATO area but worldwide. Now, with the headquarters facilities that had been steadily built up over the years at Northwood, Middlesex, and were known by the unlovely acronym OPCON (short for Operational Command and Control), it was he, through his staff, who would plan and operate the activities of the Navy's deterrent and fighting arm.[1]

The shore staff were numerous and of high calibre. A Chief of Staff, either a vice or rear admiral, headed a cluster of captains and commanders, some of them seaman specialists and some with engineering or supply duties; there was a Captain of the Fleet, of whom more later, to provide the Commander-in-Chief's grass-roots contact with the ships. A vast team of communications experts manned the web of equipments by which the fleet was controlled. The Secretariat, under Captain Don Beadle who had accompanied Lewin from Whitehall, dealt with the mass of paperwork that inevitably accompanied this complex and widespread command.

It was an organisation in which it was very easy to become impersonal and remote, and Lewin lost no time in emphasising his individual style to ensure this did not happen. An officer who was one of the most junior on the staff at the time recalled that after all the ceremony of the turnover of command:

By mid-afternoon the whole [Northwood] base was as quiet as a middle watch at Fountain Lake jetty in Portsmouth ... the Duty Lieutenant Commander [DLC] arrived in the wardroom to enjoy his one beer of the day ... three sips into his beer he got the message that 'there was a bit of a flap on' as the Commander-in-Chief himself was 'down the hole' (the secret underground part of the base). No one had been at the main gate to salute him ... The DLC was off faster than a greyhound leaving its trap ... The armed Royal Marine guard on duty confirmed that the Commander-in-Chief had indeed passed earlier, dressed in slacks and a sweater ... [the DLC] eventually found Admiral Lewin sitting back to front on a standard typist's chair casually chatting to one of the on-watch Wren communicators ... genuinely surprised that just his presence on 'his' base could cause so much consternation.[2]

The only subsequent 'flap' was to get enough milk for the duty watch to have a cup of tea with their new admiral.

At sea, the Commander-in-Chief had three subordinate commanders, the Flag Officers of the First and Second Flotillas and the Flag Officer Aircraft Carriers. These had administrative, and often operational, control over the ships and aircraft subordinated to them and it was they who would take units to sea, including deployments for major cruises or exercises. Their staffs were necessarily small. This was a relatively clear-cut organisation. That for submarines was less so. The Flag Officer, Submarines was subordinate to the Commander-in-Chief but was still located at Gosport and had a good deal of autonomy; the situation was complicated further by the fact that the Polaris cell was at Northwood. Operational command and control of submarines, with their natural mode of operation as lone wolves, was a chronically difficult problem to solve, as was to be demonstrated sharply several times within the next decade.

Two other flag officers were closely associated with the Commander-in-Chief of the Fleet. The Flag Officer Sea Training at Portland was responsible for delivering fully worked-up ships to the fleet after they had recommissioned or undergone substantial crew changes. Here too there was a large degree of autonomy. There had been times in the past when the necessarily high tempo, and requirement for quantified results, had resulted in a rigid attitude and rejection of anything that was not the 'staff answer'.[3] This needed watching. The other authority was the Flag Officer Naval Aviation, whose headquarters was at Yeovilton in Somerset; he was responsible for all shore training of naval air squadrons, and the closest liaison had to be established between his staff and that of the Fleet to ensure that aircraft operating from ships were at maximum efficiency and utilisation.

There was, then, a great deal of networking to be done at all levels if the Fleet was to carry out its national tasks to the best of its potential. But that was not all. The Commander-in-Chief of the UK Fleet was also a NATO Commander. He was the Commander-in-Chief Eastern Atlantic Area (CINCEASTLANT), a sub-command of the Allied Command Atlantic but comprising nearly half of that vast area and, arguably, the most important bit, with all the approaches to northern Europe and the strategically vital Norwegian Sea; and he was also the Allied Commander-in-Chief, Channel (CINCHAN). By a curious historical anomaly, CINCHAN was a higher-grade command than CINCEASTLANT, since the Channel area came under neither of the Supreme Allied Commanders, Atlantic or Europe, and CINCHAN therefore ranked with them though, it had to be acknowledged, as a rather poor relation. CINCEASTLANT, on the other hand, was a subordinate commander to the Supreme Allied Commander Atlantic.

While neither of these NATO commands was activated except for exercises or in time of crisis, both needed care and feeding. They had permanent staffs at Northwood drawn from the nations of the alliance and headed by a Chief of Allied Staff who reported to the Commander-in-Chief and would in time of tension or war assume exceptionally heavy responsibilities. Here Lewin was singularly lucky in having as his COAS Rear Admiral Pierre Besnard of the Royal Netherlands Navy.[4] Tall, courteous and calm, Besnard sometimes gave the impression of a diplomat in uniform, but his manner hid an astute professionalism and Lewin regarded him very highly.

There was one further vital link, and that was with the Royal Air Force. The Royal Navy and Coastal Command – now 18 Group RAF – had since before the Second World War been accustomed to working together, and had steadily developed their procedures and command relationships. Co-location of their headquarters at Northwood had improved matters further. Now, with the responsibility for operational support of the Fleet by combat as well as patrol aircraft passing more and more to the Royal Air Force, Strike Command, with its head-quarters at High Wycombe, came more into the picture. Here again Lewin was fortunate in his colleagues. In charge of 18 Group was Air Vice Marshal Doug Lowe, a vastly effective and pragmatic figure; and at High Wycombe was the welcome presence of Air Chief Marshal 'Splinters' Smallwood, now Commander-in-Chief, Strike Command. As has been shown,[5] there was strong mutual confidence between him and Lewin, cultivated during difficult times as Vice Chiefs of Staff of their respective services.

A Commander-in-Chief may long to get afloat, but has few oppor-tunities to do so. It is not possible to control all the activities, much less the administration, of a widespread and still numerous fleet from a flagship, however sophisticated, and links with politico-military direc-tion from Whitehall are weaker. Most of the business of the Fleet there-fore has to be handled by the rear link in the shore headquarters, if the Commander-in-Chief is away at sea or on representative duty. Mutual trust and understanding between the boss and his supporting staff is essential and Lewin was always careful to emphasise this. He relaxed the custom of receiving daily situation reports from the Chief of Staff and encouraged more junior members to make their own decisions.[6] He paid great attention to the confidential reports on his staff officers, seeking to ensure that merit was recognised.

The first opportunity for a full-scale fleet visit occurred in February 1974. Admiral of the Fleet Sir Michael Pollock was leaving the post of First Sea Lord after an exceptionally difficult three and a half years[7] during which his acknowledged wisdom and good humour had been fully tested. It was right that the Fleet should say goodbye to him in a fitting manner, and an assembly at Virgin Gorda in the West Indies was to be the occasion. Plans for the assembly had been made by the Flag Officer First Flotilla, Rear Admiral Iwan Raikes, and his staff.

The assembly began with the arrival of Raikes in HMS *Blake* (whose behaviour had improved, under careful management, in recent years) on 12 February, and built up steadily to a gathering of nine major surface units, a submarine and three RFAs. The Commander-in-Chief arrived by helicopter and hoisted his flag in HMS *Kent*.[8] The big day was 14 February, with the arrival of the First Sea Lord flying his flag in HMS *Bulwark*, still in her role as a commando carrier. His busy schedule included visits to five ships of the assembled force, a reception by the Fleet chief petty officers and chief petty officers on board *Kent*, watching boat competitions of varying degrees of professionalism and versatility, and a final sports session on the flight deck of the *Bulwark* which included the 'horse-racing under floodlights' that had been so popular in the *Hermes* under Lewin's command almost ten years before.

On 15 February the ships proceeded to sea and carried out the traditional steam and fly-past, cheering their First Sea Lord on his way. It had been a grand send-off and something of a family occasion for the Navy. If commentators thought it just another example of mucking about in boats, they were entitled to their opinion. For Terry Lewin, it had been an ideal opportunity to sense the pulse of the fleet and to begin impressing his own personality upon it.

He found little to disturb him greatly. Already he had recognised that the slight lightening of the reins, suited to his style of command, had paid dividends in encouraging initiative and confidence. As for the Fleet's fighting efficiency, the steady introduction of the Principal Warfare Officer scheme was sharpening the all-important area of timely command and control, and was soon to be matched by a similar change in the rating structure with the formation of the Operations Branch.[9] Operational readiness and the state of maintenance of the ships was always a worry, but the transition from steam to gas turbine propulsion in new construction gave promise that it would be less so in future.

One matter, however, was of some concern and he discussed this with his Captain of the Fleet, Tom Baird. It was to do with drink. The

Navy's rum issue, the 'tot', had been abolished in 1971 with remark-ably little fuss, in spite of dire predictions from some.[10] It was gener-ally recognised that the issue of an eighth of a pint of spirit at midday, every day, was simply not tolerable in a highly technical navy that depended for safety, as well as fighting efficiency, on precise mainte-nance and operation of equipment. The move had been accompanied by a considerable relaxation of the rules about consumption of other forms of alcohol, notably in chief and petty officers' messes.

Lewin's attitude to these changes had been entirely positive; he had anticipated them in *Hermes*. However, it is clear that he was surprised by the amount of alcohol consumed at the Virgin Gorda assembly, and evidence that in some cases privileges were being abused. Both he and Tom Baird had had experience of deaths due to excessive drinking,[11] and even though these dated from the era of the 'tot' and the associ-ated 'sippers' or 'gulpers' on special occasions,[12] they resolved to do their best to check any ill-effects from the new liberal regime.

The medium chosen was the Captain of the Fleet's Newsletter, an innovation of Roddy Macdonald's when he had the job and now regu-larly circulated throughout the fleet. It addressed concerns that Baird, on his frequent and always sympathetic visits to ships, had found most affected sailors. Each newsletter began to contain 'Salutary Tales' where people had fallen short in their duty or discipline, or worse still ruined their health. A typical piece of lateral thinking was introduced by Terry: 'Tom, have we got this the wrong way round? Why not have a "sensible drinking" campaign?'[13] One way and another, it worked: not completely, as in the nature of things it could not, but a more sensible attitude emerged and incipient excess was checked.

On drugs, Lewin and Baird perceived less of a problem. The Fleet, as it trailed away from the Far East at the end of the 1960s, had been by no means free of both soft and hard drug abuse, but determined efforts by the provost departments at home had helped to diminish the incidence, and so had the attitude of the great majority of sailors: basically, they were against three things, theft, buggery and drugs, and would be more likely to shop their chums for those than for anything else.[14]

While the Fleet went about its business in accordance with its planned programme, in Britain it was anything but business as usual. The economic situation had greatly worsened in the last few months of 1973 and the first two of 1974; the miners' strike and the three-day working week caused by power shortages led in March to a general election and the fall of the Heath government. A Labour government under Harold Wilson took office. Roy Mason was the new Secretary of State for Defence and Denis Healey Chancellor of the Exchequer. A further defence review was the inevitable outcome.

However, the effects were not felt in the Fleet anything like as violently as they might have been. Mason proved a robust Secretary of State, and he was backed by an exceptionally able team of Chiefs of Staff, with Field Marshal Sir Michael Carver as CDS, Admiral Sir Edward Ashmore as CNS, General Sir Peter Hunt as CGS and Air Chief Marshal Sir Andrew Humphrey as CAS. The combined intellectual power of these men was formidable, and Carver ensured that it stayed combined, regarding it as his most important task to hold the Chiefs of Staff together.[15] They established a 'Critical Level' beneath which the respective forces could not be allowed to sink without endangering the cohesion of NATO, and this not only safeguarded the main British Fleet strength which was the largest ready contribution to the EASTLANT area, but also the amphibious force which had now established itself as the most credible means of reinforcing northern Norway in time of crisis.[16]

Moreover, no obstacle was put by the new government in the way of further Group Deployments. These were supported by the Foreign Office, who liked to feel that the Royal Navy was helping to maintain the influence of Britain abroad, and the departments connected with trade and industry, who could see some spin-off for the economy, whether related to arms sales or to exports in some less direct way. Rear Admiral Clayton's group reached Australia, without any attempt to recall it or modify its itinerary, at the end of May 1974[17] and preparations went ahead for a further deployment under Rear Admiral Henry Leach in the autumn.[18] The foundations laid by Lewin as VCNS for retaining an element of worldwide reach for the Royal Navy were paying off.

During the summer of 1974, ironically, the fleet was heavily involved in one of the areas the Carver/Mason review set out as no longer being 'critical' to the UK defence effort in the NATO context. This was the eastern Mediterranean, where in June the Turkish government, alarmed by a takeover of the Cyprus government by a radical Greek faction with consequent threat to the large minority Turkish-Cypriot population, mounted a full-scale invasion of northern Cyprus. The consequent evacuation of some 1500 expatriates, of 29 different nationalities, from Kyrenia was handled by HMS *Bulwark* and 41 Commando Royal Marines, supported by HM Ships *Devonshire, Andromeda, Rhyl* and *Brighton* and the Royal Fleet Auxiliaries *Olna, Olwen, Gold Rover* and *Regent*. 815 and 845 Squadrons provided the helicopter lift.[19] It was a remarkable demonstration of naval versatility.

Operational contingencies or not, the Commander–in-Chief had to visit and tour extensively if he was to do his full job of keeping in touch with his fleet, fostering alliances and meeting as many as possible of the people who might be useful to the Navy or the nation in the future. NATO meetings were a high priority; he was in the Brussels area on average once a month, and there was immensely impressed, as so many others were, by the then Secretary-General, Joseph Luns. A tall, articulate Dutchman of commanding presence, Luns was a dominant figure in the NATO of the 'Seventies and was of enormous benefit to the alliance. The admiration was mutual: when Lewin left the job of C.-in-C. Fleet, Luns wrote a charming note saying that he had shown 'a keen understanding of Alliance affairs ... a reassuringly broad grasp of the political as well as the military facts of life in the Alliance'.[20]

Another powerful figure was General Al Haig, the Supreme Allied Commander, Europe. His history as a Nixon aide at the time of the Watergate scandal in the USA had not predisposed the alliance to welcome him with open arms, but his evident competence and political skill had quickly commanded respect and he and Terry Lewin got on well.[21] It was a state of mutual respect and trust that was to have critical results later.

On 11 October 1974 the second general election of the year resulted in the return of a Labour government with an increased

majority. Southern Africa was one of the foreign policy preoccupa-
tions of this fourth Wilson government. There was growing irritation
over the ineffectiveness of the Beira Patrol in stopping shipments of
oil reaching Rhodesia, still clinging to illegally declared independence. Frank Judd, the Navy Minister, had visited ships on the patrol
in the summer and no doubt sensed frustration.[22] The South African
regime was regarded as Rhodesia's chief accomplice in the devious
arrangements whereby oil got to Rhodesia[23] and was in any case
tainted with apartheid.

Only a few days after the election, the next Group Deployment left
the United Kingdom for a nine-month operational tour of the Indian
Ocean and Far East. It was the largest yet, consisting of *Blake*, five
frigates and three Royal Fleet Auxiliaries, and the nuclear-powered
submarine *Warspite*.[24] Since the Suez Canal was still closed, the force
was scheduled to round the Cape of Good Hope and a visit to Simonstown, near Capetown, was included in the plan. This caused a considerable political stir and newspaper headlines: why had Rear Admiral
Henry Leach, the Flag Officer First Flotilla and in charge of the
deployment, allowed his ships to visit the pariah regime in South
Africa, fire a national salute, offer and accept entertainment?[25]

Back in Northwood, Lewin stood the fire patiently, distinguishing
carefully between an 'operational' and an 'informal' visit (the group's
was 'operational', the kind that had least diplomatic overtones), and
emphasising the need for stopovers on an extended deployment like
this. He took the trouble, too, to reassure Henry Leach's wife Mary,
who had been assailed by the Press in her garden at Sutton Scotney and
given a robust interview in consequence, that he fully supported her
and that her words had done much good.[26]

This deployment was the only one that ran from start to finish
during Lewin's time in command of the Fleet, and it was natural that
he should take particular interest in it. Its emphasis was on the Indian
Ocean and the CENTO alliance figured prominently. CENTO was an
ill-assorted association of states each with its own agenda. Apart from
the USA and UK, it consisted of Iran, Turkey and Pakistan. Iran, still
under the Shah, thought it an aid to establishing a dominant position

in the Gulf; Pakistan would have liked it to buttress her against the perceived threat from India, but the USA was reluctant to recognise any threat but the Soviet; and Turkey regarded it as a stabilising influence to the south-east but not much more. In spite of these disparate objectives all three regional members benefited enough from the alliance, through arms supplies and training support, to make it worth their while.[27]

Leach's deployment was scheduled, after its controversial call at Simonstown and a less politically fraught one at Mombasa, to take part in Exercise Midlink, the annual CENTO event in the north-west Indian Ocean, in November 1974. This was an unusually large Midlink, with over 50 ships taking part, and a good opportunity for Terry Lewin to meet some of his ships as well as the CENTO authorities. He accordingly flew to Karachi for the first leg of a carefully planned tour, visited ships of the deployment and attended the post-exercise discussion. Relaxation took the form of Burns Night with the Karachi Caledonian Society, haggis included.[28]

There followed a whirlwind tour of the Indian Ocean. First came a visit to Diego Garcia, where in this British Indian Ocean Territory a leased US base was building up and British presence and nominal authority was maintained by a small naval party of 26 men. Then there was a 48-hour stay in Mauritius, where he had a more serious task. He visited the Communications Centre that had for many years served the Royal Navy's needs in the East, but was now being superseded by new communications methods including satellite, and announced its planned closure. Mauritius was rightly a prized draft for a lucky few, and there must have been some sadness here. After that Lewin flew to the Gulf, visiting first the RAF base at Masirah, then two frigates operating in those waters, then the Iranian base at Bandar Abbas where an impressive British training team was working up Iranian ships.[29]

It had in all taken ten days. Everywhere he went, the Commander-in-Chief had met not only the British units in his widespread command, but local and allied authorities. Such tours are often regarded, by those who have never had the responsibility of them, as swanning around in rather pleasant conditions and chatting amiably with a few like-minded people. It is not quite like that. Not only is constant travel tiring; so is meeting new faces, establishing rapport quickly – for there never is much time – putting one's own and one's country's message across, and, just as important, listening to the concerns of others.

Back at Northwood, there was as always much to be done and a steady entertaining load for both Terry and Jane. Not only were there the local (and particularly the NATO) staffs to be recognised, there were constant visitors from other commands in the United Kingdom, and from ships and flotilla staffs; and when foreign ships visited British ports their senior officers would generally call on the Commander-in-Chief. Contrary to some assertions, the Lewins did not 'run Admiralty House as a mess'[30] and the immensely devoted and loyal staff found themselves fully employed.

The remoteness of Northwood from the sea and ships was an evident anomaly, which had persisted for over 20 years. Some regarded it as more apparent than real; road and rail communications with outports were acknowledged not always to be convenient, but given Northwood's central position they were more or less equally inconvenient for everybody, and communication by telephone and radio was improving all the time. Others took the view that the proper place for a Fleet Commander was by the sea, and in 1973 the then Commander-in-Chief had put forward a plan for the headquarters to move to the Portsmouth area.[31] One of the claimed advantages was that it would have then been unnecessary to move the Flag Officer Submarines, already based at Portsmouth.

Lewin's view on this proposal, which rumbled on in his first year as Commander-in-Chief, was that the link with the RAF was more important than any other factor, and would be badly damaged by a naval move to Portsmouth. He and Smallwood had recently instituted flag and air officers' meetings, with the slogan 'There are no problems at the sharp end which starts here'. All that confidence would have had to be rebuilt. Additional to this were the effects on NATO staff, who liked being close to London; the loss of proximity to Whitehall; the increased difficulty of getting to other outports in the United Kingdom;

and, as always, the initial cost. Thus he took the opposite view, and strongly supported a move by the Flag Officer, Submarines to Northwood. However he felt he did not need to work too actively against the Portsmouth proposal: 'Let others squash it,' he said,[32] and others – and money – did.

The year 1975 saw him as active as ever. Arctic deployments by the Royal Marines were exercised every winter, and he visited 45 Commando on Exercise Clockwork in northern Norway in February. In early March he was for three days with a Fleet gathering in Gibraltar, somewhat reminiscent of the combined fleet events before and after the Second World War. Sixteen warships were assembled to take advantage of the better weather for weapon training and, when in harbour, for inter-ship and squadron sports, with a race to the top of the Rock as the crowning event.[33]

It was time to begin planning for the return of Henry Leach's Group Deployment to the United Kingdom. The furore over the South African call on the way out had been such that any sort of visit there seemed out of the question, and indeed when even the possibility of sending a RFA tanker to Durban for mail was broached, this was refused by ministers.[34] The Suez Canal was still closed, although British mine clearance teams were continuing their collaborative work. Lewin was most keen that the group, which had worked extremely hard as well as seeing the world from Japan to the Arabian Gulf, should have a final bright-lights visit.

The solution he hit upon could scarcely have been simpler. *Ark Royal* (still running, in spite of forebodings for at least the last ten years), *Hampshire* and three RFAs were due to visit Brazil in May; why should Leach's group not join up with them in Rio de Janeiro? The compliment to the Brazilians would be well received; the joint exercises with their navy would be bigger and better; and Rio was big enough, and bright enough, to take such a visit. So the staff got to work, the necessary diplomatic negotiations were conducted, and the visit happened, and was memorable.[35]

During the summer the decision to proceed with the Sea Harrier was finally announced.[36] A ship of the Fleet, in a prominent place, was needed to mark this momentous event. The Assault Ship *Fearless* was the ship, and Greenwich the place, on 24 June, to coincide with an Atlantic Treaty Association seminar at the Royal Naval Staff College. A Harrier duly landed; Terry Lewin was host at a reception on board; there was an exhibition of naval equipment.[37] It was not inappropriate that *Fearless* was now the Dartmouth Training Ship, successor to Lewin's squadron in the early 'Sixties. A role closer to that originally planned for her was to come in 1982, but it would have needed a crystal ball to see that.

Lewin now knew what his next appointment would be. He was to be relieved by Admiral Sir John Treacher in October 1975, and would become Commander-in-Chief Naval Home Command in succession to Admiral Sir Derek Empson. This had initially been very unwelcome news. The Fleet was a highly attractive command, and he would have done less than two years; the Naval Home Command, though varied and interesting with its emphasis on shore training and administration, could scarcely be regarded as so exciting or professionally rewarding, and it looked remarkably like a dead end. Admiral Sir Edward Ashmore, the First Sea Lord, was able to give some reassurance (through their respective secretaries)[38] that he wished simply to widen Terry's experience, though without of course offering any guarantee that he would eventually reach the top job.

So it was time for a final surge by the Commander-in-Chief. The next Group Deployment, consisting of a guided missile destroyer, five frigates and three RFAs, left the United Kingdom on 22 July. It was under the command of Rear Admiral John Fieldhouse, who had been Lewin's commander in *Hermes* and a much-respected Director of Naval Warfare when Lewin was VCNS. It would go round the world, making transits of the newly reopened Suez Canal and the Panama; it would exercise in the Mediterranean, the South China Sea, Australian waters and the west coast of the USA; it would see the West Indies at the best time of year, January and February. The staffs looked to have done well on this one.

Lewin built his own last tour as Commander-in-Chief around this deployment, planning to visit them as they went through Singapore and on to his familiar exercise grounds in the South China Sea. But it was to take in much more than just the Fleet, since he too would go round the world; and Jane was to come as well.

They travelled in a Comet of RAF Transport Command; it is said this was the last time such a privilege was extended to a Commander-in-Chief. They touched down at Doha in the Gulf, night-stopped at Gan in the middle of the Indian Ocean, went on to Singapore and visited the group with warm welcome and goodwill. Then it was on to Hong Kong and near-disaster, when after the notoriously steep approach to Kai Tak airport the aircraft burst three tyres on landing and finally stopped too close for comfort to the waters of Hong Kong harbour. Once the damage was rectified, they went on to the Philippines, to Guam and the large American base there, to Wake Island and Hawaii. In all these places there was great interest from the US authorities in the activities of the British Fleet both in and outside the NATO area, and very general approval of the policies being followed. They flew on to San Diego, the main west coast base of the US Navy, discussing the forthcoming group visit and meeting Royal Navy officers on exchange, with their families, and then to Ottawa where a return to the NATO fold was signalled. The final event of a memorable tour was a birthday party for Lady Lewin over the Atlantic.[39]

In October 1975 Lewin turned over command of the Fleet to Admiral Sir John Treacher, an aviator behind whose cheerfulness and youthful manner lay both judgement and determination. No one could be in doubt that a first-class outfit was being bequeathed to a worthy successor.

Terry Lewin had, then, achieved much during his Command-in-Chief. The 'sharp end' of the Royal Navy was in good shape and in good heart, an instrument well suited for the support of alliances and the furtherance of national objectives. He had satisfactorily established a pattern of operations that maximised the Fleet's potential, and its fighting efficiency was not in doubt.

Yet he would have been the first to say that it was, in the end, all about people. The administration and machinery of command might be all right, and he saw to it that it was, but the spark of leadership was the essential element to keep the Fleet thoroughly happy and effi-cient, and this he provided in his unique way.

Few incoming Commanders-in-Chief would have asked an incumbent flag lieutenant whether he preferred to live in Admiralty House, or independently; they would have given direction one way or the other. Lewin asked,[40] and readily assented to John Lippiett, his flag lieutenant's, living out. Nor would many have so gracefully accepted Lieutenant Lippiett's one peccadillo, when after oversleeping he appeared breathless, unbreakfasted but immaculately dressed, just in time for a very formal NATO parade. 'Missed you at breakfast,' murmured Terry, and gave him an alarm clock for Christmas.

Formality was not, in any case, one of Terry Lewin's traits. On the contrary, he made known his dislike of unnecessary pomp and circumstance.[41] He tended to arrive for quite important national visits in a beret and the 'woolly pully' that was standard officers' working dress, and if he stipulated a more formal procedure – guard, band and full ceremonial – it was always for a reason, usually to ensure that a ship or establishment about to embark on some event that demanded pomp could do it properly. There were occasions when his staff found it necessary to explain apparent inconsistencies in policy:[42] he thought that a price worth paying.

During Fleet visits, he was always particularly keen to sound out the view of senior ratings. The rate of Fleet Chief Petty Officer had been introduced some five years before, and this had enhanced the status of all the Navy's middle management. Lewin had long been convinced of their key position and his easy informal manner ensured that they did not hold back in voicing their concerns. Many informants have commented on his personal interest in individuals, and his phenomenal memory for names and faces. Some important people have a knack of making everyone in a large gathering feel they are the one person the visitor has come to see: Terry Lewin was one of these. It stems generally, and in Lewin's case certainly did, from a genuine interest in people as individuals, and the natural warmth that goes with that: and goodwill, always goodwill.

Examples of this exceptional touch are legion, and one or two will have to do. A tour of northern Norway in winter was disrupted, savagely and not without danger, by blizzards. Lewin to the naval attaché, as the hosts reordered the programme: 'Remember that single magpie we saw this morning?'[43] An introductory call at Northwood by a junior commander-in-command of an ancient frigate yielded the information that her Beira patrol was likely to be cancelled. 'What would you like to do instead?' asked Terry – and they got their heads together over a chart and outlined a tour for her to Singapore and Hong Kong. 'Fine,' said the Commander-in-Chief, 'I will talk to the planners and we will make it work if we can.'[44] It did; but not many a C.-in-C. would get things moving in such a way.

Another call was by the prospective commanding officer of the communications station at Mauritius, tasked with managing its closure in due course. This was after Terry's Indian Ocean circuit of November 1974. 'There', he said, 'is a memento of my visit which I treasure.' It was a framed pencil drawing that looked like a pair of chicken's legs. He explained that he had visited the Naval School to speak to the pupils and that afterwards the headmaster had invited them to draw pictures of the admiral's visit. Among them was this picture of his legs, which was all the smallest children, sitting in the front, could see of him.[45]

It was no wonder everyone was charmed: and all the more so because the warmth came from inside, was never artificial or assumed. In this Jane willingly supported him. She too disliked pomp and circumstance, but she took a great deal of personal trouble to look after her guests at every level; and she established true friendships, for example with Lady Smallwood at High Wycombe and Angie Baird at Northwood. Spontaneity was never far away: at an airfield near Ottawa on their round-the-world tour, with the Commander-in-Chief about to leave in full fig for an official event, she broke away from the 'ladies' programme' saying, 'I haven't said goodbye to Terry', crossed an expanse of tarmac and gave him a hug.[46]

It was no wonder their personal staff worshipped them and worked their socks off. Lewin was beginning to establish a more widespread 'following': Captain Don Beadle had now been his Secretary in two appointments, Chief Steward Jack Frost was becoming a fixture;

Rodney Stannard of the Royal Marines was his driver eventually for eight years. Among many other things he taught Jon to drive.[47] They all felt they were 'treated as family'; Limes Cottage would always provide breakfast or supper as occasion required, but more importantly company and companionship.

If the Fleet had been a 'people job', so, in spades, would be the Naval Home Command. Terry Lewin took up his new appointment on 11 November 1975.

THE NAVAL HOME COMMAND 1975–1977

The functions and organisation of the Naval Home Command, and its relationships with other entities, both naval and national, made those of the Fleet look simple by comparison. The Command's core responsibility was the Navy's training and support structure ashore. But in meeting that responsibility it had to be responsive to policies that stemmed from the Ministry of Defence, from the Second Sea Lord's department to do with training and personnel, and from the Chief of Fleet Support to do with stores and supplies. The operation of the great naval bases at Portsmouth, Devonport, Rosyth, Faslane and (still) Chatham was even more complex, with almost every part of the ministry involved, and the Fleet, and a thousand and one local interest groups: but those in charge of the bases answered primarily to the Commander-in-Chief, Naval Home Command.

For Admiral Sir Terence Lewin it was, even more than the Fleet, a people job. More than half the Navy's people were stationed ashore.[1] Many were undergoing new entry training, in the West-country schools at the Britannia Royal Naval College, Dartmouth, and HMS *Raleigh* and HMS *Fisgard* in Cornwall. Many more were at the schools around Portsmouth where advanced training was carried out, both in the technical and warfare branches. All these establishments had large instructional staffs because the instructor/pupil ratio was necessarily high. Then there were the maintenance teams that did front-line servicing for the ships of the Fleet, the establishments that organised drafting and pay, and dozens of units from organisations such as the Sea Cadets and the Royal Naval Reserve, all requiring staff involvement even if the number of serving personnel in the units themselves was minimal.

It was not, either, a matter of uniformed people alone. The Navy employed very large numbers of civilians; in the late 1960s the general manager's department of Devonport dockyard employed 18,000.[2] Not all these were the direct concern of the Commander-in-Chief Naval Home Command, but many were, and he had always to consider relationships with civilian organisations, including the trades unions, in his work. Finally – and, as will be seen, it was to Terry Lewin a matter of very high priority – the families of sailors both ashore and at sea were a concern of the Commander-in-Chief. Their welfare and well-being were a prime ingredient for a contented and efficient Navy, and it was the Home Command that had the main responsibility for those matters.

He found to his great delight that his Chief of Staff, during his first few months as Commander-in-Chief, was to be Rear Admiral Roddy Macdonald. They had met on their very first day in the Navy and had remained firm friends ever since. Roddy had had a rougher ride than Terry; he once wrote that Terry had been 'denied the useful experience of toad under harrow'[3] in the same way as he. Macdonald's experience in the Second World War, under a captain whose conduct ranged from the difficult to the impossible, has been chronicled elsewhere.[4] He had risen above that, as much later he rose above a serious collision during an exercise at sea of which, after court martial, he had been fully acquitted. Now his energy and grasp of essentials would prove of tremendous value and support to his new Chief: their career paths might have widened, their friendship did not diminish.

The first major matter that arose was a piece of unfinished business. The 'Constrain' plan, formulated by Lewin as ACNS(P) some six years before, had not yet been fully implemented. Some elements of it had indeed come to pass; for example, the new School of Maritime Operations at HMS *Dryad*, in a fold of Portsdown Hill north of Portsmouth, had been inaugurated in 1974.[5] But previous Commanders-in-Chief had been reluctant to apply the final recommendations, including the eventual closure of one major establishment, the Torpedo School at HMS *Vernon*, as well as several smaller ones; it was always easy to find reasons for delay, and reactionary elements were not slow to put them forward.

Macdonald already had a plan for this further implementation, and within the first few days of Lewin's tenure put it to him. After careful and probing discussion, the Commander-in-Chief gave approval for the plan to go ahead, and the Chief of Staff presented the decision to the assembled captains of the schools.[6] The predictable protests were overridden, Lewin firmly backing Macdonald throughout, and the closures and relocations went ahead. Implementation still took some years to complete,[7] but the essentials had been done. The linkage between this development and the Principal Warfare Officer system of training and management of operations at sea, so near to Lewin's heart, cannot be sufficiently emphasised.

A quite different issue, and even more of a people matter, was that of family welfare. In 1972 a committee under the chairmanship of Lord Seebohm had been invited to study this aspect of the Navy's organisation. It had concluded that while the existing Naval Family Welfare Organisation had a history of dealing effectively with crisis cases, expansion was needed in 'the level and scope of other welfare support ... particularly for the benefit of wives and families during periods when husbands are away at sea. Accordingly the Committee recommend[ed] the formation of a Naval Personal and Family Service, staffed in the main by trained social workers ...'[8] The government accepted this recommendation and planned a three-year transition, with the existing organisation continuing to cater for crisis management while simultaneously a number of trained social workers would be recruited for the new service. Some current staff would be sponsored for professional training.[9]

There was, understandably, a good deal of heart-searching over this. There was a fear, not only in the Family Welfare Service but in the Navy generally, that it would be 'undermined by long-haired, handbag-waving social workers of both sexes'[10] – and that is a quotation from an officer who eventually became one of the new scheme's chief architects. Misgivings were overcome by several factors.

The first was the appointment of Miss P. M. Baker as the Head of the Naval Social Service,[11] later called the Naval Personal and Family Service (NPFS). Described by Lewin's then secretary as a 'formidable but able lady',[12] she worked tirelessly to establish confidence in the new organisation and its staff, visiting ships as well as quarters and communities ashore. When the NPFS was fully inaugurated on 1 April 1977 it was a generally trusted organisation.

The other key element was the support of Sir Terence Lewin and his suggestions as to the structure of the NPFS. He was fully aware of the opposition to, and downright unpopularity of, the measures in some quarters, and could easily, in the view of one who was intimately concerned, have 'put it quietly to bed'.[13] But both he and Admiral Sir David Williams, the Second Sea Lord, could see the positive elements of the proposals and supported them.

On the matter of subordination and control, however, he and Williams did not see eye to eye. Williams would have preferred the service to answer to the Second Sea Lord's department directly, acting outside the Naval Home Command structure. Lewin thought this would be too remote from the situation on the ground, where so often the issues were local or regional and where base commanders already controlled or were in touch with many of the factors involved such as quarters, wives' clubs and community groups. His alternative was control by the Commander-in-Chief Naval Home Command, through local commanders to regional directors of the NPFS.[14]

This was a genuine difference of opinion between two people of goodwill who were, moreover, close personal friends. There was nothing of attempted empire-building or power-struggle about it. It was put, quite properly, to the Admiralty Board and they ruled that the regional structure should be adopted.[15] It was, accordingly, announced in November 1975.[16] Regional Directors of the NPFS would be responsible through the commodores at Portsmouth and Plymouth, and the captain of HMS *Cochrane* at Rosyth; there would be special arrangements for the Fleet Air Arm and Royal Marines. In the view of one (perhaps not entirely unbiased) observer, 'Not for the first time, the Royal Navy led the way. Slowly but surely the other services have followed suit.'[17]

The NPFS was not the only organisation aimed at keeping in touch with the concerns of the Navy's people. Lewin spent much time visiting married quarters estates and community centres near the naval bases, and ensured that links between them and officialdom became stronger and more effective. He set up a Personnel Information Office in HMS *Nelson* at Portsmouth, a kind of naval Citizens' Advice Bureau to answer queries from sailors and their families.[18] He gave extra responsibility to the immensely able Superintendent of WRNS on his staff, Vonla McBride, in making her the staff officer responsible for housing.

Those were matters of organisation and structure, even though they stemmed from the Commander-in-Chief's own inquiry and interest. Sometimes the intervention was on a more personal level. On one occasion Lewin, accompanied by a staff officer, visited a married quarter to find a young wife distraught, with no one immediately to turn to. Her petty officer husband, convalescing from 'flu, had been recalled to sea in emergency while she was doing the shopping. She collected some things her husband had forgotten and set off to post them, but during this expedition the car had caught fire and burnt out. Fortunately the children were elsewhere with a minder and the wife was unharmed, but her distress was extreme. Lewin 'immediately took over ... whilst [the staff officer] put the kettle on'. The Commander-in-Chief 'spent nearly an hour ... [arranging] for another neighbour to come and collect her as well as telephoning the baby sitter that all was well, under control and that Mum would be home shortly',[19] ensuring that the police and insurance company were fully informed, and sending a personal signal to the petty officer concerned, telling him what had happened and not to worry. It was no doubt what any good neighbour would have done, but Terry Lewin had to be a good neighbour to about seventy thousand people.

Another incident reached the pages of the *Navy News*. Tom Baird, who had relieved Macdonald as Chief of Staff in the rank of rear admiral, became aware one day, through a crossed telephone line, of a welfare problem in HMS *Gurkha*, far away east of Suez. It was the death of a rating's loved grandmother back in Britain, with much family distress. Lewin personally intervened and the necessary passages were arranged.[20] It probably was not an isolated event, though the circumstances were peculiar; and although it undoubtedly made good copy for the lively and buoyant *Navy News*, it does not appear that the publicity was sought, much less manufactured, by the authorities.

One asset that helped maintain and improve morale at home was the Sailors' Fund, which had been instituted, with considerable and unexpected Treasury generosity, on the abolition of the 'tot'.[21] It totalled £2¾ million, and the income, administered by a board whose membership was overwhelmingly drawn from the lower deck, was available to fund sailors' amenities. Lewin had his own views about policy for the Sailors' Fund: he believed it should finance large capital projects rather than boost minor amenities which ought either to be self-supporting once they were up and running, or to be financed by existing arrangements. The contrary opinion was that a much wider spread, including meeting or subsidising running costs – for example, the replenishment of ships' and establishments' sports gear – would benefit, and be seen to benefit, a higher proportion of people. Lewin saw the force of this and withdrew his objections; satisfactory compromise was reached whereby each ship's and establishment's welfare or sports fund received some Sailors' Fund money but the bulk was still available for the larger projects.[22] One such that reached fruition during Lewin's time as C.-in-C. Naval Home Command was the Southwick Park Recreation Centre alongside HMS *Dryad*, with a golf course, camping, fishing, boating and riding facilities. It was opened in July 1976, although in the arid summer of that year the golf course had to wait another couple of months[23] before it was ready for play.

The good name of the Navy, as much as the morale and welfare of its people, was an important concern for the Commander-in-Chief. At the upper end of the scale, he had a unique asset in his flagship, HMS *Victory*. Lord Nelson's flagship at the Battle of Trafalgar, she had been saved from destruction in 1922 by the Society for Nautical Research, which set up a Save the Victory Fund to provide money for her preservation that government was too mean to supply. She had since rested in No. 1 Dock at Portsmouth, still a ship in commission and in the mid-'Seventies manned by regular naval personnel, but open to the public and a national monument of the first importance. Lewin took a great deal of interest in the ship and her maintenance, for which government finance was now available, supplemented by the still-existing Save the Victory Fund.[24] But she was much more than just an historic asset. Dinner in the Great Cabin of HMS *Victory*, with the Commander-in-Chief as host, was an event no guest would want to miss or would ever forget, and Lewin ensured, as did his predecessors and successors, that the guest lists included both British and foreign persons of great influence.[25]

For the wider public, Navy Days at Portsmouth were an annual feature, normally held over the period of the late August Bank Holiday. In 1976 twenty ships were open to the public, and each of seventeen establishments or shore units contributed a static display.[26] The Commander-in-Chief's staff provided the infrastructure and overall organisation, but much was left to individual units in the way of making their exhibits interesting and crowd-pulling. Later in the century, Navy Days tended to give way to less frequent, but more spectacular, events in the home naval bases.[27]

A less transient way of fostering public interest in its Navy was the Royal Naval Museum at Portsmouth. Terry Lewin took a very personal interest in this. It had begun as an adjunct to HMS *Victory* in the 1930s, in a quite small but specially designed building facing the ship. Under the enterprising and energetic Captain Jimmy Pack, and with the critical intervention of Admiral Sir John Frewen, it had in the late 1960s taken on the range of eighteenth-century storehouses to the south of the Victory Museum, and had acquired in the early 1970s a magnificent collection of Nelsoniana from Mrs Lily Lambert McCarthy, an American benefactress.[28] Lewin, with his strong sense of history, supported all the museum's activities and initiatives, and so did the Navy Ministers, Frank Judd and later Patrick Duffy, who successively chaired the trustees.

The museum steadily expanded both in size and scope, seeking eventually to tell the whole story of the Royal Navy from earliest times to the present day. During Lewin's time the Society of Friends was formed and continued to flourish a generation later. Lewin's contribution to the museum's development was recognised by the naming of its twentieth-century gallery after him.

Lewin sponsored one further initiative that has had lasting effects. Lieutenant-Commander 'Bushy' Arnold-Shrubb, who had been an

Assistant Secretary in his outer office when he was VCNS, began to transform a rather pedestrian Admiralty record of naval anniversaries into an illustrated Book of Days, and the work was taken up by Captain Tony Sainsbury, RNR, when serving as Staff Secretary to Lewin as C.-in-C. With his enquiring mind and wide and detailed knowledge of naval history, Sainsbury was able to enlarge *The Royal Navy Day by Day*, which has since gone through two editions, supplying material for a multitude of after-dinner speeches as well as increasing almost by osmosis the general awareness of history throughout the service.

In 1976 began the planning for the Jubilee Naval Review of Her Majesty the Queen, to be held in the Solent in June 1977. This, though primarily a demonstration of loyalty and affection, was also a means of bringing the Navy into the public consciousness. Many organisations and government departments were involved in the plans, but the principal co-ordination lay with the Commander-in-Chief Naval Home Command, and it was in Portsmouth that the planning team was set up under Captain Gordon Walwyn.[29] Every aspect of the event – anchor berths for the British and foreign ships attending, the timetable from assembly through the Royal progress along the lines to the final firework display, arrangements for embarkation of guests, orders for 'cheer ship', gun salutes, and a thousand other details – had to be meticulously set out. With his Royal Yacht experience none of this would have been unfamiliar country to Terry Lewin, but as usual, having made his assessment that the staff were approaching things in the right way, he trusted them to get on with the detail of what was to be a great national event.

It was during his time, too, that the Reserves and Cadets came within his jurisdiction. During the early 1970s the role and composition of the Royal Naval Reserve had come under scrutiny. They were a widespread body, eleven units each operating its own coastal minesweeper, with at that time a great deal of residual experience either in the Second World War or subsequently among national servicemen. This was beginning to erode as younger people joined. In 1973, while Lewin was still VCNS, the Admiralty Board had initiated reconsideration of the force and a committee was set up under Captain Geoffrey Mitchell in March 1974.[30] This recommended that the RNR should continue to have a seagoing role as a 'part-time element in the single naval service' and – on Lewin's insistence against stodgier opposition – that 'a voluntary service should contain an element of fun'.[31]

Another important recommendation of the Mitchell Committee was that the post of Admiral Commanding Reserves should be abolished and that in future administration of the RNR should come under the Commander-in-Chief Naval Home Command, while its seagoing vessels should be operated by the Commander-in-Chief, Fleet. The very numerous Sea Cadet and Combined Cadet Force units round the country would also come under the Commander-in-Chief Naval Home Command. Lewin realised that the change would be unpopular with many units fearing the effect of the removal of 'their' admiral. He wrote to every Reserve unit commanding officer and every chairman or officer in charge of a Cadet unit, topping and tailing every letter personally, telling them they had not lost a two-star (rear admiral) so much as gained a four-star (full admiral) to look after them. He also took pains to attend as many Reserve and Cadet conferences as he could.[32]

Most unhappily, before the change of command occurred, the tragic loss of HMS *Fittleton*, which at the end of a NATO exercise in September 1976 was overrun by HMS *Abdiel* with heavy loss of life,[33] cast a shadow over the scene, which meant that the new structure got away to a more difficult start than would otherwise have been the case. Nevertheless Lewin was able to pass on to his successor a Reserve force that was capable of serving the country in emergency in a multitude of ways.

He was always concerned, as he spoke to the Reserves or the Royal Naval Auxiliary Service (another, and somewhat separate, set of units that he valued highly), that they were part of the deterrent structure of the country's defences. 'Deterrence', he would say, 'is the name of the game.' Captain Peter Kimm, in charge of the RNXS at the time, produced a cartoon of two young persons of uncertain ethnic origin with one saying to the other, 'Dat man, he say de Terence is de name of de game', and TTL striding away in the background.[34] Political Correctness was still fifteen years away.

He did, indeed, do a great deal of travelling throughout his command and throughout his time. He went afloat occasionally: at the 1976 Cowes week he flew the Trinity House flag in HMS *Achilles* (he was now an Elder Brother).[35] But mostly it was in the way of inspections of shore establishments and other units, from the Stores Depot at Copenacre to the Britannia Royal Naval College at Dartmouth. Some of them were conducted by the Chief of Staff on his behalf, but most he did himself.[36] He enjoyed them: people were his profession, after all.

But perhaps it was his visit to Dartmouth that seemed best. The place was in good heart under his erstwhile first lieutenant in *Urchin*, now Captain Paul Greening; the first WRNS officers' course was going through the college after more than a generation's segregation; and he had a telephone call. It told him that he was to be the next First Sea Lord.[37]

He was to be relieved by Admiral Sir David Williams in the spring of 1977, and there was some hope that he might have a long spell of leave before taking up the top appointment in the Navy. It was not to be. Marshal of the Royal Air Force Sir Andrew Humphrey, an officer of outstanding quality, had become Chief of the Defence Staff in October 1976,[38] and much was hoped for under his leadership. But early in 1977, after an arduous visit to northern Norway in the depth of winter, he fell ill and died on 25 January. After lengthy discussion it was decided that Admiral Sir Edward Ashmore, then First Sea Lord, should hold the post of CDS for a few months and be followed by Air Chief Marshal Sir Neil Cameron for a 'standard' two-year tenure.[39] This would make Lewin a front-runner for the post of CDS after Cameron, since it would be the Navy's 'turn' as was still then the custom.

But it was early days to be thinking about that. The immediate effect was a sharp telescoping of the relief programme. Ashmore would take over as CDS in February, so Williams must take over as C.-in-C. Naval Home Command and Lewin as First Sea Lord in March. In the meantime, Admiral Sir Raymond Lygo, the Vice Chief of Naval Staff, would be acting First Sea Lord. Even that short interregnum was unusual: the Foreign Office may have its *Chargés d'Affaires* in such cases, but the Navy tries not to.

There was one final matter to attend to, and it was typical of Terry Lewin. At an inspection of the naval drafting and records centre in Gosport a few months previously, one of the junior officials had claimed that they could recover any record, however obscure, about the personal entitlements of serving or retired personnel. 'All right,' said Terry, 'what medals is my wife entitled to?' The commodore in charge of the centre had to admit that this information was not immediately to hand, but 'They'd find out, Sir'.

They did; and on the day he was relieved by Admiral Sir David Williams, Sir Terence Lewin presented war medals (which they had never received) to Wren Paul (later Angie Baird) and to Leading Wren Lewin. As an end to a People Job, it could not be bettered.

16

FIRST SEA LORD
1977–1979

Someone once heard him say it was the dullest job he ever had in the Navy. It may have been said tongue-in-cheek, but like most such statements there was reason behind it. The First Sea Lord, as the professional head of his service, is responsible for its readiness, efficiency and morale, but that is exercised through his Commanders-in-Chief; as the Chief of Naval Staff, he is responsible for the service's smooth administration and responsiveness to the directives and desires of government, but that responsibility is exercised by and through a vast number of officers both naval and civilian. The complexity of the organisation ensures that opportunities for hands-on leadership or administration are strictly limited.

That would have applied at any time in the last thirty years. But the end of the 'Seventies had their own peculiarities for Britain, a cusp of time like the calm before a typhoon when, as the Admiralty Sailing Directions famously had it, 'There is an indescribable feeling that all is not well.' The country's economic difficulties had in 1976 caused the government to submit to stringent conditions laid down by the International Monetary Fund.[1] These included severe cuts in public spending and very tight pay restraint in the public sector. The services had, with the help of a new and subsequently much-maligned Secretary of State, Fred Mulley, not suffered disastrously from the spending cuts so far as equipment was concerned, but could not escape the near-freeze on pay.[2] Yet at the same time the government was showing itself sensitive to NATO demands (led by the United States) for a 3 per cent increase in defence spending, year-on-year and in real terms. These and many other internal contradictions gave the whole period a kind of uneasy breathlessness that must have made the post of First Sea Lord an unusually frustrating one.

Another aid to *ennui* would be revisiting topics and programmes that had been in their earlier stages during his previous appointments in the ministry – or, worse still, recognising that they had not progressed at all or even had moved further from the point of solution. It was a common Whitehall syndrome, and Lewin had been in Whitehall more often than most officers, even the senior ones.

Finally, there was the thudding pressure of business. Every Tuesday there was a meeting of the Chiefs of Staff Committee, under the chairmanship of the Chief of Defence Staff (Admiral of the Fleet Sir Edward Ashmore, followed in late 1977 by Marshal of the Royal Air Force Sir Neil Cameron), with Terry's counterparts General Sir Roland Gibbs and Air Chief Marshal Sir Michael Beetham. Most Thursdays there would be a meeting of the Navy or Admiralty Board. For all such meetings there would be written briefs, oral briefings, detailed papers to be read and analysed. And that was simply the standing framework: round it would be grouped every other aspect of naval and inter-service business, as well as the busy representational duties of a service head.

Terry Lewin had brought with him from the Naval Home Command his devoted and invaluable Secretary, Captain Don Beadle, and had also the services of a high-grade Naval Assistant, initially Captain Ben Bathurst and subsequently Captain John Coward. Grouped round the First Sea Lord were the naval staff: The Vice Chief, Vice Admiral Anthony Morton; the Assistant Chiefs, initially Rear Admirals Bryan Straker (Policy), Stephen Berthon (Operational Requirements) and Roger Gerard-Pearse (Operations); and beneath them, the Directorates of Naval Plans, Naval Warfare, Operational Requirements and Naval Air Warfare. The departments of the Second, Third and Fourth Sea Lords – Admiral Sir Gordon Tait (Personnel), Admiral Sir Richard Clayton (Materiel) and Vice Admiral James Eberle (Support) – were equally fully staffed.

Parallelling them, as they had since the time of Samuel Pepys, were the civilian officers, whose business it was to reflect the views and wishes of ministers and to see they were incorporated in policy and planning; and, as important, to ensure that financial control was exercised in accordance with budgetary limits, and that unauthorised programmes and expenditures did not go forward. There had been some change of ethos in this area in the past decade and a half. Before

1964, when there was an Admiralty, civil servants remained in that department throughout their careers and developed a great loyalty to it and to the naval service. They could be relied upon not only for financial, drafting and management skill and advice, but for expert knowledge of the naval case and what would and would not run with the other services and with ministers. After the Mountbatten co-location, with the establishment of the Permanent Under Secretary to the Ministry of Defence as the overall accounting officer, it became the policy to appoint middle-ranking civil servants away from the departments they had previously served in, so that their loyalties were to the ministry rather than to a particular service; moreover after 1968, with the decisive shift to NATO as the focus of British defence effort, all the brighter stars were deliberately sent to NATO appointments for some of their careers.[3] Rightly or wrongly, the officers of the fighting services felt themselves less well supported than they had previously been, and found it necessary to become much more involved in the detail of costings and policy statements than before.[4]

Many threads ran right through Lewin's time as First Sea Lord, and well before and long after it too. One of these, to which he gave paramount importance, was the strategic nuclear issue. As was suggested in Chapter 13, he had not been concerned with the detail of this as Vice Chief of Naval Staff, preferring the minutiae to be handled by ACNS(P), but matters had moved on since then. In 1974, on moving into the appointment of First Sea Lord, Admiral Sir Edward Ashmore had become alarmed at the escalating cost and lack of management of the Polaris Improvement Programme, codenamed Chevaline.[5] He had been alerted not only by his predecessor Sir Michael Pollock, but by the Deputy Controller (Polaris), Rear Admiral David Scott, who had identified at least six major concerns, some on safety, some on design complication, and some on operational penalties.[6]

Ashmore set up, in consultation with the Chief Scientific Adviser Sir Hermann Bondi, an independent inquiry under Fred East, a senior scientist, with Captain Peter Herbert, an experienced Polaris submariner. This reported in March 1976[7] and the result was a drastic change in management. The organisation was renamed the Polaris

Executive, with Scott as its chief, and no longer answered to the Controller but to the Admiralty Board.[8] Both East and Herbert were brought on to the Polaris Executive full-time, East to handle the technical detail and Herbert to oversee operational and safety matters.[9]

It was too late to check entirely the runaway costs that had been incurred by chaotic management and over-enthusiastic scientists over the previous five years. In the event, having been assessed as £600 million in 1976, they finished up at rather over £1 billion by 1982. But at least some sort of control had been established and during Lewin's time as First Sea Lord was maintained. Lewin, it is clear, had Scott's full trust[10] – not the easiest of achievements, after all Scott had been through – and backed the Polaris Executive through all its troubles.

Over the whole business had hovered the shadow of the Poseidon alternative. As mentioned in Chapter 13, this had been considered a serious option in 1971, and there is evidence[11] that Rear Admiral Levering Smith USN, head of the United States Strategic Systems Projects Office, assured the then First Sea Lord that a request for purchase of Poseidon in, say, 1973 would receive a positive response from the US authorities. It had not been pursued because Leach, the ACNS(P), had been persuaded that Chevaline was the better option. But even in the mid-'Seventies the possibility of Poseidon was regarded by some as still faintly there, much attenuated because a Labour government was by then in office and not ready or willing to countenance a new generation of missiles – as opposed to warheads, which were the extent of the Chevaline development – and the balance of opinion in the USA had hardened.[12]

There were two downstream effects of this whole sorry story. Generally, most of those in the know regarded the Chevaline project, particularly after what they considered to be the premature rejection of Poseidon, as something of a job creation scheme for British defence scientists. The fact that the project had been allowed to run out of control only sharpened this perception. It was not by any means the first, nor was it to be the last, time a British development had been handled in this way,[13] and the resulting suspicion was pervasive and damaging.

The other effect was more specific to Lewin himself. He became sceptical about any strategic deterrence system that had a large technical British input. The British had proved themselves capable of producing warhead-sized thermo-nuclear explosives and detonating them, and that, with the country's proven nuclear propulsion techology for submarines, was enough to ensure that a British strategic deterrent system could claim to be independent. He did not, in a future system, want any hostage to fortune in the shape of national add-ons.[14]

Thinking about a future system was, indeed, overdue in 1978. Harold Wilson, when Prime Minister, had recorded his Cabinet's decision ten years before that it was not intended to replace the Polaris submarines.[15] He had been succeeded by James Callaghan in 1976, and in the interim – including four years of Conservative government – nothing, except Chevaline, had stirred. There was no money in the Long Term Costings earmarked for a Polaris replacement.[16] The first Polaris boat was ten years old, and there were already signs of ageing.[17]

In 1978 James Callaghan took the courageous decision to charge officials with considering the future of the British strategic deterrent force. A group was set up under Sir Anthony Duff, a senior official of the Foreign Office, with Sir Clive Rose of the Cabinet Office, Michael Quinlan the Deputy Under Secretary (Policy) at the Ministry of Defence, and a commodore from the Defence Policy Staff[18] as members. After some meetings they were joined by Professor Sir Ronald Mason, the Chief Scientific Adviser at the Ministry of Defence. Their Secretary was Richard Mottram, of the Defence Secretariat. Their task was to consider and report on the rationale for a British independent nuclear deterrent and the criteria that would need to be met to make it credible. They were enjoined to make no recommendations as to whether a system was required or not. Within that limitation, however, they produced convincing reasoning for another generation of British nuclear deterrence.[19]

The Duff Group having reported, the Mason Group, with Professor Mason in the chair, was then formed with a larger membership, but one drawn almost entirely from within the Ministry of Defence, and much more weighted towards the scientific and technical side. Its remit was to state which system or systems, likely to be available within the timeframe for replacement of the Polaris/Chevaline system (an in-service date of the early 1990s), would meet the criteria established by the Duff Group for a credible British independent nuclear deterrent.

The Mason Group quickly disposed of two possibilities: all-British solutions to the problem, and collaboration with France for the next generation of systems.[20] In brief, the first was too technically risky and the second would overturn a carefully constructed set of arrangements with the Americans, stretching over more than twenty years: the political implications were immense, and the benefits uncertain. Almost as quick was the rejection of a ground-based missile force. This could only employ the American cruise missile, already in prospect as an intermediate-range system at the top of the *theatre* part of NATO's nuclear armoury, and, after the Guadeloupe summit of January 1979, likely to be deployed in that role in Britain[21] as an essential part of the 'twin-track' approach to arms control in the field of theatre nuclear weapons. The idea of giving it a British nuclear warhead as a *strategic* national deterrent would hope-lessly stir up already muddy waters. An airborne cruise-missile solution was almost as quickly set aside; it would require very expensive round-the-clock air deployment and its bases would be vulnerable. The same critical shortcoming applied to any missiles mounted in surface ships.

That left only submarine-based solutions. Even within these limits there were several alternatives. One was put forward by Scott himself: re-engining the existing Polaris missiles with the fuel used in the modern American Trident missiles, to give them much longer range, and continuing to operate the 'R' class submarines with this improved Polaris. Scott argued that this would spread replacement costs so that when the time came to replace the submarines themselves, there would be less financial pain.[22] But it would have been a very largely British system; American help was likely to be reluctant at best; it would be riskier and riskier to operate the old submarines through the 1990s; and it would continue to use far outdated control technology ('How can you think of using *analogue* computers in the year 2000?' asked Terry Lewin). The suggestion was rejected.

Two contenders were left. The first was the American Trident ballistic missile system, which in its then current C-4 version gave entirely adequate range and up-to-date Multiple Independently-Manoeuvring Re-entry Vehicles (MIRV) to combat the anti-ballistic missile defences around Moscow or any expected development of them. It would need new submarines to carry it, and the initial expense would be heavy, but the operating cost would not be high, operating patterns and control procedures were already tried and tested, and updates would not be expected for many years.

The other candidate was the submarine-based cruise missile. The first-generation Tomahawk had first attracted public attention in the mid-'Seventies, notably in Britain in a carefully argued paper for the Royal Institute of International Affairs in 1977.[23] The cruise missile was (and still is) essentially a small pilotless aircraft with a terrain-hugging flight profile. It was claimed to be virtually undetectable by ground radars. It had very precise navigation that would lead it to its designated target; at that time the system depended on preset survey-derived information. It was not expensive in unit cost, and no difficulty was expected in designing a British warhead for it. However, the Tomahawks then available had only a limited range, which meant submarines carrying them would have to lie relatively close off enemy shores and even then could not conduct attacks on the centres of power in the Soviet Union. Moreover no Western submarine had been designed to carry large banks of cruise missiles. It might be feasible for each nuclear-powered submarine to carry a few, but then the complication arose of which ones were to be deployed specifically for deterrence and which were to be treated as tactical units. Finally, the data on which the navigation and targeting systems operated were in the hands of the USA.

These objections to adoption of the cruise missile were elaborated at length by the Mason Group, but boiled down to one hyphenated word coined by Michael Quinlan: 'assumption-sensitive'.[24] There simply were too many unknowns. However complex nuclear rationales might be, however much doubt there might be in the minds of both deterrers and deterrees in conditions of peace, tension or war –

and doubt is a necessary ingredient – the deterrent structure must be built on technical and material certainty: that the system cannot be neutralised by a pre-emptive strike, that it will be within range of its targets when needed, that the missiles will fly, that a sufficient number of warheads will penetrate, and that the charges will go off. That certainty was not there in the cruise missiles, and the Mason Group unhesitatingly recommended Trident.

There is no doubt at all that this conclusion was fully endorsed by Terry Lewin, as First Sea Lord and subsequently as Chief of Defence Staff. He regarded the British strategic deterrent as a key element of defence policy, requiring the bedrock of technical and material certainty on which the complex philosophies and postures of deterrence could rest. In his view, only Trident gave it. Both then, and in many subsequent writings,[25] he argued strongly against those who put forward the case that cruise missiles were sufficient.[26]

The Mason Group's recommendations were put before the Labour government before the end of 1978, but no final decision had been made before the change of government in May 1979. There, for the time being, discussion must be left, to be resumed in the next chapter.

Another strand that ran through Lewin's time as First Sea Lord was the vexed question of service pay, and its downstream effects. Government policy was to impose the most severe pay restraint nationwide. This would, it was held, help to get the economy back on its feet after the buffeting it had suffered over the past decades, and would in addition satisfy the International Monetary Fund who were almost in the position of Britain's paymasters in 1976–7. In the private sector, restraint was largely ineffective, because it could be circumvented by employees moving from one job to another more highly paid one, often in another firm or organisation. In the public service, with its much more rigid structures, the policy bit deep. Comparability with the private sector was measured throughout by the Armed Services Pay Review Body, and by March 1978 the gap between service and comparable private pay had widened to 37 per cent.[27]

The result was predictable. Servicemen and women left the armed services in droves. The newspapers were not slow to point out the irony of the situation. A 3 per cent increase in defence spending, requested by NATO and granted by Her Majesty's Government, could not be handled by the services because government's own policy had unmanned them. Ships, even though authorised, could not be built fast enough, and when they were built there would be no one to take them to sea.[28] Similar problems arose in the other services; flying in the RAF was restricted owing to shortage of aircrew, and tanks and guns were withdrawn into reserve by British forces in Germany.[29]

The policy limped on, in spite of modifications that gave some relief to the most disadvantaged sections of the services, through the so-called Winter of Discontent in 1978–9, and it was in large part the contradictions in the government's stance that led to its fall in the spring of 1979. One of the first acts of the incoming Thatcher government was to restore pay comparability to the services, and although welcome and indeed essential, this had its own downstream effects, as will be seen in the next chapter.

Operationally, Lewin's period in the office of First Sea Lord was generally quiet. The unfortunate and ultimately unsuccessful 'Cod Wars' to support the British distant-water fishing industry in the face of Iceland's steadily expanding fishing limits – 12 miles in 1958, 50 miles in 1972, 200 miles in 1975 – were over, with many lessons learned. In international law, it was not enough to think one had won a case before the International Court of Justice, when the tide of custom was flowing in the opposite direction.[30] In politics, it was not enough to hope for support from powerful allies if they also had a stake in the facilities provided by the other side.[31] In ship management, it was not enough to deploy thin-skinned frigates designed for fleet or convoy escort to take on sturdily built gunboats optimised for fishery confrontations. Lewin had learned some of the lessons when he commanded the Fleet. He was glad to see the 'Island' class Offshore Patrol Vessels (OPV), which he had done so much to initiate as VCNS, coming into service. Not much more could be done within the resources available, though two bigger and more capable 'Castle' class (OPV 2) were in prospect.[32] OPV 3 was somewhere on the drawing board, but it did not survive later insistence on 'front line' units.

There were two perturbations of the normal pattern of operational deployments and exercises. The first was in 1977. Argentina at the time was governed, as in 1982, by a military junta which from early 1976 had applied spasmodic pressure on foreign interests in the south-west Atlantic. The British civilian research vessel *Shackleton* had been fired on by the Argentine Navy;[33] a Bulgarian trawler had been arrested, and other fishing vessels harassed; an illegal Argentine presence had been established on South Thule. The Falkland Islands, the principal British possession in the area, were believed by the British government to be the ultimate focus of these activities. Talks had been requested by Argentina and the first round, conducted by the Foreign Office Minister Ted Rowlands, took place in March 1977.[34] In spite of the apparent success of these, the general assessment of the Foreign and Commonwealth Secretary, David Owen, was that Argentina was pursuing a policy of soft words while being ready to take hard actions. He successfully, and rightly, lobbied the Defence Secretary for a stay of execution on the naval patrol vessel *Endurance*, which was due to pay off.

In October the situation, coinciding with further talks with the Argentine authorities, was judged to have deteriorated, and this went on through November. With further talks scheduled for December, a critical state might be reached quite quickly. The Foreign Secretary requested that a nuclear-powered submarine (SSN) should be sent to the area as a precautionary deployment, as he put it, 'for the defence of British shipping and for the eventuality of an Argentine invasion of the Islands and their dependencies'.[35] Lewin as First Sea Lord argued that 'a balanced force of two frigates and a submarine, with appropriate logistic ships, would provide a greater range of options than a single submarine'.[36] This advice was endorsed by the Chiefs of Staff and accepted, and the frigates *Phoebe* and *Alacrity*, the nuclear-powered submarine *Dreadnought* and the RFAs *Olwen* and *Resurgent* were duly deployed during the last week of November. It appears that the surface ships were held in an area some 1000 miles from the Falklands while the SSN may well have been a good deal closer.

Rules of Engagement were drawn up and approved by ministers, after consultation with the Law Officers. They were based upon the

assessment that the most likely threat was harassment of British shipping, that other possibilities were limited incursions in the Dependencies, and finally that there could be armed invasion of the islands
themselves. Lewin recorded:

> The instructions the commanders were given were based on the
> minimum use of force in response to an Argentinian hostile act
> ... If invasion was attempted, Argentine ships could only be
> forcibly stopped within the territorial waters of the Falklands,
> three miles from their coast, and then only after a warning ...[37]

Several points arise from this statement. First, what was the extent of
'minimum force' envisaged? From a military point of view, it must be
the minimum force necessary to achieve the objective. But this calls for
a great degree of professional judgement, and the availability of a wide
spectrum of weapons – far wider than the single, lethal torpedo option
of a submarine – to the commander involved.

Second, the perennial difficulty of distinguishing between 'hostile
intent' and 'hostile act' is clearly visible. Even in harassment situations,
such things are not easy to define; shooting is a hostile act, but does
pointing a gun unmistakably indicate hostile intent? The argument can
be interminable and in the missile age is even more acute and
involved.[38] Again, confusion is far less likely on a frigate's bridge than
through a submarine's periscope.

Finally, in the case of threatened invasion, 'hostile act' might well
have been defined as entering the territorial sea after being warned not
to do so. But who was to deliver the warning? The thought of a nuclear
submarine surfacing to deliver such a warning would be, to most
submariners, quite ludicrous. A submarine's whole potency lies under
water; and, as Lewin so cogently wrote, 'A submarine by itself is a
blunt instrument.'[39]

It is clear that Lewin's professional advice of making a balanced
deployment in this situation was entirely sound, and could if events
turned sour have saved grave embarrassment to Her Majesty's
Government. However, the question remains: would it have been

adequate in case of escalation? Lewin himself thought it would not have prevented invasion, if that had been contemplated; and the politically decreed 1000-mile distancing of the surface force from the islands – two days' steaming – reinforces this view. But, he maintained, the intelligence assessment at the time put invasion low on the list of contingencies. For harassment or limited incursions, the deployed force could well have held the ring until reinforcement arrived or the situation quietened.

The other unanswered question was whether the deployment should have been covert or overt. In fact it seems to have been a bit of both. All were agreed that it should not be blazoned in the Press. The Foreign Secretary wished it to be absolutely covert, purely precautionary, in order not to prejudice negotiations with Argentina either then or later.[40] The Prime Minister favoured letting the Argentines know covertly through intelligence channels, although whether this happened is uncertain.[41] However, there is evidence that the Argentine Navy was informed, discreetly, by the British Naval Attaché in Buenos Aires.[42] That was probably the best way to do it. Naval attachés are not just striped-pants cookie-pushers. However it was handled, no military action was taken by Argentina.

The other operational foray was, in hindsight, a minor affair, but at the time took up just as much of the ministry's attention. The small territory of Belize in Central America, at that time still some way away from full independence from Britain, was under threat from Guatemala, whose stance ranged from mild to acute sabre-rattling. The small garrison could hope to deter and possibly delay any assault, but timely reinforcement would be needed if deterrence looked like failing. In 1977, during an acute phase of tension, the frigate *Achilles* was sent to the area,[43] and in 1978 the carrier *Ark Royal*, fresh from her final period of deep maintenance, was held at readiness to go thundering across the Atlantic in support. The incidents are notable only because they were successful examples of the all-level deterrence that Lewin had long preached.

He had some opportunity to put forward his ideas in speeches and public statements while he was First Sea Lord. But the head of a fighting service in Britain is even more circumscribed by ministerial policy than are more lowly officials, because what he says is more likely to be regarded as *ex cathedra* and will make headlines if there is any deviation from the government's line. In consequence it was always necessary to get 'clearance' for what he would say.[44] Experienced listeners could sometimes hear between the lines, though, of the necessarily guarded statements.

An example was the Thomas Gray Memorial Lecture he gave at the Royal Society of Arts on 21 March 1979, with his old friend Air Chief Marshal Sir Denis Smallwood in the chair.[45] Having in mind an audience of largely scientific bent, he touched only lightly on strategy and Soviet maritime expansion, and concentrated on the nature of maritime warfare. He turned first to anti-submarine warfare and explained the complexities of the detection–localisation–tracking–destruction cycle, putting the role at the top of the priority list. He went on to the air defence question, carefully explaining the need to deal with shadowers (still the Sea Harrier's official primary role) and then incoming aircraft and missiles in what would later be called layered defence, though Lewin did not use the term on this occasion. It would require shore-based fighters, area and point defence missiles, and electronic counter-measures. He then dealt with countering the surface threat, both by attacking surface ships themselves and by shooting down, confusing or seducing any missiles they might fire. There was more than a passing reference to mines and counter-measures against them. He went on to describe the personnel of the Navy and Royal Marines, for whom he had much praise: but 'We have currently a problem of crisis dimensions with keeping our people' due to the pay situation. He ended on a sombre note: 'I do see extremely grave dangers ahead of us which require us to look very carefully at the level of our defences.'

Whether this passage was extempore or in the 'cleared' speech is not certain. It was reported in the *Daily Telegraph* two days later, to the exclusion of most of the rest of the speech. It does not appear that, if it was a late insertion, he was hauled over the coals for it; his appointment as Chief of Defence Staff had already been announced so he must have felt on fairly firm ground.

But as so often happens, and it is something for which service lecturers are always on the alert, the question period gave some scope for things he would not have wished to put forward for clearance. There were two particular moments when Lewin might have most honestly replied: 'That's a good question – I'm glad you asked that question.' The first was from the Director of the Air League, who suggested that the balance between submarine and surface forces should be further shifted in favour of submarines. Lewin's reply was robust:

> I would not agree with you that the submarine is the best anti-submarine unit to have. You need the lot. You need Nimrods ... big ASW helicopters, conventional submarines ... SOSUS, the small helicopter to deliver the weapon, you need ships, and you are going to need ships with very long range sonar in the future, because who knows how long SOSUS is going to last?

The other question was so welcome it might have been planted, though there is no evidence that it was. From a Canadian in the audience, it asked whether 'the navy's world role [was] still valid and true'. Lewin readily agreed: 'I see the threat to our interests as global', and went on to describe the course of recent Group Deployments, emphasising their frequent exercises with foreign navies and the afloat support they took with them on their nine-month absences from the United Kingdom. 'So,' he said, 'the White Ensign is still seen around.'

Representing the Royal Navy was, of course, an integral part of the First Sea Lord's duties. Two Royal occasions must have given him particular pleasure early in his tenure: the launch by Her Majesty the Queen of HMS *Invincible* at Vickers' yard in Barrow on 3 May 1977, with an attendant flypast by a Sea Harrier and Sea King helicopters trailing white ensigns; and her Silver Jubilee Review on 28 June, when the Royal Navy appeared at its brightest and best and many foreign and merchant ships came to pay their respects.

There were, too, many visits by other Chiefs of Naval Staff. The preceding First Sea Lord had found it convenient to hold on to the

Mall House flat, overlooking Admiralty Arch, as an official residence when he became Chief of Defence Staff. This posed no problem for the Lewins, who were offered instead the Dean's House at the Royal Naval College, Greenwich. Many staff and sea officers experienced their kind hospitality there. However, when an overseas Chief visited, it was customary for him to be 'dined' by the Admiralty Board at Admiralty House in London, and sometimes by the Commander-in-Chief Naval Home Command on board HMS *Victory* as well. There was always the problem of a suitable gift to remember the visit by: Lewin enlisted the help of the Hydrographer of the Navy, who provided in each case a print of an original Royal Naval survey of the appropriate country's coastline, which was framed for presentation.[46]

Representing the Navy in the best possible way sometimes had its lighter side. In December 1977 there was a lift mechanics' strike in government offices. All and sundry in the Ministry of Defence had to climb the stairs. 'Resting chairs' were placed on the half-landings. One of these bore, for a brief space of time, the legend 'Fred Mulley slept here' – a reference to the unfortunate moment earlier in the year when a Press photographer had caught the Secretary of State with his eyes closed during a RAF flying display. *The Times* did not get wind of that, but it ran a piece under the title 'Heavy Breathing'[47] alleging that the Permanent Secretary, Sir Frank Cooper – 'a heavy smoker' – would be glad when the strike was over. Sir Frank wrote to the paper that he was 'cut to the quick', since he had given up smoking 105 days before, and added that he was looking for an admiral to walk up with him to the sixth floor. Four commanders from the Directorate of Naval Operational Requirements at once weighed in, championing their First Sea Lord who, they said, took the six flights two steps at a time (Terry thanked them privately in green ink, saying, 'It is only that I like to get the pain over quickly that projects me upwards').[48] The upshot was a concerted climb by Cooper and Lewin, gleefully reported by London's evening newspaper on 14 December.[49] It ended, predictably, in a diplomatic dead-heat.

A function of more *gravitas*, but equally good for the Navy's image, was a dinner at Greenwich held on 24 October 1978 to commemorate the 250th anniversary of the birth of Captain James Cook. Terry

Lewin had personally initiated this and it was a glittering occasion with High Commissioners, presidents of learned societies and many other distinguished guests present. Lewin's comprehensive notes, mostly in his own hand, demonstrate the care he took over his own speech and the depth of his research.

There was academic recognition six weeks later when he was admitted to the degree of Doctor of Science *honoris causa* by the City University. This was a tribute not only to his own merits – which included, said the Presentation in a particularly happy note, 'the rare gift of making those less well equipped than himself to shine beyond their wildest dreams'[50] – but to the close and important association between the university and naval students of the Systems and Management degree course, an enlightened venture that ran for many years. It was one of Terry's delights thereafter to include in his letter-head the DSc next to his DSC – the sign, no doubt he would say, of a true all-rounder.

Like many busy men, he always seemed to have time for simple acts of kindness. Their next door neighbour at Limes Cottage, where they still escaped at weekends whenever possible, was ageing and found it difficult to cut his grass: the First Sea Lord cut it for him. Ungrateful Fate handed out a backlash when he broke the crank of the family Flymo running over a metal stake. He handed over the remains to Tim as a gift 'to avoid wasting it', which cost Tim the price of a replacement engine. The Flymo was one of the earliest models: 'He loved all new technology.'[51]

The Navy Minister for most of Lewin's time was Patrick Duffy, who had long taken an interest in the Royal Navy and was one of its staunchest friends and supporters. He and Lewin struck up a great rapport[52] and saw eye to eye on all major issues. Duffy was in favour of a Lewin innovation whereby the Commanders-in-Chief of the Fleet and Naval Home Command attended most Admiralty Board meetings.[53]

Some First Sea Lords regard their most important single task as placing senior officers in the correct appointments. Certainly it is something for which only they can take the final responsibility, and the critical decisions can be, as one of Lewin's predecessors said, 'very lonely'.[54] To help him the First Sea Lord has only one standing adviser, the Naval Secretary, a rear admiral usually in his first post as such and traditionally assured of another decent appointment to follow. He is therefore to an extent above the battle in a way that almost no other senior or flag officer could be.

For much of Lewin's time the Naval Secretary was Paul Greening, well known to him from days in the Dartmouth Training Squadron. He recalled that Lewin knew most of the individuals involved, 'right down the captains' plot', and had very firm ideas about who could do what.[55] Sometimes, when a name was suggested for a responsible position, Terry would complain, 'But he's never commanded *anything*' – and that would set a well-defined limit to future employment. He was always imaginative. Two candidates were put forward as captains of the old Gunnery and Torpedo Schools, still soldiering on in the final stages of Plan Constrain. A Gunnery Officer was to go to *Excellent*, a Torpedo Officer to *Vernon*. Lewin switched them. It worked.[56]

But it was the succession to the top jobs, the Board members, that was of supreme importance. The composition of the Sea Lords had remained quite stable for most of Lewin's tenure, and in 1979 several changes would be necessary in the ordinary course. Sir Gordon Tait, Second Sea Lord and Chief of Naval Personnel, who had staunchly and urbanely weathered the worst of the pay problem and its inevitable after-effects, was due to retire and would be relieved by Admiral Sir Desmond Cassidi, an aviator of sharp intellect and great firmness of purpose. Sir Richard Clayton, the Controller, would be succeeded by Vice Admiral John Fieldhouse, moving very smartly through the Flag List after a series of successful appointments; a submariner, he had been commander of the *Hermes*, long ago. Anthony Morton, the Vice Chief, was moving 'sideways' to be Vice Chief of the Defence Staff and his successor would be Vice Admiral William Staveley, whose charm and ability to get on with the other services was well known.

The successor to Lewin himself was the most critical question of all. There were several candidates of the highest quality. Admiral Sir Henry Leach, the Commander-in-Chief of the Fleet, was described by a contemporary from another service as 'as high principled as he was able, and a charming man',[57] a description that cannot be bettered. But at the Naval Home Command was Admiral Sir David Williams, immensely skilful in the Whitehall wars and with steely determination behind his sometimes mordant humour; and there was support too for the brilliant and human Richard Clayton,[58] though he was rather young at this juncture.

Lewin settled eventually on Henry Leach as his successor. The important post of Governor of Gibraltar was fortunately in the Navy's gift at the time, and he was sure David Williams would fill this superbly, which he did. Clayton went on to the Naval Home Command, while James Eberle took command of the Fleet. Leach was, Lewin knew, 'sound on Trident' – an absolute precondition so far as the new Chief of Defence Staff was concerned. Leach's firmness and fairness were well known, and his capacity for detail undoubted. All his good qualities would be tested to the limit in 1979–81, and triumphantly proved in 1982.

So, in September 1979, Sir Terence Lewin was to be Chief of the Defence Staff of the United Kingdom. Under him the Royal Navy had carried out what Denis Healey is reputed to have said was the first duty of any armed service in peacetime: it had survived. It had done so with heart and, even at the darkest times, with humour.

Perhaps a good way to end this chapter is a tale from the Winter of Discontent in 1978–9. Neil MacEacharn, Terry's Staff Officer (Operations) in the Far East in 1969–70, was now a commodore and in charge of the Clyde Naval Base where the Polaris submarines were berthed and serviced. There had been trouble all through the summer with boats being periodically 'blacked' by the unions,[59] threatening their operational cycle, although this was never critically affected. Early in the winter, a similar crisis arose, with sit-ins, lock-outs, crossed telephone calls and general mayhem. MacEacharn sent the only signal, personal to the First Sea Lord, that he deemed possible in the circumstances.[60] It was handed to Terry in the middle of a fraught crisis meeting at No. 10. It read: 'Attention is drawn to Bersatu Padu Vol. 4 Chap. 6 para 4'.

If chased by an elephant, run downhill.

CHIEF OF DEFENCE STAFF
1979–1982

One evening in the spring of 1979, when almost all the staff had gone home, Terry Lewin sat on the edge of the desk of June Light, the highly efficient personal assistant who had adorned the outer office of several successive First Sea Lords, and said to his Assistant Secretary Lieutenant-Commander David Smith: 'I'm sacking you.'

When the shock had subsided, he added 'But you won't be going very far – I mean, six doors away.' That, as Smith knew, was the office of the Chief of the Defence Staff. Terry wanted him to be his Flag Lieutenant. He had 48 hours to think it over, but it was scarcely necessary: the admiral's 'following' would willingly go with him to tougher places than the sixth floor of the Ministry of Defence.[1]

That is not to say it was not going to be tough. When Lewin took up his post in September 1979, the Conservative government under Margaret Thatcher had been in office for five months. The economic situation was seen as dire and the state of the nation uncertain; many of the papers circulated in those months were headed 'Our Legacy', and all were gloomy. Inflation was high,[2] the balance of payments was adverse, industrial relations were bad, and the manufacturing base of the country was showing signs of eroding. Monetarist solutions and other measures were bound to take time to work through, and meanwhile there would be financial misery for all government departments.

This did not, however, deter the new government from honouring its pledge to restore pay comparability to the services. That was done in full and in a remarkably short time.[3] It was absolutely necessary in order to arrest the haemorrhage of trained people from all three services, and it must have been a comfort to the new Chief of Defence Staff, but as a realist with great Ministry of Defence experience he would have been the first to understand that what the Treasury gives with one hand, it takes away with the other – and then holds out one hand, or both, for more.

The financial background will dominate this chapter, as indeed it dominated Lewin's time as Chief of the Defence Staff, except for the time of the Falklands conflict – which merits a chapter of its own. It has been necessary to outline it here; details will recur throughout, but the underlying perception of continuing crisis and desperately hard choices must be kept always in mind.

There were three principal concerns for Admiral of the Fleet Sir Terence Lewin, as he now was, during his time as Chief of the Defence Staff. They were the replacement of Britain's strategic nuclear deterrent; the review of Britain's defence structure in the light of heavy and conflicting demands for expenditure and of financial stringency, particularly during the tenure of John Nott as Defence Secretary; and the higher organisation of the Ministry of Defence. They ran to an extent in that sequence, although, as generally happens, they overlapped and interacted.

Trident: the Replacement for Britain's Strategic Deterrent

Chapter 16 explained how the Callaghan government had commissioned the Duff and Mason reports. The resulting recommendation that Trident best fitted the criteria for a next-generation deterrent had been under examination by ministers when the government changed. There had been some optimism that the four ministers who formed the inner core group looking at the recommendations would come down in favour of going ahead, although one, the Foreign Secretary, was known to advocate a lower targeting criterion and the theoretically cheaper cruise missile solution.[4]

When the government changed, it was generally thought in the Ministry of Defence that a decision to go for Trident was a foregone conclusion. The Election Manifesto had said that a Conservative government would 'not hesitate to spend what is necessary on our armed forces'[5] and surely, it was argued, the strategic deterrent would be regarded as 'necessary'. If Labour ministers had seemed warm towards replacement then, *a fortiori*, the Conservatives would approve.

Lewin was not so sure. He knew how heavy the other financial demands of the services were for re-equipment programmes. The Army needed a new battle tank and means of combating new Soviet armour, which intelligence claimed was frighteningly efficient; the Royal Air Force was moving into the heaviest part of the massive expenditure on its Tornado combat aircraft programme, and in addition the Nimrod 3 Airborne Early Warning project was in the same runaway cost situation as Chevaline had been some years earlier; and the Navy was not only in the middle of fitting-out the three 'Invincible' class carriers but had a rolling programme of construction and modernisation of ships and fleet submarines. All these items had been carefully and often painfully fed into the ten-year Long Term Costings by which defence provision was ruled. *Trident had not.*[6]

In consequence, Lewin for the first few months of his time as CDS was extremely uneasy about Trident on several counts. First, he wanted to make quite sure there was no backsliding amongst the Ministry of Defence officials – including the Navy. Sandy Woodward, then a captain and the influential Director of Naval Plans, said that if he had been asked whether he was for or against Trident, he would have 'sat on his hands and looked vague'[7] on the grounds that it was 'a political lever and not a military weapon system'. There was an arguable tactical reason for such a stance: if the Navy was not seen to be advocating it as a part of the Navy, then it might, just might, escape meeting the bulk of the cost.

Yet neither Lewin nor Leach believed this was a tenable position; they considered that any demonstration of doubt might seriously weaken the chances of getting the system. Those who were 'unsound on Trident' were not welcome to influential positions on their staffs. They were glad to have the wholehearted support not only of the other Chiefs of Staff but of both the Permanent Under Secretary and the Chief Scientific Adviser, and it was a troika of these two plus Lewin who presented the proposal to a relatively small committee of ministers.[8] The project was approved in principle there and then, and announced to Cabinet later; a mild caveat was entered by the then Trade Secretary, John Nott, that some more substantial briefing would have been preferable.[9]

The next steps were in two directions. One was, clearly, to approach the Americans to ask if they would be willing to sell this sophisticated system to Britain. The links established and maintained at all levels over very many years came into action and delegations went back and forth across the Atlantic. The negotiation proceeded remarkably smoothly, with no need for intervention on Lewin's part. The Carter administration, shaken by the fall of the Shah, battered by the hostage crisis in Tehran and shocked by the Soviet invasion of Afghanistan all within the space of little over a year, had few illusions left about foreign policy and anything that would buttress its position was welcome. Britain's desire to maintain a robust deterrence, and provide a 'second centre of nuclear decision making' in NATO, was to be encouraged. An exchange of letters agreeing the purchase of Trident C4 and supporting components was published on 15 July 1980.[10]

The other step was more difficult, and that was to work out how it was to be paid for. At a fairly early stage it was made clear at Chief of Staff level that the Army and Royal Air Force would not willingly give up any of their planned and costed programmes to help finance the project, whose total cost spread over fifteen years was stated to be around four and a half to five billion pounds.[11] The estimate was stated in very careful terms as 'capital costs ... at today's prices' and no one in the ministry was under any illusion that it represented the full amount that could be attributed to the development. Seven and a half billion was even then regarded as a more realistic total figure, and as events turned out, and allowing for inflation and variations in the exchange rate, that was pretty much how it stayed throughout.

Where was it to come from? The original submission to ministers had included, with the Chief of Defence Staff's full agreement, a plea that because Polaris replacement had not, for political reasons, been in the Long Term Costings, and because it was a national politico-military requirement outside the normal business of defence provision, it should be paid for by a special subvention separate from the general defence budget. Neither the staff officer concerned, nor Terry Lewin, nor Sir Frank Cooper thought it had much chance of succeeding, particularly in the current economic climate, but it was worth a shout.

The few people who knew about this thought it had subsequently been allowed to run into the sand. However, there is some evidence now that a considerable fight was put up, even in Cabinet. An official close to John Nott, who by that time was Secretary of State for Defence, recalled that a special subvention was argued for;[12] and Lord Howe, who was then Chancellor of the Exchequer, records a limerick scribbled by Lord Carrington, the Foreign Secretary, at the Cabinet table:

The spendthrift and bellicose Nott
Is involved in a nuclear plot;
He's impaled on the fork
Of his Tridential talk
And Howe has to finance the lot.[13]

It would scarcely have been put like that if Nott had been saying the defence budget could handle it. Moreover, 'spendthrift' and 'bellicose' were not adjectives normally applied to the Defence Secretary, in the ministry or outside it.

Fight or not, no special subvention was forthcoming. The cost of Trident would have to be found from within existing defence provision. Moreover, that provision was lower than the projections of the past few years had led the services to expect. These had been based on the continuation for another seven years of the 3 per cent increase, in real terms, agreed at the behest of NATO in the late 1970s. Such increments would have given at least some headroom for accommodating the Trident programme, though it would still have been very difficult to keep all the other projects in place and up to the required speed.

However, Treasury sleight of hand had scaled the increase from the defence outturn (not the budget) in one particular year when there had been a severe underspend owing largely to the pay-restraint policy.[14] This sharply cut back the expectations of the services and made the Long Term Costing crisis acute; it was followed up by a demand for a further short-term cut. In late 1980 the Chiefs of Staff exercised their prerogative of meeting the Prime Minister personally to voice their concerns.[15]

Lewin's notes for this meeting[16] indicate the very strong line he took. He argued that any budget cut in one year would, if used as a baseline, affect the next ten, and showed just how great – running into billions – that effect would be. His summary was in the broadest strategic terms and not related to Trident (though he had stressed that factor earlier) or any other specific project:

> A reduction in our base line such as [is] proposed [would] require another major reshaping of our programme. [It is] certain that we could no longer meet our present commitments at the level we consider necessary. [It would be] asking our people to take on the Russians inadequately equipped and inevitably the nuclear threshold – already dangerously low – would be lowered still further. All this at a time when alliance is in a shaky state and at a time of increasing danger.

Soon afterwards, no relief having been achieved, the Defence Secretary Francis Pym left office to become Leader of the Commons, and his place was taken by John Nott. This led to a further budgetary blow that critically affected Trident. Nott, coming into office in early 1981, viewed the projections in the light of the expected development of the British economy as a whole, and concluded that a 3 per cent increase – even from the depressed baseline – in the later years of the Long Term Costings was unrealistic and most unlikely to be achieved. He therefore, with the agreement of his civil servants, ruled that it must not be made an assumption.[17]

Two further perturbations were to be dealt with before the final decision was made on the Trident programme, although the second came after the settlement of the question of who was to pay. The first concerned the size of the submarine force that was to carry the system. Here Lewin took a strongly personal line. He remembered well the initial planning for the Polaris force, which for some time in the early 'Sixties had been for five boats, giving normally two at sea with consequent insurance in the admittedly unlikely event of accident to or elimination of one. The argument had been long and tortuous, and the fifth boat was popularly dubbed *Reconsideration*.[18] It had been removed from the programme on the advent of the Wilson government in 1964. Lewin recognised the immensely superior capability of Trident over Polaris, but it had to last until 2020 or thereabouts. Much could happen in that time. He was fully briefed on developments in Soviet anti-ballistic systems and was, still, convinced of the need for maximum insurance against mishap. He argued strongly for a five-boat Trident force.

There was no doubt an element of deliberate over-insurance in this. The real fear among defence staff as a whole was that the government would eventually settle, given all the financial problems, for a three-boat force, which would stretch operating cycles to the absolute limit in order to keep one on patrol, and allow no margin at all for the slightest unserviceability if the continuity of deterrence – and therefore its credibility – was to be maintained. Lewin might have thought himself in the position of the stores officer who asks for five in order that he may get four, knowing that four will do unless there is a total disaster. That, in the event, was what he got; Howe recorded with some glee: 'We cut back extravagant plans for the new Trident base and knocked out the fifth submarine.'[19]

The other concern was the design and nature of the missile. The C-4 Trident-I had been recommended to ministers as the right deterrent for Britain, and this accorded with American advice at the time. As one US official said, 'It will give you as much as you want for as long as you want it.' Britain knew well that the USA was developing the Trident-II D-5 missile, but it was bigger, more sophisticated, could carry more warheads and was so accurate that arms control experts, let alone nuclear disarmers, might suspect it of having a 'first-strike' role in taking out Soviet strategic ground-based missiles. Moreover, it would require larger submarines and more complex maintenance facilities. It over-fulfilled the Duff-Mason criteria.

However, in November 1980 Ronald Reagan was elected President of the USA, and one of the first decisions made by the new administration was to accelerate the development and production of the D-5 so that by the middle of the 1990s the C-4 would almost completely have disappeared from US service. This was precisely the period when the British Trident submarines were due to go on patrol for the first time.[20] The British were faced with an unpleasant dilemma. Did they continue with C-4 and saddle themselves with a unique system for a whole generation, with steadily eroding and increasingly reluctant support from both industry and the US authorities; or did they go for D-5, building larger submarines to fit into the small base at Faslane, finding some solution to the very real problems of maintaining these big missiles in our tight little island, and being prepared to answer charges that far from furthering the cause of arms control, Britain was fuelling a nuclear arms race?

Lewin came down firmly on the side of D-5. He had had enough of uniqueness with the Chevaline development, and the re-motoring of Polaris that had also proved necessary. The thought of saddling a remote successor with similar problems was deeply distasteful. He supervised a way out of the maintenance dilemma by negotiating an agreement to share the American facilities at King's Bay, Georgia.[21] He ensured that the submarine designers would have no difficulty in incorporating a missile compartment of the required diameter, and with Michael Quinlan, the Deputy Under Secretary (Policy) and Group Captain Willie Rae of his own staff, prepared a detailed case to answer the contention that British acquisition of D-5 was escalatory. The increase in capital cost was of the order of £400 million, but it was argued that this would be more than offset through the life of the force by the benefits of commonality with the USA; and in any case the inflation effect, plus a sharp adverse movement in the exchange rate, had made the initial cost estimates wildly out of date. The new, realistic prediction of £7500 million for the whole programme including D-5 was paradoxically easier to accept than previous figures.

All these points were put together by Terry Lewin in his presentation to ministers in late 1981. It was suggested by at least one observer[22] that if it had not been he who advocated the proposal, it is unlikely that government would have approved what has turned out to be a far-sighted decision. An exchange of letters followed between Prime

Minister and President, and the plan to equip the British deterrent force with Trident D-5 was announced in March 1982.[23]

This was one more burden for the Navy to shoulder. For in the spring of 1981, and well before making any other final decisions in his review of defence, Nott had ruled that the cost of Trident should be borne on the naval vote alone.[24] In hindsight, the writing had been on the wall ever since the submission to ministers had been discussed in the Chiefs of Staff Committee. No one had expected the idea of a special subvention to run, and the other service chiefs had turned to the First Sea Lord and said, 'If you want it, Henry, you'll have to pay for it.' But the Navy had always hoped there would be a change of heart. When it was not forthcoming, from Cabinet, the Secretary of State or – it must be said – through any intervention from the Chief of Defence Staff,[25] the sense of betrayal in the higher reaches of the Naval Staff was deep. Its effect was to be present in all that subsequently occurred.

The Nott Defence Review of 1981

'Nott' puns naturally abounded in the Ministry of Defence and the services after the new Secretary of State for Defence took office in January 1981. One of the most appropriate was that his radical reappraisal of the defence programme, carried out in the first half of that year, was 'Nott a Defence Review'. The term was steadfastly avoided by authority, but those involved were entitled to wonder what else it could possibly be. Some sort of nuance is provided by the Prime Minister's memoirs: Nott was appointed 'with the remit of getting better value for money from the huge sums spent on defence'.[26] That might be thought limiting to the extent of precluding root-and-branch strategic reappraisal. Earlier in the same page of her book Margaret Thatcher noted that just such a review, *NATO-wide*, had been suggested by the British Foreign and Defence Secretaries in 1980 and rejected by Chancellor Schmidt of West Germany. Possibly this was thought to foreclose any large shift in Britain's position in the Alliance.

In the context of Terry Lewin's tenure as CDS, these are not passing academic points. One staff officer of another service, who worked close to him almost throughout his time in the post, said Lewin had arrived with 'very dark blue' ideas.[27] These may well have included a re-weighting of the British contribution to NATO towards the maritime 'pillar' of the Alliance; persuading the NATO authorities to accept not only that there was a maritime threat outside the NATO area but that steps must be taken to counter it; and negotiating in a downward direction the responsibilities of British forces in Germany. All these might have been thought appropriate to a maritime Chief of Defence in a maritime nation like Britain. They may well have been in the back of Lewin's mind in any support he gave Carrington and Pym in their *démarche* on NATO strategy. But this had got nowhere, and in the course of 1980, as is clear from his notes for the November meeting with the Prime Minister, he was steadily moving to a much more 'purple' line, giving full weight to the demands and worries of the Army and Air Forces on the central front.

So there was a good deal of common ground as Nott approached, with great speed and energy, the task that had been set for him by the Prime Minister. His initial enquiry, on flying back from Indonesia which he had been visiting as Trade Secretary, was 'What is the strategy?'[28] He was quickly briefed on the 'four pillars' of the British contribution to NATO – the strategic nuclear deterrent, the defence of the home base, British Forces Germany, and the maritime effort in the Eastern Atlantic and Channel – with the extra 'half-pillar' of amphibious support to the Northern Flank of the Alliance in time of tension or war. Subsequently he worked on and within those parameters as the determinants of British force structures, while accepting that there were other things the forces could do. Then, according to one of his closest advisers, he looked at the task as solving a 'resource and priority allocation problem'.[29]

This, with the added constraint of the budgetary limits Nott himself set, created a pretty tight jacket in which the review was to take place. There was scarcely any strategic headroom, and no financial flexibility. That did not mean he wanted atrophy within the strategic framework. On the contrary, it was there that he expected radical thinking and if necessary restructuring. Lewin summed up the approach in lecture notes made at the end of 1981: 'Individual style – makes own decisions; doesn't like long papers, big meetings, monolithic bureaucracy; gets on with job, tends to concentrate on one issue at a time to exclusion of all else; very, very able politician; Nott (pun) a military genius or defence expert, nor does he have to be.'[30]

All the service staffs, used to deliberate and generally cheeseparing re-examinations of their existing programmes, were to some extent put off balance by this disturbance of their underlying assumptions. A meeting at Greenwich, lasting two days, between Nott, Cooper, Mason, Quinlan and the Chiefs produced more questions than answers and resulted in a remit for further studies, to be handled by the central staffs after single-service consultation.[31] But already there was a sense that Nott believed 'the answers might lie in concentrating Britain's limited military resources on continental defence, virtually abandoning any maritime pretensions now that most of Britain's residual overseas commitments had been liquidated'.[32]

It was not only the sense that this was the way things were going, rather quickly percolating through the Naval Staff, that caused their forebodings. The decision to saddle the naval budget with the cost of Trident, as has been suggested, had greatly shaken their confidence and their feeling that loyalty did not extend downwards from their political masters. The Navy department tended to turn inwards, dealing with questions in the way they had come to know best, which was to adjust existing programmes in the most limited fashion that resource constraints would allow. This was not what Nott said he wanted; and he complained, then and later, that he found it impossible to hold an open and intellectually satisfying discussion with anyone in the higher reaches of the Naval Staff. His relations with Leach were at best coolly polite,[33] and when he tried to reach further down the naval tree he found, in his view, none of the flexibility, penetration or judgement he sought.

It was not that, in this initial phase of what turned out to be a headlong process, the General and Air Staffs were producing anything much more imaginative. But then they did not have to, to anything like the same extent as the Navy. From the very outset of NATO the Army had a mandate to defend some 75 km of front in north Germany, and the Air Force to provide the bulk of the Second Tactical Air Force and its commander. There were well-defined force levels and goals written firmly into NATO plans. They could easily rest on these and indeed press for improvements to them, to keep up with what was seen as an increasing Soviet threat. The Navy, although it too appeared in the NATO force goals, was in a far more 'contributory' role – and how big was a contribution, particularly when the powerful United States Navy so often talked as though it could control the Atlantic on its own?[34]

At the heart of the strategic debate, when this was conducted (as it was) within the strait-jacket of NATO scenarios, lay a conundrum. Rightly or wrongly, whenever a battle on the Central Front was 'gamed' by NATO, by the Defence Operational Analysis Establishment, or by the Staff Colleges, given the accepted intelligence assessments, the situation within seven days or so was so desperate for NATO that they were forced to initiate the use of tactical nuclear weapons.[35] If this conclusion was correct, it meant that reinforcement by shipping across the Atlantic, which was a main plank of the naval case, would be too late to prevent a catastrophe. It also meant – again if it was correct – that by accepting the likelihood of a short war ending in at best a tactical nuclear exchange, and at worst the horror of a strategic exchange, NATO was in fact planning, if not to lose, at least to accept a highly unsatisfactory outcome.

The only way to get out of the conundrum was to strengthen NATO's conventional forces on the ground in Europe *and* ensure that naval forces in the Atlantic were strong enough to safeguard reinforcement. So much was made clear in a book published in 1978 called *The Third World War*,[36] written by retired officers of all three services under the aegis of General Sir John Hackett, an outspoken ex-Commander of the British Army of the Rhine. It was a polemic aimed at a massive increase in defence spending throughout NATO, far greater in extent than the modest 3 per cent to which NATO was (in the case of many of its members half-heartedly) committed. While the imagination that went into the book was widely commended, its financial implications were clearly judged to be politically unacceptable.

Subsequent reappraisal of Warsaw Pact capabilities, particularly after the end of the Cold War, has suggested that there was a more or less gross over-assessment of their efficiency and organisation. Even at the time there was some feeling that the intelligence estimates were overblown, and moreover that some of the allied ground forces, notably the Bundeswehr, were better furnished than they let on. However, such suspicions were regarded as unworthy and highly detrimental to NATO solidarity, and the general perception that the group of Soviet forces in Germany represented a beetling menace has to be acknowledged in any account of this period.

Lewin of course, as the tri-service Chief of Defence Staff, was fully aware of all these arguments. He probably had reservations about them in their extreme form, but could not ignore them. He could also have doubts about the concentration on the Central Front and the single NATO scenario when all experience showed this was the least likely contingency, and these he did express, but he was up against a British defence policy that had been set in 1968 and had been endorsed by government over and over again.

He was getting no help from the single-service staffs, and neither was Nott. The studies set in train by the Greenwich meeting soon became bogged down in the Central Staffs when single-service inputs proved incompatible. Lewin, with his own very small staff of briefers, confessed later to feeling 'both impotent and frustrated'.[37] Nott became increasingly impatient. He and Lewin visited Washington in February to call on Caspar Weinburger, the new Defence Secretary, and Al Haig, now the Secretary of State; Lewin already knew Haig and good relations prevailed. Lewin persuaded Nott to go down to Norfolk, Virginia for two hours with the Supreme Allied Commander Atlantic.[38] The outcome is not recorded.

On the way back Nott stopped over in Bermuda, with only his Private Secretary David Omand, for a Parliamentary conference. His patience was now exhausted. On a wet Sunday afternoon, waiting for the aircraft, they drafted the document that became known as 'the Bermudagram' and was the basis for all subsequent developments in the Review. It was issued on 16 March 1981.

The precise wording of the Bermudagram will presumably remain closed until 2011, when no doubt it will be minutely analysed by historians. There have been varied accounts of its contents.[39] In summary, it appears to have set out two main directives: the assumptions on which defence provision was to be based, and the cash limits on which the services were to base their proposals for future force levels. These proposals, it was made clear, were to be radical, 'bottom-up' restructuring resulting in a 'core programme based on capabilities vital to our defences'.[40]

None of the services found response easy, because they were not used to this way of looking at themselves. There was good reason for this; military forces are long in gestation, the life cycles of equipment generally being measured in decades, and concepts of operation likewise showing much continuity. Step changes are regarded, often rightly, as disruptive and dangerous. In consequence they preferred, when invited to inflict cuts upon themselves as they so frequently were, to adopt a 'top-down' approach, lopping off their least desirable projects in what was familiarly known as a Pain and Grief Exercise.

The Army and Royal Air Force, however, were not unduly alarmed by the Bermudagram, for several reasons. First, an assumption embedded in the directive was that the Brussels Treaty commitment to British Forces Germany was not renegotiable. There might be room for trimming and economical reorganisation but that was all. Moreover, the continental commitment appeared firmly as third in the order of the 'four pillars', the first two being Trident and the defence of the home base; and finally, the budget ceilings did not pose unmanageable threats to existing forward programmes. They were able to present their relatively modest restructuring as 'bottom-up' without too much difficulty.

The Navy was in a quite different situation. The Eastern Atlantic and Channel 'contribution' came fourth on the list of pillars,[41] and the extra half-pillar of amphibious support for the flanks of NATO appeared, if at all, in attenuated form.[42] The budgetary limits would have been tight even had it not been for the inclusion of Trident; and with that in the programme too, the Navy department judged the whole thrust of the Bermudagram to be unacceptable.

According to Nott,[43] the Naval Staff then did what he had asked them not to do: they embarked on a Pain and Grief Exercise, putting forward as candidates high on the list for lopping-off such politically sensitive items as the Royal Yacht, the assault ships *Fearless* and *Intrepid* and the South Atlantic patrol ship *Endurance*. Acrimonious meetings at staff level between the Navy and the Centre followed.[44] The Navy's conclusion remained that meeting the budgetary targets would lead to a complete undermining of the fighting arm of the service; it would not even meet the 'core requirement'.

Eventually, Nott took matters into his own hands and largely through his Scientific Adviser, Sir Ronald Mason, instituted his own conception of what maritime forces for the Eastlant role should be like. Influenced by studies at the Defence Operational Analysis Establishment (DOAE), the dictum was formulated that 'the balance of our investment between platforms and weapons needs to be altered so as to maximise real combat capability'.[45] This quasi-scientific conclusion was to be brutally tested in the South Atlantic less than a year later; however, for the time being it carried credence with Nott, particularly in the context of a putative Eastlant battle. Emphasis would swing away from the traditional pattern of escorted convoy that had been effective over the centuries, towards a far more open scheme of defence employing mainly maritime patrol aircraft and submarines as anti-submarine vehicles. This was untried in war, but DOAE thought it would be all right.

This was, to Nott, an attractive concept because it would allow quite deep cuts to be made in the destroyer and frigate force, and obviate what he regarded as disproportionately expensive modernisations of much of it.[46] It would also allow the reduction of the carrier force to two ships, because these were not easy to fit into the Atlantic scenario that was being evolved and for the remaining, peripheral role Nott had in mind for them, two would be enough.[47] As for the amphibious capability, he was coming to the conclusion that this should be allowed to erode, with increasing reliance on *ad hoc* arrangements.

This was the way things were seen to be going at the beginning of May 1981, and the concern in the Navy Department was extreme. The First Sea Lord, Admiral Sir Henry Leach, asked to see the Prime Minister and wrote a nine-paragraph minute in preparation.[48] It was couched in strategic terms and although many of the points it made would have been familiar to defence *aficionados*, they needed to be set out. Particularly telling were the dependence of the Alliance on British ready forces in the Eastlant area, and the damage likely be done by cutbacks forming a package which was 'militarily unsupportable, industrially damaging and politically unpalatable. The Soviets would be pleased, but SACLANT, SACEUR and CINCHAN dismayed.' The weakness of the paper, in political terms, was its answer to the inevitable question, 'What would you do instead?', because it amounted to a reduction of the British Forces in Germany, albeit presented as bringing home a large proportion of dependents and sacking locally enlisted civilians. This was a course which was bound to be bitterly opposed by the Army, and had already been discounted.

In the event, Leach did not see the Prime Minister before the next political event occurred, which was an outspoken speech by, and the subsequent dismissal of, the Navy Minister Keith Speed on 17 May.[49] A defence debate was due in two days' time and Speed may have judged that he could no longer support government policy in the House; in any case, the Prime Minster regarded his conduct as 'disloyal'[50] and he had to go. Speed's post was left vacant, all the single-service ministers being abolished some months later and replaced by two junior ministers with functional responsibilities. But in the meantime, while the Nott Review was in its final stages, the Navy alone was left without a political representative and its resentment deepened accordingly.[51]

The process ground to its inexorable close and in June 1981 the result of the Review was published. It is curious that this brief document is generally known by its number, Cmnd. 8288. Perhaps that is because the number comes trippingly off the tongue, or perhaps because its title *The United Kingdom Defence Programme: The Way Forward* turned out to be rather quickly overtaken by events. In any case, if '8288' is mentioned in any circle of people concerned in the ministry around that time, they know at once what is meant.

The main thrust of the decisions has already been discussed in some detail above, and will not be repeated. It was summarised as 'RAF better off, Army about the same, and the Navy considerably worse off'.[52] This was not quite just, as the Army lost 7000 personnel, but it was near enough. One or two extra points, not previously mentioned, need to be made.

The reduction of the carrier force to two, and the destroyer and frigate force to 'about 50' (which actually meant 42 plus eight in reserve) were clearly the most painful cuts. The amphibious capability was treated only in one short paragraph; three Royal Marines Commandos were to be retained, but the phasing out of specialist amphibious shipping was to be accelerated without any specific reprovision. In contrast to the pain in Eastlant and on the Northern Flank, there was some acknowledgement of a role beyond the NATO area. The value of the Navy, notably in Group Deployments, was mentioned, and the carriers' function in this role emphasised.[53] It is not known whether Lewin made any input here; it would have been surprising if he had not, given his background. The closure of the dockyards at Chatham and Gibraltar was announced; the former must surely have been welcome to Lewin, who had advocated it long before, and the latter may well have been thought inevitable, though the large graving docks there were a loss. Finally, and possibly the most far-reaching of all the decisions, naval personnel were to be reduced by between 8000 and 10,000 by 1986.

Reaction in the Navy generally to Cmnd. 8288 was more muted than might have been expected. In 1966, when the last great body-blow had been delivered with the cancellation of the fixed-wing carrier programme, much emotion had been displayed in sounding-boards such as *The Naval Review*.[54] Now, the same publication showed contributions from members that were much calmer in tone. The strongest criticism came from a Conservative Member of Parliament,[55] significantly an ex-Royal Marine, who dismissed as 'nonsense' the early retirement of the assault ships and the idea that their place could be taken by roll-on/roll-off ferries. Other articles, mainly by middle-ranking officers both serving and retired, sought to suggest ways in which the surface fleet might be restructured more economically and to learn lessons from what was seen as a staff failure to convince politicians of the 'naval case'.

It was inside the Ministry of Defence that trauma was most deeply felt. It was not confined to uniformed officers; the case has frequently been quoted of a civil servant, a descendant of the old school of Admiralty men, who said at a high-level meeting, not confined to the Naval Staff, that the reduced fleet was not the sort he would send any son of his to sea in.[56] Many others in the ministry saw clearly what the downstream effects of the decisions were likely to be, and feared that it would not end there but that, once the integrity of the balanced fleet was breached, further disproportionate cuts in the Navy would follow. The ultimate nightmare, the 'Navy reduced to a coast defence force', seemed all too close. The other services' nightmares – the Army deprived of its regimental traditions, the Air Force abolished and absorbed into the two older services – were by comparison remote.

But there were no resignations beyond that of the courageous Keith Speed. The First Sea Lord, Admiral Sir Henry Leach, felt more deeply than anyone that the Navy had been unfairly treated, that the allocation of funds (particularly over Trident) had been inequitable, the strategic basis of the decisions was unsound and the operational concepts flawed. He was encouraged to resign by two former First Sea Lords. But he recalled how little stir the resignation of Luce had caused in 1966, and took the view that it would be the braver course to carry on and make the best of the situation, retrieving as many losses as he could. He carried his Board colleagues with him in this decision.[57]

Inevitably the question, a critical one in the context of this biography, must be asked: did Terry Lewin at any time consider resignation, as the senior serving naval officer? More broadly, did he during the Nott Review fight hard enough for the service he so patently loved and had preserved, throughout his career, as a balanced autonomous force of worldwide reach?

The answer to the first of these questions is almost certainly No. None of Lewin's closest confidants have suggested that he seriously contemplated resignation, and according to Tim, his son, Terry specifically said he was not a resigner and did not regard it as an option. If he felt the need to rationalise the decision, his reasoning probably was on the same lines as that of Henry Leach: it would have had almost no public effect and would have horribly disrupted an already damaged and dispirited organisation. But lest it be thought that he did not feel deeply about what had occurred, it is worth repeating something he said near the end of his life.[58] Had it not been for the Falklands conflict, he had intended to refuse the peerage that is customarily offered to a retiring Chief of Defence Staff. It was the only gesture he could usefully make, and he would have made it.

The second question is more difficult to answer. It was posed countless times during research for this book, and many witnesses, from all the services and from political and civil life, either asked it themselves or readily discussed it – usually in the form 'Yes, why didn't he fight harder?'

One reason could have been that he was intellectually convinced of the rightness of the reasoning in Cmnd. 8288. That would have meant his full acceptance, strategically, of the overriding nature of the NATO commitment, the primacy of the Central Front, the inevitability of a short-war scenario, and the reduction of the flanks role to an *ad hoc* sideshow; and at the grand tactical level, the early use of theatre nuclear weapons, the reduction in importance of transatlantic reinforcement, the abandonment of convoy, and entrusting anti-submarine warfare largely to a combination of air and submarine units that was untried in war. All the evidence of his career, and of his public utterances over the years, suggests that this was a most unlikely set of assumptions for him to accept. Examples of his statements are scattered throughout this book and it is not necessary to labour them. But for the most basic assumption of all, the near-exclusive NATO commitment, there is more concrete, contemporary evidence of his scepticism. In notes written in his own hand for a lecture he gave at the end of 1981, he set out the four and a half pillars of Britain's contributory 'strategy' – and then the green ink explodes in block letters: FIFTH PILLAR?[59] This could only mean, in the context, a *national* capacity for taking independent action within and beyond the NATO area. Indeed, it is likely that he ensured at least partial acceptance of such a role in Cmnd. 8288, and the Navy's part in it.[60]

If then Lewin was not intellectually convinced by the rationale of the Review, why did he accept it with apparently so little demur? Three possible reasons can be advanced. The first, and simplest, is that he believed Nott had come into office with the fixed intention of accepting financial stringency, and of making the Navy bear the brunt of it. Trident was a *sine qua non*; the Prime Minister had asked Nott if he was 'sound' before he became Secretary of State.[61] The defence of the home base was an irreducible commitment. As between the Central Front and the Eastern Atlantic, all Nott's political instincts (and advice, including advice at Cabinet level) would point to the former. Lewin is likely to have judged that damage limitation was the best he could hope for; and Trident, the nuclear submarine force and the beyond-the-NATO-area provisions were well worth having.

The second reason is that Lewin was Chief of the *Defence* Staff. It was his business to co-ordinate, within the then limits of the organisation, the defence interest as a whole. As Chairman of the Chiefs of Staff Committee, he had to take a strictly impartial position, reconciling, so far as he could, often radically different points of view without fear or favour. Any partisanship would be very quickly detected and his credibility with the other Chiefs would be fatally undermined. The fact that, in the circumstances of the Nott Review, the balance of opinion amongst his colleagues would almost always be two to one – the Army and Air Force against the Navy – would increase his difficulty in advocating any naval line. He was not placed in the same position as Carver had been in 1974, when the ultimate in salami-slicing had been achieved by the device of the Critical Level; in the Nott Review, the claims of Central Front and Eastlant were deliberately set against each other.

The third possible reason, and it is a much more contentious speculation, is that Lewin believed the Navy's situation post-8288 was retrievable. It still had substantial forces capable of the highest level of hostilities; the Trident force was secure, the nuclear-powered fleet submarine programme was not to be reduced, two carriers were to remain. The lowering of both the numbers and the modernity of the destroyer and frigate force was serious, but modernisations in particular can, in whole or part, sometimes be added back into the programme, and future frigates could be cheaper in both capital cost and manpower, with consequent accretions in numbers. The Royal Marines were not to be decimated or dissolved. All was not lost; there was a tomorrow.[62]

There is less evidence for Lewin's embracing this third reason than the other two. If he did, he would, given his ready grasp of reality, have detected some flaws. The biggest gap had been exposed by Sir Patrick Wall: the provisions for amphibious shipping even in the medium term were almost non-existent. In the event, a brilliant *coup* by Henry Leach sent Nott to visit *Fearless* on the one day the Secretary of State could spare to see the Navy at sea; Nott was hugely impressed, and the assault ships were consequently reprieved for a few years[63] – so addbacks were, indeed, possible. Nevertheless there were no plans to replace specialist shipping in the long term. Another gap was in the manpower bill: with the severely reduced numbers projected, it would not be possible to man an increased fleet with trained people even if it were to be built. Finally, there was the nightmare: given the blow to the concept of a balanced fleet, would the remains be a further bait for Treasury jackals? In particular, if the carriers were now to be dedicated to an out-of-area role, how long would they survive a further withdrawal of British defences into the NATO shell? Sir John Nott maintained in 1999 that there was no intention to dispose of them;[64] but, as is well known, Secretaries of State come and go, and new ones bring their own ideas.

Thus, there were valid reasons for Terry Lewin's not overtly taking the part of the Navy during the Nott Defence Review. Much more light may be thrown when all the papers are available. After all, some very personal and individual advice was being given by other actors, notably Cooper and Mason, and there was good reason for the Chief of Defence Staff, however unconstitutionally, to have acted similarly in the circumstances. Lewin may or may not have put his views on paper, but there has been no hint of it in oral or written research. For now, it can only be said that he did all he believed he could. This, incidentally, included the time-honoured Whitehall stratagem of seeking delay; when the terms of Cmnd. 8288 were on the Cabinet table and clearly were likely to be approved, Lewin urged that no final decisions should be taken until allies had been consulted.[65] 'We knew that most of our European allies were in the same resource trouble as we were, and were engaged on similar reviews of their own programmes. Surely it made sense to consult together? ... Cabinet accepted the logicality of this, but deemed it politically impossible.' The summer recess was approaching.

Some with naval backgrounds thought at the time that he had not done enough. The feeling was strongest among senior officers on the retired list. Many were not in a position to know just how strongly the NATO jacket had tightened over the past thirteen years, nor how narrowly the strategic assumptions were now drawn. They looked at what they saw as the more lasting verities. At all events, when Terry Lewin spoke at a dinner of the Royal Navy Club of 1765 and 1785, he was frostily received; an aide at the time described it as a 'terrible evening'.[66]

But about one aspect of the Nott Review, which had given Lewin deep concern, he felt something could be done. He had recorded feeling 'impotent and frustrated' because he, as Chief of Defence Staff of his country, had not been in a position to tender impartial, independent advice to government, calling upon proper and detailed staff work under his own control. On coming into office, he had had some ideas about this; his views had been immensely hardened by his experience since. Changing the organisation for the better was the next task he set himself.

The Central Organisation of Defence

Lewin as CDS was almost uniquely well qualified to look at the Central Organisation for Defence. It was his seventh tour in Whitehall. He had experienced the old Admiralty, the Ministry of Defence as it passed through and emerged from the Mountbatten reforms and co-location, and the way it had handled successive policy reviews and changes, as well as the almost constant pressures on its resources. From the beginning of his time as Chief of Defence Staff, he was moving towards proposals for change.

It went without saying that he had to go quietly about this business.[67] The Chiefs of Staff were jealous of their autonomy and a direct set of radical proposals from someone who was constitutionally simply their chairman, even though he was acknowledged as *primus inter pares*, would have had as dusty an answer as Mountbatten received in 1962. Lewin adopted a more roundabout approach. In the inaugural Mountbatten Memorial Lecture, given at the Royal United Services Institution on 7 July 1980,[68] he did, as his then Military Assistant recalled,[69] designedly insert some 'teasing' passages indicating, to those who cared to read, the way in which his thought was moving. While dismissing sweeping unification – he specifically mentioned Canadian experiments in that direction – he said:

> I doubt if there would be disagreement that evolutionary improvements to the organisation are inevitable, to accommodate the increasing complexities of defence planning and resource allocation ... Our Armed Forces are more closely integrated today than they have ever been ... But, defence is a dynamic business and there is no certainty that what appears basically sound today will meet tomorrow's needs.

He ended by reminding the audience of the title of his address The Common Cause.

The events of the next eleven months were to show how difficult it was for the Chiefs of Staff, under the extreme pressures to which they were subjected, to keep that common cause in mind. Indeed, it was often apparent that they did not agree what it was. The Chief of Defence Staff ought, in Lewin's view, to have been able to formulate it for them, but he had neither the authority nor the staff to allow him to do so. The single-service staffs were numerous and strong, and even the so-called Central Staff did not serve the Chief of Defence Staff as such, but the Chiefs as a whole.[70] The Chiefs themselves had a dual role, never so clearly set out as by Professor Michael Howard many years before: 'to give professional advice on the making of national defence policy, and to act as supreme guardian of [his] own service'.[71] It was a quotation often used by Lewin, as expressing cogently the dilemma in which the Chiefs so often found themselves.

It was for him a fortunate spin-off from the Nott Review – perhaps one of few – that the organisation had been so clearly demonstrated to be ineffective. It enabled him to formulate, and carry through, a fundamental shift in responsibility and accountability in a remarkably short space of time. As has been indicated, he had been thinking about it ever since he got into the chair; but between July 1981 and February 1982 he put it into execution, and that by Whitehall standards was rapid. He received support in principle from John Nott as Secretary of State for Defence, but Nott did not intervene with any great force.[72] Lewin commented, with uncharacteristic waspishness, near the end of his life, 'Fat lot Nott did!',[73] but probably it was wise for the Secretary of State to stay aloof; at least one Chief of Staff would have opposed the scheme much more vigorously had he been its advocate.

The reforms were introduced in a very discreet way, in a Ministry of Defence Notice to Directors and Heads of Divisions – not much more than an office memorandum – on 4 February 1982,[74] and communicated to Parliament in a letter from the Secretary of State to the Chairman of the Select Committee on Defence a week later. But they were far-reaching. The principles were never more clearly summarised than by Lewin himself, in a speech in the House of Lords on 13 June 1984, and it is right to quote this extensively:

> I made proposals which were based on five principles. The first was that the Chief of Defence Staff should become the principal military adviser to the Secretary of State and to the Government in his own right, and no longer as the chairman of a committee with collective responsibility ...
>
> From that first principle followed the second: that the Chiefs of Staff Committee would become the forum in which the Chief of Defence Staff sought the advice of his colleagues. No longer would it become the fulcrum of collective responsibility.
>
> The third principle preserved the position of the Chiefs of Staff. They would remain the professional heads of their single services, responsible for their morale and efficiency. They would remain responsible for giving advice to the Secretary of State

and to Ministers across the whole field of strategy, resource allocation and their own single service matters. They would retain
their right of direct access to both the Secretary of State and the
Prime Minister, so that if they do not like the advice the CDS
gave they had a way out to represent their own view.

The fourth principle concerned the central staff, which
before had been responsible to the Chief of Defence Staff in his
position as chairman of the Chiefs of Staff Committee, and not
to him individually. Therefore, the CDS had no staff of his
own; he had only a staff which was responsible to the collective
body. With these changes the central staff became accountable
to the Chief of Defence Staff in his own right. At last he would
have a staff of his own and could set it studies with terms of
reference which he did not have to get agreed with all the
Chiefs of Staff beforehand.

The fifth principle – and a vital one – was that the Chief of
Defence Staff should become the Chairman of a senior appointments committee which would consist of the Chiefs of Staff.
This committee would have responsibility for overseeing the
promotion and appointments of all three- and four-star officers
– Lieutenant-Generals, Generals and their equivalent – and the
appointments of some two-star officers to important posts. This
is essential to preserve the careers and the promotion prospects
of those officers who might serve with objectivity in central
appointments to the disappointment of their own services ...

The notice itself followed these principles precisely, defining the duties
of both the CDS and the single-service Chiefs of Staff and making clear
the subordination of the Central Staffs to the CDS. It was amended
after the Falklands operation to clarify the chain of command in operations, which even in the case of single-service operations was subsequently to run through CDS.[75]

Lewin was able to comment further on the way in which his
reforms had worked when he appeared before the Defence Committee
of the House of Commons on 19 July 1984. It is clear from a note on

the cover of his copy of the committee's Report[76] that he regarded this appearance as very important. It 'is an expression of my faith. Do read it.'[77] No stronger statement from this man of moderate language can be recalled.

The committee's enquiries were in the context of follow-up reorganisation, published as a White Paper on 18 July 1984.[78] Lewin, in evidence that covered twelve pages, was able to explain not only the principles already covered in his House of Lords speech, but the way they had worked and the relative positions that had now been achieved by all the principal actors. A great deal of the discussion centred on the strength of the respective staffs: would the single services be able to call on enough professional advice under the follow-up proposals? Lewin pointed out that the single-service heads would be able to consult the Central Staffs, and gave his view that they must themselves control sufficient staff expertise to draw up the essential operational requirements for their own services.

But he was able to make his most telling comments in a wider field. He pointed out:

> With only single-service staffs to form a view of the whole range of policy and strategy, then the single-service staff will, I think, only be able to put in a single-service gloss ... Now the Chief of Defence Staff will be able to require papers, set the terms of reference himself ... this is likely to produce much more valuable advice than ... the lowest compromise which you could get all to agree to.

He stressed that 'War is no longer a matter for single services.' So far as the influence of the military was concerned, he believed it had been strengthened by the reforms: in previous times, including his own as CDS, the Chiefs had hardly ever attended meetings of the Defence and Overseas Policy Committee (DOPC) of the Cabinet, but now 'it has become normal practice for the CDS to attend meetings of the DOPC which is as it should always be'.

A better example scarcely exists than this Report of Lewin's extraordinary clarity of thought and utterance. Where others, including his interlocutors, fumbled for words, interjected asides and lost the thread, his articulation and logic flowed almost without a flaw – and these reports are, as is well known, verbatim. At the very end of his evidence he was subjected to a singularly testing and abrasive set of questions from an ex-minister, some of them clearly designed to draw him into an indiscretion, and he dealt with them with robust but unruffled urbanity. It was the sort of performance that makes one long to have been there.

It should not be thought that his reforms went unopposed by his colleagues. The Chief of the Air Staff, Air Chief Marshal Sir Michael Beetham, was strongly against the erosion of the influence of the Air Force; on the other hand, General Sir Edwin Bramall, the Chief of the General Staff, was in favour on principle: he was acknowledged to be far too big a man to be influenced by the fact that he was next in line for the post of CDS.

This left the First Sea Lord, Admiral Sir Henry Leach. He regarded the reorganisation as the only aspect of his long and harmonious relationship with Lewin that caused real disgreement.[79] But on further enquiry, it appeared that by far the strongest point of contention was the procedure for selection of the CDS. Leach was still, seventeen years later, passionately in favour of the system of rotational appointments to the post, irreverently called Buggins's Turn. His argument was that if this continued, each service would plan its promotion and career patterns to bring a Buggins of appropriate quality to the top at the right time, and this would ensure independence of thought and deed. A neutral selection of 'the best man for the job', even if nominally conducted by the Senior Appointments Committee, would be subject to the final approval of the Secretary of State, who would be all too inclined to want a yes-man. In the hands of such a person, the new centralised organisation would become too malleable by politicians and Treasury.

It is the consensus that that contingency has not so far arisen. There have been misgivings among the ex-Chiefs of Defence Staff,[80] but they have been about service and not individuals, and there has been no recent evidence of military advice being ignored. Instead, the word 'joint' has come to the top of the British military vocabulary with the full approval of the politicians, and the Strategic Defence Review conducted in 1998[81] showed a more concerted view of defence, from the military, civil servants and politicians, than any similar document for many a year. In some ways it may be regarded as the posthumous culmination of Lewin's organising work as CDS: the development of a really efficient instrument for the formation of coherent defence policy.

To return this narrative to the end of February 1982, Terry Lewin had been in office as CDS for nearly two and a half years. It had been a taxing time. Apart from the exceptionally testing major events that have been described, there was an endless round of more humdrum business, an immense paper load, not always interesting but necessary to be read if tricks were not to be missed and nonsenses not allowed to go by default. Two cases went home with him, either to the house at Greenwich or to the cottage in Sussex, every night.[82] His time management was of the highest order, aided by his excellent memory.[83]

If business were not enough, he had a massive representational load. His terms of reference were making no idle statement when they included 'Representing Her Majesty's Government when appropriate'. In fact his personal staff calculated that on average he was out of the office, on representational tasks, one week out of every four.[84] NATO meetings, tours to meet his counterparts worldwide, visits to fighting units of all three services on exercises or, more rarely, ceremonial occasions, all took up time. Moreover, they took up energy: the sapping effect of such excursions has already been noted.

Reciprocal visits by Chiefs of Defence were another aspect of the job. There was always entertainment as well as discussion. Government hospitality was reasonably funded, and dinners at Admiralty House, in the old building on the west side of Whitehall, were standard. But sometimes the host had to deal with a domestic crisis. The story is told of a dinner for an important visiting delegation when the Chief Steward murmured in Terry's ear that the fish course, on its way from the kitchens down below, had got stuck in the lift. With total aplomb, the Chief of Defence Staff took his guests on a conducted tour of the collection of pictures in the dining and reception rooms. Many of them were the magnificent record by Hodges of Cook's voyages. Terry kept a brilliant commentary going for twenty minutes until the fish arrived, and none of the guests suspected that it was anything but a delightful variation on the normal dinner-party pattern.

He could not possibly have kept this pace, and this standard, going without the support of Lady Lewin and the family. It was the secure base from which he operated. Tim was now successfully established in the commodities market, a coffee trader with the market leader in that field, keeping a careful eye on the weather in Brazil. Susie, trained as a journalist, was now bringing up her delightful young family. Jon was ending his time at university, doing 'just enough to get through his exams', as his father wrote,[85] not without pride and affection. To some extent it was an extended family too: not only David Smith, but Rodney Stannard the driver and the small retinue of stewards and cooks all regarded themselves as friends as well as supporters. Loyalty travelled both ways. 'He brought out the best in us all,' said one.[86]

So that was how things stood at the beginning of March 1982. He had six months more to go. He could look back on some good things done; Trident was secure and he was convinced that his reform of the organisation for defence would prove itself. There had been some severe disappointments too, the Nott Review cutting deepest. Perhaps they had been inevitable in the circumstances but that did not lessen the pain. Now, it seemed, there would be a summer of routine business and preparation for a clean handover to his successor, General Sir Edwin Bramall. But The Unexpected – that refuge of the military planner confronted with simple scenarios by pundits and politicians – was just around the corner.

'SEVENTY DAYS OF MY LIFE'
5 APRIL – 14 JUNE 1982

That was the way Lord Lewin spoke of the Falklands conflict.[1] Like many things he said, it contained much in a few words. It was a statement of dedication: for those seventy days all his mind and energy were concentrated on a single objective. Yet it was also a statement of modesty: there was no suggestion in it that this was in some way the heroic culmination of a military career, rather that it was something that a man in his position could expect to be called upon to do. Yet again, it was statement of due proportion: there were many other things he had done in that long career, some of which might in the long run turn out to be just as important as a campaign in the South Atlantic. He knew to the end of his life that it was for the Falklands he would be first remembered by Britain and the world;[2] they might ultimately be wrong, but that would be for history to judge. He felt strongly enough about it to dictate a last audiotape[3] giving some unique personal information, which throws new light on how he approached and conducted that remote but all too real war at the other end of the world.

It had started – when had it started? Conceivably in 1690, when a British sea-captain had named the islands, 400 miles off the east coast of South America, the Falklands. Or perhaps in the 1760s and 1770s, when France, Britain and Spain were involved in settlement, counter-settlement, seizure and counter-seizure,[4] culminating in Britain's abandoning the islands but maintaining her claim to sovereignty. Or, more certainly, when Britain seized the islands from a short-lived Argentinian settlement in 1833. Since then the islands, Las Malvinas to Argentina, the Falklands to Britain, had been under British occupation but claimed by Argentina.

The dispute found new impetus in 1964 when Argentina brought it to the notice of the United Nations as a colonialist situation.[5]

Minor incidents, some of them bordering on farce, and negotiations, some of them bordering on constructive, continued for the next decade and culminated in the near-crisis in 1977 which has already been described.[6] Negotiations continued for the next four years, spanning the change of government in Britain and centred now on a concept first suggested in 1975, that sovereignty should be transferred to Argentina with a simultaneous leaseback for a period of years.[7] The British Foreign Office saw this as the best way out, and the Ministry of Defence – fully aware of the expense of establishing a 'Fortress Falklands', and of the great difficulty and risk of any attempt to recover the islands if they were seized by Argentina – were not opposed. The trouble was that the 1800 islanders, nearly all of British stock, were not at all disposed to countenance any transfer of sovereignty, and there was a vociferous lobby in the British Parliament supporting them. Thus it was very hard for ministers to negotiate any solution that would satisfy both the aspirations of the islanders and those of Argentina.

In December 1981 a new administration took office in Argentina. It was still in effect a military junta, as it had been for a decade and more, but now was headed by General Galtieri, the Commander-in-Chief of the Army. Significantly, Admiral Jorge Anaya, the Commander-in-Chief of the Navy, by repute had the strongest voice in the junta, and he was known to take a hard line on the Malvinas.

It is now clear that from its first meeting on 5 January 1982, the junta considered that an invasion of the islands was an option,[8] and planning on a contingency basis and in great secrecy was put in hand in the middle of the month. The junta was encouraged by the decisions of the Nott review to withdraw HMS *Endurance* from service in mid-1982 and not to replace her, and to phase out the assault ships shortly afterwards. But it appears that no one in Argentina at that time envisaged the possibility of a very early descent on the islands; the instructions to the planners spoke of a July date, after a period of intense diplomatic negotiation. Interestingly, this was not all that far from the British Ambassador in Buenos Aires' assessment that the period before

January 1983, the 150th anniversary of the British occupation of the islands, might be a critical time.[9]

There were two main prongs to Argentine plans. The first to be executed was the occupation of the British dependency of South

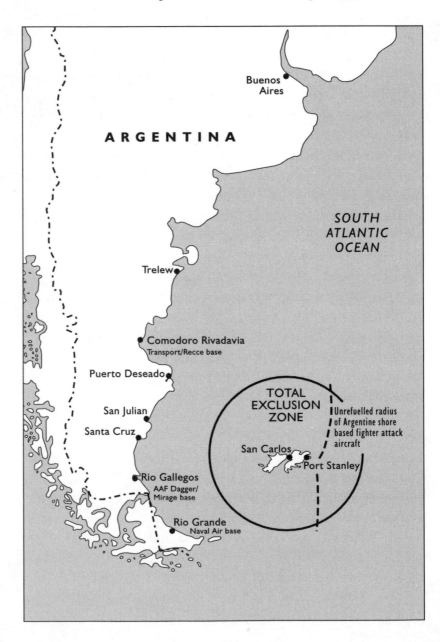

Georgia, the second the invasion of the Malvinas themselves. The lever to be used for the first phase was a scrap merchant called Davidoff, who had a contract to dismantle an old whaling station there; he would be the cover for a paramilitary force that would establish an Argentine presence which the limited British resources in the area would be powerless to dislodge. The next two months featured much probing on the ground and off-again-on-again orders from the junta,[10] alongside negotiations with the British in New York in February which met equally contradictory reactions from Buenos Aires,[11] including a particularly hard-line *communiqué* on 1 March. At this stage there was some concern in Whitehall, and the Prime Minister was informed of the disposition of British ships in the Atlantic on 8 March; apart from *Endurance*, none was within 20 days' steaming for normal deployment.[12]

The Argentines then accelerated the pace of events, for reasons that are still not clear. They were perhaps experiencing the kind of self-reinforcing escalation that affects military regimes: the military make a move, the Press play it up, any counter-moves are presented as 'provocation', public opinion is inflamed, the military are pushed into a further move, and so on. At any event, in mid-March Davidoff and a mixed party of workers and military personnel landed from the *Bahia Buen Suceso* at Leith. They were detected on 19 March by four scientists from the British Antarctic Survey,[13] who observed that an Argentine flag had been hoisted and stores in the British Custom House broken into. The Argentines assured the British party that they had permission to land. This was only partly true; the British Embassy in Buenos Aires had been formally notified but the Argentines had not gone through the proper procedures on arriving at South Georgia. In any case, the BAS party reported the matter, the report reached London without much delay and diplomatic protests were made, including one directly from the Governor of the Falkland Islands to Captain Briatore of the *Bahia Buen Suceso*.

It was at this point, on 20 or 21 March,[14] that Lewin as Chief of Defence Staff first came into the picture personally. He was telephoned by the Duty Officer in the Defence Operations Staff and informed of the situation. He gave, or endorsed, instructions for *Endurance* to sail from Port Stanley in the Falklands to South Georgia, the best part of three days' steaming. She was reinforced by embarking a small detachment of Royal Marines. When she arrived she found the situation had apparently calmed down; the Argentine flag had been lowered, most of the Argentine party seemed to have been re-embarked, and the *Bahia Buen Suceso* had sailed from Leith. The British Foreign Office took the view that the matter had been resolved; this differed quite sharply from the assessment of the governor and the captain of *Endurance*, which was that the train of events since Christmas and before indicated a steady build-up of Argentine activity designed to lead to a permanent presence in South Georgia.[15]

The view that Lewin took was, perforce, the one prevalent in Whitehall. He had access to all the intelligence reports, the telegrams, and the advice from the Foreign Office. Had he been gifted with second sight he might have taken the assessments of those on the spot as more accurate. Even then, however, that would only have been applicable to South Georgia, a local difficulty; for as is now known, the junta's decision to invade the Falklands was not made until 23 March[16] and the order to execute the operation was not given until 26 March.

So it was that the Chief of Defence Staff, with the Defence Secretary, departed for a meeting of the NATO Nuclear Planning Group at Colorado Springs, USA, early in the week beginning 22 March. The party, which included Lady Lewin, travelled by RAF Comet via Washington where there were meetings with United States defence officials; by now both Lewin and Nott knew Defence Secretary Weinberger well and relations were cordial.[17] After Colorado Springs the Lewins, with Air Commodore David Brook and Captain Lockwood in attendance, went on by Comet over the Pacific, calling at Honolulu for a breakfast meeting with the American C.-in-C. Pacific. They arrived in New Zealand where CDS was to witness a Five Power Defence Agreement exercise.[18]

During the next week the schedule allowed for a couple of days in Fjordland, New Zealand, and an opportunity to revisit some of the places surveyed by Captain Cook, followed by two days' talks with the New Zealand defence authorities in Wellington. The programme had been arranged months before. But reports from Britain were increasingly disturbing. The lull in the South Atlantic had been short-lived; a silly insult to the Argentine flag, displayed quite legitimately in an office in Port Stanley, had inflamed Argentine public opinion;[19] bellicose noises were being heard.

Brook telephoned London every night and asked not only for situation reports but for advice as to whether Lewin should fly home early. The response was consistent: he should not. The Foreign Office was still desperate to keep things cool, and took the view that recalling CDS which was bound to get out in the Press – would be paraded as a provocation. The advice of the Permanent Under Secretary to the Ministry of Defence was similar.[20]

Back in Wellington, Lewin could not escape the Press interest that was building up. He adopted a standard response to any suggestion of military action: 'I cannot believe two civilised countries could settle such a difference by anything but negotiation.' It was a statement of conviction rather than gullibility. But, during a final dinner with the Prime Minister of New Zealand on 3 April, a message was passed to the CDS saying that the Argentines had landed in force on the Falklands and were in occupation of the islands. He announced this to a sombre and sympathetic audience.

It was high time to go. They flew next day via Christchurch to Hong Kong, where he had been booked to stay for two days with the Commander of the British Forces. Lady Lewin remained for the scheduled visit, but Lewin with Brook transferred at once to a commercial flight for London.

During that long flight, where the sun overtakes the aircraft so slowly that night takes most of the seventeen hours, he had, as he said, 'plenty of time to think'. One thought recurred over and over: *It must not be another Suez.*[21] He had had plenty of time to think during Suez, too, in *Corunna* on the bottom of a dry dock in Malta, and was convinced that the services had been let down by government, principally through its failure ever to formulate a clear objective and to think through what the end result would be. That would not happen while he was Britain's defence chief.

On landing, he was met by Captain Peter Abbott of his briefing staff. Abbott had attended the often stormy meeting of the House of Commons on Saturday 3 April,[22] and left his Chief in no doubt as to the mood in the country – well described later by Lord Whitelaw as 'feelings of shame and disgrace', leaving 'really no alternative to preparing and sending a Task Force to the South Atlantic'.[23]

Abbott was also able to tell the CDS what had happened operationally in the past few days. The First Sea Lord, Admiral Sir Henry Leach, had found his way into a meeting at Prime Ministerial level on the eve of the Argentine invasion, and persuaded Margaret Thatcher that it would be possible to assemble a naval task force capable of retaking the islands.[24] Two nuclear-powered submarines had already been deployed; a group of surface ships assembled at Gibraltar under Rear Admiral Sandy Woodward for a routine exercise, Springtrain, could be sent south straight away; *Hermes* and *Invincible* could be made ready quickly as the core of the fighting force, and amphibious ships with troops embarked could follow shortly after. Ships would need to be taken up from trade for auxiliary purposes; arrangements were already in hand and the naval staff would 'hit the ground running' in making them.[25] Leach had been authorised by the Prime Minister to proceed and had instructed the Commander-in-Chief of the Fleet, Admiral Sir John Fieldhouse, that the main Task Force must be ready to sail on Monday 5 April.

All this was entirely welcome to Terry Lewin, but he was concerned with the core issue: what was the aim? At a meeting of his advisers shortly after arriving in London, he drafted it personally:

> The overall aim of Her Majesty's Government is to bring about the withdrawal of Argentine forces from the Falkland Islands and dependencies, and the re-establishment of British administration there, as quickly as possible. Military deployments and operations are directed to the support of this aim.

Later that morning he attended the first meeting of the so-called War Cabinet. He recalled being met on the steps of No. 10 by Mrs Thatcher with 'Hello, Terry – did you have a good flight?' (He had not realised she even knew his Christian name: it set the tone for a remarkable relationship.) During the meeting he was quickly able to make his point: 'You need an objective: here it is.' They approved it there and then.[26]

'War Cabinet' was media shorthand for the South Atlantic subgroup of the Cabinet's Defence and Overseas Policy Committee, short title OD(SA). That was a more accurate title because, although there was a quite strong presumption that Britain might have to go to war, it was considered possible for the first few weeks after the Argentine invasion that some means might be found of restoring the *status quo ante* without fighting. That was one of the virtues of Lewin's draft objective; it did not preclude negotiation while the Task Force moved south.

OD(SA) consisted of the Prime Minister, the Home Secretary William Whitelaw, the Foreign and Commonwealth Secretary Francis Pym (who had succeeded Lord Carrington on the latter's resignation), the Defence Secretary John Nott, Cecil Parkinson as the point of contact with the Conservative Party, and Lewin as Chief of Defence Staff.[27] The Attorney General, Michael Havers, attended when advice on international law was required, which was frequently. Like all such committees, OD(SA) operated on more than one level; there was a group of high officials, designated ODD(SA), which consisted of the Permanent Secretaries of the Cabinet Office, Foreign Office, and Ministry of Defence, with Sir Michael Palliser – recalled to service after recent retirement as the Prime Minister's special adviser – and, again, Terry Lewin as Chief of Defence Staff. Sir Anthony Parsons, the UK's Ambassador to the United Nations who performed brilliantly throughout the whole affair, attended when he was in London. This committee was in close touch too with Sir Nicholas Henderson, the Ambassador at Washington, another key figure.

The pace was unrelenting. Lewin, living in his quarters at Greenwich, would begin the day at 6 am, going through the signals over breakfast[28] and arriving in the ministry at about 7.15. He would receive an intelligence and operational brief that lasted perhaps an hour, and that would be followed by a telephone conversation on a secure line with John Fieldhouse, who had been designated joint

Commander-in-Chief. This too could take an hour;[29] much would have happened since the previous day. The OD(SA) meeting would follow at 9.30 am; Lewin would be accompanied by the Secretary to the Chiefs of Staff to ensure the rapid subsequent dissemination of decisions within the Ministry of Defence.[30] A meeting of the Chiefs of Staff would follow later in the forenoon, and in the afternoon there would generally be a meeting of ODD(SA), where the question most frequently asked was 'Where do we go from here?'[31]

It was not just the sequence of daily events that ensured, as one of his aides put it, that Lewin would emerge from ODD(SA) meetings more 'drained and exhausted' than he did from any others.[32] The questioning and probing from these senior civil servants, people at the pinnacle of their careers and in their exalted positions for very good reasons of both character and intellect, was a tremendous challenge. Lewin knew that if he could win them over, then he would most likely be able to carry his proposals in OD(SA) itself. He showed himself fully equal to the challenge. Many times, he recalled, the Prime Minster said: 'If that's what CDS wants, he must have it.'[33]

Curiously, in a complete reversal of normal Whitehall practice, 'what CDS wanted' in the way of resources was the easiest of the problems. Treasury control was largely set aside for the duration. Materiel and supplies that would normally have taken years to approve were improvised, developed and provided in days. Much of this flowed without the personal intervention of the CDS, but he was always there to put a shoulder behind a reluctant wheel. The gears of policy ground more slowly, though, and it was there that the relationship between Margaret Thatcher and Terry Lewin was most critical.

Fortunately, trust between the Prime Minister and her principal military adviser was established early and remained secure. It was founded upon common purpose, goodwill and honesty, but it had its human aspect too. Lady Thatcher remembered a combination of 'competence and sympathy'[34] that she found immensely reassuring; Lewin in turn recalled her firmness of purpose and ready grasp of all the problems involved.

They were not, as the Task Force went south, all military by any means. Lewin's well-known dictum, that there is no such thing as a purely military operation, that all operations are politico-military, was never truer than in 1982. The position of the United States was critical.[35] Their diplomatic support was essential; it had been shown early on in their endorsement of United Nations Security Council Resolution 502, calling on Argentina to withdraw forces unconditionally, but it needed to be sustained, and some in the State Department were known to be lukewarm.[36] But beyond diplomatic support, it was essential to have practical American help with material and with communications. The two most striking examples were supply of the AIM 9-L Sidewinder missile[37] and the diversion of a submarine communications satellite from its normal orbit,[38] but there was a host of others. In these vital, linked matters the relationships built up by Terry Lewin over the years were highly important. He knew Al Haig, the American Secretary of State, from NATO days when Lewin was CINCHAN and Haig SACEUR, and they got on well and trusted each other. Similarly his relations with Weinburger, the Defence Secretary, and Lehman, the Secretary of the Navy, were close and cordial: they would do a lot for him, as they knew he would back them in difficulty. Even with this basis, everything had to be fine tuned. There was no room for bluster, and equally none for weakness when firmness was called for. By every account Terry Lewin made hardly a single error of timing or nuance.

There was one occasion when he was overruled, and it illuminates several facets of the delicate structure of OD(SA). John Nott had early decided, and cleared with the Prime Minister, that the military voice in OD(SA) should be that of the CDS and not the Defence Secretary. He himself might sometimes take on the role of devil's advocate if he thought political sentiment was getting too hawkish, but generally he would keep a low profile.[39] On one occasion, however, he intervened to delay by two days the sailing of the force south from Ascension when it appeared that there might be some chance of Haig's latest initiative (one more spin of the 'Haig Shuttle') succeeding. This, he knew, would irritate all the naval authorities because they were working to a desperately narrow window of opportunity which, given all the speed, time and logistic limitations involved, opened for a landing in the Falklands only between 16 and 25 May.[40] But he reasoned that if the Task Force sailed south and it then turned round because there had been a settlement, it would look as though it had turned tail in defeat.[41] It remains a 'what if' of history. The Falklands provided many.

Rules of Engagement were a constant concern. Before sailing for the Falklands Captain Jeremy Black of HMS *Invincible* said to his wife, 'Two things: I think we are going to have to fight, there are two sides here who can't step down; and, I think we are going to be strapped by Rules of Engagement.'[42] His second foreboding was incorrect. He recalled: 'We always had the right RoE, due to Terry's judgement.' It was not done without the most constant care and attention to detail.

Much of it took place at a level below ODD(SA), in a group that does not seem to have had a name or set of initials but was composed of the Assistant Chiefs of Staff (Operations), a Foreign Office representative, John Weston, and a senior Ministry of Defence civil servant, Moray Stewart. These thrashed out, almost day by day, the rules appropriate to the immediate future.[43] They used the NATO rules initially, but because these were devised for a quite different set of situations they needed extensive caveats. It is clear from Lewin's Falklands notebook that he went deeply and personally into the detail of these rules and that the OD(SA) did too.

They were to a large extent governed by what was a Falklands singularity at that time, although it has been much in vogue since:[44] the Exclusion Zone. A Maritime Exclusion Zone, a circle drawn on a 200-mile radius from a geographical point more or less at the centre of the islands, was announced by Britain on 12 April. It applied to Argentine ships only: they were liable to attack if they entered the Zone. On 30 April the same area became a Total Exclusion Zone: any ship or aircraft within the Zone was liable to attack if it was carrying supplies or reinforcements to Argentine forces in the Falklands.[45] Both these announcements were accompanied by an additional clause that the measures were 'without prejudice to the right of the UK to take whatever additional measures may be needed in its exercise of the right of self-defence, under Article 51 of the UN Charter'.[46]

Between these two announcements, on 23 April, came a somewhat broader message to the Argentine Government:

> In announcing the establishment of a Maritime Exclusion Zone around the Falkland Islands, Her Majesty's Government made it clear that this measure was without prejudice to the right of the United Kingdom to take whatever additional measures may be needed in the exercise of its right of self-defence under Article 51 of the United Nations Charter.
>
> In this connection, Her Majesty's Government now wishes to make clear that any approach on the part of Argentine warships, including submarines, naval auxiliaries, or military aircraft which could amount to a threat to interfere with the mission of British Forces in the South Atlantic will encounter the appropriate response.
>
> All Argentine aircraft including civil aircraft engaging in surveillance of these British Forces will be regarded as hostile and are liable to be dealt with accordingly.

All the evidence is that the military establishment, including Lewin, went along generally with this set of declarations. They appealed particularly to the Foreign Office because they maintained title to the islands and conferred legitimacy on British actions, but they were thought to have military advantages too; Henry Leach thought of them as a 'means of concentrating the enemy'[47] and both Woodward and Black regarded entry into the Zone as a defining moment for themselves and their people.[48] Fieldhouse is said to have advocated such a Zone from 4 April,[49] 'in order to blockade the invaders'. Lewin's view was closest to that of Fieldhouse. He wrote five years later:

> The Total Exclusion Zone was a complete blockade by another name aimed at stopping reinforcement by whatever means. What a pity we couldn't call it a blockade, but the lawyers told

us we couldn't do that unless we were in a state of declared war, which no one wanted for all sorts of reasons – Art. 51 was our guiding light.[50]

He might have added that the Exclusion Zone much simplified the old bugbear of differentiating 'Hostile Act' and 'Hostile Intent': for any Argentine unit entering the Zone was by definition committing a Hostile Act.

Those were the advantages of the Exclusion Zone, along with the all-important overriding declaration of 23 April, as seen by those in Whitehall. They were probably aware of its disadvantages too. These lay in two directions. First, the public perception would be that the Zone was a sort of jousting area, within which battle could be joined but outside which there was sanctuary for all participants. That was supposed to be modified, and critically so, by the 23 April declaration, but all the evidence is that in the public mind it never was. Second, the jousting/sanctuary idea was to some extent reinforced by the fact that the Rules of Engagement were quite radically different inside and outside the Zone, and relaxations outside it had to be justified by reference to the highest authority.

Lewin was, without doubt, exercised by these difficulties; one of his close advisers believed that after his initial approval, he became increasingly sceptical of the value of the Exclusion Zone as the conflict went on.[51] And some years later, he expressed what appeared to be positive antagonism to the concept. But that was in a brief conversation with the author, whose opinions on such zones were known to be unorthodox,[52] and it may have been little more than a polite aside. The best judgement must be that he recognised the two-edged nature of the Exclusion Zone idea.

Meanwhile, amongst all these matters of the highest policy and sensitivity, there was more pressing operational business. The British dependency of South Georgia had, after a spirited resistance by a small party of Royal Marines, been captured by the Argentines on 3 April.[53] The Argentine force, occupying the main base at Grytviken, was known not to be in great strength and the Commander of the Task

Force detached the guided missile destroyer *Antrim* (Captain Brian Young), the frigate *Plymouth* and the fleet tanker *Tidespring*, with a total of three helicopters and a company of Royal Marines, to recapture the territory. They were joined on their way south by the *Endurance*, which had evaded capture.[54]

The operation was named 'Paraquat', planned in a separate cell at the Northwood headquarters and approved by OD(SA). It was very necessary to make sure there were no Argentine naval forces in the area, and two days were spent in doing this, with the aid of the nuclear-powered submarine *Conqueror* and an RAF Victor sortie from Ascension, between 18 and 20 April. On 21 April an SAS party was landed on the Fortuna Glacier some ten miles from Leith, but the weather was even more adverse than had been expected and after a night in appalling conditions, their mission had to be abandoned. The sense of potential disaster was much sharpened when the two troop-carrying helicopters were wrecked attempting to land in order to extract the SAS men.

Back in London, where they were kept closely informed, it was one of the worst moments of the whole seventy days. The Prime Minister must have heard echoes from the fiasco of Desert One, the attempted helicopter rescue of US hostages from Tehran a few years before. It was at moments like these, and there would be more before it was over, when she drew most on Terry Lewin's strength and war experience. He reminded her, as he had done from the start, that reverses were to be expected, but his conviction that Britain would win was unshaken.[55]

As it turned out, within a few hours the position was transformed. By unparalleled flying skill Lieutenant-Commander Stanley, pilot of the last Wessex helicopter which was not even a troop carrier but an old anti-submarine machine, managed to extract the whole of the SAS unit without any casualties; a Special Boat Section reconnaissance party was successfully inserted; and two days later, with the crippling of the old Argentine submarine *Santa Fe* by a combination of the *Endurance* and *Antrim* helicopters, and in the face of evident superiority of force, the Argentine resistance collapsed. The Prime Minister made her famous 'Rejoice' broadcast; as she later wrote, it was really expressing relief, but was taken by some sections of the Press as triumphalism.[56]

The part played by the Press in the Falklands conflict was, indeed, an interesting one. Lewin had no doubt that media representatives would have to accompany the Task Force. He himself was at reasonable ease with the Press. He had given interviews where others might not, notably a 'Profile' piece to Christopher Lee before taking up his appointment as Chief of Defence Staff.[57] He was fully aware that a free and responsible Press is part of the process of any democratic country, and knew that a free ride could not be given to Argentine propaganda. Thus he raised no objection to the embarkation of Press representatives in the carriers, and some RFAs, of the Task Force; the eventual number was 29.[58]

Yet he was in no doubt, either, that irresponsible reporting could cause much damage. He set out two requirements: the paramount importance of not making public any information which would prejudice future operations, the lives of our people, or the interests of their next of kin; and ministers' need to make sure Parliament was informed before the public. At the same time he recognised the media's own interest to inform the public or, 'it sometimes seemed to us, the competition between various parts of the media to further their own interest, their circulation, or their popularity'.[59] That was a statement of fact, not of censure.

The reception given to the media on board ships of the Task Force varied, but in some it reflected a view that was less charitable than that of the Chief of Defence Staff. The Ministry of Defence appointed some seven civilian officers from its Public Relations staff to accompany the Press representatives and these, quickly known as 'minders', had the difficult task of trying to meet the requirement for reticence – if necessary through censorship – and at the same time maximising the facilities available for reporting back to London. Inevitably, given the limited resources of the Task Force – particularly in communications and in helicopter transport – frustrations arose.[60] Although they were subsequently voiced by the Press with much more force (and often venom)[61] than by the service people involved, there was undoubtedly much resentment on both sides.[62] The Press felt they were being unfairly, unsympathetically and inconsistently treated, and the military and the minders thought the Press were making disproportionate demands on resources and that their reticence could not be relied on.

Should Terry Lewin have intervened to improve matters in what was arguably the first maritime media war? There was little enough he could do about the situation in the ships; they were thousands of miles away, and those who were manning them had their hands more than full with operational problems. An intervention from Whitehall, on behalf of correspondents that were sometimes seen by the Task Force to be acting as though the war was being conducted for their benefit, would have been a quite serious undermining of his own people. As for the situation in London, there was a high-level group in charge of the release of information and it was available 24 hours a day; and twice he attended meetings of editors when he found them 'extremely understanding'.[63] There is little doubt that two decades on, a Chief of Defence would probably spend a higher proportion of his time in cultivating the media in similar circumstances; what that has to say about the current state of democratic machinery is a matter of opinion.

As May approached, so did the Task Force towards the Exclusion Zone, and so faded any hope of a negotiated settlement. South Georgia had provided no catalyst for an acceptable Argentine response. The hard line Argentina had adopted, even in response to an emollient set of proposals that emanated from the Foreign Office,[64] remained unchanged. They had now disposed their naval forces around the western half of the Exclusion Zone: the ex-British carrier *25 de Mayo* to the north-west, the ex-American cruiser *General Belgrano* to the south-west, each with surface escorts, and a force of three light frigates to the west. Some ships in each group were thought to be fitted with French Exocet missiles, with a maximum range of about 25 miles; but the main extended-range threat came from the aircraft of the *25 de Mayo*. Her A-4s could go at least 250 miles there and back, with an adequate bomb-load, under any normal conditions.

Here lay one of the traps of the Total Exclusion Zone, if it was taken too simply and literally. This was of course appreciated by the Fleet, Naval and Defence Staffs, and once Argentine dispositions were known Lewin sought approval to make the carrier an exceptional target under the 23 April declaration. 'We had a certain amount of difficulty', he wrote later, 'in persuading ministers that the *25 de Mayo* was a ship with guns with a range of 250 miles ... The Attorney General, with six years' wartime Fleet Air Arm experience, in fact carried the day on my behalf!'[65] OD(SA) duly authorised the Task Force to attack the carrier anywhere outside the Argentine twelve-mile territorial sea limit, south of 35 degrees South and east of 48 degrees West.[66]

The first blow of the main Falklands campaign was dealt by the Royal Air Force. They had done great service in ferrying supplies and people to the airhead at Ascension Island, and had provided reconnaissance to the best of their ability, but were keen to take an operational part. From Ascension they mounted an elaborate operation, 'Black Buck', involving two Vulcan bombers and eleven supporting Victor tankers, in order to plant one stick of bombs across the runway of the only major airfield in the Falklands, near Port Stanley, at dawn on 1 May.[67] Although only one bomb hit the runway, the psychological effect on the islanders was immense; it was the best indication they had had that help was on the way. It was also, of course, politically important, for the British were simply claiming that they were putting out of action their own airfield, for the purpose of denying its improper use to anyone else.

The attack was quickly followed by action from closer at hand; Harriers from *Hermes* and *Invincible* struck the landing strip at Goose Green and installations round Port Stanley. Neither 'Black Buck' nor the Harrier strike suffered any casualties; Brian Hanrahan of the BBC, in the *Hermes,* made his famous broadcast, 'I counted them all out and I counted them all back', which many might have thought justified, on its own, every bit of Press hassle before and after.

Woodward had a subtext to his plans for this phase of the conflict. He hoped to convince the Argentines that an early landing near Port

Stanley was likely, and thereby draw their air force into combat on the least advantageous terms for them – starting from zero against full-strength, fresh and well worked-up British squadrons. He also wanted cover for landing his Special Forces, which were needed to give intelligence on Argentine ground dispositions.[68] He therefore detached a bombardment group consisting of *Glamorgan, Alacrity* and *Arrow*, not only to do further useful work on the Stanley runway but to keep up the perception that there might be an early landing.

It worked quite well, to the extent that the Argentine Air Force mounted towards evening a major attack on the Task Force. In confused air-to-air combat the British forces came out distinctly in front. No Harriers were lost, while the Argentines lost several aircraft of various types and, much more importantly, lost confidence in their ability to match the Harrier armed, as it was, with the latest Sidewinder missiles.[69]

So far as both Argentine and British military authorities were concerned, the war had started. On the Argentine side, preparations were made for a strike against the Task Force by aircraft from the *25 de Mayo* the next morning, 2 May. If this was even partly successful, the *Belgrano* group could exploit the opportunity – a classic pincer movement. From the known Argentine dispositions, that plan had been patently obvious to the British for some days[70] and the military necessity of relaxing the Rules of Engagement, so that either claw of the pincer could be taken out, was apparent. But timing was of the essence; Lewin had had enough difficulty persuading the OD(SA) to allow attack on the *25 de Mayo* outside the Exclusion Zone, and extension to the *Belgrano* group, a less self-evident long-range threat, must be carefully presented.

It became all the more important when it was realised that the two nuclear-powered submarines detailed to shadow the *25 de Mayo* were no longer in contact. But the third submarine, *Conqueror*, was in contact with *Belgrano*. On Sunday 2 May, therefore, all kinds of impetus were working towards a decision to allow attack on the Argentine cruiser. Woodward sent a signal, well beyond his delegated authority, to *Conqueror* ordering her to attack. This was intended simply as a stimulus to Northwood; Woodward knew it would be countermanded.[71] At the same time, both Fieldhouse and Lewin were coming to the conclusion that it was time to make a *démarche* to ministers. Woodward's signal may have tipped the scales. At any event, at an informal meeting at Chequers of most members of OD(SA), following an earlier review of the situation by the Chiefs of Staff,[72] the Rules were changed to 'permit attacks on all Argentine naval vessels on the high seas, as had previously been agreed for the *25 de Mayo* alone'.[73]

After some communication difficulty and confirmation of the order, HMS *Conqueror* torpedoed the *General Belgrano* at about 6 pm that evening. By one of the many ironies of the Falklands, the sophisticated 'platform' *Conqueror* employed a crude 'system', two Mark 8 torpedoes, designed in 1923 – a dramatic refutation of one of the tenets of Cmnd. 8288. They did their work; the cruiser sank less than an hour later, with the loss of over 300 lives. After a brief attempt to counter-attack and a somewhat belated rescue of some 700 survivors, the Argentine surface forces were called back to harbour, as were the northern group including the *25 de Mayo*. They did not emerge again for the rest of the war.

Lewin was never in doubt about the necessity of the decision to attack the *Belgrano*. Years later he put it in forthright terms:

> A catastrophe like the sinking of a major unit was bound to happen sooner or later once the Argentines had invaded and the Task Force sailed. They must have realised the risks, we certainly did, and it was my job to ensure that if possible it didn't happen to us first.[74]

He greatly regretted the loss of life, which in hindsight was disproportionate because the actions of the escorts might have been better-judged; but 'such things happen in war'.

And war it was. Subsequent claims that the junta had 'called a pause' on the night of 1–2 May, believing that a British descent on the islands the previous day had been called off,[75] are entirely at variance with evidence that a strike by A-4s from the *25 de Mayo* was bombed-up and ready to go at dawn on the 2nd.[76] In the event, a fortuitous calm and the carrier's lack of speed made it impossible for them to get airborne; but if the attack had developed, they were not simply going to fly past the Task Force making rude gestures. Moreover, there had been an abortive submarine attack on the Task Force the previous night. In fact, so many acts of war had occurred in the past 36 hours that the military men on either side could have been in no doubt that battle was joined.

Technically, the sinking of the *Belgrano* was no doubt an escalation. It was the first major unit to be destroyed on either side, and the first time the underwater medium had been seen to be used. Lewin's point of view was that something of the sort was bound to happen, and it should not be our own forces that would suffer if he had anything to do with it. As for any last-gasp diplomatic moves that were going on at the time – the 'Peruvian initiative' with which so much play was made later[77] – Lewin wrote:

> We didn't know about it before the *Belgrano* saga and even if we had, taking all the other circumstances into consideration, it was too vague to be taken seriously ... this is borne out by analytical hindsight, it didn't have a chance of success.[78]

So far as the Task Force was concerned, the *Belgrano* was an important event. Captain Jeremy Black in *Invincible* regarded it as the best single piece of news of the whole war:[79] his acute tactical sense told him it was virtually the end of the Argentine surface threat. It was mingled with sadness at the waste of lives,[80] and some foreboding that the next casualty might be British.

It was not long in coming. The Argentine fleet might have been neutralised, but their air force still had to be reckoned with. Their very limited stock of airborne Exocet missiles, mounted in Super Etendard aircraft, was their principal asset, and on 4 May it was used with deadly effect against the Task Force. HMS *Sheffield*, one of three Sea Dart destroyers stationed up-threat from the main body, was surprised and hit, with 20 killed. She caught fire and subsequently sank.[81]

It was the first British ship loss and made sombre news in London. Politicians had been carefully briefed in preparation for the inevitable casualties; Fieldhouse, Leach and Lewin had all been asked the question, 'What losses can we expect/afford/sustain?' They had given remarkably similar answers: six major units were likely to be lost but somewhat higher losses could be afforded.[82] Nevertheless, the first loss was bound to cause trauma, and Lewin wisely drew on his war experience, reminding the War Cabinet that in 1942 Operation Pedestal had lost two-thirds of the merchant ships involved, but had still saved Malta.[83]

Lord Lewin recalled:

Cecil Parkinson said he would go on lunchtime television to explain that casualties were necessary in war, but Mrs Thatcher said 'No no, they'll never believe a politician, CDS must do it.' So I was sent out to Northwood on what was ostensibly a routine visit to discuss matters with John Fieldhouse. We emerged from the Headquarters to be surrounded by television reporters and I said my little piece. It was the only time during the Falklands that I appeared on TV.

The next seventeen days were of anxious preparation in both the South Atlantic and London. The Task Force was lucky because the weather severely restricted flying from the Argentine mainland and, while it was waiting for the amphibious force to join from Ascension, it could operate further to the eastward anyway.[84] Special Forces were active (a recurring item in Lewin's notebook is 'What are SF up to?'), a brilliant raid on Pebble Island in West Falkland being one of the more reportable events.[85] But the main effort was concentrated on planning the landing that was now viewed as inevitable to recover the Falklands.

There was remarkable unanimity among all the military people concerned. Woodward, as the commander on the spot, looked at all the options for landing places, took every factor he could think of into account,[86] and discussed them with Vice Admiral David Hallifax, Fieldhouse's Chief of Staff, over the secure satellite link.

Hallifax put them to the military and air deputies, Major-General Moore and Air Vice Marshal Curtiss, and they then went through the Commander-in-Chief to the CDS and Chiefs of Staff. The place chosen was San Carlos Water. It was 60 miles from Port Stanley, but that was its main disadvantage. All the other characteristics – space, depth of water, accessibility for ships and landing craft, geographical difficulty for attacking aircraft, and long Argentine lines of communication – were in its favour. The Chiefs of Staff in full session presented the plan to OD(SA) on 18 May. It is clear that the General Staff in particular had had considerable misgivings about the risks of an opposed landing without the achievement of air superiority, and had continued to hope for a negotiated and honourable settlement, but the die was now cast and the War Cabinet was assured that if ordered, the operation would be carried through with the greatest resolution, courage and skill. The Prime Minister herself was in no doubt. She considered the plan, and its presentation by Lewin, to be a work of 'genius'[87] and it was readily approved.

After reorganising its troop loads in a complex cross-decking operation, the amphibious group, heavily escorted by gun and missile ships, entered San Carlos Water very early in the morning of 21 May. Falkland Sound, at the north end of which San Carlos lies, had been reconnoitred ten days before by the frigate *Alacrity*,[88] with the comforting intelligence that she had set off no mines. But she had set that night ringing with her attack on the supply ship *Isla de los Estados*, and it was with surprise and delight that the leading ships of the amphibious group passed Fanning Head without any reaction from the shore.

The day of disembarkation was one of frantic activity and, for the warships, hard fighting. The Argentine Air Force, and naval squadrons disembarked from the *25 de Mayo*, mounted very determined attacks throughout the day. Their policy, a seriously mistaken one as it turned out, was to attack the warships first and then pick off the transports, which included the great white bulk of the P & O liner *Canberra*, carrying several thousand troops. The warships did not succumb. The aircraft attacked at low level, partly for accuracy and partly because they knew, having some Sea Dart ships themselves, the capabilities of the British Sea Dart system which worked best against medium-level targets. Because low level entailed difficult fuze selection and setting, not all their bombs went off when they did hit. One frigate, the *Ardent*, after an exceptionally brave resistance, finally sank, and the newly arrived *Antelope* blew up when a bomb that had not exploded was set off when being defuzed.[89]

The happenings of the day were watched with the greatest anxiety in London. Consensus at the end of it was that it could have been much worse. The transports had escaped without loss – *Canberra* left Falkland Sound that very night – and nearly all the troops were ashore, without any serious opposition. Many of the warships had been wounded, but there was still enough fighting strength to go on with and reinforcement was on the way, and the core of the Task Force, the carriers, was intact.

Many people nevertheless took the view that the next day would be critical. If the Argentine Air Force returned in strength to San Carlos it could still do much damage to a weakened battle force and the quite large number of transport units remaining. But almost nothing developed in the way of air attacks. At least one member of OD(SA) recorded his amazement at Argentine inactivity on 22 May.[90] It must have been of the greatest comfort to Terry Lewin. He had always been sure of winning, and it now looked as though it might be done with fewer casualties than had been feared. He confided to David Smith, his ex-flag lieutenant, not long afterwards that he thought 'we were nearly through'.[91]

He spoke prematurely, for 25 May was Argentina's National Day and it was a day of considerable success for the Argentine Air Force. Still very concerned to protect the assembly of ships in San Carlos, Woodward had stationed a '42/22 combo', consisting of a Sea Dart fitted Type 42, the *Coventry*, and a Sea Wolf fitted Type 22, the *Broadsword*, to the north of Falkland Sound to draw off attacks from the Sound itself, to direct Harrier fighters, and to impose a high rate of attrition on Argentine aircraft. The group had performed well during the day, but in the evening, aided by some over-confidence and clumsy manoeuvring on the part of the British, four Argentine Skyhawks penetrated the missile defences and mortally struck the *Coventry*. She turned over and sank quickly, but astonishingly over 90 per cent of her ship's company were saved.[92]

It was not the end of the day's setbacks. The Argentines had hardly any airborne Exocets left, and now deployed two in a roundabout, and very well-planned, attack on the main body of the Task Force. They did not succeed in hitting a carrier, which was their objective, but did hit an extremely important unit, the *Atlantic Conveyor*, a big, specially adapted roll-on roll-off ship which was carrying the bulk of the Chinook helicopters, desperately needed for transport over the difficult Falklands terrain. She had also carried reinforcing Harrier aircraft, but these had fortunately been disembarked already. The ship burned fiercely and several of her crew, including her gallant sixty-plus Captain North, were lost; she sank next day. Lady Thatcher remembered this as one of the worst days of the campaign.[93]

This was a galling set of reverses for a team that had thought it was set to win, and it was made worse by what Terry Lewin afterwards admitted was an error in the public information field. Both he and Henry Leach wished to withhold the identity of the *Coventry* until details of the casualties were known. The Defence Secretary was so persuaded. What then happened was that the loss of an unnamed ship was announced, in sombre tones, to the House by John Nott, and more lugubriously still on television by the Ministry of Defence spokesman. The Northwood telephone exchange was jammed all night by calls from the families of the entire Task Force,[94] and many people went to bed that night thinking we had lost a carrier.

In spite of reverses and resource difficulties, the British military machine began to roll forward. Goose Green was captured by the 2nd Battalion the Parachute Regiment, with the loss of its heroic commanding officer H. Jones, VC, on 28 May, and 45 Commando Royal Marines and 3 Para set off on their march along the north of East Falkland. 42 Commando leapfrogged to Mount Kent. The Scots Guards, Welsh Guards and 1/7 Gurkha Rifles were nearing operational readiness. In spite of reduced mobility because of the lack of helicopters, ground troops were closing inexorably on the main Argentine concentration around Port Stanley. Air support was increasingly available from the Harriers, now that the Argentine Air Force had more or less shot its bolt, and naval gunfire support was being provided by ships of the Task Force, giving Argentine troops little rest.

At this point it was decided, without the full knowledge of the overall land force commander, to make a leap forward along the southern flank with 2 Para, followed by the 1st Battalion the Welsh Guards, brought round by sea from Falkland Sound to Fitzroy and Bluff Cove, only 15 miles from Stanley.[95] The sea movement was complicated by the unwillingness of the Commander-in-Chief to allow either of the valuable assault ships to be in this exposed position in daylight, and complex ferrying arrangements had to be made. On 8 June the situation was that the Welsh Guards, tired after a rough sea crossing, were in a position to disembark from the logistic landing ship *Sir Galahad*, with *Sir Tristram* also present, in Bluff Cove. It was decided to allow the men some rest before disembarking and this proved fatal. The ships, unprotected by anti-aircraft fire, were caught by five Skyhawks and bombed, with many soldiers killed and others dreadfully burned. The scene was caught on film and remained one of the enduring images of the war.

Terry Lewin was profoundly saddened by this episode, most of all because it was unnecessary. Those in charge of the troops, he said, had disregarded the guidance of General Wolfe, long ago before Quebec: the duty of a soldier on board a ship is to get off it as soon as he can, and go about his business on shore. They had, too, disregarded more immediate advice from Major Ewen Southby-Tailyour, who had urged them to get off as soon as possible, if necessary by Mexeflote.[96] It had been a dreadful price to pay.

So the campaign came towards a conclusion which in spite of Lewin's conviction was never foregone, which had needed some luck as well as immense skill, energy and courage on the part of all concerned. The hills in front of Stanley fell one by one; the Argentine soldiers retreated towards the port. There were casualties, and one final one to the British ships, now weary indeed. *Glamorgan*, after conducting a night bombardment, tried to cut a corner around a known area of danger where a shore-mounted Exocet lurked; it hit her a glancing blow, killing thirteen men.

It was 12 June, the day of Trooping the Colour in London. The Prime Minister had been hoping for good news of the continuing attacks on the outposts of Stanley; instead, there was a disturbing first report about damage to *Glamorgan*, which made her very anxious. She was preparing for a difficult forenoon when Terry Lewin arrived at No. 10, about 7 am by her recollection,[97] to reassure her that things were not all that bad: there had been casualties, but the ship was afloat and steaming, she would not be lost.

It was a measure of the relationship that had grown up between the Prime Minister and her Chief of Defence Staff in the past ten weeks. Some said afterwards that they were the two most powerful people in the country over that time.[98] It is hard to gainsay that. It is ironic that, had the war occurred even three months before, Lewin would have been simply Chairman of the Chiefs of Staff Committee and the War Cabinet would have had either all the Chiefs in it, or none. Either way, according to Sir Frank Cooper, who went through it all, 'it would have been a shambles'[99] – not because of any lack of competence or motivation on the part of the Chiefs, but simply because the organisation would have been too cumbersome. As it turned out, it was the finest operational test there could possibly have been for Terry Lewin's concept of how the Chiefs of Staff should work, and it worked.

So, as the Argentine troops trailed towards Stanley on the 14th June and the white flags began to go up, he could look back on one more task, the toughest of all, well done. He had had unstinting support from all around him in the defence field, not only the services but all those connected with them in industry and administration. The spirit in the country had been remarkable and heartening for him. Most of all he had had support from his close family: he had telephoned his son Tim twice a day. Lewin may have been the greatest strength of the War Cabinet, together with the Prime Minster herself, but he drew strength from the depth of sentiment surrounding him.

On 14 June, at 9.30 pm local time, General Menendez signed the instrument of surrender. The British flag was to be restored; international law was to be restored; the principle of deterrence was to be restored. The way the war ended for Terry Lewin is best told in his own words:[100]

> We sat in the PM's room with a telephone patched through to Hereford where the SAS had a satellite link to Jeremy Moore in Port Stanley, where he was negotiating the surrender. Eventually we got the details of the surrender document and at 10 o'clock, the time for a statement to be made, Mrs. T went into the House and I was taken to stand behind the Speaker's Chair to hear her make the announcement that the Argentinians had surrendered.

NOT REALLY RETIRED
1982–1998

Admirals of the Fleet do not retire. The names of those holding the rank – seldom more than eight at a time – occupy a special section of the active Navy List. If a reason needs to be sought, it is that public life, even if not active service, may return to claim them at any time. That was certainly the case with Terry Lewin.

He was, in any event, not scheduled to leave the post of Chief of Defence Staff until October 1982. The ceremonial aftermath of the Falklands, mentioned briefly below, took up some of his time, but most of the business was preparing to reconstitute the British forces after what had been a wearing and testing conflict.

This was a matter of reconstituting ideas as well as material. A defiant little Foreword was inserted into the 1982 *Statement on the Defence Estimates*,[1] saying (after a brief tribute to the Falklands forces and their supporting elements):

> The events of recent weeks must not, however, obscure the fact that the main threat to the security of the United Kingdom is from the nuclear and conventional forces of the Soviet Union and her Warsaw Pact allies. It was to meet this threat that the defence programme described in Cmnd. 8288 was designed. The framework of that programme remains appropriate.

This, signed by John Nott, was dated four days after the Argentine surrender.

That view was not shared by Lewin, nor by his successor, Field Marshal Sir Edwin Bramall. Bramall later described graphically the dangers, made so apparent in 1982, of 'jettisoning the principle of maintaining balanced forces ready and able to met the unexpected in favour of single-minded concentration on European defence'.[2] During the next few years, he managed in his own phrase to 'nudge' Whitehall into a more open acceptance of the out-of-area role.[3] He might have had more difficulty had Nott remained in office, since Nott could be expected to hold to the fully NATO-orientated line.[4] However, he left politics at the 1983 election and his successor, Michael Heseltine, was more interested in matters of organisation and management.

In the material field, however, the particular abilities of John Nott were fully and beneficially employed during Lewin's last few months in office. By skilful lobbying and use of central contingency funds, Nott was able to improve the forward finances of defence to enable full replacement of war losses, the retention of the third carrier and the provision on a permanent basis of Airborne Early Warning helicopters, to mention only the most important naval items.[5] Henry Leach believed that damage to the Navy would have been three times worse had it not been for these Falklands 'addbacks'.[6] The Army and Royal Air Force benefited too, not only by replacement and enhancement of material but by reorganisation giving a more flexible ability to respond to crises.

Thus Lord Lewin (he had been ennobled in the Falklands Honours List) was able to hand over to his successor forces in good heart and with their reputation sky-high. That had been amply shown in the numerous events and parades of the summer. Britain had lost 255 people, Argentina many more; triumphalism was avoided as far as possible, and Thanksgiving, Remembrance and Reconciliation were the themes of the Falklands Islands Service in St Paul's on 26 July.

A further honour was to fall to him next year: one which had rarely been accorded to an admiral. Since 'Black Dick' Howe in the wake of the Battle of the Glorious First of June, 1794, it had been received only by Queen Victoria's second son, the Duke of Edinburgh, and the Earl Mountbatten, among naval officers. This was the Knighthood of the Garter, announced on 22 April 1983. The installation was on 13 June; one of his supporters was Field Marshal Sir Richard Hull, the other Marshal of the Royal Air Force Lord Elworthy – a truly joint occasion.

By now he had also taken his seat in the House of Lords, one of his sponsors being Admiral of the Fleet Lord Hill-Norton. He had taken the title of Lord Lewin of Greenwich, a place with which he had had such long association; although he no longer occupied quarters there, the links were to continue. There were tributes to his past too in his coat of arms, where beneath somewhat conventional blue and white waves and a naval gun appeared three boars' heads – from the arms of Sir Frank Judde who had founded his school at Tonbridge in the sixteenth century.[7]

History, then, was to be a theme for the future. But the future generation must be considered; and he was concerned to set up a home where he could see much of his family, including the grandchildren. Limes Cottage in Sussex had been a haven and a bolthole from the turbulence of Whitehall, when it could be reached, but it was tiny and not a permanent place for the Lewins. They found instead, after search, and advice from those they trusted, a house in Suffolk, beyond Ipswich and Woodbridge in the village of Ufford, called Carousel. It was near the River Deben. There could be a boat to muck about in. Jane would be Head Gardener and Terry, he said determinedly, Under Gardener. The long low house, which had been the home of an architect, had one curious feature, a kind of central eyrie reached by a spiral staircase. This was to be Terry's 'bookroom'. They would not move house again.

The immediate past would not let go of him easily. During the 'Eighties he found himself addressing, sometimes in more controversial circumstances than he would have liked, several topics that arose directly from his time as CDS. The broadest was the question of British strategy as a whole. His views on this were best expressed at a conference on the Future of British Sea Power, held at the Royal Over-seas League in London in November 1983. His contribution, one of 27 papers, was entitled 'The Maritime Defence of Britain', but as his summary shows, it was more broadly-based than the title implies:

Our priorities should be first, the maintenance of our independent strategic deterrent (which requires the co-operation of the United States), secondly, a respectable defence of the home base, thirdly an ability to contribute to the protection of our own and Western interests and the preservation of stability throughout the world.

In meeting our present NATO commitment we should endeavour to adjust our contribution to encompass these national priorities, as a hedge against an uncertain and increasingly unpredictable future.[8]

The emphasis on national capacity and roles was a long way from the hidebound 'four pillars in support of NATO' that continued to appear in Defence White Papers for years to come, and much closer to the strategy that emerged after the Berlin Wall came down in 1989.

The second matter was the defence of the Trident programme. Strategic nuclear arms control had been a hot topic since the mid-'Seventies but had largely passed Britain and France by, because their arsenals were so much smaller than those of the superpowers. With Britain's expected acquisition of Trident D-5, some commentators in Britain and America made common cause with the out-and-out nuclear disarmers in claiming that the number of accurate warheads then available to Britain would disturb the nuclear balance. The case was put in an article by two respected American writers in the summer of 1984.[9] Lewin spent a great deal of time, consulting widely, in putting together a refutation, and this appeared in a much-edited form in America in 1985. At the same time he constructed for *The Times* a bottom-up article entitled 'Why Britain Needs Trident', which he found more satisfactory.[10] It generated, as it was bound to do, considerable correspondence. One or two admirals, as well as more predictable dissentients, weighed in against it, and were rounded upon by Lewin's defenders in their turn. He perhaps most appreciated – he certainly kept it – a letter from Sir John Nott that said, 'I have been waiting for a long time to read a decent article on Trident, and I was delighted by your views ...'[11]

It was not quite the end of strategic nuclear issues. In 1990, sparked by a Lewin article[12] in which among many other naval matters he sought to safeguard the retention of a four-boat Trident programme – even then, he still feared a cut to three – the linked questions of Polaris,

Poseidon, Chevaline and the number of SSBNs in a medium-power strategic force were forcibly resurrected in a triangular correspondence among retired submariners.[13] All was amicably settled eventually, but it was an object lesson in how long memories can be.

The third echo from the immediate past was not unexpected but must have become irksome as the years went on. Controversy over the sinking of the *Belgrano* was kept going by three sorts of people: those who were trying to make money or reputation out of it, those who were seeking to make political capital, and those who were genuinely shocked by what they saw as unnecessary violence and escalation. So far as can be made out from the papers he kept – and, interestingly, this appears to be a very high proportion of the total Press coverage of the subject – Lewin made no differentiation. Every allegation,[14] including those of duplicity and conspiracy, was dealt with courteously and firmly. He never wavered in his conviction that it was an act of military necessity, and frequently made that point. Most of the circumstances have been covered in Chapter 18, and it is unnecessary to repeat them, but one factor came out well after the event and was then played up by his critics: the westerly course, away from the Total Exclusion Zone, that the *Belgrano* was steering at the time she was attacked. It must have been irritating to Lewin to return constantly to a point obvious to any sailor, that a cruiser can reverse course in three minutes. Nevertheless he did so, with patience that seems never to have faltered.

Another echo from the Falklands was provided by the intervention of Dr David Owen in the debate on the Franks Report[15] in the House of Commons on 25 January 1983.[16] Rightly pleased with the outcome of the deployment in 1977, when there had been no Argentine action against the islands,[17] Dr Owen claimed that deployment of a nuclear-powered submarine in 1982 would have averted the crisis. He did indeed in a book published later say that for this reason 'the Falklands War was an avoidable war'.[18]

Terry Lewin personally wrote a reply to this line of argument, and this appeared in *The Daily Telegraph* in late February 1983.[19] Essentially, he argued that the situation in 1977 was different from that in

1982, the main threat in the earlier case being the harassment of shipping. There ensued some further correspondence on the 1977 Rules of Engagement,[20] Dr Owen arguing that they were in fact extremely liberal and Lewin maintaining that they were restrictive. Though politeness was preserved, the controversy was not allowed to go away and was still in Lord Owen's mind at the time of writing.[21] A judgement on the merits must await the release of the full and precise wording of the 1977 Rules of Engagement which, to the author's certain knowledge, have not been made public in their entirety.

A final reverberation from Lewin's days as CDS – apart from lectures and speeches on the Falklands, which he handled with his usual assurance and apparent ease – was the question of appointment to the post itself. He was an opponent of Buggins's Turn as a principle; but when in the 1990s it began to appear that the position of Chief of Defence Staff was becoming the prerogative of a single service, he added his voice to those of other CDSs in sounding a warning note. This was not a 'dark-blue' attitude; indeed it could be argued that the Navy usually did better in the scramble for resources when CDS was not a naval man.[22] It was much more a matter of balance and equity of expectation.

There was a brief association with industry when he became for a few years Chairman of Brooke Marine, a relatively modest shipbuilding firm at Lowestoft. The most notable happening of those years concerned the launch of the next *Roebuck*, a survey vessel, in November 1985. She was launched by Lady Cassels, wife of Admiral Sir Simon Cassels, commanding officer of the previous *Roebuck* in Dartmouth Training Squadron days. No doubt Jill Cassels already knew a good deal about the habits of that vessel, and Terry added to this from histories of previous owners of the name, most of which had come to sticky ends. The launch went well enough, but at the subsequent luncheon someone whispered urgently in Terry's ear: the new ship, true to her name, had begun to sink. Terry made a smooth exit, supervised the necessary leak-stopping and returned to the table, able to tell Jill that the ship had survived her first assault from the angry fates.[23]

History was claiming him more and more. But even here, it was mixed with administration. He had been a Trustee of the National Maritime Museum at Greenwich since 1981 and in June 1987 he took over the chair from Lord Cayzer. It was soon apparent that this was no sleeping appointment. The museum, lying between the great domes and pediments of Wren's hospital – then the Royal Naval College – to the north, and Flamsteed's Royal Observatory up the hill to the south, had long been an adornment of maritime London and its collections and library were renowned. But museums have to move with the times. Immediate problems included overstaffing, a problem common to nearly all museums then, and real estate with its multiplicity of options on and around that historic site. But there were deeper issues of policy too.

Terry Lewin must have been heartened, in what quickly began to look like a heavy task, by the composition of the Board of Trustees and the higher levels of management. He had worked with most of them during his time as an ordinary Trustee, and some of them well before that. In particular they included the Duke of Edinburgh, known from *Chequers* days, the Royal Yacht and many contacts since, and Sir Patrick Nairne, one of the most eminent of the old breed of Admiralty Civil Servants. But indeed, amongst the twelve there was a formidable spread of expertise and advice.[24] There was moreover a new director in Richard Ormond, who came from a fine arts background and brought much verve and enthusiasm to the task, and his contemporary and equally dynamic deputy director was the historian Roger Knight.

The overall policy was soon established, not so much by a statement of intent as by a change of atmosphere. It was described by one Trustee as making the museum offer 'a day out for dad and the kids'.[25] All the business of a great museum was still to be conducted – the cataloguing, storage and display of collections, the provision of visitor services, the academic, research and library work – but the staid and slightly dusty image was to be refreshed. An opportunity was ready to hand with the quatercentenary of the Spanish Armada in 1988, and the special exhibition mounted in that year was a spectacular success.

Captain Cook remained very much in the forefront of Lewin's mind. He had had close contact with Rear Admiral Andrew Robertson

RAN for many years – they were fellow gunnery officers – and advised him on setting up the Australian National Maritime Museum in 1982.[26] There had been talk then of setting up a Cook exhibition to coincide with its opening, but this had not come about although the Australian Museum was successfully launched. Late in 1987 Lewin visited Australia to give further impetus to Cook, and an exhibition opened in Brisbane in 1988. It became something of a road show, and Lewin himself opened the Perth version in February 1989.

Dynamism in the development of the National Maritime Museum would, it steadily became apparent, take two forms. For the longer term, there was an aspiration to make the permanent displays an 'experience', to make visitors do as well as look. Critics might call it 'touchy-feely', and some did, but it was very much in the mould of museums country-wide and was regarded as absolutely necessary to bring in the punters. Lewin dealt sympathetically and at length with the criticism.[27] The new philosophy, after a few false starts, resulted in plans for the development of Neptune Court, the great atrium in the heart of the west wing, to be covered with a domed transparent roof and form a focus for the modernised galleries round it. It required much money from the National Lottery, and Lewin was heavily involved in intricate negotiation that required the full deployment of his powers of reasoning and persuasion – to say nothing of patience and a charitable view of authority's actions. The work was successfully completed and the new complex opened, sadly after his death, in 1999.

The other prong of the policy was to mount more special exhibitions. Several were uncontroversial, but one was not. This was the *Titanic* event which opened in 1994. The wreck had been discovered and dived upon some years before, and artefacts recovered were said to open new vistas on the world of 1912; but many dissentients were heard to go about muttering that ghouls would be ghouls, and there was a great deal of heart-searching among the Trustees before the project was allowed to go ahead. Financially, it was a great success, and had to be extended by popular demand. There is some evidence that Terry Lewin himself had concerns about this exhibition, but he staunchly stood by the decision to mount it and was no doubt consoled by the thought that museums must pay their way.

A lasting achievement, for which Lewin as chairman was largely responsible, was the support of *The Naval History of Britain*, a monumental three-volume work by the eminent historian N. A. M. Rodger, the first volume of which was published in 1997.[28] With the Navy Records Society and the Society for Nautical Research (Lewin had close links with both these), the museum provided funding to enable this project, the first full-length venture in the field for a hundred years, to go ahead.

Sometimes the chairman's task must have seemed thankless, or worse. Lewin put immense effort into the acquisition by the museum of the Victoria Cross posthumously awarded to Able Seaman William Savage for valour during the St Nazaire Raid of 1942, only to find a national newspaper accusing the museum (and by implication, he himself) of price-fixing and thereby depriving an ailing widow of a fair price at auction. Lewin wrote a reasoned refutation, pointing out that the price paid by the museum was the highest ever paid for a naval VC,[29] but it must have remained an unpleasant memory; he kept all the papers.

He was by way of becoming an historian in his own right. While he modestly claimed to Richard Woodman that he felt out of place at the annual Garrick Club dinner for naval historians, he was a considerable authority on James Cook, and his lectures[30] on the great navigator and surveyor display not only meticulous preparation but real insight into the man's work and his character and leadership. When First Sea Lord he had gone with Lady Lewin to open the Captain Cook Birthplace Museum at Marton near Middlesbrough,[31] and he retained the connection, extending it too to Whitby where Cook had served his apprenticeship in colliers.

It was said, indeed, that Cook's style sat more easily with Terry Lewin than did Nelson's. Nelson was a hero nonetheless, and later in life Terry also became fascinated by Thomas Cochrane, Earl Dundonald.[32] He had been affected by the enthusiasm of Brazilian colleagues for 'Almirante Cochrane', who did so much for the independence struggle of South

American states in the 1820s, and studied not only his career then but in his turbulent days in the Royal Navy, heroic and outcast by turns, during the Napoleonic Wars. No record of Lewin's considered opinion of Cochrane seems to have survived; it would be interesting to find a judgement, by one great leader, of another whose style was so totally different.

Operation Pedestal was another lecture subject. In spite of his personal recollections, it received just as much research attention and preparation as did Cook. In this case he did have help from others who had survived the operation, in particular Tony Bailey while he lived and Fred Jewett, who had been an able seaman in *Ashanti*, later acquired a BA and was in 1999 still a branch secretary of the George Cross Island Association. Fred's anecdotes, including the occasion when he stepped on Rear Admiral Burrough ('a highly dangerous occupation – I never owned up to who it was – fortunately we got another E-boat attack'),[33] must have enlivened many a Pedestal lecture.

All were illustrated with a wealth of slides, put together during the years. These were an aid to the apparent spontaneity of Lewin's delivery; generally, observers reckoned he spoke without notes. That was not so, at least for lectures, though he could speak extempore if called upon to do so. He preferred to have triggers and a fairly full outline of what he was going to say. In short or after-dinner speeches, he would use cue-cards, and those sparingly; he had been known to note the number of points to be made on his knuckles.[34] But whatever the occasion, it would have been given a lot more rehearsal than it appeared to have had. One final comment on the Pedestal lectures is worth recording: 'He spoke for over half an hour ... never once mentioning his own name.'[35] It was in character.

Pedestal was something to be remembered in another way. Reunions were held on the 25th, 40th and 50th anniversaries and were very widely attended by veterans of the epic convoy. The detailed work – the correspondence occupies three huge cardboard boxes – was done from the office of Captain Desmond Dickens in Trinity House, but Terry Lewin's name and signature frequently recur in the files, lending a hand here, putting a shoulder behind the wheel there. He and Jane knew the Dickenses well and it was a happy association.[36] For Terry, too, it was a way of maintaining links with the Merchant Navy, for which he had immense respect and admiration.

There was to be a more tangible memorial. In 1987 Mr Fred Plenty, an ex-Royal Navy veteran of Malta convoys, founded the George Cross Island Association and Terry Lewin became its president. Following a suggestion from the Maltese ex-Ambassador to the Holy See,[37] they quickly developed the idea of a striking structure to be mounted in a prominent position near the entrance to Grand Harbour. The focus was to be a great bell – the Siege Bell – and the columned surround was designed by Professor Michael Sandle. Captains Tony Bailey and Ken Aylwin, Bob Looker the chairman of the GCIA, and Richard Woodman the historian, as well as a host of others gave their time and support. Within five years the memorial was completed and was dedicated by Her Majesty the Queen and President Tabone of Malta on 29 May 1992.[38] It was a quite remarkable achievement in such a short time, and required tremendous effort on the part of all concerned, not least Lord Lewin. It has not been free from controversy, before or since.[39] Lewin wrote to Aylwin in 1997: 'You are right. I should write an account of the Siege Bell memorial. It would take a book, and need to be vetted by a lawyer to protect me from libel ...'[40]

A memorial of a different sort, and one slightly easier of achievement, was the installation of a Book of Remembrance for the Special Entry at the Britannia Royal Naval College, Dartmouth. Vice Admiral Sir Roderick Macdonald had been surprised by the fact that such a book existed for the 'Darts' but not the Special Entry to which both he and Lewin belonged. Roddy enlisted Terry's help and John Beattie, another Special Entry and rugby player to boot, enthusiastically joined in. The Ministry of Defence was persuaded to cough up the money and the book, beautifully prepared and presented, was dedicated in the presence of HRH Prince Philip on 10 April 1992. That made two major events of the kind in the space of two months: 'Jane says I'm obsessed with memorials!' wrote Terry to Roddy as the projects were going ahead.[41]

And there was at least one more to come. He gave telling support to the project to erect a statue of Captain 'Johnny' Walker, the supreme anti-submarine commander of the Second World War, collaborating with Tony Sainsbury and taking many behind-the-scenes initiatives before eventually turning the sponsorship over to Vice Admiral Michael Gretton, son of another Battle of the Atlantic hero.[42] The monument was unveiled by the Duke of Edinburgh at the Liverpool Pier Head on 13 October 1998.

History did not end with one or two selected items. President of the Society for Nautical Research, he also took an active interest in the Navy Records Society, the development of Chatham Historic Dockyard and a host of other causes. But when he thought they were not viable, he would say so. Ship preservation for the sake of it was not on his agenda. Preserved ships must generate enough revenue on their own to keep them in good repair and looking right. Though sad to deny it, he could not give wholehearted support for the retention of the destroyer *Cavalier*, and wrote a typically reasoned and kind letter to Rear Admiral John Hervey, president of the *Cavalier* Association, explaining why.[43] On the disposal of the Royal Yacht *Britannia*, his views were not made public but there are very strong indications that as an ex-commander of the Yacht he would have preferred her to have had another fate.[44]

In spite of his strong interest and considerable expertise, he was always modest about his history. He would ask a 'good friend and honest critic' to give a view even on a Pedestal lecture.[45] He would introduce Alan McGowan, the erudite chairman of the Victory Advisory Technical Committee and long-time stalwart of the National Maritime Museum, as 'Here's the man who taught me naval history'; and after a lecture at which McGowan was present would anxiously enquire, 'Was that all right?'[46]

But his response to any excursion into history was always enough to stimulate further discussion and enquiry. In the early 1980s 'Chalky' White, ex-Royal Navy, in a second career as a police officer at Eridge in Sussex, sought to commemorate the 'Hunt' class destroyer *Eridge* in which he had been sunk in 1942, and enlisted Lewin's help. That was willingly given, and when White retired to Worthing he sought to do the same for HMS *Broadwater*, named after a parish of Worthing.

Lewin had been in the *Highlander* and stood by *Broadwater* when she was torpedoed in 1941. Coincidence followed coincidence, and the White/Lewin correspondence shows how interwoven naval lives can become – and the great and human interest taken by a very senior officer in the events of a distant, but not forgotten, past.[47]

It would have been quite foreign to his character if all the focus had been on the past. The future was served by association with young people, most of all through the British Schools Exploring Society. That, under its previous name, had given him a formative experience in 1938.[48] There had been further contact, mostly through old shipmates, thereafter; the most substantial was a report on the Ellesmere Island expedition of 1980, sent to him in the middle of the Falklands conflict. Not only did he find time to acknowledge it, but he had 'a happy hour or two' reading it.[49] Now, from 1985, he became the society's president. For the next fourteen years he took the most lively and detailed interest in all its activities, and ensured that it maintained its objectives of scientific enquiry as well as giving young people opportunities to develop their personality and abilities.[50] Many other organisations of a similar nature have grown up since the foundation of the society but it kept its distinctive character. Lewin was a patron of the Millennium Expedition to Antarctica, scheduled for 1999–2000,[51] and it was a sadness of his last days that he would not be there to welcome it back.

Other bodies to which he belonged abounded, even though he did his best to keep commitments down. He greatly prized his appointment as Life Colonel Commandant of the Royal Marines, a corps so bound up with the Royal Navy that in his experience they stood or fell together. The Skinners' Company had close associations with the Judd School, and he became a freeman in 1976; later in life it gave him great delight that his grandson Cosmo Roe was his apprentice and was to be admitted to the company in due course. In 1976, too, he was made a 'Stowaway Member' of the Southampton Master Mariners' Club. This was a great honour; the list was short and immensely eminent.[52]

By the middle of the 1990s, even his horizons were beginning to close. He retired from the chair of the National Maritime Museum in 1995.[53] He had given a great deal of himself in his seven years of office, not only in administration and development but in leadership. His cheerful, helpful presence always seemed to be about; everyone on the museum staff knew their admiral.[54]

His departure coincided with the government's decision to dispose of the Royal Naval College. This was the greatest sadness of his later years. He had lived there, as his London residence, for the best part of ten years. It was deeply offensive to him to think that the white ensign would no longer fly in the Grand Square, and much worse that those noble buildings would no longer be a place where people from all three defence services would meet, study and discuss the complexities of strategy and command. Reasons might be advanced for the disposal, but he saw many of them as spurious. He allowed himself to become quite outspoken on the subject; it was one of the very few occasions in his life when a substantial number of people thought he had gone over the top.[55] He was not entirely mollified by the foundation of the Maritime Institute of the University of Greenwich, set up on the site in 1999. Time will tell.

Woodbridge saw more of him. He and Jane had always treasured the privacy of their home life and now there was more of it. Local matters became prominent; he spoke at the Remembrance Service in Ufford church, lectured in the village hall and secured the future of the nine-hole golf course by a well-timed squeeze on the National Lottery. He was often about in the town, with a modest, almost diffident 'I'm Terry Lewin' as an introduction. He was talking one day to Jimmy Ferguson, an ex-Royal Irish Fusilier, member of the George Cross Island Association and friend of the family. A passer-by gave Jimmy a pat on the shoulder and said, 'You will never talk to a nicer man.' 'I pay him to say that,' said Terry.[56]

The family increased. His seventieth birthday had seen all the children now married; Jon, embarked on a career in broadcasting, had married Madeleine Marsh who worked in the same field. Susie was beginning to embark on her work for the Woodland Trust which benefited immensely from her enthusiasm and dedication. Tim was breaking new ground in Russian development, frustrating and satisfying by turns. There was a total of four grandchildren who gave great delight. All the family lived in the south of England so close touch could be maintained. It was some late compensation for years apart.

Of course, the wider world still figured. He was always a soft touch for a Foreword; old shipmates or acquaintances would not be turned away, even for work of variable quality. He would always have something constructive and encouraging to say, and once said that all his Forewords, gathered together, might make a book in themselves. In other fields, old shipmates often turned up; he had a long correspondence with Leo Lee, ex-*Ashanti*, water-colourist and enthusiast for all things naval.[57] Modest ceremonial still occurred, as it did at the 1805 Club's bicentennial commemoration of the award of the Garter to Lord Howe in 1797, arranged by the historian Stephen Howarth. Terry confided to Peter Warwick, the club's secretary, that the regalia he was wearing had been those previously held by Earl Mountbatten, and likened them to naval stores on Permanent Loan.[58]

One thing he did not do much was attend the House of Lords. There was criticism of him for this;[59] some people in high places felt his counsel and wisdom would have been well employed. He was heard to say the Lords was boring,[60] and clearly felt all he could contribute was what is irreverently called in the navy the Old Dark Blue Bang-On or, at best, the New Joint Defence Bang-On. He could have been right, but the other view was that 'When he spoke, people listened'.[61]

Nor did he comment much on three issues concerning the services which exercised the media in the 1990s. On women at sea, none of his acquaintances can recall his expressing a negative opinion, and one or two heard a carefully positive one. Extrapolating, it is probable that he considered the Navy had been told what to do, and had better maximise the benefits while minimising the disadvantages. This is what the Navy has in fact done. On homosexuality, he did state an opinion on the BBC's *Today* programme: he pointed out that experience showed how closely it was linked to indiscipline in ships. Few who had been at sea would be found to disagree with him. As for racism, it was so foreign to his nature that it would have seemed almost indecent to raise it; he would have been the first to say that example was the best means of teaching how to treat every individual with dignity. 'It is all done by goodwill.'

Two causes he did take up were connected with his old friend and colleague Tony Sainsbury. The first was the book *The Royal Navy Day by Day*, which has already been mentioned.[62] Sainsbury was now its sole editor, bringing out a second edition in 1992. Lewin continued to take the closest interest – he refreshed his memory from the book frequently and delighted in surprising people with unfamiliar facts about whichever day it happened to be – and was joint holder of the copyright. There was only one quotation on which Sainsbury consulted Lewin for clearance, and that was *The Times*'s parody of Belloc at the time of the Falklands:

> *Whatever happens, they have got*
> *The Exocet, and we have Nott.*

Keep it in, said Terry.

The other was a tribute to a forgotten legion. Near the end of the Second World War some young men were conscripted to serve, in lieu of military service, in the coal mines which were an important part of the war effort. They were known as the Bevin Boys, and Sainsbury was one of them. They had always been saddened by the refusal of the authorities to allow them to march in the Remembrance Day parade; they had, they thought, served their country as it had thought fit to demand of them. In 1997 and 1998 Terry enlisted the help of Roy Mason, now Lord Mason of Barnsley, himself an ex-miner, and together they overcame objections not least from the Royal British Legion. The Bevin Boys marched in the 1998 parade.[63]

But by then 1998 had turned out not to be a good year. In September Jane was suddenly taken seriously ill. Callers heard a telephone message: they were off to Addenbrooke's Hospital; it was hoped all might yet be well; a rear link was established with Pete and Susie who would give callers up-to-date information. The message, at once serious, buoyant, hopeful and practical, was a marvellous example of Terry Lewin. It is sad that no one probably recorded its exact wording. Hope was rewarded. Jane, by miracles of care and resolve, was restored, and was back at Carousel within the month.

By now, however, Terry himself was feeling unwell. He complained to someone, at a meeting of the Shipwrecked Mariners' charity of which he was still an active president,[64] that he felt he had been kicked by a horse. Hospital tests followed, and inoperable cancer was diagnosed.

His reaction was predictable, given his character, but it still had all those who experienced it staggering in admiration. One cheerful telephone call followed another, to every friend high and low, rich and poor, saying he had had a wonderful life, was sad at the prospect of leaving it, still hoped for a miracle – and then went on to talk about what *they* might need to do, in the wake of what was likely to happen. There were arrangements to be made for a new chairman of this, president of that; no orders were given, just gentle reminders of what would have to be done. Many were moved to write in reply, and some kept closer touch in the weeks that followed; Henry Leach and Roddy Macdonald, for example, faxed memories to him (he had always been a great exponent of the fax machine) which he greatly appreciated.

And, of course, he asked for this book to be written. He had concluded some time before that autobiography was a dubious game and had, in effect, rejected it. Recording his memories for the benefit of a biographer was a different matter, and in his last six weeks he dictated some 55,000 words of audiotape that have formed the basis, and the best, of what has been written here. Moreover, with the help of a devoted granddaughter, Emily Roe, who abandoned a holiday in the West Indies to return to Carousel, he put together a list of over thirty contacts who had had most to do with his career and were the foundation for what he knew would be a widespread interviewing programme. It was one final piece of work, amongst so many others; one hopes it was not distracting, rather a pleasant occupation of recall.

Throughout this time Jane was a citadel of fortitude. She had always been the sure foundation of his personal life, the guardian and centre of the family, and their love had survived all the many buffets that a career in the naval service had to offer. It was a sure shield now. Terry Lewin died in peace on 23 January 1999.

On 13 April there was a gathering in the Chapel of the Royal Naval College at Greenwich such as it has seldom seen. The Service of Thanksgiving for the life of Admiral of the Fleet Lord Lewin of Greenwich was attended not only by the great and good, but by shipmates and associates from every walk of life. A row of Admirals of the Fleet, in full uniform, listened approvingly as a Commodore told them Terry was the best of them all. Prince Philip was there, and Lady Thatcher. Tim Lewin introduced the service with the utmost dignity and courtesy. Cosmo Roe read a lesson, superbly. Roddy Macdonald gave an inspiring and reminiscent address, Roger Knight a forward-looking and insightful one. But perhaps what would have delighted Terry most was that afterwards, his beloved Painted Hall was packed full of friends.

'A MAN OF
TRUE RESOLUTION'

The chapter heading comes from a tribute by Libby Purves that appeared in *The Times* on 26 January 1999, written because she found the many obituaries, seen the day before, too sober and too passionless to commemorate such a man. Many naval people felt she was right, and any attempt to sum up Terry Lewin's life and work must acknowledge what she wrote that day.

Lewin's life, like any other, has to be looked at in two ways: what he did, and what he was. Terry as a man of action would no doubt have wanted what he did to be recorded first. Forget the detail: that is in what has gone before. There are three main themes, each with a powerful second subject.

More than any other senior officer, he brought the Royal Navy into modern times. Technically, he ensured it remained in the front rank of innovation: nuclear and gas turbine propulsion, guided missiles, jump-jet aircraft, the strategic nuclear deterrent, and all the changes in training and organisation that went with them, were given his wholehearted impetus even if he had not actually initiated them. But, he wrote near the end of his life, 'equally dramatic was the Navy's social change – much more egalitarian, relaxed, family-conscious, yet we have achieved this without – I hope – losing the Navy's traditions and heritage'. On the telephone, about the same time, he put it another way: 'What I would like to be remembered for is a real improvement of attitude and mutual respect between officer and rating, and the effect this has had on the well-being and efficiency of the Navy.' It was not, of course, done single-handedly. The trend was there in the social fabric of the nation, and others, notably admirals like LeFanu and Twiss, had gone before. But no one did more than Terry Lewin, the ex-grammar school boy, to ensure that the change was carried through with conviction and goodwill.

The second subject to this theme of change within the Navy was very much his own work, with that of LeBailly and Dunlop. The initiation of the General List concept set out an officer structure that has in essence survived to the present day, and has served the Navy and country well. He recalled it with some pride, writing to the first captain of Dartmouth of the engineering specialisation (in 1989) of his pleasure at the appointment, 'as an avid proponent of the General List'. Like any good concept, the General List was capable of development and will no doubt be altered further, but its principles endure and are a tribute to Lewin's far-sightedness.

The second theme of change was in the wider field of defence. Lewin's reappraisal of the function and powers of the Chief of Defence Staff, and his consequent reorganisation of the higher direction of defence in late 1981, were not matters that would hit the headlines. Yet they proved of the most far-reaching importance, operationally in the Falklands and subsequent conflicts, and in the policy and planning field from that day to this. They were overlaid by subsequent changes in staffing and organisation, but the basic principle was set out by Lewin and has not altered. He himself thought it one of the most far-reaching things he had ever done.

The second subject to the defence theme is even broader. By his reorganisation, Lewin created the conditions for a much more joint-service approach to all defence questions, and this has flourished ever since. The single services have kept their identity, but now there are no single-service staff colleges; all basic doctrine is joint although it has subsets in the land, air and maritime fields; joint headquarters and operational command and control are common currency. The same approach applies to development and procurement of materiel. It could not have happened so readily, indeed it might not have gone ahead at all, if it had not been set in train in 1981. Had it not happened, or happened with obstruction and acrimony, all the services would have been in a much less good state than they are in now.

Finally, the third main theme was not one of change so much as conservation. Lewin managed to preserve, throughout his naval service, a balanced fleet capable of worldwide reach. It could not possibly be as powerful a fleet as he would have wished, but it just about kept pace with the true requirements of the country, which were so markedly different – as operation after operation proved – from the narrow laid-down parameters set by politicians and civil servants. Its range of abilities stretched from the height of strategic nuclear deterrence to the Offshore Tapestry, and he was a prime mover in both. But in between, its balanced main force, supported by a well-maintained Royal Fleet Auxiliary and nurtured by Group Deployments – another Lewin tenet – was a national asset, often under threat, always preserved.

The second subject to this theme was, of course, the Falklands conflict and the Nott Defence Review that preceded it. In that war, the balanced fleet that had been so carefully preserved proved its worth. Whether the balance would have been sufficient if the conflict had occurred a year later – whether, indeed, it would have been possible a year later – is not easy to judge. In that, as in so many other matters, the Falklands was a near-run thing and raises a 'what-if' of history. In the event, it can be said, the Navy and Terry Lewin deserved their luck.

So that, all too briefly, was the nub of what he did. What he was is no easier to summarise. It may bring us a little closer to think of three headings: leader, thinker, operator.

Leaders decide what is to be done, and instruct and inspire the led to do it. Terry Lewin's technique of leadership was exemplary. He never was known to raise his voice, except on the parade ground at Whale Island. His calm, often in situations of turmoil, was something of a legend, but it was accompanied by an alertness and speed of reaction that had been learnt in the school of war. His professional knowledge was all-embracing, helped by a prodigious memory and deep study of the essential problems. Within those parameters, he trusted people; an adviser who showed himself competent would be consulted, a subordinate would be allowed to get on with the job. He never, by all accounts, sacked anyone. That was partly because everyone who served him would do their best for this human, friendly, open man with his own vast and obvious ability. Henry Leach, a great leader in his own right, said, 'The mortification of having let him down was enough', to ensure that only one's very best was done. More than all this, there was a quality that can only be called magnetism. His arrival in a room full of people was an event, owing nothing to pomp and everything to personality. The effect was always positive.

As a thinker, Lewin had one of the clearest minds most people, even in the higher reaches of government, can remember. Lord Carrington, no mean judge, said, 'There was an intellect there.' Terry penetrated swiftly to the essentials of any problem, and articulated solutions pithily. If they needed elaboration, the staff would probably be sent away to do that. Similarly, he would not necessarily write out speeches himself; there was no time. But he made sure they said what he wanted to say. Extempore, he could be brilliant. The coherence of his thought and argument, supported by wide background reading, knowledge and experience, was formidable. Probably he shone least in setting out visions for the future; they were there, as his performance consistently showed, but he kept them largely to himself, partly because any form of pretension was not his style, and partly because they might be hostages to fortune.

As an operator, whether at sea or ashore, he was supreme. Not only was he an expert communicator, he ensured that he was communicating with the right people or groups. He brought outlying flag officers into staff meetings in the Ministry of Defence. He sought always to bring more people into the picture than less. Their views might not always be accepted, but they were always listened to with courtesy and a total lack of pomposity. His energy and stamina in seeking out all the factors affecting a problem were prodigious; he left his staff breathless with admiration. In the end, the solution would be a matter for his judgement; and if one had to choose an outstanding operator's quality out of many, it could well be that. For he was, with all his experience and professional knowledge, a master in judging what would run and what would not, what battles were worth fighting and what were bound to be lost. It was not to the taste of the more hot-headed, who would battle on for lost causes they believed to be right; but Terry Lewin was playing the wider, longer game.

In the 1990s it is called networking; there will be another catchword for it in ten years' time; in Lewin's case it was, anyhow, much more than that. He would give equal attention to a sailor in the ranks of a guard, the Fleet Dental Officer and the Commandant General of the Royal Marines. He had that quality, given to few, that made everyone in the room think they were the one person he had come to see. It comes always from inside, from a warm and genuine interest in people.

It was accompanied by what many perceived as an inner peace, a core without which the vitality must sometimes have been vain and the interest hollow. That had to come from a family life that was satisfying and complete, founded upon his love for Jane and for their children and grandchildren. No naval marriage is easy, its demands always beyond those of what ought to be more tranquil associations, and the Lewins' had posed a heavier load than most. Not only did it survive, but it added a dimension to his own sympathy for all those in the naval service, and that included those who remained at home.

This ready, real, immensely human sympathy seems to me to come close to the essence of this great man. There were (and perhaps still are) officers, some of them very senior indeed, whom one might not unfairly call manufactured. They have adopted many of the techniques and mannerisms of leadership and management without any real desire or direction. Terry Lewin was totally different. The openness, the humour, the innate modesty and courtesy, combined with assured confidence to form a personality that was as lovable as it was commanding: but it all came from inside, it was totally genuine, a man of integrity and completeness, alive and whole.

As his great friend Roddy Macdonald said in April 1999:

'They don't come often.'

NOTES

Chapter 1. A Candidate for War, 1920–1941

1 Sources for this section are audiotapes dictated by Lord Lewin in December 1998 and January 1999, and a videotape made some months earlier.

2 Information supplied by John Beattie, a contemporary of Lewin in the Special Entry to the Royal Navy.

3 Videotape, n. 1.

4 *The Juddian*, December 1936.

5 See W. S. Churchill, *The Gathering Storm* (Cassell, 1948), p. 77.

6 *The Juddian*, March 1937.

7 Ibid., March 1938.

8 School report, December 1937.

9 British Schools Exploring Society, *Memorandum and Articles of Association* (1994), p. i.

10 The date may have been 29 July; Lewin's account in *The Juddian*, December 1938, gives the 29th, but his Expedition Notebook states the 28th.

11 Commander Murray Levick's notebook of the Newfoundland Expedition of 1938, in the possession of the British Schools Exploring Society.

12 BSES Expeditions *Annual Report*, 1997–8.

13 Levick's notebook, n. 11, manuscript report on Lewin, notes that he was 'very useful on survey having a sound knowledge of mathematics'.

14 'Hoosh' was expedition slang for the permanent supper stew.

15 The base line, an essential element of surveys, had been set up earlier.

16 Levick notebook, entry for 10 August.

17 *The Juddian*, December 1938.

18 Letter from Lieut. Cdr. D. C. Eve RN, 7 April 1999.

19 Lewin notebook, 30 August.

20 Quoted in Churchill, op. cit. n. 5, p. 286.

21 Videotape, n. 1.

22 John Beattie, speech at the 45th Anniversary of SE 47, 1984.

23 Audiotape, n. 1.

24 Beattie, n. 2.

25 Videotape, n. 1.

26 Commander Ian Browne, interview, 15 March 1999.

27 Commander John Casson, interview 17 February 1999.

28 Rear Admiral T. R. Cruddas, interview 8 May 1999.

29 *Vindictive* Magazine, July 1939, p. 11.

30 Ibid., p. 43.

31 Audiotape, n. 1.

32 Beattie, n. 2.

33 Vice Admiral Sir Roderick Macdonald, address at the Service of Celebration for the life of Lord Lewin, 13 April 1999.

34 S. W. Roskill, *The War at Sea*, Vol. 1, p. 67.

35 See Clay Blair, *Hitler's U-Boat War*, p. 122, for an account of the success of the 'duck' U-boats including Frauenheim's *U-21*.

36 Audiotape, n. 1.

37 Midshipman Lewin's *Journal*, 19 February 1940. All midshipmen were required to keep a journal; the demise of the requirement was regarded by Lord Lewin in later years as a grave error.

38 Roskill, op. cit. n. 34, p. 163. Roskill's account of the subsequent

campaign (to p. 203) is still one of the most accurate and comprehensive available.

39 *Journal*, n. 37, 14 June 1940.
40 Vice Admiral Sir Roderick Macdonald, letter of 15 November 1999.
41 *The Somerville Papers* (Navy Records Society, 1996), pp. 136–9.
42 Audiotape, n. 1.
43 Letter from Adrian Holloway (midshipman in HMS *Valiant*, 1940), 29 March 1999.
44 *The Cunningham Papers* Volume 1 (Navy Records Society, 1999), p. 60.
45 Macdonald, n. 40.
46 Admiral Sir David Williams, interview 16 March 1999; audiotape, n. 1.
47 Audiotape, n.1; letter from Mr. R. E. White, 29 March 1999; Roskill, op. cit. n. 34, p. 472.
48 Audiotape, n. 1.

Chapter 2. *Ashanti*, 1942–1945

1   See Edgar J. March, *British Destroyers* (Seeley Service, 1966), pp. 322 ff., for full details of the class.
2   Martin Brice, *The Tribals* (Ian Allan, 1971), p. 46.
3   Dr Peter Baly, interview 25 February 1999.
4   Audiotape, Chapter 1 n. 1.
5   S. W. Roskill, *The War at Sea*, Vol. 1, p. 513.
6   Fred T. Jewett BA, letter of 21 May 1999.
7   Lord Lewin, interview 14 December 1998.
8   Brice, *The Tribals*, p. 40.
9   Jewett, loc. cit. n. 6.
10 Audiotape, n. 4.
11 Ibid.
12 Letter from Sir John Moore, 2 June 1999.
13 Bob Ruegg and Arnold Hague, *Convoys to North Russia 1941–1945* (World Ship Society, 1992), p.20.
14 Roskill, *The War at Sea,* Vol. 2, p. 130.
15 The Russian Convoys Club, based in London, has done much to encourage research by Russian authors and archivists.
16 Roskill, op. cit. n. 14, p. 139.
17 Ibid., pp. 64–72; Peter C. Smith, *Pedestal* (4th edn., Crecy Publishing, 1999), pp. 25–34.
18 Lord Lewin, lectures on Operation Pedestal, and interview with the Oral History department of the Royal Naval Museum, Portsmouth. Much of the following detail is based on this material.
19 Lecture notes, n. 18.
20 Oral history tape, n. 18.
21 Smith, op. cit. n. 17, p. 87.
22 See J. R. Hill, *Anti-Submarine Warfare* (Ian Allan, 1984), p. 40, for a general discussion of the problem.
23 Lecture notes, n. 18.
24 Smith, op. cit. n. 17, p. 130.
25 Ibid., p. 134.
26 Jack Greene and Alessandro Massignani, *The Naval War in the Mediterranean 1940–43* (Chatham, 1998), p. 257.
27 Lecture notes, n. 18.
28 See Chapter 18; Captain Desmond Dickens, interview 16 April 1999.
29 Smith, op. cit. n. 17, p. 185.
30 Roskill, op. cit. n. 14, p. 307.
31 Lecture notes, n. 18.
32 Brice, *The Tribals*, n. 2, p. 54.
33 Ruegg and Hague, op. cit. n. 13, p. 43.
34 Roskill, op. cit. n. 14, p. 281.
35 Brice, op. cit. n. 2, p. 55.
36 Audiotape, n. 4.
37 Ibid.
38 R. G. O. (Admiral Sir Richard Onslow), 'A Tale of Two Tribals', 56 *The Naval Review* (1968), p. 127 ff. The narrative of the tow is based on this account.
39 Ibid.
40 Audiotape, n. 4.
41 R. G. O., loc. cit. n. 38, p. 129.

42   Audiotape, n. 4.
43   Dr Peter Baly, interview 25 February 1999.
44   R. G. O., loc. cit. n. 38, p. 133.
45   *London Gazette*, 25 August 1942.
46   *London Gazette*, 1 December 1942.
47   Audiotape, n. 4.
48   Roskill, op. cit. n. 14, pp. 312–37.
49   On rugby, F. T. Jewett, letter to Lord Lewin, 8 December 1998; generally, audiotape, n. 4.
50   Audiotape, n. 4.
51   Letter from S. R. Kennedy, 11 March 1999.
52   Brice, op. cit. n. 2, p. 58.
53   Telephone conversation with Dr Stevenson, May 1999.
54   Audiotape, n. 4.
55   Brice, op. cit. n. 2 p. 59, records that *Ashanti*'s radar was defective and that 'A' mounting had ripped a strip out of the forecastle deck-head.
56   Churchill had been convalescing from pneumonia 'in the ruins of Carthage' after the Tehran Conference: W. S. Churchill, *Closing the Ring* (Cassell, 1952), p. 407.
57   Stevenson, n. 53.
58   Captain Basil Jones, DSO, DSC, *And So To Battle – A Sailor's Story* (B. Jones, 1980), Chapter 13.
59   Brice, op. cit. n. 2, p. 60.
60   Audiotape, n. 4.
61   John Watkins, 'Actions against "Elbings", April 1944', (81 *The Mariner's Mirror* (May 1995), p. 195ff.) The account of the action is based on this excellent article, on which Lord Lewin was extensively consulted. Professor Watkins was at the time of the action a sub-lieutenant in the *Ashanti*.
62   Stevenson, n. 57.
63   Lewin to Watkins, 28 July 1990.
64   Audiotape, n. 4.
65   Brice, op. cit. n. 2, p. 62.
66   Jones, op. cit. n. 58, p. 83.
67   John Watkins, 'Destroyer Action, Ile de Batz, 9 June 1944' (78 *The Mariner's Mirror* (August 1992), p. 307ff.) at p. 319. The account which follows is based upon Jones (n. 58) and Watkins, with Watkins taking precedence where there is conflict.
68   Lewin to Watkins, 20 September 1990.
69   Jones, op. cit. n. 58, p. 75; Brice, op. cit. n. 2, p. 60.
70   Roskill and Brice both quote this ship as ex-*Callenburgh*. However, Watkins and Lewin were both convinced she was *Tjerk Hiddes*.
71   PRO ADM 1/15784.
72   Leo Lee, letter 10 March 1999.
73   Lewin to Watkins, 20 September 1990.
74   Jones, op. cit. n. 58, p. 87, quoting the Senior Officer of the Third German Naval Defence Division.
75   Audiotape, n. 4.
76   Brice, op. cit. n. 2, p. 64.
77   *London Gazette*, 29 August and 14 November 1944.
78   Captain John Wells, *The Royal Navy: An Illustrated Social History 1870–1982* (Alan Sutton, 1994), p. 253.

Chapter 3. Gunnery Officer, 1945–1951

1   See Jon Tetsuro Sumida, *In Defence of Naval Supremacy* (Unwin Hyman, 1989), for an exhaustive examination of surface fire control developments before 1914.
2   Audiotape, dictated by Lord Lewin December 1998.
3   See Chapter 2 for early developments in Action Information.
4   Audiotape, n. 2.
5   Ibid.
6   Information supplied by J. H. Beattie.
7   Lieut. Cdr. L. G. Hooke, RNR,

letter of 7 June 1999.

8   Gregory Haines, *Cruiser at War* (Ian Allan, 1978), chapter by Captain W. D. S. White.

9   J. R. Hill, *The Royal Navy Today and Tomorrow* (Ian Allan, 1981), p. 20.

10 Eric J. Grove, *Vanguard to Trident* (The Bodley Head, 1987), p. 21.

11 Audiotape, n. 2.

12 Author's personal experience, 1948 (cricket only).

13 Audiotape, n. 2.

14 Ibid.

15 Ibid.

16 HMS *Excellent*, 'flimsy' No. 5, 5 January 1949.

17 Rear Admiral A. J. Robertson, RAN, letter of 13 June 1999.

18 Edgar J. March, *British Destroyers* (Seeley Service, 1966), p. 424.

19 J. R. Hill, in *The Oxford Illustrated History of the Royal Navy* (OUP, 1995), p. 383.

20 Not only the Palestine emergency, but the Corfu Channel incident of 1946 when HM Ships *Saumarez* and *Volage* were mined: see Leslie Gardiner, *The Eagle Spreads His Claws* (Blackwood, 1966), and James Cable, *Gunboat Diplomacy 1919–1991* (Macmillan, 1994), p. 179; the provision of a presence to keep the peace in Trieste; and a steady mine clearance programme throughout the Mediterranean.

21 Vice Admiral Sir Roderick Macdonald, letter of 19 November 1999.

22 Lord Lewin, television programme 'The Real Philip', Channel 4, June 1999.

23 Basil Boothroyd, *Philip* (Longman, 1971), p. 144.

24 Admiral Sir Simon Cassels, interview 12 April 1999.

25 Information supplied by John Beattie, a member of the same team.

26 Commander J. H. Walwyn, HMS *Chevron*, October 1951.

27 Boothroyd, op. cit. n. 23, p. 105; Channel 4, n. 22.

28 HMS *Chequers*, 'flimsy' No. E/16 dated 10 October 1951.

29 Vice Admiral Sir Anthony Troup, note of December 1998, and interview, 25 February 1999.

30 Author's personal recollection as navigating officer of HMS *Chevron*.

31 See Chapter 10 for the culmination 16 years later.

32 Cable, op. cit. n. 18, p. 215: 'the use of local force to create or remove a *fait accompli*'.

33 Troup, n. 29.

34 Audiotape, n. 2.

35 'Cantor', 'The Persian Gulf – Past and Present', 37 *The Naval Review* (1949), p. 41.

36 Audiotape, n. 2.

37 Ibid.

Chapter 4. Introduction to Whitehall, 1952–1955

1   Audiotape dictated by Lord Lewin, December 1998.

2   Rear Admiral P. G. LaNeice, *Not a Nine to Five Job* (Charltons, 1992), p. 120.

3   Tim Lewin, interview 6 May 1999.

4   Vice Admiral Sir Roderick Macdonald, interview 23 March 1999. Audiotape, n. 1.

5   S206 dated 20 August 1953.

6   Audiotape, n. 1.

7   PRO ADM 1/24713.

8   770/FES/3/30 dated 18 November 1949, in the same.

9   Admiralty Board Memorandum B833 of 5 May 1953, in the same.

10 Gradatim, 'The New Officer Structure', 44 *The Naval Review* (1956), pp. 6–15. 'Gradatim' was the pseudonym of Vice Admiral Sir Aubrey Mansergh himself.

11 Audiotape, n. 1.

12 PRO ADM 116/5998, Minutes of COST Meetings. 321 meetings are recorded in all, the rate being

sometimes two a day.
Commander Dunlop is mentioned
first in the Minute of the 141st
meeting, Lewin in the 154th.
Thereafter their names appear
more and more frequently.

13 Gradatim, loc. cit. n. 10, p. 7.
14 Pierrot, 'The New Officer Entry'
    42 *The Naval Review* (1954), pp.
    395–403. The identity of 'Pierrot'
    is not clear since *Naval Review*
    records did not regularly attribute
    pseudonyms to authors until
    January 1955, but he clearly
    wrote with authority.
15 Gradatim, loc. cit. n. 10, p. 6.
16 Audiotape, n. 1.
17 Ibid.
18 Gradatim, loc. cit. n. 10, p. 10.
19 For example, Fxle (Commander J.
    P. Ellison), 'Wet or Dry', 47 *The
    Naval Review* (1959), pp. 157–9.
20 Rear Admiral Colin Dunlop,
    interview 18 March 1999.
21 Audiotape, n. 1.
22 John Winton, 'Life and Education
    in a Technically Evolving Navy',
    in J. R. Hill ed., *The Oxford
    Illustrated History of the Royal
    Navy* (OUP, 1995), p. 276.
23 Captain John Wells, *The Royal
    Navy: an Illustrated Social History*
    (Alan Sutton in association with
    the Royal Naval Museum,
    Portsmouth, 1994), pp. 59–60.
24 Vice Admiral Sir Louis LeBailly,
    From Fisher to the Falklands
    (Marine Management (Holdings)
    Ltd for the Institute of Marine
    Engineers, 1991), p. 12.
25 Wells, op. cit. n. 23, p. 62.
26 Winton, loc. cit. n. 22, p. 278.
27 LeBailly, op. cit. n. 24, p. 36.
28 Dunlop, interview, n. 20.
29 Gradatim, loc. cit. n. 10, p. 10.
30 Ibid., p. 11.
31 Ibid., p. 13.
32 Vice Admiral Sir Louis LeBailly,
    interview 15 March 1999;
    Dunlop interview, n. 20.
33 PRO ADM 116/5998, Minutes of
    the 141st, 142nd and 145th
    Meetings, September 1954.

34 Winton, loc. cit. n. 22, p. 274;
    Wells, op. cit. n. 23, p. 236.
35 PRO ADM 116/5998, 180th
    Meeting.
36 Ibid., 227th Meeting.
37 PRO ADM 116/5997 and 5998.
38 Opinions differ as to whether the
    chief drafter was Sendall, the
    secretary of the main committee,
    or Moses, the civil service coun-
    terpart of the Ferrets. An order as
    complex as AFO 1/56 probably
    involved many drafting meetings.
39 Le Bailly, op. cit. n. 24, p. 122.
40 Audiotape, n. 1.

Chapter 5. Destroyer Command:
HMS *Corunna*, 1955–1957

1 Audiotape, dictated by Lord
   Lewin, December 1998.
2 Stephen Chumbley ed., *Conway's
   All the World's Fighting Ships
   1947–1995* (Conway, 1996).
3 Tim Lewin, letter of 22
   November 1999.
4 PRO ADM 53/140813, Log of
   HMS *Corunna*, November 1955.
5 Audiotape, n. 1.
6 *Corunna* log, n. 4.
7 Audiotape, n. 1.
8 PRO ADM 53/140814, December
   1955.
9 Admiral Sir Frank Twiss, ed. Chris
   Howard Bailey, *Social Change in
   the Royal Navy 1924–1970*
   (Sutton, 1996), pp. 18–19.
10 PRO ADM 53/143543, Log of
    HMS *Corunna*, February 1956.
11 Commander Rex Phillips, inter-
    view 7 April 1999.
12 Audiotape, n. 1.
13 PRO ADM 53/143546, May
    1956.
14 Details of the visit are in HMS
    Corunna's Report of Proceedings
    dated 14 May 1956, supple-
    mented by Audiotape, n. 1.
15 Phillips interview, n. 11.
16 Mr H. F. A. Tree, letter dated 4
    March 1999.
17 Report of Proceedings, n. 14.

18 Audiotape, n. 1.
19 S206 dated 30 March 1956.
20 PRO ADM 53/143547, Log of HMS *Corunna*, June 1956.
21 Audiotape, n. 1.
22 Eric J. Grove, *Vanguard to Trident* (The Bodley Head, 1987), pp. 177–8.
23 See Chapter 4.
24 Audiotape, n. 1.
25 Philip Ziegler, *Mountbatten* (Collins, 1985), Chapter 41.
26 Letter from I. S. Sandeman, 1 March 1999.
27 Letter from John Melia, March 1999.
28 PRO ADM 53/143552, Log of HMS *Corunna*, December 1956.
29 Audiotape, n. 1.
30 Hilary Foxworthy, letter of 24 February 1999.
31 Ibid.
32 Audiotape, n. 1.

Chapter 6. The Royal Yacht, 1957–1958

1 Walter Bagehot, *The English Constitution* (first published 1872; Nelson edn., 1912), p. 74.
2 Brian Hoey, *The Royal Yacht Britannia* (Patrick Stephens, 1995), p. 46.
3 Audiotape dictated by Lord Lewin, December 1998.
4 HM Yacht *Britannia 1954–1997* (Decommissioning Book, 1998).
5 Captain C. H. H.Owen, letter of 22 February 1999.
6 Audiotape, n. 3.
7 *Britannia*, n. 4.
8 PRO ADM 53/146002, Log of HMY *Britannia*, May 1957. Most of the detail of the succeeding passage is based on this document.
9 Audiotape, n. 3.
10 Ibid.; confirmed by HRH the Prince Philip, Duke of Edinburgh, audience 10 March 1999.
11 Prince Philip, n. 10.
12 Author's personal recollection, as

second navigator of HMS *Albion*.
13 Andrew Morton, *The Royal Yacht Britannia: Life on Board the Floating Palace* (Orbis, 1984), p. 72.
14 Hoey, op. cit. n. 2, p. 67.
15 PRO ADM 53/146004, July 1957.
16 Audiotape, n. 3.
17 Log, July 1957, n. 15.
18 Audiotape, n. 3.
19 Ibid.
20 Morton, op. cit. n. 13, p. 77.
21 Cmnd. 214, 4 April 1957; see Eric J. Grove, *Vanguard to Trident* (The Bodley Head, 1987), pp. 202–3.
22 The Third Destroyer Squadron in the Mediterranean, at the same time as Lewin was gunnery officer of the First. He had a reputation for tautness then, and it is probable that Lewin was well aware of it.
23 Audiotape, n. 3.
24 Owen, n. 5.
25 Audiotape, n. 3.
26 Print, *Passages of HM Yacht Britannia during 1958*, copy provided by Captain C. H. H. Owen.
27 Audiotape, n. 3.
28 Ibid.
29 Commander R. A. Clarkson, letter of 12 April 1999.

Chapter 7. Back to the Ministry, 1959–1961

1 Audiotape dictated by Lord Lewin, December 1998; Admiral of the Fleet Lord Hill-Norton, interview 16 March 1999.
2 Vice Admiral Sir Louis LeBailly, *From Fisher to the Falklands* (Marine Management (Holdings) Ltd for the Institute of Marine Engineers, 1991), p. 151.
3 See Eric J. Grove, *Vanguard to Trident* (The Bodley Head, 1987), Chapter 5.
4 Tim Lewin, letter of 22 November 1999.
5 Hill-Norton interview, n. 1.

6   J. R. Hill, 'The Realities of Medium Power', in J. R. Hill ed., *The Oxford Illustrated History of the Royal Navy* (OUP, 1995), p. 385.

7   Grove, n. 3, p. 254.

8   PRO DEFE 13/113, Defence Committee 26 July 1960.

9   Audiotape, n. 1.

10 Norman Friedman, *The Post-War Naval Revolution* (Conway, 1986), p. 87.

11 PRO ADM 1/27685, on which the following paragraphs are based.

12 See Grove, op. cit. n. 3, pp. 122–3, and Friedman, op. cit. n. 10, pp. 46–7.

13 A further class, the Type 14, was a 'third-rate' frigate designed for economy. It proved reasonably successful in service, though uncomfortable and unpopular with ships' companies. It plays no part in the Lewin story and therefore is not mentioned further. Neither is the second-rate 'Tribal' class which, unlike its predecessors which bore that designation, was deliberately of limited capability.

14 D. K. Brown, *A Century of Naval Construction* (Conway, 1983), p. 203.

15 Audiotape, n. 1.

16 Norman Friedman, 'The Royal Navy and the Post-War Naval Revolution', in J. R. Hill ed., op. cit. n. 6, pp. 429–30.

17 See K. Purvis, 'Post War RN Frigate and Guided Missile Destroyer Design 1944–1969', *116 Transactions of the Royal Institution of Naval Architects* (1974), p. 189; and telephone conversation with Ken Purvis, May 1999.

18 Brown, op. cit. n. 14, p. 206.

19 Audiotape, n. 1.

20 Purvis, conversation, n. 17.

21 Audiotape, n. 1.

22 See J. R. Hill, *The Royal Navy Today and Tomorrow* (Ian Allan, 1981), pp. 51–3.

23 PRO ADM 1/27818.

24 Audiotape, n. 1.

25 Mr John Shillidy, Civilian Junior Directing Staff, 1966. The author was a member of the Junior Directing Staff at that time and some of the detail in this passage stems from that experience.

26 *Imperial Defence College Register*, 1927–1967.

27 Audiotape, n. 1.

28 Captain J. B. Frewen, 1957 course.

29 Admiral Sir Deric Holland-Martin, 1966.

30 Audiotape, n. 1; Tim Lewin, interview 6 May 1999.

31 Audiotape, n. 1.

Chapter 8. The Dartmouth Training Squadron, 1961–1963

1   See Chapter 4.

2   Vice Admiral Sir Louis LeBailly, *From Fisher to the Falklands* (Marine Management (Holdings) Ltd for the Institute of Marine Engineers, 1991), p. 139 ff.

3   The speech is quoted in *47 The Naval Review (1959)*, p. 337.

4   P. J. Fox, *The Britannia Magazine*, Easter 1962, p. 10.

5   See Chapter 7.

6   Fox, loc. cit. n. 4.

7   Admiral Sir Simon Cassels, interview 12 April 1999.

8   Author's recollection, 1958–9.

9   PRO ADM 53/158883, Log of HMS *Urchin*, February 1962.

10 Cassels interview, n. 7.

11 Based on the logs of HMS *Urchin*, audiotape dictated by Lord Lewin in December 1998, and the author's personal experience.

12 Audiotape, n. 11.

13 See Chapter 2.

14 Audiotape, n. 11.

15 Lieutenant-Commander Tom Troubridge, 1959.

16 Commander J. P. T. Torr, letter, March 1999.

17 Fox, loc. cit. n. 4, p. 7.
18 Audiotape, n. 11.
19 Rear Admiral Sir Paul Greening, interview 19 April 1999.
20 Confirmed by Fox, loc. cit. n. 4, p. 8, and John Davis, interview 22 June 1999. Also Captain D. J. Farquharson, telephone conversation 10 August 1999.
21 Davis, n. 20.
22 Fox, loc. cit. n. 4, p. 9.
23 Log, n. 9.
24 Audiotape, n. 11.
25 Log, n. 9.
26 See Chapter 14.
27 Andrew Gordon, *The Rules of the Game* (John Murray, 1997), p. 184.
28 Torr, n. 16, detailed a Lewin weekly routine not unlike that of Connolly Abel Smith's when the Royal Yacht was in refit, see Chapter 6.
29 J. M., in *The Britannia Magazine*, July 1962, p. 9.
30 Audiotape, n. 11.
31 PRO ADM 53/158887, Log of HMS *Urchin*, June 1962.
32 J. M., loc. cit. n. 29, p. 13.
33 Lieutenant-Commander Jeremy Grindle, telephone conversation June 1999.
34 Audiotape, n. 11.
35 Notably Captain Jack Broome, *Make a Signal* (Putnam, 1955).
36 e.g. Toby Harnden, *The Independent*, 25 January 1999.
37 Grindle, n. 33.
38 PRO ADM 53/160871, Log of HMS *Urchin*, January 1963.
39 Audiotape, n. 11; confirmed by Tim Lewin, interview 6 May 1999.
40 Raymond Roberts, *The Britannia Magazine*, April 1963, p. 7.
41 Audiotape, n. 11.
42 PRO ADM 53/160872, Log of HMS *Urchin*, February 1963.
43 George Morralee, interview 7 April 1999.
44 Roberts, loc. cit. n. 40, p. 8.
45 Morralee interview, n. 43.
46 See Chapter 7.
47 Audiotape, n. 11.
48 Ibid.
49 PRO ADM 53/160801, Log of HMS *Tenby*, May 1963.
50 Raymond Roberts, *The Britannia Magazine*, July 1963, p. 17.
51 Audiotape, n. 11.
52 Ibid.
53 PRO ADM 53/160802, Log of HMS *Tenby*, June 1963.
54 PRO ADM 53/160803, Log of HMS *Tenby*, July 1963.
55 Audiotape, n. 11. There is some discrepancy between the audiotape and the ship's log at this point. From the log it appears that it was Bush who was on the jetty and Madden who was on board.
56 Tim Lewin, telephone conversation November 1999.
57 Audiotape, n. 11.
58 Commander J. P. T. Torr (first lieutenant of *Urchin/Tenby* 1963), letter March 1999.
59 Commander Peter Cotes (secretary to Captain (F), 1962–3), letter 13 April 1999.
60 W. G. Tapley (chief engine room artificer, *Urchin*), letter 5 March 1999.
61 Torr, n. 58.
62 Tapley, n. 60.
63 Log, n. 54.
64 R. Gorman (physical training instructor, *Urchin*), letter 6 April 1999.
65 Commander Peter Cotes, letter 13 May 1999.
66 Cotes, n. 59.
67 Sir Michael Moore, letter 2 March 1999.
68 Rear Admiral Sir Paul Greening (first lieutenant *Urchin*, 1962), interview 19 April 1999.
69 Admiral Sir Simon Cassels (commanding officer, *Roebuck*, 1962), interview 12 April 1999.
70 See Richard Baker, *Dry Ginger* (W. H. Allen, 1977), passim.
71 Captain A. R. Barnden, interview 4 August 1999.
72 Roberts, loc. cit. n. 50, p. 19.

Chapter 9. Tactical and Weapons Policy, 1964–1966

1   See Chapter 8.
2   Audiotape dictated by Lord Lewin, December 1998.
3   Captain G. G. W. Hayhoe (FOST Staff, 1963), interview 1 February 1999.
4   Audiotape, n. 2.
5   Tim Lewin, letter of 22 November 1999.
6   For the best account of this period in Whitehall see Bill Jackson and Dwin Bramall, *The Chiefs* (Brassey's, 1992), Chapter 10, pp. 313ff.
7   Eric J. Grove, *Vanguard to Trident* (The Bodley Head, 1987), p. 258.
8   *The Higher Direction of Defence*, Report by Lord Ismay and Sir Ian Jacob, 20 February 1963, covering note, para 4.
9   Ibid., main report, para 70.
10 They are still there in 2000, showing marked Germanic, 1930s, influence. They were the subject of much ribaldry and elaborate painting plans by the younger Ministry of Defence officers.
11 e.g. PRO DEFE 10/471 and 10/472, WDC papers for 1965. Fifteen major papers concern naval projects, and do not include CVA 01 itself, which was subject to different treatment.
12 'My Impressions of DTWP': Vice Admiral Sir Roderick Macdonald to Lord Lewin, 20 October 1998.
13 Ibid.
14 Notably Grove, op. cit. n. 7, as the title of his seventh chapter, covering this period.
15 See J. R. Hill, 'British Naval Planning Post-1945', in N. A. M. Rodger ed., *Naval Power in the Twentieth Century* (Macmillan, 1996), p. 219.
16 Vice Admiral Sir Louis LeBailly, *From Fisher to the Falklands* (Marine Management (Holdings) Limited for the Institute of Marine Engineers, 1991), p. 179.
17 Captain D. J. I. Garstin (Ship Department at Bath, 1963), letter 7 May 1999.
18 PRO ADM 1/28639, Thorney-croft to the Chief Secretary of the Treasury, 14 October 1963.
19 Joint Minute by DCNS and VCNS No. 506, 26 November 1964.
20 Audiotape, n. 2; Eric Grove, 'Partnership Spurned: The Royal Navy's Search for a Joint Maritime-Air Strategy East of Suez 1961–63', loc. cit. n. 15, p. 227ff.
21 One of the best accounts, among many, is in Jackson and Bramall, op. cit. n. 6, pp. 364–8. For more detail see Grove, op. cit. n. 7, pp. 268–77.
22 Grove, op. cit. n. 7, p. 269.
23 Audiotape, n. 2.
24 J. R. Hill, 'The Realities of Medium Power' in J. R. Hill ed., *The Oxford Illustrated History of the Royal Navy* (OUP, 1995), p. 391.
25 PRO DEFE 13/589.
26 Sir Patrick Nairne, telephone conversation June 1999.
27 Loc. cit. n. 25, Minute of 4 August 1965.
28 Ibid., Note by CAS of 12 August 1965.
29 Ibid., Note by CGS of 17 August 1965.
30 Audiotape, n. 2.
31 Secretary Vance to Healey, 3 September 1965.
32 Audiotape, n. 2.
33 Loc. cit. n. 25, CNS to S of S, 8 September 1965.
34 Ibid., CNS to S of S, 28 October 1965.
35 Macdonald, n. 12.
36 Admiral of the Fleet Lord Hill-Norton, interview 16 March 1999.
37 CNS to S of S, 17 September 1965.
38 See Chapter 7.
39 Mayhew to Healey, 7 January

1966, in DEFE 13/589.

40 Grove, op. cit. n. 7, p. 275.

41 *Statement on the Defence Estimates 1966*, Cmnd. 2901.

42 Jackson and Bramall, op. cit. n. 6, p. 370.

43 Audiotape, n. 2.

44 'Cecil', 'Self Inflicted Injury', 54 *The Naval Review* (1966), pp. 181–2.

45 'Vox non Incerta', 'Aircraft Carriers – The Sell Out', 54 *The Naval Review* (1966), pp. 183–6.

46 'Vox non Incerta', 'Ministerial Touchdown', 54 *The Naval Review* (1966), p. 291.

Chapter 10. Carrier Command, 1966–1967

1 See John Winton, *Carrier Glorious* (Leo Cooper, 1986).

2 PRO ADM 1/28597.

3 Bill Whitton, 'Thoughts of a Shipmate', Fleet Air Arm Officers' Association *Newsletter,* Spring 1999.

4 Audiotape, dictated by Lord Lewin December 1998.

5 Ibid.

6 Ibid.

7 HMS *Hermes* Third Commission Book, p. 7.

8 Audiotape, n. 4.

9 PRO ADM 53/165723, HMS *Hermes* Log, September 1966.

10 Rear Admiral L. Middleton, interview 16 April 1999.

11 Commission Book, n. 7, pp. 18–19.

12 See Chapter 11.

13 Middleton interview, n. 10.

14 PRO ADM 53/165725, HMS *Hermes* Log, November 1966.

15 Commission Book, n. 7, p. 67.

16 PRO ADM 53/167563, HMS *Hermes* Log, January 1967.

17 Captain Richard Sharpe, letter of 1 March 1999.

18 Log, n. 16; Audiotape, n. 4.

19 Middleton interview, n. 10.

20 Audiotape, n. 4.

21 Captain M. T. Prest, letter 17 June 1999.

22 Log, n. 16.

23 Commission book, n. 7, p. 67.

24 PRO ADM 53/167564, HMS *Hermes* Log, February 1967.

25 Middleton interview, n. 10.

26 Commander D. C. Isard, interview 17 March 1999.

27 Audiotape, n. 4.

28 Ibid.

29 Middleton, n. 10, recalled differences of opinion continuing for several months.

30 Audiotape, n. 4.

31 Commission book, n. 7, p. 27.

32 Log, n. 24.

33 PRO ADM 53/167565, HMS *Hermes* Log, March 1967.

34 Middleton interview, n. 10.

35 Audiotape, n. 4.

36 Ibid.

37 March Log, n. 33.

38 Commission book, n. 7, p. 59.

39 Audiotape, n. 4.

40 PRO ADM 53/167566, HMS *Hermes* Log, April 1967.

41 Audiotape, n. 4.

42 PRO ADM 53/167567, HMS *Hermes* Log, May 1967.

43 Walter Laqueur, *The Road to War* (Weidenfeld & Nicolson, 1968), pp. 47–63.

44 Admiral of the Fleet Sir Edward Ashmore, ed. Eric Grove, *The Battle and the Breeze* (Sutton with the Royal Naval Museum, 1997), p. 160.

45 CinCME 191237Z May, in PRO DEFE 11/528.

46 Report of the UN Secretary General, 18 May 1967.

47 A discussion is in Case Study F of J. R. Hill, *The Rule of Law at Sea* (Defence Fellowship thesis, King's College London, 1972).

48 Laqueur, op. cit. n. 43, p. 93.

49 Commander David Isard, interview 17 March 1999.

50 PRO ADM 53/167567, Log for May 1967.

51 PRO DEFE 11/528.

52 Trevor McMullan, ship's

company HMS *Hermes*, telephone conversation 31 July 1999.

53 Commission book, n. 7, p. 35.

54 Ibid., p. 72.

55 FO2 45/10, Flag Officer Second in Command Far East Fleet's Report of Proceedings for 4–31 May 1967.

56 Richard Baker, *Dry Ginger* (W. H. Allen, 1977) pp. 201–5.

57 PRO ADM 53/167568, HMS *Hermes* Log for June 1967.

58 FO2 45/10, Flag Officer Second in Command Far East Fleet's Report of Proceedings for 1–22 June 1967.

59 Isard interview, n. 49.

60 CinCME 060836Z June, situation report in PRO DEFE 11/528.

61 Baker, op. cit. n. 56, p. 205.

62 June Log, n. 57.

63 Commission book, n. 7, p. 39.

64 Ibid., p. 73.

65 Trevor McMullan, letter of 1 August 1999.

66 FO2 45/10, Flag Officer Second in Command Far East Fleet's Report of Proceedings for 17 July–7 August 1967.

67 Audiotape, n. 4.

68 Ashmore, n. 44, p. 161.

69 FO2FEF Report of Proceedings, n. 66; Commission book, n. 7, p. 62.

70 Ashmore, n. 44, p. 160.

71 Eric J. Grove, *Vanguard to Trident* (The Bodley Head, 1987), p. 299.

72 Audiotape, n. 4.

73 FO2 45/10, Flag Officer Second in Command Far East Fleet's Report of Proceedings for 19 August–16 October 1967.

74 Ibid.

75 PRO ADM 53/167571, HMS *Hermes* Log, September 1967.

76 Audiotape, n. 4.

77 Ibid.

78 September Log, n. 75. The succeeding paragraphs are based on this reference.

79 R. E. Amory, letter of 31 March 1999.

80 Audiotape, n. 4.

81 Ibid.

82 This paragraph draws on J. R. Crole, letter of 5 April 1999; Brian Wines, letter of 23 February 1999; M. T. Prest, letter of 17 June 1999; D. J. Melhuish, letter of 7 April 1999; R. E. Amory, letter of 31 March 1999; Bill Whitton, 'Thoughts of a Shipmate', FAAOA *Newsletter* Spring 1999.

83 It was discontinued in 1971; see Admiral Sir Frank Twiss, ed. Chris Howard Bailey, *Social Change in the Royal Navy* (Sutton with the Royal Naval Museum, Portsmouth, 1996), pp. 194–201, and A. B. Sainsbury ed., *The Royal Navy Day by Day* Second Edn., p. 219.

Chapter 11. A Non-Job Restored: Assistant Chief of Naval Staff (Policy), 1968–1969

1 Audiotape dictated by Lord Lewin, December 1999.

2 Eric J. Grove, *Vanguard to Trident* (The Bodley Head, 1987), pp. 277–8.

3 Cmnd. 3357.

4 Grove, op. cit. n. 2, p. 282.

5 See Chapter 7.

6 Admiral of the Fleet Lord Hill-Norton, interview 16 March 1999.

7 Grove, op. cit. n. 2, p. 283.

8 Bill Jackson and Dwin Bramall, *The Chiefs* (Brassey's, 1992), p. 374.

9 Grove, op. cit. n. 2, p. 294.

10 Jackson and Bramall, op. cit. n. 8, p. 374.

11 J. R. Hill, in *The Oxford Illustrated History of the Royal Navy* (OUP, 1995), p. 387.

12 NATO Military Committee document MC 14/2.

13 MC 14/3.

14 For a near-contemporary assessment, see David Fairhall, *Russian Sea Power* (Gambit, Boston, 1971); for a later appraisal, Bryan Ranft

and Geoffrey Till, *The Sea in Soviet Strategy* (Macmillan, 1983).

15 Author's personal experience. The work of Commander Kit Baker, NATO desk in the Plans Directorate, should be noted.

16 113 *Journal of the Royal United Services Institution* (August 1968), pp. 202–9.

17 *For the Record: a navy news summary current affairs supplement*, September 1968.

18 Hill-Norton interview, n. 6.

19 Grove, op. cit. n. 2, p. 175.

20 Cmnd. 4290, *Statement on the Defence Estimates 1970*, p. 58.

21 David Owen, *Time to Declare* (Penguin, 1991), p. 151.

22 Audiotape, n. 1.

23 Owen, op. cit. n. 21, p. 150.

24 Rear Admiral P. G. LaNeice, *Not a Nine to Five Job* (Charltons, 1992) pp. 204–5.

25 Rear Admiral LaNeice, interview 28 April 1999.

26 Admiral of the Fleet Sir Edward Ashmore, ed. Eric Grove, *The Battle and the Breeze* (Sutton with the Royal Naval Museum, 1997) p. 173.

27 LaNeice, op. cit. n. 24, p. 205.

28 LaNeice, interview, n. 25.

29 Cmnd. 4290, p. 51.

30 Jackson and Bramall, op. cit. n. 8, p. 431.

31 Audiotape, n. 1.

Chapter 12. The Far East Fleet, 1969–1970

1 58 *The Naval Review* (1970) p. 69.

2 Captain Neil MacEacharn, interview 15 March 1999.

3 Captain P. T. Sheehan, interview 25 February 1999.

4 Norman Friedman, *Navies in the Nuclear Age* (Brassey's, 1993), p. 45.

5 Audiotape dictated by Lord Lewin, December 1998.

6 *Naval Review*, loc. cit. n. 1, p.

70; Rear Admiral G. S. Ritchie, 'The Cook Bi-Centenary', *Navy*, November 1969, pp. 392–5.

7 Audiotape, n. 5.

8 Ibid.

9 Ibid.

10 Admiral of the Fleet Sir Edward Ashmore, ed. Eric Grove, *The Battle and the Breeze* (Sutton with the Royal Naval Museum, 1997), p. 170.

11 Ibid.

12 Ashmore, op. cit. p. 175; conversations with Vice Admiral Sir Lancelot Bell Davies, summer 1999.

13 Bell Davies, n. 12.

14 Sheehan, n. 3.

15 MacEacharn, n. 2.

16 Rear Admiral Sam Salt, conversation 22 June 1999.

17 Rear Admiral L. E. Middleton, interview 16 April 1999; MacEacharn, n. 2.

18 Rear Admiral Roger Gerard-Pearse, letter of 14 April 1999.

19 Bell Davies, n. 12.

20 UN Security Council Resolution 217 (1965).

21 J. R. Hill, *The Rule of Law at Sea*, Defence Fellowship thesis, University of London King's College 1972, Case Study E.

22 Audiotape, n. 5.

23 Norman Friedman, *The Post-War Naval Revolution* (Conway, 1986), pp. 113–16.

24 For a good description of seaborne helicopters and their operation in this period see Lt.-Cdr. J. M. Milne, *Flashing Blades over the Sea* (Maritime Books, 1981).

25 Audiotape, n. 5.

26 MacEacharn, n. 2.

27 See Alastair Couper ed., *The Times Atlas and Encyclopaedia of the Sea* (Times Books, 1989), p. 56.

28 Audiotape, n. 5.

29 Sheehan, n. 3.

30 Audiotape, n. 5.

31 MacEacharn, n. 2.

32 Ibid.
33 Audiotape, n. 5.
34 See Nicholas Rodger, *The Wooden World* (Collins, 1986) for discussion of the system.
35 58 *The Naval Review* (1970) pp. 376–7.
36 MacEacharn, n. 2.
37 Ibid.
38 *Naval Review*, n. 35.
39 MacEacharn, n. 2.
40 David Owen, *Time to Declare* (Penguin, 1991), p. 162.
41 Audiotape, n. 5.
42 Sheehan, n. 3
43 Ibid.
44 Audiotape, n. 5.
45 Ashmore, n. 10, p. 176.
46 Audiotape, n. 5.
47 Ibid.
48 MacEacharn, n. 2.
49 Ibid.
50 Sheehan, n. 3.
51 Ibid.
52 Captain D. W. Foster, letter of 26 February 1999.
53 Audiotape, n. 5.
54 Sheehan, n. 3.
55 Audiotape, n. 5.
56 Admiral Sir David Williams, interview 16 March 1999.
57 Ibid.
58 Admiral of the Fleet Lord Lewin, 'Chapter Headings', notes prepared for the author, December 1998.

Chapter 13. The Heat of the Day: Vice Chief of Naval Staff, 1971–1974

1   Admiral of the Fleet Sir Edward Ashmore, ed. Eric Grove, *The Battle and the Breeze* (Sutton with the Royal Naval Museum, 1997), p. 177.
2   LeFanu had issued a short statement called 'PIM 69'. 'PIM' stands for Position and Intended Movement.
3   Ashmore, loc. cit. n. 1.
4   David Owen, *Time to Declare* (Penguin, 1991), p. 147.
5   Cmnd. 4592, *Statement on the Defence Estimates 1971*.
6   Ibid., paras 15–25.
7   See Chapter 11.
8   Author's recollection.
9   Ashmore, op. cit. n. 1, p. 180.
10 Eric J. Grove, *Vanguard to Trident* (The Bodley Head, 1987), p. 319.
11 Bill Jackson and Dwin Bramall, *The Chiefs* (Brassey's, 1992), p. 377.
12 Benbow, 'Benbow's Column', 60 *The Naval Review* (1972), p. 8.
13 *Sunday Telegraph*, 28 November 1971.
14 Grove, op. cit. n. 10, p. 319.
15 *Yorkshire Post*, 13 December 1971.
16 The reporter on board *Rapid* was Desmond Wettern, a well-known advocate of fixed-wing naval aviation.
17 VCNS Meeting Notebook, undated. 'DPR(N) [Director of Public Relations (Navy)] sparking on *Sunday Telegraph*. How did Wettern know the aims of High Wood? Is he PR sponsored? Was High Wood offered to Fleet Street?'
18 Group Captain R. A. Mason, *The Royal Air Force Today and Tomorrow* (Ian Allan, 1982), Chapter 4.
19 *Liverpool Daily Post*, 3 January 1972.
20 Elmo R. Zumwalt Jr., *On Watch* (Quadrangle, 1976), p. 106.
21 [US] *Navy Times*, 1 March 1972.
22 *Jane's Fighting Ships 1997–98*, p. 818.
23 Captain Don Beadle, interview 7 April 1999.
24 Cmnd. 4891, *Statement on the Defence Estimates 1972*, Part II para 7c.
25 Ashmore, op. cit. n. 1, p. 222.
26 Beadle, n. 23.
27 J. R. Hill, in *The Oxford Illustrated History of the Royal Navy* (OUP, 1995), p. 391. See also James Cable, *Britain's Naval*

Future (Naval Institute Press, 1983), pp. 60–1.

28 Beadle, n. 23.
29 See Chapter 12.
30 Beadle, n. 23.
31 *Glasgow Herald*, 28 May 1973.
32 Ashmore, op. cit. n. 1, p. 210.
33 P. R. Odell, 'Oil and Western European Security', *Brassey's Annual 1972*, p. 75.
34 UN Convention on the Continental Shelf, 1958, Art. 5(4).
35 Exchange of Notes between the British and Icelandic Governments, 11 March 1961.
36 R. B. Clark, *The Waters around the British Isles: Their Conflicting Uses* (Clarendon Press, 1987), p. 179.
37 Captain Arnout Wepster of the Dutch merchant marine, and of the Institute of Navigation, ran a questionnaire before putting the scheme forward, and over 80 per cent of the master mariners questioned approved the proposal. Information given to the author, 1976.
38 Still operating at the end of the century: see *Jane's Fighting Ships 1997–98*, p. 773.
39 J. R. Hill, *The Royal Navy Today and Tomorrow* (Ian Allan, 1981), p. 96.
40 'The United States Coast Guard', *World Survey No. 47* (Atlantic Education Trust, 1972).
41 Weaver, 'The Offshore Tapestry', 62 *The Naval Review* (1973), p. 122.
42 The *Braer* (1993) and *Sea Empress* (1996) incidents. See Lord Donaldson's *Safer Ships, Cleaner Seas* (Cm2560, 1994) and *Review of Salvage and Intervention and their Command and Control* (Cm 4193, 1999) for a view of the complexity of the issues involved.
43 Beadle, n. 23.
44 E. D. Brown, *The International Law of the Sea, Vol. 1* (Dartmouth, 1994), p. 10.

45 United Nations Law of the Sea Convention, 1982, Part II Section 3 (Innocent passage) and Part III Section 2 (Transit passage through straits).
46 Lewin to the author, 1973.
47 Author's recollection. See J. R. Hill, *Anti-Submarine Warfare* (First Edition: Ian Allan, 1984), p. 110.
48 Cmnd. 4891, *Statement on the Defence Estimates*, 1972.
49 Bryan Ranft and Geoffrey Till, *The Sea in Soviet Strategy* (Macmillan, 1983), pp. 197–8.
50 *Yorkshire Post*, 28 May 1973.
51 Captain A. B. Sainsbury, information supplied in November 1999.
52 *Daily Telegraph*, 18 April 1973.
53 Cmnd. 5231, *Statement on the Defence Estimates*, 1973, shows SSNs 7 and 8 to reach acceptance during the year, 9 and 10 under construction.
54 Grove, op. cit. n. 10, p. 320.
55 Ashmore, op. cit. n. 1, p. 223.
56 *Navy International*, July/August 1999.
57 Cmnd. 4592, *Statement on the Defence Estimates*, 1971.
58 J. R. Hill, *Air Defence at Sea* (Ian Allan, 1988), p. 69.
59 Captain Chris Craig, *Call for Fire* (John Murray, 1995), p. 275.
60 *Daily Telegraph*, 19 June 1973.
61 An accurate prediction of the *Daily Telegraph* article, n. 60.
62 Hill, *Air Defence*, n. 58, p. 33.
63 Grove, op. cit. n. 10, p. 307.
64 See Chapter 18.
65 See Chapter 10.
66 Ashmore, op. cit. n. 1, p. 223.
67 Very numerous references exist. Amongst those bracketing the period of Lewin's tenure as VCNS are David Fairhall, *Russian Sea Power* (Gambit, Boston, 1971); Bryan Ranft and Geoffrey Till, *The Sea in Soviet Strategy* (Macmillan, 1983); J. R. Hill, *Anti-Submarine Warfare* (Ian Allan, 1984); Norman Friedman, *Submarine Design and*

Development (Conway, 1984).

68 See Richard Compton-Hall, *Submarine versus Submarine* (David & Charles, 1988). Though written a decade and a half after Lewin's time as VCNS, it illustrates principles which were already becoming clear at that time.

69 Donald C. Daniel, *Anti-Submarine Warfare and Superpower Strategic Stability* (Macmillan, 1986), pp. 123–4.

70 Friedman, op. cit. n. 67, pp. 171–2.

71 Rear Admiral Martin Wemyss, 'Submarines and Anti-Submarine Operations for the Uninitiated', RUSI *Journal*, September 1981.

72 Friedman, op. cit. n. 67, pp. 76–88.

73 e.g. the British Sea King Mark 5.

74 The 'Barra' was a sophisticated passive directional sonobuoy using advanced beam-steering techniques: Hill, *Anti-Submarine Warfare*, n. 47, pp. 82–3.

75 Compton-Hall, op. cit. n. 68, p. 37, with many subsequent scenarios, for submarine towed arrays; Hill, n. 47, for surface ship towed arrays.

76 North Atlantic Assembly, *NATO Anti-Submarine Warfare: Strategy, Requirements and the Need for Co-operation* (1982).

77 Notes left by Lord Lewin as 'Chapter Headings', 1998.

78 Compton-Hall, op. cit. n. 68, p. 145.

79 Sherry Sontag and Christopher Drew, *Blind Man's Bluff* (Public Affairs, New York, 1998), pp. 281–3.

80 Rear Admiral Tony Whetstone, interview 1 February 1999.

81 *Liverpool Daily Press*, 21 May 1973.

82 Beadle, interview n. 23.

83 See particularly Peter Nailor, *The Nassau Connection* (HMSO, 1989) and Captain J. E. Moore ed., *The Impact of Polaris* (Richard Netherwood, 1999), *passim*.

84 Cmnd. 4290, *Statement on the Defence Estimates*, 1970, p. 17.

85 Colin McInnes, *Trident – The Only Option?* (Brassey's, 1986), p. 4.

86 DS12/215/6/1 of 13 January 1967.

87 PRO DEFE 11/437.

88 MO 26/10/6, in the same.

89 McInnes, loc. cit. n. 85.

90 Minute to the Foreign Secretary, 24 July 1967, loc. cit. n. 87.

91 COS 1702/11/8/67.

92 McInnes, op. cit. n. 85, p. 5.

93 Sir Hugh Mackenzie, in Captain J. E. Moore ed., *The Impact of Polaris* (Richard Netherwoood, 1999), p. 113.

94 Interviews, Lord Lewin 14 December 1998; Admiral of the Fleet Sir Henry Leach, 19 January 1999.

95 Admiral Sir Anthony Morton, interview 19 January 1999.

96 Estimated in 1972 at £175 million: *Ninth Report of the Committee of Public Accounts, Ministry of Defence, HC 269, 1981–2*, p. 1.

97 Leach interview, n. 94. Unhappily, Leach's autobiography *Endure no Makeshifts* (Leo Cooper, 1993) gives no detailed account of his time as ACNS(P), confining it to one paragraph at p. 155.

98 McInnes, op. cit. n. 85, p. 5.

99 Lawrence Freedman, *Britain and Nuclear Weapons* (Macmillan, 1980), pp. 46 and 50.

100 Leach interview, n. 94.

101 See Chapter 16.

102 Admiral Sir John Woodward, telephone conversation June 1999.

103 Lewin's notebooks, numerous entries.

104 R. E. C., 'The Royal Navy Presentation' 61 *The Naval Review* (1973), pp. 45–9.

105 Beadle interview, n. 23.

106 See Chapter 11.

107 61 *The Naval Review* (1973), p. 295.

108 Beadle, n. 23, as the basis for this

and succeeding paragaphs.

109 Lord Carrington, interview 8 April 1999.

110 Admiral of the Fleet Lord Hill-Norton, interview 16 March 1999.

111 Lewin to Captain A. B. Sainsbury, fax dated 27 March 1998.

Chapter 14. Fleet Command, 1974–1975

1 Norman Friedman, 'The Royal Navy and the Post-War Naval Revolution' in J. R. Hill ed., *The Oxford Illustrated History of the Royal Navy* (OUP, 1995), p. 416, and *Navies in the Nuclear Age* (Conway, 1993), p. 182, for a description of OPCON in the tactical mode. More generally, it was the day-to-day means of exercising overall control of fleet activity, normally through subordinate commanders at sea or ashore.

2 Mike Critchley, letter 3 March 1999.

3 Admiral of the Fleet Sir Henry Leach, *Endure no Makeshifts* (Leo Cooper, 1993), p. 141.

4 Captain Don Beadle, interview 7 April 1999.

5 See Chapter 13.

6 Beadle, n. 4.

7 Leach, op. cit. n. 3, p. 163.

8 *Navy News*, April 1974.

9 *Navy News*, September 1974.

10 Admiral Sir Frank Twiss, ed. C. Howard Bailey, *Social Change in the Royal Navy 1924–70* (Alan Sutton with the Royal Naval Museum, 1996), pp. 194–201.

11 Vice Admiral Sir Thomas Baird, interview 22 March 1999.

12 The terms are self-explanatory. A popular rating, offered 'gulpers' by several members of his mess on, say, his birthday, would be in grave danger.

13 Baird interview, n. 11.

14 Ibid.

15 Sir Frank Cooper, interview 17 February 1999.

16 Bill Jackson and Dwin Bramall, *The Chiefs* (Brassey's, 1992), p. 379.

17 *Navy News*, July 1974.

18 Leach, op. cit. n. 3, p. 158.

19 *Navy News*, September 1974.

20 Letter of 20 November 1975.

21 Beadle, n. 4.

22 Ministry of Defence (Navy) Press Release 28/74.

23 David Owen, *Time to Declare* (Penguin, 1991), pp. 292–5.

24 *Navy News*, November 1974.

25 Leach, op. cit. n. 3, pp. 158–9.

26 Admiral of the Fleet Sir Henry Leach, interview 19 January 1999.

27 See Barry Buzan and Gowher Rizvi, *South Asian Security and the Great Powers* (Macmillan, 1986); Rasul B. Rais, *The Indian Ocean and the Superpowers* (Croom Helm, 1986); Rahul Roy-Chaudhury, *Sea Power and Indian Security* (Brassey's, 1995).

28 *Navy News*, February 1975.

29 Beadle, n. 4.

30 Ibid.; see also Admiral of the Fleet Sir Edward Ashmore, ed. Eric Grove, *The Battle and the Breeze* (Alan Sutton with the Royal Naval Museum, 1996), p. 219.

31 Ashmore, op. cit. n. 30, p. 210.

32 Beadle, n. 4.

33 *Navy News*, April 1975.

34 Leach interview, n. 26.

35 Ibid.; and Ministry of Defence (Navy) Press Release 58/75.

36 *Navy News*, June 1975. See also Ashmore, op. cit. n. 30, p. 222.

37 Ministry of Defence (Navy) Press Release 62/75.

38 Beadle, n. 4.

39 Ibid.

40 Rear Admiral John Lippiett, interview 19 April 1999.

41 Strongly expressed in 1979 in a BBC 'Profile' interview by Christopher Lee.

42 Beadle, n. 4.

43 Commander John Torr, letter of March 1999.

44 Captain N. C. H. James, 1 May 1999.

45 Captain Peter Lucas, letter of 26 February 1999.

46 Beadle, n. 4; conversation with Vice Admiral Sir John Webster, June 1999.

47 Rodney Stannard, interview 19 April 1999.

Chapter 15. The Naval Home Command, 1975–1977

1 Cmnd. 6432, Statement on the Defence Estimates 1976, Annexes B and G

2 David Owen, *Time to Declare* (Penguin, 1991), p. 149.

3 Vice Admiral Sir Roderick Macdonald, letter of 3 June 1999.

4 Vice Admiral Sir Roderick Macdonald, *The Figurehead* (Pentland Press, 1993).

5 *Navy News*, November 1975, reported celebrations of the first anniversary.

6 Vice Admiral Sir Roderick Macdonald, interview 23 March 1999.

7 *Navy News*, July 1977, gave a summary of the smaller establishments and units that went into the Naval General Training Centre at Whale Island. *Vernon* itself did not finally close until 1986, though many of its responsibilities were relinquished in 1975: see Rear Admiral E. N. Poland, *The Torpedomen* (Kenneth Mason, 1992), Chapter 21.

8 Anthony Buck, US of S for the RN, Written Answer dated 6 February 1974, in Ministry of Defence (Navy) Press Release 8/74.

9 Ibid.

10 Captain A. J. Oglesby, letter of 8 July 1999.

11 MoD (Navy) Press Release 64/74.

12 Captain Don Beadle, note of 4 June 1998.

13 Oglesby, n. 10.

14 Beadle, n. 12.

15 Ibid.

16 *Navy News*, November 1975, p. 40.

17 Oglesby, n. 10.

18 Beadle, n. 12.

19 Commander I. C. Webb, letter of March 1999.

20 'Admiral helps to solve a Problem', *Navy News* August 1976, p. 13.

21 Admiral Sir Frank Twiss, ed. Chris Howard Bailey, *Social Change in the Royal Navy 1924–70* (Alan Sutton with the Royal Naval Museum, 1996), p. 200.

22 Macdonald interview, n. 6. *Navy News*, August and October 1976. The October issue shows Lewin driving off in wellington boots: the weather had broken.

23 Macdonald interview n. 6.

24 Dr Alan McGowan, telephone conversation 5 June 1999.

25 Beadle, n. 12.

26 *Navy News*, August 1976.

27 As an example, the International Festival of the Sea held in Portsmouth in 1998.

28 Colin White, *The Nelson Companion* (Royal Naval Museum, 1995), p. xi.

29 *Navy News*, October 1976.

30 *History of the London Division RNR* (1983), p. 129.

31 Captain A. B. Sainsbury, letter of 16 October 1999.

32 Beadle, n. 12.

33 *Navy News*, October 1976.

34 Captain Peter Kimm, letter of 4 February 1999.

35 *Navy News,* October 1976.

36 Vice Admiral Sir Thomas Baird, interview 22 March 1999.

37 Rear Admiral Sir Paul Greening, interview 19 April 1999.

38 Bill Jackson and Dwin Bramall, *The Chiefs* (Brassey's, 1992), p. 381.

39 Admiral of the Fleet Sir Edward
    Ashmore, ed. Eric Grove, *The
    Battle and the Breeze* (Alan
    Sutton with the Royal Naval
    Museum, 1997), pp. 257–9.

Chapter 16. First Sea Lord, 1977–1979

1   David Owen, *Time to Declare*
    (Penguin, 1991), p. 251.
2   Bill Jackson and Dwin Bramall,
    The Chiefs (Brassey's, 1992),
    p. 382.
3   Sir Frank Cooper, interview 17
    February 1999.
4   Captain Don Beadle, interview 7
    April 1999.
5   Admiral of the Fleet Sir Edward
    Ashmore, ed. Eric Grove, *The
    Battle and the Breeze* (Alan
    Sutton with the Royal Naval
    Museum, 1997), p. 217.
6   Rear Admiral Sir David Scott,
    interview 17 February 1999.
7   Colin McInnes, *Trident – the
    Only Option?* (Brassey's, 1986),
    p. 7.
8   Scott, n. 6. Scott considered
    himself responsible to the First
    Sea Lord in person. But see also
    Ashmore, n. 5.
9   Admiral Sir Peter Herbert, inter-
    view 9 March 1999.
10 Scott, n. 6.
11 Captain R. W. Garson, letter of 1
    September 1999, covering a note
    taken on 14 May 1971.
12 Cooper, n. 3.
13 cf. The Nimrod Airborne Early
    Warning project, approved in
    1977 and cancelled seven years
    later at a cost of £1 billion, with
    nothing to show for it.
14 Admiral Lewin, conversations
    with the author, 1979–80.
15 Chapter 13, n. 86.
16 Cooper, n. 6, maintained there
    was a 'general wedge' in the
    LTCs. To the author's knowledge,
    no one in the central staffs
    regarded any such sum as avail-
    able for application to a successor
    strategic system.
17 Hairline cracks in the pipework
    of nuclear submarines, both SSBN
    and SSN, were widely reported in
    the Press. Scott interview, n. 6.
18 The author. Since the composition
    and remits of the Duff and
    Mason Groups have been vari-
    ously reported, it is thought right
    to record them as accurately as
    memory allows.
19 Later elaborated by Michael
    Quinlan in Defence Open
    Government Document 80/23 and
    other papers through to *Thinking
    about Nuclear Weapons* (RUSI,
    1997).
20 McInnes, n. 7, pp. 185–95.
21 Jackson and Bramall, op. cit. n. 2,
    p. 385.
22 Scott, n. 6. See also Jonathan
    Alford in Nailor and Alford, *The
    Future of Britain's Deterrent
    Force* (IISS, Adelphi Paper
    No.156, 1980), p. 36.
23 Ian Smart, *British Foreign Policy
    to 1985: The Future of the British
    Nuclear Deterrent: Technical,
    Economic and Strategic Issues*
    (RIIA, 1977).
24 Author's recollection; confirmed
    by Sir Michael Quinlan, April
    1999.
25 See Chapters 17 and 19.
26 A particular proponent was
    David Owen: see *Time to
    Declare*, op. cit. n. 1, p. 381, and
    Personally Speaking (Weidenfeld
    & Nicolson, 1987), pp. 148–9.
27 Jackson and Bramall, op. cit. n. 2,
    p. 383.
28 *Daily Telegraph*, 28 January 1978
    and 21 February 1978.
29 Jackson and Bramall, op. cit. n. 2,
    p. 382.
30 ICJ, *Anglo-Icelandic Fisheries
    Case*, 1974.
31 Admiral Elmo R. Zumwalt USN,
    On Watch (Quadrangle, 1976),
    pp. 470–3, shows the difficulty
    for the USA of balancing interests
    as between the UK and Iceland.

32 The 'Islands' were commissioned in 1978–9, the 'Castles' in 1981–2; *Jane's Fighting Ships, 1997–98,* pp. 772–3.

33 Eric J. Grove, *Vanguard to Trident* (The Bodley Head, 1987), p. 358.

34 Owen, *Time to Declare,* op. cit. n. 1, p. 355.

35 Ibid., p. 359.

36 Note in Lord Lewin's handwriting 'The Falklands: 1977 and All That', undated and unclassified but certainly written after the publication of the Franks Report, 1983 (henceforth 'Lewin ms').

37 Ibid. The passage quoted was 'massaged' by another hand, presumably in case of publication, but was not erased.

38 For a very early, but highly professional, excursion into this field, D. P. O'Connell, 'International Law and Contemporary Naval Operations', 44 *British Yearbook of International Law* (1970), pp. 20ff. O'Connell was a Commander RANR as well as a Professor of International Law.

39 Lewin ms.

40 Owen, op. cit. n. 1, p. 360.

41 Ibid., p. 349.

42 The late Captain Daniel Leggatt, in conversation with the author, 1982.

43 James Cable, *Gunboat Diplomacy 1919–1991* (Macmillan, 1994), p. 204.

44 Beadle, n. 4.

45 *Journal of Naval Science,* Vol. 6 No. 2, pp. 75–89.

46 Beadle, n. 4.

47 *The Times,* 9 December 1977.

48 First Sea Lord to Commander C. P. R. Belton and others, 13 December 1977.

49 *Evening Standard,* 14 December 1977.

50 Professor P. K. M'Pherson, letter of 4 December 1999.

51 Tim Lewin, letter of 22 November 1999.

52 Sir Patrick Duffy, interview 14 July 1999.

53 Beadle, n. 4.

54 Admiral of the Fleet Lord Hill-Norton, interview 16 March 1999.

55 Rear Admiral Sir Paul Greening, interview 19 April 1999.

56 Beadle, n. 4.

57 Jackson and Bramall, op. cit. n. 2, p. 390.

58 Duffy, n. 52.

59 *Daily Telegraph,* 25–29 July 1978.

60 Captain N. MacEacharn, interview 15 March 1999.

Chapter 17. Chief of Defence Staff, 1979–1982

1 Commodore David Smith, interview 27 April 1999.

2 Geoffrey Howe, *Conflict of Loyalty* (Pan Books, 1995), pp. 144–5.

3 Bill Jackson and Dwin Bramall, *The Chiefs* (Brassey's, 1992), p. 390.

4 David Owen, *Time to Declare* (Penguin, 1991), p. 381. See also Eric J. Grove, *Vanguard to Trident* (The Bodley Head, 1987), pp. 348–9.

5 Jackson and Bramall, loc. cit. n. 3.

6 Lewin always maintained this was the case, as is confirmed by his own handwritten notes for a Staff College lecture at the end of 1981 (henceforth 'Lecture notes') and this accords with the author's recollection. Sir Frank Cooper (interview 17 February 1999) believed that there was 'a general wedge' in the Long Term Costings (LTCs) that could have been used to meet part of the cost, and other civil servants then in the Defence Department (Sir Richard Mottram, interview 21 June 1999, and David Omand, interview 28 July 1999) have said

some alleviation was available. However, in view of the severe effect on the defence programme of the insertion of Trident, it is believed that such a contribution from the LTCs could not have been substantial.

7   Admiral Sandy Woodward with Patrick Robinson, *One Hundred Days* (Fontana, 1992), p. 60.
8   Cooper, n. 6.
9   Sir John Nott, interview 21 April 1999.
10 Defence Open Government Document (DOGD) 80/23, preamble.
11 Ibid., p. 25.
12 Omand, n. 6.
13 Howe, op. cit. n. 2, p. 240.
14 Jackson and Bramall, op. cit. n. 3, p. 392.
15 Ibid., p. 393.
16 Notes in Lewin's own hand and in the possession of the author.
17 Nott, n. 9.
18 Coined by Commander Martin Wemyss, of Plans Division, early 1963.
19 Howe, op. cit. n. 2, p. 145.
20 Defence Open Government Document (DOGD) 82/1, March 1982.
21 Grove, op. cit. n. 4, p. 356.
22 Omand, n. 6.
23 DOGD 82/1, preamble.
24 Omand, n. 6; Nott, n. 9; Admiral of the Fleet Sir Henry Leach, *Endure no Makeshifts* (Leo Cooper, 1993), p. 203.
25 Nott, n. 9, said specifically that Lewin 'made no demur' to the decision that the full cost should be borne by the Navy.
26 Margaret Thatcher, *The Downing Street Years* (Harper Collins, 1993), p. 249.
27 Air Vice Marshal David Brook, interview 17 March 1999.
28 Omand, n. 6.
29 Cooper, n. 6.
30 Lecture notes, n. 6.
31 Nott, n. 9.
32 Jackson and Bramall, op. cit. n. 3, p. 394.
33 Leach, op. cit. n. 24, p. 204.

34 J. R. Hill, 'The Realities of Medium Power', in *The Oxford Illustrated History of the Royal Navy* (OUP, 1995), p. 391.
35 Air Chief Marshal Sir Michael Graydon, interview 22 June 1999.
36 General Sir John Hackett and others, *The Third World War, August 1985 – A Future History* (Sidgwick & Jackson, 1978).
37 Lecture notes, n. 6.
38 Ibid.
39 Nott, Cooper and Omand interviews, nn. 6 and 9; Lecture notes, n. 6; Leach, op. cit. n. 24, p. 198.
40 Lecture notes, n. 6, *ipsissima verba.*
41 Grove, op. cit. n. 4, p. 350.
42 It has been particularly difficult to isolate this part of the directive, and the conclusion has been derived from subsequent decisions including the wording of Cmnd. 8288 itself.
43 Nott, n. 9.
44 Grove, op. cit. n. 24, p. 346.
45 Cmnd. 8288, *The Way Forward* (June 1981), para 5.
46 A point forcefully made at interview, n. 9.
47 H. C. Deb., 19 May 1981, col. 165.
48 Leach, op. cit. n. 24, pp. 207–9.
49 Grove, op. cit. n. 4, p. 347.
50 Thatcher, op. cit. n. 26, p. 250.
51 Leach, op. cit. n. 24, p. 205.
52 Grove, op. cit. n. 4, p. 346.
53 Cmnd. 8288, n. 45, para 34.
54 See Chapter 9.
55 Major Sir Patrick Wall, 'The Government's Defence Programme: A Politician's View', 69 *The Naval Review (1981)*, pp. 279–81.
56 Jackson and Bramall, op. cit. n. 3, p. 398.
57 Leach, op. cit. n. 24, pp. 212–13.
58 Admiral of the Fleet Lord Lewin, interview 14 December 1998.
59 Lecture notes, n. 6.
60 Cmnd. 8288, n. 45, paras. 32–6.
61 Nott, n. 9.
62 See the Preface to J. R. Hill, *The*

Royal Navy Today and Tomorrow (Ian Allan, 1981), a difficult piece to write. Neither Lewin nor Leach were consulted, though Leach contributed the Foreword.

63 Leach, op. cit. n. 24, p. 199.

64 Nott, n. 9.

65 Lecture notes, n. 6; Nott, n. 9.

66 Admiral Sir Peter Abbott, interview May 1999. The Royal Navy Club of 1765 and 1785 is a dining club and charitable foundation whose membership at that time was restricted to serving and retired officers of the rank of commander and above in the seaman specialisation.

67 Commodore David Smith, interview 27 April 1999, Cooper, n. 6, and Abbott, n. 66, emphasise that Lewin played the hand with great discretion.

68 125 RUSI *Journal* (December 1980), pp. 14 ff.

69 Graydon, n. 35.

70 COS RU21(1), a paper by Colonel John Lucken for the RUSI, p. 18.

71 Michael Howard, *The Central Organisation of Defence* (RUSI, 1970).

72 Nott, n. 9.

73 Marginal note on Lewin's copy of DOGD 84/03, *MINIS and the Development of the Organisation for Defence*, made almost certainly in December 1998.

74 NDHD 12/82.

75 PS/2nd PUS Memorandum No. 2nd PUS/622/82 dated 13 August 1982.

76 House of Commons, *Third Report from the Defence Committee, Session 1983–84, Ministry of Defence Reorganisation* (HMSO, 15 October 1984). Lord Lewin's evidence is at pp. 12–24.

77 Manuscript note on cover of the above, dated 13 December 1998.

78 Cmnd. 9315, *The Central Organisation for Defence*.

79 Admiral of the Fleet Sir Henry Leach, interview 19 January 1999.

80 See Chapter 19.

81 Cm. 3999, *The Strategic Defence Review*, July 1998.

82 Smith, n. 67.

83 Abbott, n. 66.

84 Smith, n. 67.

85 Lewin to Beadle, 14 August 1980.

86 Rodney Stannard, interview 19 April 1999.

Chapter 18. 'Seventy Days of My Life': 5 April–14 June 1982

1 Admiral of the Fleet Lord Lewin, interview 14 December 1998.

2 Of his obituary notices in the broadsheets (*Sunday Telegraph*, 24 January 1999; *Independent*, 25 January; *The Times*, 25 January; *Guardian*, 25 January; *Daily Telegraph*, 25 January) all headlined his part in the Falklands campaign and devoted nearly half their material to it.

3 Henceforth 'Falklands audiotape'.

4 A good chronology is in Martin Middlebrook, *Operation Corporate* (Viking, 1985), pp. 22-4.

5 See Cmnd. 8787, *Falkland Islands Review: Report of a Committee of Privy Councillors, Chairman: Lord Franks, January 1983* (Henceforth 'Franks Report'), pp. 4–8. Sir Roderick Macdonald has commented (letter of 19 November 1999) that as a commander in DNTWP, he had been expected to draft answers to Parliamentary questions on the matter.

6 See Chapter 16.

7 Franks Report, n. 5, p. 9.

8 'Grey Rock', 'Planning and Preparing a Disaster – Argentina and the Falklands', 73 *The Naval Review* (1985), pp. 115-21, analyses the report of the Interservice Commission of Analysis and Evaluation of Political and Mili-

tary Responsibilities in the War of the South Atlantic, under the chairmanship of Teniente General Benjamin Rattenbach, leaked to the weekly magazine *Siete Dias* in November 1983. The sequence of Argentine decisions is drawn from this source.

9 Franks Report, n. 5, p. 37.

10 'Grey Rock', n. 8.

11 Franks Report, n. 5, p. 43.

12 Ibid., p. 45.

13 Roger Perkins, *Operation Paraquat* (Picton Publishing, 1986), p. 46.

14 Falklands audiotape, n. 3. The tape states clearly that it was a Sunday evening, which would have been 21 March; but it also states that it was Lewin who gave instructions for the *Endurance* to sail, which she did at 0845 on 21 March (Perkins, n. 13, p. 49). Both statements, on the evidence, cannot be right.

15 Perkins, op. cit. n. 13, p. 51; Franks Report, n. 5, p. 52.

16 'Grey Rock', n. 8, p. 121.

17 David Omand, interview 28 July 1999.

18 Falklands audiotape, n. 3.

19 Franks Report, n. 5, p. 51.

20 Falklands audiotape, n. 3.

21 Lord Lewin, interview 14 December 1998; and Falklands audiotape, n. 3.

22 Admiral Sir Peter Abbott, interview May 1999.

23 William Whitelaw, *The Whitelaw Memories* (Aurum Press, 1989), p. 203.

24 Admiral of the Fleet Sir Henry Leach, *Endure no Makeshifts* (Leo Cooper, 1993), pp. 219–21.

25 I am indebted to Captain Richard Sharpe, letter of 11 March 1999, for this phrase and information. He pays tribute to Captain Brian Outhwaite, the previous Director of Naval Plans, who reorganised the arrangements for taking up ships from trade.

26 Falklands audiotape, n. 3.

27 Eric J. Grove, *Vanguard to Trident* (The Bodley Head, 1987), p. 364.

28 Falklands audiotape, n. 3.

29 House of Commons, First Report from the Defence Committee, Session 1982–3, *The Handling of Press and Public Information during the Falklands Conflict*, Vol. II, 8 December 1982, p. 351.

30 COS RU21(1), a paper by Colonel John Lucken.

31 Sir Michael Palliser, interview 30 April 1999.

32 Air Vice Marshal David Brook, interview 17 March 1999.

33 Falklands audiotape, n. 3.

34 Lady Thatcher, interview 19 May 1999.

35 Whitelaw, op. cit. n. 23, p. 206; Margaret Thatcher, *The Downing Street Years* (Harper Collins, 1993), p. 187.

36 Or worse: Lewin's Falklands notebook names at least one, but it is not appropriate to quote it here.

37 Jeffrey Ethell and Alfred Price, *Air War South Atlantic* (Sidgwick & Jackson, 1983), p. 215.

38 Admiral Sandy Woodward with Patrick Robinson, *One Hundred Days* (Fontana, 1992), p. 126.

39 Sir John Nott, interview 21 April 1999.

40 Woodward and Robinson, op. cit. n. 38, p. 93.

41 Nott, n. 39.

42 Admiral Sir Jeremy Black, interview 12 February 1999.

43 Rear Admiral A. J. Whetstone, interview 1 February 1999.

44 BR 1806, *British Maritime Doctrine, Second Edition* (HMSO, 1999), p. 54.

45 Middlebrook, op. cit. n. 4, pp. 96 and 126.

46 Statement annexed to a letter from the Prime Minister to George Foulkes MP, reported in full in *The Daily Telegraph*, 20 September 1984.

47 Admiral of the Fleet Sir Henry

Leach, interview 19 January 1999.

48 Black, n. 42; Woodward and Robinson op. cit. n. 38, pp. 128–9.

49 Grove, op. cit. n. 27, p. 362.

50 Letter from Lord Lewin dated 10 May 1987, recipient not stated.

51 Whetstone, n. 43.

52 J. R. Hill, *Maritime Strategy for Medium Powers* (Croom Helm, 1986), pp. 135–6.

53 Perkins, op. cit. n. 13, Chapter IV.

54 Grove, op. cit. n. 27, p. 363.

55 Falklands audiotape, n. 3.

56 Thatcher, op. cit. n. 35, p. 209.

57 Captain Don Beadle, interview 7 April 1999.

58 HC Defence Committee Report, n. 29, p. 7.

59 Ibid., p. 337.

60 Alan Hooper, *The Military and the Media* (Gower, 1982) pp. 155-64.

61 HC Defence Committee Report, n. 29, pp. 93–149.

62 See e.g. Woodward and Robinson, op. cit. n. 38, passim; and on p. 344 the final comment after Woodward's homecoming Press Conference: 'Christ! I suppose it's a good thing we didn't lose the war, if it's like this when you win it.'

63 HC Defence Committee Report, n. 29, p. 345.

64 Thatcher, op. cit. n. 35, pp. 206–7.

65 Lewin letter, n. 50.

66 Thatcher, op. cit. n. 35, p. 212.

67 Ethell and Price, op. cit. n. 37, pp. 45–55.

68 Woodward and Robinson, op. cit. n. 38, p. 132.

69 Ethell and Price, op. cit. n. 37, p. 72.

70 Woodward and Robinson, op. cit. n. 38, pp. 148–9; Admiral Sir Peter Herbert, interview 9 March 1999; Captain Richard Sharpe, letter 1 March 1999.

71 Woodward and Robinson, op. cit. n. 38, p. 155.

72 Bill Jackson and Dwin Bramall, *The Chiefs* (Brassey's, 1992), p. 410.

73 Letter from the Prime Minister, n. 46.

74 Lewin letter, n. 50.

75 Laurence Freedman and Virginia Gamba, *The Independent*, 2 May 1987.

76 Ethell and Price, op. cit. n. 37, p. 75.

77 HC Deb. 13 May 1983, col. 1051, among many others.

78 Lewin letter, n. 50.

79 Black, n. 42.

80 Middlebrook, op. cit. n. 4, p. 151.

81 Accounts are in all the book references quoted; a good plan is at Middlebrook, n. 4, p. 157.

82 Leach, op. cit. n. 24, p. 227; Herbert, n. 70.

83 Falklands audiotape, n. 3.

84 Ethell and Price, op. cit. n. 37, pp. 84–97.

85 Woodward and Robinson, op. cit. n. 38, p. 220.

86 Ibid., pp. 185–90.

87 Lady Thatcher, interview 19 May 1999.

88 Captain Chris Craig, *Call for Fire* (John Murray, 1995), pp. 76–86.

89 Detailed accounts of this day are in Ethell and Price, op. cit. n. 37, pp. 100–28, Woodward and Robinson, op. cit. n. 38, pp. 245–68, and many other books.

90 Whitelaw, op. cit. n. 23, p. 209.

91 Commodore David Smith, interview 27 April 1999.

92 Woodward and Robinson, op. cit. n. 38, pp. 283–88.

93 Lady Thatcher, n. 87.

94 Leach, op. cit. n. 24, p. 228; HC Defence Committee Report, n. 29, p. 348.

95 Middlebrook, op. cit. n. 4, pp. 299–311

96 Falklands audiotape, n. 3.

97 Lady Thatcher, n. 87.

98 *The Independent,* 25 January 1999.

99 Sir Frank Cooper, interview 17 February 1999.
100 Falklands audiotape, n. 3.

Chapter 19. Not Really Retired, 1982–1998

1   Cmnd. 8529-1.
2   Bill Jackson and Dwin Bramall, *The Chiefs* (Brassey's, 1992), p. 424.
3   Ibid., p. 434.
4   Indeed he did so, with some vehemence, for many years; see Sir John Nott, speech at the RUSI, 21 January 1987.
5   Cmnd. 8758, *The Falklands Campaign: The Lessons,* pp. 34–5.
6   Admiral of the Fleet Sir Henry Leach, interview 19 January 1999.
7   St George's Chapel, Windsor Castle, *Report of the Society of Friends of St George's and the Descendants of the Knights of the Garter, 1994–1995,* p. 254.
8   Geoffey Till ed., *The Future of British Sea Power* (Macmillan, 1984), p. 145.
9   George M. Seignious III and Jonathan Paul Yates, 'Europe's Nuclear Superpowers', *Foreign Policy,* Summer 1984, pp. 40–53.
10 *The Times,* 6 February 1985.
11 Nott to Lewin, 6 February 1985.
12 *The Daily Telegraph,* 10 July 1990.
13 Letters to *The Daily Telegraph* from R. W. Garson, Sir David Scott and Sir John Roxburgh, July 1990.
14 For three examples among many, see HC Deb. 13 May 1983, col. 1047 ff.; *New Statesman,* 24 August 1984; Arthur Gavshon in *The Guardian,* 28 January 1985.
15 Cmnd. 8787, *Falkland Islands Review: Report of a Committee of Privy Counsellors* (January 1983).

16 HC Deb. 25 January 1983 Col. 817.
17 See Chapter 17.
18 David Owen, *Time to Declare* (Penguin, 1991), p. 361.
19 *Daily Telegraph,* 22 February 1983, under the title 'Send a Gunboat – if there's a Fleet and a Will to Back it'. The article in Lewin's handwriting is complete and in the Lewin papers.
20 Letter from Dr Owen to *The Daily Telegraph,* 23 February 1983.
21 Lord Owen, interview 30 April 1999.
22 Field Marshal Lord Bramall, interview 9 March 1999.
23 Admiral Sir Simon Cassels, interview 12 April 1999.
24 Kevin Littlewood and Beverley Butler, in *Of Ships and Stars* (The Athlone Press, 1998), give a list at App. 1.
25 Sir Patrick Nairne, telephone conversation June 1999.
26 Rear Admiral Andrew Robertson RAN, letter of 13 June 1999.
27 Correspondence between Lewin and Rear Admiral Roger Morris, 1992; Lewin and Commander David Joel, 1995.
28 N. A. M. Rodger, *The Safeguard of the Sea* (Harper Collins, 1997).
29 *The Mail on Sunday,* 15 and 22 July 1990.
30 Comprehensive lecture notes exist for at least three lectures in 1997, and the lecture was clearly well run in by then.
31 26–27 October 1978.
32 Tim Lewin, telephone conversation November 1999.
33 Fred Jewett to Lord Lewin, 8 December 1998.
34 Rear Admiral Bill Higgins, interview 16 April 1999.
35 Captain Peter Lucas, letter of 26 February 1999.
36 Dickens to Lewin, 19 August 1975.
37 Captain E. A. S. Bailey ed., *Malta Defiant and Triumphant* (Bailey,

1992), p. 13.

38 Malta Department of Information, *Pajjizna* Supplement 1992.

39 *Times of Malta*, 26 November 1995; 13 March 1996; 19 May 1996.

40 Captain C. K. S. Aylwin, letter of 4 July 1999.

41 Lewin to Macdonald, 1 December 1989.

42 Captain A. B. Sainsbury, information supplied November 1999.

43 Lewin to Hervey, 12 January 1995.

44 James D. Ferguson, letters of 10 and 21 June 1999.

45 Sainsbury, n. 42.

46 Dr Alan McGowan, telephone conversation 5 June 1999.

47 Mr R. E. White, letter of 17 March 1999 and Lewin–White correspondence.

48 See Chapter 1.

49 Lewin to CPO S. R. Williams, 11 May 1982.

50 Information in this paragraph has been supplied by Lt.-Col. Jon Fleming, Executive Director BSES.

51 Commander Chris Furse, letter to Lewin of 4 May 1998.

52 Commodore D. M. MacLean, *Cachalots and Messmates: A Brief History of the Southampton Master Mariners' Club, 1928–1973*, p. 27.

53 Littlewood and Butler, loc. cit. n. 24.

54 Libby Purves, 'A Man of True Resolution', *The Times*, 26 January 1999.

55 Admiral of the Fleet Sir Jock Slater, interview 5 May 1999.

56 Jimmy Ferguson, letter of April 1999.

57 Leo Lee, correspondence, particularly letter of 10 March 1999.

58 Peter Warwick, telephone conversation June 1999.

59 Admiral of the Fleet Lord Hill-Norton, interview 16 March 1999; Bramall, n. 22; Captain Richard Sharpe, letter of 1 March 1999.

60 Slater, n. 55.

61 Ibid.

62 See Chapter 16.

63 Captain A. B. Sainsbury, letter of 11 June 1999, covering extensive correspondence.

64 Rear Admiral David Eckersley-Maslin, interview April 1999.

INDEX

Individuals are entered under the names by which they are most commonly known, and ranks are the highest known to have been achieved. Decorations are not included. Sub-entries are arranged in chronological order where this is clear, otherwise alphabetically. Names and classes of ships are alphabetical under the appropriate heading eg Merchant Ships, British; Warships, German.